Family Memorial. Part 1. Genealogy of Fourteen Families of the Early Settlers of New-England, of the Names of Alden, Adams, Arnold, Bass, Billings, Capen, Copeland, French, Hobart, Jackson, Paine, Thayer, Wales and White ... All These Families Are More...

FAMILY MEMORIAL.

PART I.

GENEALOGY

OF

FOURTEEN FAMILIES

OF THE

𝔈arly 𝔖ettlers of 𝔑ew-𝔈ngland,

OF THE NAMES OF

ALDEN, ADAMS, ARNOLD, BASS, BILLINGS, CAPEN, COPELAND, FRENCH, HOBART, JACKSON, PAINE, THAYER, WALES AND WHITE,

FROM THEIR FIRST SETTLEMENT IN THIS COUNTRY, TO ABOUT THE MIDDLE OF THE LAST CENTURY.

WITH OCCASIONAL NOTES AND REFERENCES, BIOGRAPH-
ICAL SKETCHES, MEMOIRS OF SOME DISTINGUISHED
INDIVIDUALS, EPITAPHS, &c.

COLLECTED FROM

ANCIENT RECORDS, MANUSCRIPTS, AND PRINTED WORKS.

All these families are more or less connected by marriage, and most of
them of late generations, the descendants of JOHN ALDEN.

PART II.

GENEALOGY

OF

𝔈𝔓𝔥𝔯𝔞𝔦𝔪 𝔞𝔫𝔡 𝔖𝔞𝔯𝔞𝔥 𝔗𝔥𝔞𝔶𝔢𝔯,

WITH THEIR

FOURTEEN CHILDREN;

FROM THE TIME OF THEIR MARRIAGE TO 1835, WITH
NOTES OF REFERENCE, &c. AS IN PART FIRST.

BY ELISHA THAYER,
DEDHAM, MASS.

> " *Aye, thus it is, one generation comes,*
> *Another goes and mingles with the dust,*
> *And thus we come and go, and come and go,*
> *Each for a little moment, filling up*
> *Some little place—and thus we disappear*
> *In quick succession, and it shall be so*
> *Till time in one vast perpetuity*
> *Be swallowed up.*"—ANON.

HINGHAM:
J. FARMER, PRINTER.
1835.

PREFACE.

THE publication of the following pages was design-
ed to perpetuate to future generations the Record of
these ancient families, and enable them to trace their
genealogy, in a direct line, back to their Pilgrim Fathers. The history of the settlement of the Old Colony,
in 1620, and of the Massachusetts in 1630, is familiar
to a large portion of the present generation, being taught
in their schools and read by their firesides ; the trials
they endured on their first arrival and for a number of
years afterwards, by sickness and death, by want of
provisions, by terror by night and day from the howl-
ings of savage beasts and more savage men, will not
cease to be interesting to their descendants to the latest
period of time.

It may not be uninteresting to give a short sketch of
the Ecclesiastical History of the first settlers of New
England, in which not only they were concerned but
all their posterity to the present day.

" The first settlers of the Plymouth Colony, (1620)
were called *Separatists,* having separated from the
Established Church of England, some years previous to
their settlement in this country."

" In 1596, they (the Separatists,) published their
Confession of Faith with the *grounds* of their *separation ;* reprinted with their Apology in 4 to 1604.

But their sufferings and writings soon increased their numbers, and more of the *warmer Puritans* embraced their Doctrines, left the public churches, and met in private houses for a purer worship. But then they lost the *name* of *Puritans,* and received that of the *Separatists*, the far greater part of the Puritans remaining still in the church, writing with zeal against the *separation;* and as *Sprint* on their behalf in 1608 expresses it :—A *separation* we deny not from the *Corruptions* of the church wherein we live, in Judgment, Profession, Practice ; for which so many of both parts, (or Parties, i. e. of *Puritans* and *Separatists*,) have suffered and do suffer so many things. But the difference is, We (i. e. the *Puritans*,) suffer for separating *in* the church ; you, (i. e. the Separatists,) out of the church."—*Prince's Annals*, 1, 235.

And those of the Massachusetts Colony, (1630) were called Puritans, as the same author says, p. 239. " Of these English Puritans were the greater part of the Massachusetts Colony. They had been chiefly born and brought up in the *National Church*, and had hitherto lived in Communion with her. As their Ministers had been ordained by her Bishops, they had officiated in her *Parochial Churches,* and till now had made no *Secession* from them."

In a Poem written by ROGER WOLCOTT, Esq., published in the Mass. Hist. Coll. 4, 263, are the following curious lines :

" But if you ask to gain intelligence
" What were the reasons why they went from hence,
" What straits they met with in their way and there ?
" These facts I think I'm able to declare,
" Religion was the cause : Divinity '
" Having declared the gospel shine (light) should be
" Extensive as the sun's diurnal shine ;
" This moved our founders to this great design."

A vast fund of information relative to the Political
and Ecclesiastical state of our ancestors may be collected from the Plymouth Memorial and other Histories of
that Colony, and from Winthrop's Journal of the Massachusetts, Hutchinson, Prince, Holmes, &c.   But after
all there is still an increasing desire "to know," as
Mr. Farmer says, "something respecting those who
have preceded us in the stage of action; and there has
begun a curiosity among many of the present generation to trace back their progenitors, in an uninterrupted
series, to those who first landed on the bleak and in-
hospitable shores of New England.   And it is not improbable that the arrival of the puritan fathers of New
England will form a more memorable epoch in history,
than the conquest of England does in that country ; and
that posterity, a few centuries hence, will experience as
much pleasure in tracing back their ancestry to the New
England colonists, as some of the English feel in being
able to deduce their descent from the Normans."

    " There is a satisfaction in recognizing our first an-
cestor from the European continent ; in knowing from
what part of Great Britain he came ; where he settled,
and the circumstances and condition of his family. Owing to the trials and hardships endured by the first settlers of New England, the uncertainty of their remaining in the country, and the little time afforded them for
recording family data and genealogical facts, there are
but few families, who have full and complete satisfaction in each of these particulars.   But some facts, even
at this late period, might be known of almost every individual who settled in any of the colonies, if suitable
patience, research, and industry were employed in collecting them.   Our earliest records and Memorials are

full of information, and in regard to minuteness and accuracy will bear a comparison with those of modern date ; and it is somewhat remarkable that so large a portion of them have escaped the many perils to which fire and the aboriginal wars exposed them."

These records are in a gradual state of decay, and many of them in a very shattered condition, many names and dates have already become obliterated, some portions lost, and probably lost forever ; every effort should therefore be made to rescue these precious relics of antiquity from the ruins of time.

The materials of the First Part were principally collected by the personal labour and research of the author, from authentic, original sources ; some small portion from tradition, and some from the written communications of persons interested in the work.

A large portion of the Second Part was collected and arranged by Dr. Samuel W. Thayer, of Thetford, Vt. more than twenty years ago, to which large additions have been made from time to time, by Stephen W. Jackson, Esq. of Boston, and others ; but nearly all the dates of births, marriages, and deaths, prior to 1760, and even later, with very many additional names, (and numerous corrections of errors,) were extracted from town records with the utmost care and precision. Many acknowledgments are however due to several distinguished individuals for their contribution of Materials, and for their encouragement and patronage towards its publication, of whom are Rev. Timothy Alden, of East Liberty, Pa. ; John Farmer, Esq. of Concord, N. H. ; Hon. John Q. Adams of Quincy ; Z. B. Adams, M. D. ; Isaac Porter, M. D., and Stephen W. Jackson, Esq. of Boston ; Rev. Jonathan French of N. Hamp-

ton, N. H. ; Hon. Naнum Mitchel of Bridgewater ;
many Town Clerks, who have generously given free
access to their records, or furnished extracts therefrom,
and others too numerous to specify.

EXPLANATIONS.

A. B. C. D. &c. denotes the successive generations
from the first progenitor of each family. A. denotes
the first generation, B. the second, C. the third, &c.
in the first part. In the Second Part, consisting of
fourteen branches corresponding with the same number
of families, in Part I. the Progenitor of each branch is
numbered 1, and *their* generations designated by the
same characters, A. B. C. &c.

In the early records it will be observed that the dates
were specified by numerical figures in many instances,
as 23 day, 2 month, 1640, or 12 month, 3 day, 1657,
see Bass No. 11, first part, &c. which method of com-
putation was continued until 1752, the year beginning
on the 25th of March, which was called the 1st month,
February the 12th, September, October, November, and
December, then having the numerical rank agreeably
to their Latin etemology, which is now done away.

To the dates of births, marriages, deaths, &c. recorded prior to 1752, eleven days should be added, to make
the old style correspond with the new. (Compare No.

1—5, Ninth Branch, O. S. with No. 62 Memoir, N. S.) This rule will apply in most instances, but there are exceptions.

In conclusion, to use the language of another, on a similar occasion—" The object of the author has been to throw light on a subject of which, necessarily, very many must have been ignorant ; and although this may not have been effected in the best manner possible, he is conscious of having done it as well as he could.   If the collection should be found in any degree useful, the purpose will be answered."

                    ELISHA THAYER.

Dedham, June 18, 1835.

FAMILY MEMORIAL.

THE FAMILY OF ALDEN.

HON. JOHN ALDEN,*

the Progenitor of all of the name of Alden in the United States, married Priscilla, daughter of Mr William Mullins, by whom "he had eight children, four sons and four daughters, who lived to enter the marriage state, who had many children and most of whom lived to a good old age."

[Alden's Collection.

1. JOHN,	5. ELIZABETH,
2. JOSEPH,	6. SARAH,
3. DAVID,	7. RUTH,
4. JONATHAN,	8 MARY.

*The Hon. John Alden was one of the pilgrims of Leyden, who came in the May Flower to Plymouth, in 1620. He was about twenty two years of age, when he arrived, and was one of those who signed the original civil compact formed and solemnly adopted by the first adventurers at Cape Cod Harbor, on the 15 November This was a few days previous to their finding and selecting a place for the commencement of their settlement in this western world. He was a single man and appears to have been an inmate in the family of Capt Myles Standish. He was *the stripling who first leaped upon the rock,* as mentioned by President Adams in a certain communication.

It is well known that of the first company, consisting of one hundred and one, about one half died in six months after landing, in consequence of the hardships they were called to encounter Mrs. Rose Standish, consort of Capt. Standish, departed this life on the 29 January, 1621. This circumstance is mentioned as an introduction to the following anecdote, which has been carefully handed down by tradition:

In a very short time after the decease of Mrs Standish, the Captain was led to think that if he could obtain Miss Priscilla Mullins, a daughter of Mr William Mullins, the breach in his family would be happily repaired. He therefore, according to the custom of those times, sent to ask Mr. Mullins' permission to visit his daughter. John Alden, the messenger, went and faithfully communicated the wishes of the Captain. The old gentle-

2

No 2. I. A.　　　JOHN ALDEN,

son of the Hon John Alden, went from Duxbury to Boston
as early as 1659, with his wife Elizabeth, by whom he had
one child.

man did not object, as he might have done, on account of the recency of Capt.
Standish's bereavement   He said it was perfectly agreeable to him, but the
young lady must also be consulted   The damsel was then called into the
room, and John Alden, who is said to have been a man of most excellent
form, with a fair and ruddy complexion, arose, and in a very courteous and
prepossessing manner, delivered his errand. Miss Mullins listened with
respectful attention, and at last, after a considerable pause, fixing her eyes
upon him, with an open and pleasant countenance, said, *"prythe John why
do you not speak for yourself ?"* He blushed and bowed and took his leave,
but with a look, which indicated more than his diffidence would permit
him otherwise to express. However he soon renewed his visit and it was
not long before their nuptials were celebrated in ample form   From them
are descended all of the name Alden in the United States   What report he made to his constituent after the first interview, tradition does not
unfold, but it is said, how true the writer knows not, that the Captain never
forgave him to the day of his death.

For a few years, the subject of this article lived in Plymouth, and then
settled in Duxbury, on a farm, which, it is a little remarkable, has remained in the possession of his descendants ever since, and is one of the best
in the town. He built his house on a rise of land near Eagle Tree Pond,
where the ruins of his well are still to be seen.

John Alden, the principal subject of this memoir, is supposed to have
been a native of some part of the Island of Great Britain   A very few of
the name however appear to have been in England   The name has probably been more common in Germany   In a certain printed catalogue of
the graduates of Cambridge University, but *one* of this name is to be found.
In that part of Calamy's account of ejected ministers and others confined
to the County of Bedford, Mr Alden a scholar of St John's College is mentioned as one who suffered from the tyranical Bartholomew Act.   In Guil-
lime's Display of Heraldry, the following armorial passage is recorded   "He
beareth gules, three crescents within a border engrailed ermine by the
name of Alden " This coat was assigned 8 September, 1607, by William
Cambden, clarencieur to John Alden, of the Middle Temple

Through a long protracted life, the subject of this article was almost
continually engaged in public employments. In the patent for Plymouth,
in New England, dated 16 January, 1629, and signed by Robert Earl of
Warwick, Myles Standish, Edward Winslow, John Howland, and John
Alden or any of them, are named as the true and lawful attornies of the
council established at Plymouth, in the county of Devon   Accordingly,
John Alden entered into some part of the tracts specified in the patent,
took possession in due form, and delivered the full and peaceable possession and seizen of the same to William Bradford, Governor of the Old
Colony, his heirs, associates and assigns, *secundum formam chartæ*

He was one of the Court of Assistants in 1633, and successively for a
number of years   From 1641 to 1649 inclusively, he was chosen to rep-
resent the town of Duxbury in the General Court of the Old Colony.   In
1653, and for several succeeding years, he was one of the Council of War,
appointed on account of danger apprehended from the Indians   In the
year 1650, he was again elected one of the assistants to the Governor, and

1. MARY, born 17 Dec. 1659.

John Alden married Elizabeth Ewrill, widow of Abiell Ewrill deceased, 1 April, 1660.

every year after till 1686 In December of the last mentioned year, Sir Edmund Andros arrived with an extensive Commission from King James II. appointing him Governor of all the New England Colonies. Of course the liberties of the people of the Old Colony were supposed to be at an end. The measures of Sir Edmund were very disgusting to the free born sons of this western world; and at length he was seized and imprisoned at Boston. In 1688, a happy revolution took place, William and Mary came to the throne of England, and Andros had leave to depart from the country. This colony then resumed its original powers, and elections by the people took place till May, 1692, when the charter, uniting the Old Colony of Plymouth with Massachusetts, arrived The Governor, Lieut. Governor and Secretary, were after appointed by Royal Authority

The subject of this memoir was an assistant to all the Governors of the Old Colony, except Carver, who early fell a victim to the distressing calamities which afflicted the adventurers on their first arrival at Plymouth For thirty six years without interruption he was elected to this office, and for the twenty last years of his life, from 1666 till the liberties of the people were infringed, through the folly of James the second, he was the senior assistant.

From tradition as well as from the annexed elegy occasioned by his death, this aged and venerable puritan was distinguished by his holy life and conversation He was a meek, humble, sincere, pious, and faithful follower of the blessed Redeemer, and his end was peace and triumph.— The object which in his youthful days he anxiously sought, was fully attained. He came to the howling wilds of America to enjoy the sweets of religion, pure and undefiled Like the saints of old he was willing to endure hardships with the people of God, while he might be instrumental in extending the Kingdom of Immanuel, and looking to a better and an eternal state of existence for the rewards of grace Here he was unmolested in the exercise of the rights of conscience and in the worship of the Most High In addition to his spiritual blessings he was crowned with that competence which is vital to content, with an uncommon length of days, and with a goodly number of children, all of whom delighted in the ordinances of God and finally left that good name in the world which is better than precious ointment.

The following lines with which this article is closed are supposed to have been written by the Rev John Cotton of Plymouth, and are respectful to the memory of one of the pious and worthy fathers of New England. They have been several times given to the public from the press, and are more valuable on account of the rich sentiments they contain, than the style in which they are composed:

ELEGY,

On the death of the Honorable John Alden, for many years a Magistrate of the Old Plymouth Colony, who died on the 12 September, 1687, probably in his 90th year.

The staff of bread and water eke the stay,
From sinning Judah God will take away ;
The prudent Counsellor, the Honorable,
Whom grace and holiness makes delectable,

2. John,	born 20 Nov.	1660	5. William,	born 16 March,	1664
3 Elizabeth,	" 9 May,	1662	6 Elizabeth, 2d	" 9 April,	1665
4. John, 2d,	" 12 March,	1663	7. William, 2d,	" 5 March,	1666

The Judge, the prophet, and the ancient saint,
The deaths of such cause sorrowful complaint
The earth and its inhabitants do fall,
The aged saint bears up its pillars all
The hoary head in way of righteousness
A crown of glory is   Who can express
The abundant blessings by disciples old !
In every deed they're more than can be told
The guise 'tis of a wanton generation
To wish the aged soon might quit their station
Though truth it be, the Lord our God does frown,
When aged saints by death do tumble down.
What though there be not such activity,
Yet in their prayers there's such fervency
As doth great mercy for a place obtain,
And gracious presence of the Lord maintain.
Though nature's strength in old age doth decay,
Yet the inward man renewed is day by day.
The very presence of a saint in years,
Who lifts his soul to God with prayers and tears,
Is a rich blessing unto any place,
Who have that mercy to behold his face.
When sin is ripe and calls for desolation
God will call home old saints from such a nation
Let sinners then of the aged weary be
God give me grace to mourn most heartily,
For death of this dear servant of the Lord,
Whose life God did to us so long afford,
God lent his life to greatest length of days,
In which he lived to his Redeemer's praise.
In youthful time he made Moses his choice,
His soul obeying great Jehovah's voice,
Freely forsook the world for sake of God,
In his house with his saints to have abode.
He followed God into this wilderness ,
Thereby to all the world he did profess
Affliction with his saints a better part
And more delightful to his holy heart,
Than sinful pleasures, lasting but a season ,
Thus said his faith, so saith not carnal reason
He came one of the first into this land
And here was kept by God's most gracious hand.
Years sixty seven, which time he did behold
To poor New England mercies manifold
All God's great works to this his Israel
From first implanting that to them befell ;
Of them he made a serious observation
And could of them present a large narration
His walk was holy, humble and sincere,
His heart was filled with Jehovah's fear ,
He honored God with much integrity,
God therefore did him truly magnify.
The hearts of saints entirely did him love,

8. Zachariah, born 8 March, 1667 | 11. Zachariah, 2d born 18 Feb. 1673
9. William, 3d " 10 Sept. 1669 | 12. Nathan, " " 17 Oct 1677
10. Nathaniel, ? " about 1670 | 13. Sarah, " " 27 Sept. 1681

John Alden, Senior, died 14 March, 1702.

His uprightness so highly did approve,
That whilst to choose they had their liberty
Within the limits of this Colony,
Then civil leader him they ever chose
His faithfulness made hearts with him to close
With all the Governors he did assist ,
His name recorded is within the list
Of Plymouth's pillars to his dying day.
His name is precious to eternal ay'
He set his love on God and knew his name,
God therefore gives him everlasting fame
So good and heavenly was his conversation,
God gave long life and showed him his salvation.
His work now finished upon this earth ,
Seeing the death of what he saw the birth,
His gracious Lord from heaven calls him home,
And saith, my servant, now to heaven come ,
Thou hast done good, been faithful unto me,
Now shalt thou live in bliss eternally.
On dying bed his ails were very great,
Yet verily his heart on God was set
He bare his griefs with faith and patience
And did maintain his lively confidence ,
Saying to some, the work which God begun,
He would preserve to its perfection.
His mouth was full of blessings till his death
To ministers and christians all his breath
Was very sweet by many a precious word
He uttered from the Spirit of his Lord.
He lived in Christ, in Jesus now he sleeps,
And his blest Soul, the Lord in safety keeps.

JOHN ALDEN. ANAGRAM—END ALL ON HI.

Death puts an *end* to *all* this world enjoys
And frees the saint from *all*, that here annoys
This blessed saint hath seen an *end* of all
Worldly perfections. Now his Lord doth call
Him to ascend from earth to heaven *high*,
Where he is blest to all Eternity
Who walk with God as he, shall so be blest,
And evermore in Christ, his arms shall rest
Lord spare thy remnant, do not us forsake,
From us do not thy Holy Spirit take.
Thy cause, thy interest in this land still own
Thy gracious presence ay let be our crown

J. C. (Alden, 264)

No. 3.   IV. B.   JOHN ALDEN,

son of John and Elizabeth Alden, married Elizabeth ——
and settled in Boston.

1. Elizabeth,	born	7 Nov.	1687	8 Nathaniel,	born	6 July,	1700
2. Hannah,	"	20 Nov.	1688	9. Thomas,	"	13 Aug.	1701
3 John,	"	20 Sept	1690	Died same day			
4. Mary,	"	15 Dec.	1691	10 Katharine, 2d	"	17 Feb.	1704
5. Katharine,	"	19 Aug.	1697	11 Thomas, 2d	"	1 March,	1707
Died 31st October, 1702.				12 William,	"	9 May,	1710
6 Gillam and 7 Ann,	"	7 July,	1699	Died 27 December, 1714.			

No. 4.   III C.   JOHN ALDEN,

son of John and Elizabeth Alden, 2d, married Anna ——
by whom he had two children, born in Boston.

1 Anna, born 29 January, 1722 | 2 Benjamin, born 18 Sept. 1724

This John Alden, must have been the same who went
to Needham, purchased a farm and married Thankful Parker, 26 Nov 1728, (a second wife,) his name does not oc-
cur again in the Boston Records   The children of John
and Thankful Alden, were

1. Jemima,	born	9 March,	1730	7. Moses,
2. John,	"	9 Oct.	1731	8. Moses, 2d.
3 Alice,	"	12 July,	1733	9 Thomas,
4. Henry,	"	27 Nov.	1734	10. Thankful,
5 Silas,	"	23 Oct.	1736	11. Mary.
6. Samuel,	"	——	1743	

No. 5.   I. D.   JEMIMA ALDEN,

the first child of John and Thankful Alden died in infancy.

No. 6.   II D.   JOHN ALDEN,

the second child of John and Thankful Alden settled in
Vermont.

---

*This must have been the Capt. John Alden mentioned by Hutchinson,
(vol 2 p. 50) as follows: "Towards the end of the month of May, 1692,
Capt. John Alden, of Boston, commander of a sloop in the colony service,
employed for supplying the posts East with provisions and stores, was ac-
cused of *Witchcraft*, and thereupon sent down to Salem, although the Justices allowed that he always had the character of an honest man.   Alden
in his account says, that the accuser first pointed to another man and said
nothing, but the man who held her stooped down to her ear and then she
cried out Alden ! Alden!   All were ordered into the street and a ring
made, and then she cried out, "There stands Alden, a bold fellow, with
his hat on, sells powder and shot to the Indians."******   After examination he was committed to gaol, where he lay fifteen weeks and then was
prevailed on by his friends to make his escape and to absent himself until
the consternation should abate, and the people recover the use of their
reason "

No. 7. III. D. ALLICE ALDEN,
the third child of John and Thankful Alden was married to
Jonathan Capron of Attleborough, Mass

No. 8. IV. D. HENRY ALDEN,
the fourth child of John and Thankful Alden lived and died
in Needham, Mass.

No. 9. V. D. SILAS ALDEN,
the fifth child of John and Thankful Alden, married Margaret Capron a sister of Jonathan Capron before named,
and settled in Needham. He was a deacon of the church.
His children were,

1. Moses, who married Elizabeth Whiting, and settled
in Marlborough, N H

2. Elizabeth, whose husband was Enoch Mills of Watertown

3 Paul, who married Rebecca Newell, and settled in
Newton, Mass.

4 Silas, who married Mary Gay, and settled in Templeton.

5. Amasa, who married Martha Davenport, and settled
in Dedham

6. Lydia, whose husband was Fuller Mills. She lives
in Boston.

7. Rebecca, whose husband was Timothy Pike, of
Dudley.

8. Simeon, who married Elizabeth Cook, and settled
in Newton.

9. Samuel, who married Lavina Ausdale, and lived in
Needham

10. George, who married Hannah Wright, and settled
in Needham.

Dea. Silas Alden died in March, 1826, aged about 90.

No. 10. VI. D SAMUEL ALDEN,
the sixth child of John and Thankful Alden, married Susannah Coller, and settled in Needham. His children were,

1. Hannah, born 9 April, 1772 | 4 Susannah, born Sept 1777
2. Susannah, " about 1771 | 5 Sarah, " 28 Nov. 1778
And died the next year. | 6. Priscilla, who died in infancy.
3. Abigail, " 15 Jan. 1776 | 7. Samuel, born 1 June, 1792

Mr. Samuel Alden died in June, 1797.

No 11. IX. D THOMAS ALDEN,

the ninth child of John and Thankful Alden, married Polly Cheney, and settled at Otter Creek, (now Middlebury) Vt

No. 12. X. D THANKFUL ALDEN,

the tenth child of John and Thankful Alden, was married to —— Pratt.

No. 13 XI D. MARY ALDEN,

the eleventh and youngest child of John and Thankful Alden, was married to Samuel Paine of Roxbury.

No. 14 IX B WILLIAM ALDEN,

son of John and Elizabeth Alden, married Mary Drewry in 1691, and settled in Boston.

1. Mary,   born 14 Feb. 1693 | 4. Lydia,   born   22 Dec.   1701
   Died 27 October 1702 | 5. Mary,   "   12 June,   1706
2. Elizabeth, born 10 March, 1695 | 6. Drewry,   "   12 May,   1708
3. William,   "   23 July, 1697 | 7. John,   "   22 Jan.   1711

No 15 X. B NATHANIEL ALDEN,

son of John and Elizabeth Alden, married Hepzibah Mountjoy in 1691, and settled in Boston.

1 Mary,   born 20 Aug.   1692 | 3. Elizabeth, born ————————
2 Nathaniel, "   6 Aug.   1694 | 4. Hepzibah, "   ————————

No 16. II. C. NATHANIEL ALDEN,

son of the preceding, married Mary ——, and settled in Boston, and had one daughter
1. Elizabeth, born 3 Aug 1730, and perhaps other children

No 17 XI B ZACHARIAH ALDEN,

son of John and Elizabeth Alden, was graduated at Harvard College, in 1692. In 1700, he married Mary Viall, and settled in Boston.
  1. Zachariah, 11 Oct 1701.

NOTE.—William, son of Henry and Deborah Alden, was born in Dedham, 14 August, 1709 —[*Dedham Records*
Henry Alden deceased Feb ye 18, 1730
Mary ye daughter of William and Ruth Alden, deceased May 29. 1740.
Ruth Alden, ye wife of William Alden, deceased Ded ye 17, 1766.
This Henry was probably a son of John Alden, senior, of Boston.
[*Needham Records.*

No 18 I. C.   ZACHARIAH ALDEN,
son of the preceding, married Jemima ——, and settled
in Boston
  1. Mary, born 8 March, 1725 *

No. 19. II. A.   JOSEPH ALDEN,
the second son of the Hon. John Alden of Duxbury, whose
wife was Mary Simmons, was one of the original settlers
of Bridgewater.† His children were, 1 Isaac 2. Joseph.
3. John

No. 20. I. B   ISAAC ALDEN,
son of Joseph Alden, married Mehitable, daughter of Samuel Allen, 1685, and settled in East Bridgewater, their
children,

1 Mehitable,	born	1687	6. John,	born	[1694]
2 Sarah,	"	1688	7. Mercy,	"	1696
3 Mary,	"	1691	8 Abigail,	"	1699
4 Isaac,	"	1692	9 Jemima,	"	1702
5. Ebenezer,	"	1693			

No 21. I. C.   MEHITABLE ALDEN,
was married to Benjamin Richards, in 1711

No. 22. II C.   SARAH ALDEN,
was married to Seth Brett, in 1712, and Dea Recompence
Cary, in 1727.

No. 23. III. C.   MARY ALDEN,
was married to John Webb of Braintree, 1720. She died
a widow 1772, aged 82.

---

* Lydia, daughter of Zachariah and Lydia Alden, was born in Milton, 3
June, 1730.—[Milton Records.
  This was probably the same man with a second wife.

† The first improvements in this place, which were begun in 1651, were
in what is called the West parish, which for a time was known by the
name of Duxbury plantation.
  The Sachem who deeded this township, went with the purchasers upon
a certain hill, in the East parish and made his conveyance in this manner,
mentioning the consideration, "I give you all the land South seven miles
all the land West seven miles· all the land North seven miles, and all the
land East to where the white men live."
  Joseph Alden departed this life 8 Feb. 1697, at the age of about 73
years, leaving a widow and three sons above named
                                        [Alden's Collection. 2, 207.

3

No. 24.   IV. C.   ISAAC ALDEN,
lived to old age, a Bachelor, and left a large real estate.

No. 25.   V. C. Capt. EBENEZER ALDEN,
married Anna, daughter of Joseph Keith, 1717, their children,

1 Ann,	born	1718	4. Nathan,	born	1727
2. Susanna,	"	1719	5. Ezra,	"	1732
3. Abigail,	"	1721			

No. 26.   I. D.   ANNA,
was married to Eleazer Washburn.

No. 27.   II. D.   SUSANNA,
was married to Ephraim Cary.

No. 28.   III D.   ABIGAIL,
was married to Ebenezer Byram, Jr. Esq. all at the same
time, 1738.   The mother died 1775, aged 79 ; the father
1776, aged 83, and was the surviving member of the church
in East Bridgewater, when it was first gathered in 1724.

No. 29.   IV. D. Dea NATHAN ALDEN,
son of Capt. Ebenezer Alden, married Mary, daughter of
Daniel Hudson, 1750 ; their children 1. Nathan, born 1751.
She died 1755, and he married Lydia, daughter of Benjamin Richards, 1757.   (See No. 21.)   2. Isaac, born 1758 *
The father died 1807, aged 80.   The second wife died
1823, aged 90 years and 7 months.

No. 30.   I. E.   NATHAN ALDEN, Esq.
married a Barrell for his first wife, and settled on the
homestead of his father, and has three sons.   1. Marcus.
2. Isaac.   3. Lucius.   His second wife was a widow.

No. 31.   V. D.   EZRA ALDEN,
son of Capt. Ebenezer Alden, married Rebecca, daughter
of Josiah Keith of Easton, 1756 ; their children, 1. a son,
1757.*   2. Abby, 1759.*   3. Abigail, 1761.   4 Isaac, 1763.
5. Susanna, 1766.

No 32.   III. E.   ABIGAIL,
was married to George Vining, 1778.

---

* This star denotes their early death.

No. 33. V. E. SUSANNA,

was married to Jacob Allen, 1784, and both removed to Plainfield. The father died and the widow was married to John Bisbee, 1771, and died 1777, aged 41.

No. 34. VI. C. JOHN ALDEN,

son of Isaac and Mehitable Alden, married Hannah, daughter of Henry Kingman, 1727 ; their children, 1. John and 2 James, born 1729.* 3. Isaac, 1731. 4. Jonathan, 1733. 5. Hannah, 1736. 6. Adam, 1738 * 7. another son, 1740.* 8. Abigail, 1742.* 9. Keziah, 1743. The mother died 1744, and he then married Rebecca Nightingale, 1745. 10. Rebecca, 1745. 11. John, 1747. 12 Esther, 1749.* 13. James, 1751. 14. Adam, 1754. 15. Joseph, 1755. 16. Benjamin, 1757. The father died 1762, aged about 67.

No 35. X. D. REBECCA,

was married to John Sprague, 1767, and they with the mother and *John* went to Warwick, *James, Adam, Joseph* and *Benjamin* went to Claremont, N. H.

No. 36. VII. C. MERCY,

daughter of Isaac Alden, was married to Zacheus Packard, 1725. (See Cary, p. 25,) and settled in N. Bridgewater.

No. 37. IX. C. JEMIMA,

sister of the preceeding, was married to Dea. Thomas Whitman, 1727.—[*Hon. Judge Mitchell.*

No. 38. II. B Dea. JOSEPH ALDEN,

who spent his days in the South Parish of Bridgewater, was the second son of Joseph Alden, noticed in Article No. 19. He married Hannah, daughter of Daniel Dunham of Plymouth, about 1689, a native of Middleborough. Their children,

1. Daniel Alden, Esq who died at his seat in Stafford, at the age of 80 years.

2. Eleazer Alden, who died on his farm near Pine Hill, in the South of Bridgewater, at the age of 79 years.

3. Samuel Alden, who died on his farm at Titiquot, at the age of 80 years.

4. Capt. Seth Alden, who inherited and occupied the farm of his father, and died at the age of 75 years.

5 Hannah Alden, the wife of Mark Lothrop of Easton, who died in her 81st year.

6 Mary Alden, the wife of Timothy Edson of Stafford, who died at the age of 80 years

7. Mehitable Alden, the wife of Barnabas Eaton of Middleborough, who died at the age of 30 years.

In Memory of
Deacon Joseph Alden, who deceased 22 December, 1747.
in the 80th year of his age.
Memento Mori.
[*Alden's Collection.* 2. 208.

No. 39. I C. DANIEL ALDEN, Esq
son of Deacon Joseph Alden, had seven children, viz :

1. Joseph Alden, who lived at Stafford, and died at Worcester, at the age of about 50 years.

2 Daniel Alden, Esq who removed to Lebanon in the vicinity of Dartmouth College, in the latter part of his life, and died at the age of 70 years ; was the father of Dr. Ebenezer Alden, and others.

3 Zephaniah Alden, who spent his days in Stafford, and died at the age of about 80 years

4. Barnabas Alden, who lived at Ashfield, and died at the age of 60 years

5 Ebenezer Alden, who died at Stafford, at the age of 21 years.

6. Abigail Alden, who was the wife, and is now, (1814) the widow of the late venerable Dea Whitman of Abington.

7. Hannah Alden, who was the wife of Joshua Blodget of Stafford, and died at the age of 70 years.—[*Ib.* 3. 28.

No. 40. I. E. EBENEZER ALDEN,*
a Physician of distinguished reputation in Randolph, in Mass. was born at Stafford, in Conn. 4 July, 1755 He was a son of Daniel Alden, Esq of Lebanon, in New Hamp-

* The following is from a sketch drawn by the Rev. Dr. Strong, pastor of the church and congregation in Randolph

"Having gone through a regular course of study, preparatory to the practice of physic, he removed to Braintree, (now Randolph,) Mass in the year 1781, where he commenced the duties of his profession. These he discharged with reputation to himself, and with great usefulness to his employers. His circle of business, though small at first, gradually increased, until it became very extensive.

As a Physician, he was remarkably attentive, prudent, and successful During the latter part of his life, his advice was sought and much respect-

shire, and grandson of Daniel Alden, whose name stands at the head of the preceding article. The subject of this article received his acidemical education at Plainfield, under the tuition of Ebenezer Pemberton, Esq. a gentleman, who, for his urbanity, talents, acquirements, and wonderful ability in his profession, is greatly esteemed and venerated by all who have ever had the honour and the happiness to be under his instruction, and whose numerous pupils, not a few have risen to the most elevated rank, in Church and State. He married his wife from one of the first families in Randolph, (Sarah, daughter of Col. Jonathan Bass, and also a descendant of the Hon. John Alden. See Bass, Nos. 32 and 34,) by whom he had two sons and one daughter, viz : *Ebenezer, Henry Bass,* and *Susan.*

---

ed by his brethren of the faculty in his vicinity. No Physician, in this part of the country, possessed the love and confidence of his patients to a higher degree This was evident from the universal sorrow occasioned among them by his death They felt as though they had lost, not only their able and beloved Physician, but a most important friend and useful member of society. Such indeed was the subject of this biographical sketch."

Amidst all the rage of political party spirit, he never betrayed the interests of his country. He was a disciple of Washington, whose principles he revered and uniformly supported. As a husband, Dr. Alden was kind and affectionate ; as a parent, tender and faithful. He was a firm, unshaken believer in the truth of divine revelation, for about twenty years previous to his death, a member of the Church of Christ. He was never absent from public worship on the Lord's day, unless imperious necessity required it He believed in the necessity of regeneration by the special influence of the Holy Spirit, in order to future happiness. A hope that he had experienced such an internal change, and was interested in the merits of the Redeemer, supported him during his last sickness, and enabled him to meet death with coolness and fortitude. He was not only a Christian in theory but in practice. Whenever he conversed about himself, he did it with the greatest modesty and self abasement Instead of resembling the bold confident professor, who generally out-lives his religion and deeply wounds the cause of Christ, he resembled the little trembling tree which often takes the deepest root in the garden of the Lord and bears the most and best ripe fruit.

The writer of these memoirs, who was intimately acquainted with the subject of them for many years has seldom known a person who appeared to act more conscientiously in the various concerns of life, and whose daily conduct would better bear the test of examination. He proved the sincerity of his faith by his works.

In his dying address to his children he earnestly exhorted them to seek first the kingdom of God and his righteousness, assuring them that if they did thus, all other needful things would be added. In truth it may be said he has left behind him that good name which is better than precious ointment " Mark the perfect man and behold the upright, for the end of that man is peace."—[*Alden's Collection* 3, 29.

No. 41. II. C. ELEAZER ALDEN,*

the second son of Dea. Joseph Alden, married in the year 1720, Martha, a daughter of Joseph Shaw, and a sister of the late Rev. John Shaw, and settled in South Bridgewater —[*Alden's Col.* 2, 209.

Their children and descendants were,

A. * No. 42. I D. *Jonathan,* was born 22 June, O. S. 1721, and settled on a farm in Greenwich, Mass. where he died at the age of 84 years. His wife Experience, was a daughter of Nathaniel Howard of South Bridgewater, his native place, and died in December, 1809, in the 91st year of her age Their children were,

1 Col. Amos, who settled in Enfield, Conn. whose first wife was Hannah Bush. Their children were Mary, Hannah, Amos, Seth, and Lovice His second wife was Elizabeth, a daughter of Lemuel Kingsbury, and widow of Elisha Pitkin, Esq. of Hudson.

2 Jonathan, whose wife was Mary Merrill of Stafford.

3. Mary, whose husband was Moses, a son of Deacon Simon Stone, and settled in Ruport, N. Y.

4. Caleb, who died at the age of 21 years.

5. Azuba, whose husband was a son of Jacob Ramsdale.

6. Huldah, whose husband was Rufus Bush of Enfield.

7. Seth, who died at the age of 14 years.

8. Howard, a Physician in Suffield, whose wife was Rhoda, a daughter of Capt. Consider Williston. Their children were Sarah, Sidney, Edwin, Delia, Leonard, Howard, Eliza Pitman, John Newton, William Henry, George Williston, Sarah King, and Julia.

9. Experience, whose husband was Rendall Wheeler of Greenwich.

B. No 43 II D *Eleazer,*† was born 30 August, O. S.

---

* Children marked A B. C &c.

†His epitaph as well as the next following, was written by the late Rev. John Shaw of Bridgewater .

HERE LIES BURIED	HERE LIES BURIED
MR. ELEAZER ALDEN,	MRS. MARTHA ALDEN,
Who died 29th Jan. 1773 in the 79th year of his age.	the wife of Mr. Eleazer Alden Who died 6th Jan 1769 aged 69 years.
Laid in the dust he must abide,	The resurrection day will come, [tomb ;
Thus sleeping by his consort's side.	And Christ's strong voice will burst the
Ye children living, come and see,	The sleeping dead we trust will rise
Where both your once loved parents be,	With joy and pleasure in her eyes,
Then follow in the path they trod,	And ever shine among the wise.
Till you shall rest with Christ in God	[*Alden's Col* 2, 269

1723, and settled on a farm near his father's, where he died at the age of 80 years Sarah, his wife, who lived to the age of 91 years, was a daughter of Nicholas Whitman of East Bridgewater Their children were 1 Martha, who was born 17 July, 1752, and died 29 May, 1802, whose husband was Sylvanus Blossom. Their children were Alden, Libeus, and Sarah, whose husband was William Snell, Jr

2. Mary, who was born 2 July, 1754, and who died unmarried after many years' great bodily infirmities.

3. Abigail, who was born 23 August 1756, and whose husband was William Snell, Esq Their children were William, Seth, Smerdis, Eleazer, Alden, and Martin

4. Sarah, who was born 29 March, 1759, and died 8 Aug 1778

5 Hannah, who was born 13 March, 1762, whose husband was Levi Latham. Their children were, Nathaniel, Cyrus, Susanna, Marcus, Robert, Marcus, Lewis, and Hannah.

6. Eleazer, who was born 21 March, 1767, and whose first wife was Deborah Churchill. Their children were, Lewis, Isaac, and Rebecca

C. No. 44. III. D. *Abraham,* who died at the age of two years.

D. No 45 IV D *David,* was born 18 June, O S. 1727, and settled on a farm in Ashfield, near Mount Owen, where he died at the age of 80 years His wife was Lucy, a daughter of Noah Thomas of Middleborough, and survived her husband Their children were,

1. Isaac, a magistrate, who died in Warren County, Pennsylvania, at the age of 70 years, and whose wife Irene, was a daughter of the Rev Ebenezer Smith Their children were, Philander, Philomela, the wife of Dr. Rathbone of Camden, N Y ; Joshua, for many years in the service of the patriots in South America, Pliny, Isaac, who owns and occupies an extensive plantation in Louisiana, thirty miles from Nachitoches; Hiram, a physician in Ripley, N Y.; Richard, a magistrate in Pine Grove, Penn.; Enoch and Philo

2. David, of Batavia, Ohio, whose wife Susanna, was a daughter of John Ward of Buckland Their children were, Ezra, Lucy, Chandler, Mary, Lydia, Enoch, Susanna, Hannah, and Sarah

3 John, a minister of the Baptist denomination, who in-
herits and occupies his paternal estate, and whose first wife
was Nancy, a daughter of Jonathan Gray of Pelham Their
children were, Arion, Elizabeth, Eunice, Nancy, Armille,
Cyrus, Lucy, Willard, and Minerva
    4 Lydia, the wife of Jonathan Gray, a brother of Nan-
cy Their children were, Elias, Irene, David, Lucy, Lydia,
Levi, Nancy, and Naomi
    5 Enoch, a Physician in Redfield, N Y whose wife was
Lucy Elmor

E. No 46 V D *Joshua,* was born 19 April, O S 1729,
inherited and occupied his paternal farm, near Pine Hill,
in South Bridgewater, where he died at the age of 80
years His wife was Mary, the widow of Seth, the son of
Capt Seth Alden, and a daughter of Eleazer Carver She
died 2 Dec 1811, about 63 years of age. He had no chil-

---

*Lieut Alden, like some others of the name, and like many of the de-
scendants from the pilgrims of Leyden, had a great fondness for the history of New England
    The hazardous enterprize, the uncommon trials, the exquisite sufferings,
the noble christian heroism of those venerable worthies, who forsook the
endearments of their native land, and fled to this western world, the haunt
of savages and beasts of prey, and encountered hardships, which would
have immortalized a Roman band, were subjects, which deeply interested his feelings, as they invariably must those of every one, who is a friend
to liberty of conscience, and to religion, pure and undefiled
    He was a farmer of intelligence, and blessed with that competence which
is *vital to content.* He enjoyed the society of his friends and was much
esteemed by all who knew him
    From 1756 to the beginning of 1809 he kept an accurate bill of mortal-
ity for the South parish of Bridgewater, from which it appears that that
part of our country is remarkable for longevity This fact will be duly
noticed in a historical discourse which Dr. Sanger is preparing against
the close of the first century from the gathering of the church in that
parish —[*Alden's Col* 2. 210

EPITAPH.

Beneath are deposited the remains of Lieut Joshua Alden, who died
21st March 1809 in the 80th year of his age
    He led a sober and regular life, was a friend to peace and good order,
a steady attendant on public worship and a valuable member of society.
    In his last will and testament, after some deductions, he bequeathed a
tenth part of his property to the South congregational society in Bridgewater, of which one hundred dollars were for the use of the church, of
which he was a member, two hundred dollars for the encouragement of
psalmody, and the remainder for the fund of said society
    To perpetuate his memory and to express the gratitude due to an exam-
ple so worthy of imitation, it has been thought fit to erect this monument.
                                                        [*Ibid,* 2, 210.

dren upon whom to bestow his estate, a tenth of which
he bequeathed to the congregational church of which he
was a member

F. No. 47. VI D. *Caleb,* who died at the age of two
years.

G. No 48. VII D. *Ezra,* was born 22 June, O S 1734;
a deacon in the congregational church at Greenwich, where
he settled on a farm, and died at the age of 84 years. His
first wife was Miriam, a daughter of Uriah Richardson of
Stafford, and grand-daughter of the Rev. Jacob Green of
Hanover, N J Their children were,

1. Sarah, the wife of Daniel Alden, Jr. originally of Stafford, but afterwards of Lebanon, N H a son of Daniel Alden, Esq Their children were Daniel, Ezra, John, Sarah,
Roxena, Elam, Julius, and Dorothy

2 Judith, the wife of James, a son of Col James Stone.
Their children were James, Jemima, Miriam, Abigail, Elizabeth, and Sarah

3 Eunice, the wife of Capt Abijah Powers Their
children were John, Sarah, Benjamin, Horace, and Alva

4 Ezra, whose wife was Achsah, a daughter of Dea. Nehemiah Stebbins of Longmeadow Their children were Pliny,
Samuel, Alma, Jason, Abel, and Emery Dea Alden's sec·
ond wife was Sarah, the widow of Abel Harwood, and
daughter of Capt Benjamin Ruggles of Hardwick His
children by her were Miriam, Dorothy, the wife of Ebenezer Eaton of Montville, Conn , Anna, the wife of the Rev
Caleb Knight of Monson , Abel, Alice, and Miriam.

H. No 49 VIII D *Timothy,* was born 24 Nov O S.
1736, was graduated at Harvard University, 1762, was ordained pastor of the congregational church in Yarmouth,
Mass 13 Dec 1769, and died 13th Nov 1828, having nearly completed the fifty-ninth year of his pastorate, and the
ninety-second of his age On his grave stone, kindly
erected by his much esteemed people, it is stated that "He
was a faithful and beloved pastor , a man of prayer ; of a
mild, cheerful, amiable disposition, sanctified by grace ; of
great humility ; and exemplary in the various walks of a
long life All his hopes rested on the merits of Jesus Christ,
and his end was peace The memory of the just is blessed " His wife was Sarah, a daughter of the Rev Habijah
Weld of Attleborough, lineally descended, according to
Guillim, from Edrick Sylvaticus, anglicised, Wild or Weld,

a saxon of renown in the days of Harold and William the Conqueror, whose father was Alfrick, a brother of Edrick of Stratton, Duke of Mercia, and in the maternal line, from John Fox the Martyrologist She died 28 Oct 1796, in the 59th year of her age —[*Alden's Coll* *Ant* 60

Their children were,

No 50. 1. Timothy, who was born 28 August, 1771, was graduated at Harvard University, 1794, was ordained a colleague with the Rev. Samuel Haven, D D in the South Congregational Church of Portsmouth, N H 20 Nov 1799 ; was honorably released from his pastoral charge, 31 July, 1805, by the advice of a mutual Council ; was afterwards Principal of an academy for both sexes in Portsmouth ; of a young ladies' academy in Boston, and of the young ladies' boarding academy at Newark in New Jersey; was inaugurated President and Professor, in several departments of Alleghany College at Meadville in Pennsylvania, 28 July, 1817 resigned his connexion with that Institution, 11 Nov 1831, and in 1834 became Principal of the East Liberty Institute, located in a pleasant village, four miles East of the city of Pittsburgh, where, in separate buildings, both sexes are taught in a variety of branches of literature and science His first wife was Elizabeth Shepherd, the only child of Capt Robert Wormsted of Marblehead —[*See Alden's Coll* *Ant* 525

Their children were 1 Martha Wright, who was born at Marblehead, 19 May, 1798, the second wife of the Hon. Patrick Farrelly of Meadville, a native of the County of Caven in Ireland, who died at Pittsburgh, on his way to Congress, 12 Jan 1826 They had one daughter, who died in infancy, and one son, Patrick Alden, who was born 11 August, 1821 Mr Farrelly's former wife was Elizabeth, a daughter of Gen David Mead, the pioneer to French Creek, and the first settler of Meadville By her he had two sons, David Mead and John Wilson, both graduates of Alleghany College, and are in the practice of the law at Meadville. 2 Elizabeth Shepherd Wormsted, who was born at Portsmouth, 23 Nov 1800, the wife of John Gibson, a merchant in Meadville. They had five children, all of whom, except Elizabeth Shepherd, died in infancy. 3. Timothy John Fox, who was born at Portsmouth, 12 April, 1802, was an alumnus of the first class of Alleghany College, which was admitted to the baccalaureate in 1821, and to the degree of Master of Arts in 1824, and settled in the practice of the law at Meadville His wife was Priscilla

Dunn, a daughter of Cornelius Van Horne, originally from New Jersey, one of the first company of settlers on French Creek. Their children were, Timothy Cornelius Wormsted Farrelly, Josephine Willis, Cornelius Van Horne, who died 14 Jan. 1834, at the age of six years, and Harriet. 4. Robert Wormsted, who was born at Portsmouth, 30 Jan. 1804, a graduate of the first class at Alleghany College, for several years a Midshipman in the U. S Navy, and afterwards in the whaling service. 5. Sarah Weld Josephine Nau, who was born at Newark, N. J. 30 Dec. 1812, the wife of Peter Joseph Maitland, a native of Philadelphia, who settled in Pittsburgh. They have one daughter, Mary, who was born 28 Dec 1833.

Mr. Alden's second wife, Sophia Louisa Luker, a native of Farringdon in Berkshire, was the only child of George Mulcock, a merchant, born in Wiltshire, near Highworth, in Great Britain, who brought his family to the United States in 1795, and died at Philadelphia, 21 Dec. 1805, at the age of 44 years. By her he had one daughter, Caroline Ann Grier Mulcock, who was born at Meadville, 31 Jul , 1823.

No 51. 2 Isaiah, who was born 22 Sept 1772, was graduated at Harvard University, in 1799 ; in 1817 settled in Meadville, and has devoted his life to the instruction of youth. His wife was Susanna, a daughter of Barnabas Hedge of Yarmouth Their children were, 1 Betsey, the wife of Augustus Bradley of Meadville Their children were, Adeline Elizabeth, Warren Hedge, Augustus, Susanna, and Harriet, who died in infancy. 2 Eunice Weld. 3. Sarah Weld, the wife of the Rev. James Grier Wilson, a graduate of Alleghany College. 4. Weld Noble.

No 52. 3. Martin, who was born 17 Oct. 1773; was graduated at Harvard University, in 1799 ; was ordained a Congregational Minister of the gospel, without a pastoral charge.

No. 53. 4. Oliver, who was born 9 March, 1775, was educated a merchant in Charleston, S. C. in the house of Crocker & Sturges, whose wife Lucy, was a daughter of David Alden, Jr. formerly of Williamstown, Mass but subsequently of Batavia, Ohio. Their children were Nancy Ward, Julia Ann, David Chandler, Oliver Noble, Henry Williams, Charles Fox, Lucy, and Clinton. Mr. Alden was a magistrate many years, and was engaged in mercantile pursuits till 1829, when he removed to Aldenia, a new village pleasantly situated on the western shore of Konneyaut Lake, Pennsylvania.

No. 54. 5 Sarah Weld, who was born 17 Dec. 1776, the second wife of Capt. Isaac Matthews of Yarmouth, who died at sea, 5 Oct. 1827, as he was returning from a voyage, in the 55th year of his age.

No. 55. 6 Martha Shaw, who was born 8 Jan. 1778, the wife of Capt. Jeremiah Taylor, a native of Yarmouth, who having abandoned a sea-faring life, settled on a farm in Hawley, Mass. where he died. Their children were, 1. Oliver Alden, an alumnus of Alleghany and Union Colleges, and a graduate of both, a theological student at Andover, where he has resided for some time, engaged in translating German authors for the press. 2. Mira, who died in her fourth year. 3. Sarah. 4. Martha 5. Mary Fox, who died in her second year. 6. Timothy Alden, a member of Amherst College. 7 Rufus, a member of Amherst College. 8 Mary Joice.—[*Rev T Alden. M. S.*]

No 56. III C.   SAMUEL ALDEN,
the third son of Dea Joseph Alden, settled at Titiquot, in Middleborough, and had four sons, 1. Samuel, who settled in North Bridgewater ; 2. Josiah ; 3. Simeon ; 4. Silas, who died in the 22d year of his age.

No. 57. I D   SAMUEL ALDEN,
was son of Samuel Alden of Titiquot, (who was a descendant of John Alden of Duxbury,) one of the first settlers in Bridgewater. He married a Williams, had seven sons, Daniel, Silas, Joseph, Samuel, Williams, Seth, and Hosea, and one daughter Hannah, who married James Cary.
   Samuel Alden died in 1816, aged 81.
   1. Daniel, married a Cary, had three sons, Otis, Daniel, and Alpheus, and one daughter Sally, who married a Burr. Otis married an Adams, Daniel 2d, married a Southworth. He and Alpheus live in Randolph.
   2. and 3. Silas and Joseph live in Jay, state of Maine.
   4. Samuel 2d, married a Ford, has one son Sanford, and three daughters, Mehitable, Hannah, and Sally.
   5 Williams, married a Linfield, has three daughters, Mary, Lavina, and Clarissa.
   6 Seth, married a Southworth, and lives in Stoughton.
   7 Hosea, married an Edson.—[*Cary's Genealogy*, 42.

No. 58.   II D.   JOSIAH ALDEN,
son of Samuel Alden of Titiquot, had three sons, Elijah,
Hazael, Josiah.

No. 59.   III D.   SIMEON ALDEN,
brother of the preceding, had eight sons, 1. Simeon, who
married Rachel French   (See French, No 18, 7.)   2. Alpheus ; 3. Silas, who married Polly French, (see French,
No. 5, 9,) for his first wife, and Mrs. Charlotte, widow of
Ezra Thayer, deceased, for his second. (See Thayer, No.
26, 8, and French, No. 18, 8)   4. Solomon ; 5. David ; 6.
Jonathan ; 7. Isaac ; 8. Lot.

No. 60.   IV C.   Capt SETH ALDEN,*
the youngest son of Dea. Joseph Alden, had four sons, 1.
Oliver ; 2 Seth, whose wife was Mary Carver. (See No.
46.) 3. Caleb ; 4. Joseph.

No. 61.   III B   JOHN ALDEN,
the third son of Joseph Alden of Bridgewater, married
Hannah, a daughter of Capt Ebenezer White of Weymouth. (See White, No. 30)   Their children were,
    1. David, who married Juda Paddleford, and settled in
Middleborough
    2. Priscilla, whose husband was Abraham Borden.
    3. Thankful, whose husband was Francis Eaton.
    4. Hannah, whose husband was Thomas Wood.
    5. Lydia, whose first husband was Samuel Eddy, and
second John Fuller
    6 Mary, whose husband was Noah Thomas.
    7. Abigail, whose husband was Nathan Thomas.
    8. Joseph, who married Hannah Hall , settled in Mid-
dleborough.
    9. John, who married Lydia Lazell for his first wife,
and Rebecca Weston for his second, and settled in Middleborough.

---

* HIS EPITAPH.

In memory of Capt. SETH ALDEN, who departed this life 6 September,
1784, in the 75th year of his age.

> The corpse in silent darkness lies,
> Our friend is gone, the Captain dies '
> In peace he lived, in peace he died
> Sleeps sweetly by his consort's side.
> In this dark cell, they both must lie,
> Till th' archangel rends the sky,
> And saints ascend to Christ on high.   [Alden's Col.

10 Ebenezer, who married Anna Whitaker for his first
, wife, and Rebecca Smith for his second.   At twenty years
of age, he went with many others from New England, on
the expedition to Cuba, where he was taken prisoner, and
suffered great hardships, not being released under ten
years.   He settled in Ashfield

11. and 12. Samuel and Nathan, who died at an early
age.

13. Noah, was settled in Bellingham, as a Minister of
the Gospel.—[*Alden's Collection.*   3, 67.

No. 62.   IX C   JOHN ALDEN,
son of John and Hannah Alden, was the subject of the following memoir, which was published in the Christian
Watchman, of April 14, 1821, as follows .

In Middleborough, the venerable John Alden, in the 103d
year of his age   His great grandfather, whose name he
bore, as did also his grandfather* and father, was one of
the first settlers of New England, being one of the number
who accompanied the Rev Mr. Robinson† from Europe to
America in 1620, and is said to have been the man who firs
stepped upon the Plymouth Rock   His grand mother wa
the daughter of Mr. Peregrine White,‡ who was the fi
male child born in New England   Mr Alden was marr
young, and his first wife, by whom he had five child
died at the age of 27.   By his second and last wife he
14 children.   His descendants are 19 children—62
children—134 great grand children, and 7 of the fift
eration, 47 of this number we believe have decease
172 are now living.   When his century sermon was
ed, he is understood to have said that he had read
his bible in course as many times as he was years
retained his bodily strength and mental energy
markable degree   When more than one hund
old, he would converse with great propriety upo
and occasionally repeat whole chapters and qu
ous passages from the sacred scriptures.   He
est man in the Old Colony, and probably the
Commonwealth.   He had been a professor o
connected with a church upwards of 78 y
probably the oldest church member in the
" We understand," says the editor of the

---

*His grandfather was Joseph Alden of Bridgewater.
†Mr. Robinson did not come to this country, but died in
‡His mother was a daughter of Capt Ebenezer White
perhaps she was the grand daughter of Peregrine White.

zette, "that his likeness was taken by a skillful portrait
painter a few weeks before his death, to be deposited in
the gallery of curiosities belonging to the Pilgrim Society,
at Plymouth."

The above memoir was probably taken from a manu-
script book of the venerable John Alden, now in possession
of Solomon Alden, Jr. Esq. of Bridgewater.

No 63.   XIII C.   Rev NOAH ALDEN,

the youngest son of John and Hannah Alden, was born in
that part of Middleborough, called Titiquot, 31 May, 1725,
and in time of a great revival of religion in 1741, became
a convert, and, soon after, a preacher of the gospel of the
baptist denomination.   He was ordained over a society in
Stafford, on the 5 June, 1755, and held his pastoral relation in that place for ten years.   He was dismissed by
the advice of a council, 28 August, 1765   He then travelled and preached in various places till he was installed
in Bellingham, 12 November, 1766, where he was useful,
as long as he lived.   In December, 1763, he went through
Woodstock and only preached one sermon there, but it was
blessed for the conversion of one young man, who had been
a leader in vanity, and he then became so in religion, and
was afterwards a minister of the gospel

"Mr. Alden was a member of the convention which formed the Massachusetts' constitution of government, and so
he was of that which adopted the constitution of the United States   But the affairs of the church of Christ, and
watching for souls, as one who must give an account to
God, were his great concern, until he died, with great
peace of mind, 5 May, 1797, nearly 72 years old."

The subject of this article married Joanna Vaughan, by
whom he had three sons and several daughters

[Alden's Collection. 3, 66.

No 64.   III A.   DAVID ALDEN,

the third son of Hon John Alden, was the representative
of Duxbury for a number of years, in the Old Colony Court,
and in 1690 one of the assistants.   He had two sons, Benjamin and Samuel, and one daughter Alice, who was married 5 December, 1706, to Judah Paddock of Yarmouth, now
Dennis, grandfather of the present Judah Paddock, Esq

No. 65.   I B   BENJAMIN ALDEN,

had four sons and one daughter, Mary, who was the wife
of Doct. John Wadsworth, and the mother of John Wads-

worth, A. M. a much beloved tutor at Harvard College. The sons of Benjamin Alden, were David, Bezaleel, Wrestling, and Abiathar ; the first and last of whom removed to the District of Maine. Abiathar, a Physician, and a man of uncommon metaphysical talents, to Scarborough, the other two spent their days in their native place.

[Alden's Collection. 3, 267.

No. 66. II B. Capt. SAMUEL ALDEN,*

was the second son of David Alden, and brother of Benjamin Alden, before mentioned. He was the father of Col. Ichabod Alden, a brave revolutionary officer, who fell at the time of the destruction of Cherry Valley.

No. 67. IV A. Capt. JONATHAN ALDEN,†

the fourth son of the Hon John Alden, inherited and occupied the ancient homestead. He died in February, 1697, at the age of about 70 years. From the Duxbury records it appears that he married Abigail Ralat, 10 Dec 1672, by whom he had four sons,

---

* It is a remarkable circumstance that Capt. Samuel Alden, and Mrs. Alice Paddock, his sister, two of the grand children of one of the first settlers of the Old Colony, should have been upon the stage at the commencement of the revolutionary war They lived to see the country peopled with three millions of white inhabitants, and successfully opposing the ungenerous usurpation and tyranny of the parent empire. Had any one told the first adventurers, who were often in the utmost jeopardy from then surrounding enemies, that some of their grand children would live to witness such an astonishing population in the vast and dreary region which they beheld, overspread with unknown numbers of savages and beasts of prey, and establishing national liberty and independence, they would have considered it as a thing utterly improbable, if not totally impossible.

This gentleman was remarkable for his strength of mind, soundness of judgment, and exemplary deportment through life He was a pious man, and was ever cheerful through the Christian hope which he had attained. He lived till he was impatient to depart and enter a happier state, though he suffered but little bodily distress

"In memory of Capt. Samuel Alden, who died 24 February, 1781, aged 92 years, 2 months and 3 days."—[Ibid, 3, 274

†Capt Jonathan Alden was buried under arms, 17 February, 1697, on which occasion an address was delivered at the grave, by the Rev. Ichabod Wiswall of Duxbury, a copy of which is still preserved, and from which the following paragraphs are selected :

"Neighbors and friends, we are assembled this day in a posture of mourning, to solemnize the funeral of the present deceased, to pay our last tribute of respect to a person well known among us. I need not enlarge upon his character, but in brief am bold to say thus much. He stepped over his youth without the usual stains of vanity. In his riper years, he improved himself a good Commonwealth's man, and which is the crown

1. Andrew, who settled in Lebanon, Connecticut

2. Jonathan, who also removed to Lebanon, and whose son Dea. Austin Alden, settled at Gorham, in the vicinity of Portland.

3 John, who inherited the place of his father, was a Colonel of the militia, and died 24 July, 1739, at the age of 58 years.

4. Deacon Benjamin Alden, who was drowned near the Gurnet, 14 April, 1741.

No. 68.   I B.   ANDREW ALDEN,

the oldest son of Capt. Jonathan Alden of Duxbury, settled at Lebanon in early life. He married Lydia Stanford, in his native place, and was more than 80 years of age at the time of his death. Their children were, 1. Jabin Alden.

of all, a sincere christian, one whose heart was in the house of God, even when his body was barred thence by the restraints of many difficulties which confined him at home. He could say in truth, Lord I have loved the habitation of thy house   He earnestly desired the enlargement of Jerusalem, and inwardly lamented that the ways to Zion did mourn, because so few did flock to her solemn feasts, but is now united to that general assembly, where is no more cause of sorrow on that account

"As to his quality in our militia, he was a leader, and I dare say, rather loved, than feared of his company, etc etc.

"Fellow Soldiers, you are come to lay your leader in the dust, to lodge him in his quiet and silent repose. You are no more to follow him in the field. No sound of rallying drum, nor shrillest trumpet will awaken him till the general muster, when the Son of God will cause that trumpet to be blown, whose echoes shall shake the foundations of the heavens and the earth, and raise the dead!

"Fellow Soldiers, you have followed him into the field, appeared in your arms, stood your ground, marched, countermarched, made ready, advanced, fired, and retreated, and all at his command. You have been conformable to his military commands and postures, and it is to your credit. But let me tell you, this day he has acted one posture before your eyes, and you are all at a stand! No man stirs a foot after him · but the day is hastening wherein you must all conform to his present posture, I mean, he laid in the dust."

After offering various serious exhortations, with many scriptural references, Mr. Wiswall concludes his address in this manner ·

"Fellow Soldiers, Oh, consider how dreadful it will prove, if, after you have, with a matchless bravery of spirit, acted the part of soldiers on earth, you should in the mean time, forget your christian armour and discipline, and be numbered among those mentioned in Ezek 32—26, 27, who, having been the terror of the mighty in the land of the living, yet went down to hell with their weapons of war, their iniquities remaining upon their bones' which, that you may all escape, follow your deceased leader as he followed Christ, and then, though death may, for a short space of time, tyrannize over your frail bodies in the grave, yet you shall rise with him in triumph, when the great trumpet shall sound, and appear listed in the muster roll of the Prince of the Kings of the earth, the Captain of our eternal salvation.—[*Alden's Collection*, 3, 276.

2 John Alden, whose wife was Elizabeth Ripley, and whose children were Parthenia, the wife of Woodbridge Little, Esq., Violetta, the wife of Isaac Fitch, John, Judah, Captain of a company in the revolutionary war. Hon. Roger Alden of Meadville, Elizabeth, twin sons, Elizabeth.

3. Prince Alden, whose wife was Mary Fitch, and whose children were Mary Mason Fitch, Abigail, Sarah, Lydia, and Andrew.

4. Andrew Alden, whose wife was Rebecca Stanford, by whom he had one daughter, Fear

5. Walter Alden, whose wife was the widow Irene Blackman.

6. Lydia Alden, whose husband was SETH ALDEN, a son of Jonathan Alden, before mentioned, and whose children were Seth, Sybil, Jonathan, Lydia, Felix, Joab, Melissa, Sarah, Christian.

7. William Alden, whose wife was —— Metcalf, and whose children were Eunice, William, Jabin, Sarah, Lydia, and Andrew.—[*Alden's Collection.* 4, 140.

No. 69.   II. B   JONATHAN ALDEN,
the second son of Capt. Jonathan Alden, whose wife was —— Arnold of Marshfield, by whom he had three sons, SETH, Austin, Josiah, also removed to Lebanon, where he departed this life at a great age.—[*Ib.* 4, 140.

No. 70.   III B.   Col. JOHN ALDEN,
the third son of Capt. Jonathan Alden, had four sons,

1. John Alden, who died in infancy.

2. Capt. Samuel Alden, who was master of a merchant ship, and died at Bristol, England, where he married Edith —— and died about the year 1744.

3. Capt. Judah Alden, master of a vessel, who died on his passage to Scotland.

4. Col Briggs Alden, who owned and occupied the ancient seat of his ancestors, and died in October, 1797, at the age of 74 years.

He also had three daughters.

5. Abigail, the wife of Benjamin Loring, who died at the age of 88 years.

6. Deborah, who died a young woman in 1730.

7. Abigail ? (quere) the wife of Col. Anthony Thomas of Marshfield.

No. 71   IV C.   Col. BRIGGS ALDEN,
son of Col. John Alden, had nine children, viz:

1. Hannah, who was the wife of Capt John Gray of Boston, and died in 1790, at the age of 47.

2. John, who was drowned in 1766, at the age of 21.

3 Deborah, whose first husband was Caleb Coffin of Nantucket, and second, Isaac Belknap of Newburgh, in the state of New York, where she died in 1792.

4. Judah, a member of the General Court of Massachusetts, and Justice of the Peace.

5. Nathaniel. 6. Edith. 7. Abigail, the first wife of the Hon. Bezaleel Hayward of Bridgewater.

8. Samuel, who died in November, 1778, by a wound he received in the Penobscot expedition, under Gen. Lovell.

9. Amherst, who died in 1804, at the age of 45 years.

No 72. V A. ELIZABETH ALDEN,

the oldest daughter of the Hon. John Alden, was the wife of William Paybody of Little Compton, in the state of Rhode Island.

The following paragraph is from the Boston News-Letter, 17 June, 1717, and is retained in Judge Sewall's Phœnomena Quœdam Apocalyptica, published in 1727, in connexion with sundry other statements, in evidence of the longevity of the first settlers of the Old Colony, and of their immediate descendants :

" Little Compton, 31 May. This morning died here, Mrs. Elizabeth Paybody, late wife of Mr. William Paybody, in the 93d year of her age. She was a daughter of John Alden, Esq. and Priscilla his wife, daughter of Mr. William Mullins This John Alden and Priscilla Mullins were married at Plymouth, in New England, where their daughter Elizabeth was born She was exemplary, virtuous, and pious, and her memory is blessed. She has left a numerous posterity. Her grand daughter Bradford, is a grand mother."—[Alden's Collection, 3, 279.

No. 73. VI A. SARAH ALDEN,

the second daughter of the Hon. John Alden, was the wife of Alexander Standish, a son of Capt. Myles Standish.

[Ib 3, 267.

NOTE —While the memorial of Plymouth survives, the name of Alden, a brief account of whom is found in Eliot and Allen, cannot be forgotten. Many of his descendants are in honorable place in various parts of the United States, of whom one is an indefatigable antiquary, the President of a College at Meadville, in Pennsylvania, to whose collection of Epitaphs, many acknowledgments are due. The ancestor and his genealogical series down to the present hour, are found in Vol. III. 264—271. [Winthrop's Journal, Vol. I. p 131, by James Savage]

No. 74. VII A.   RUTH ALDEN,

the third daughter of the Hon. John Alden, *was the wife of John Bass of Braintree,* (now Quincy) *a son of Dea. Samuel Bass.* (See Bass, Nos. 1 and 11.—[*Alden's Coll.* 3, 267.

No. 75. VIII A.   MARY ALDEN,

the youngest daughter of the Hon. John Alden, was the wife of Thomas Dillano.*—*Ib.* 3, 268.

---

*Delano, Philip Plymouth, 1623. The name was first spelled De la Noye, by which we may conclude that he was a French protestant, who had united himself to the church of Leyden

[Savage, M. S. Note. Farmer]

THE FAMILY OF ADAMS.

No. 1.   HENRY ADAMS,*

the ancestor of a numerous posterity in this country, came to Mount Wollaston, (now Quincy, but originally a part of Boston. He was accompanied to New England by eight sons, viz.

1. Henry, born in 1604 ; 2. Samuel—3. Thomas—4. Peter—5. Edward—6 Jonathan—7. John—8. Joseph, born in 1626.

No. 2. I A.   HENRY ADAMS,†

son of Henry Adams, married Elizabeth Paine, 17, 8, 1643, at Braintree, and had three children born there, viz.

| 1 Eleazer, | born 5, 6, | 1644 | 3. Elizabeth, | born 11, 9, | 1649 |
| 2 Jasper, | " 23 June, | 1647 | | | |

Children born in Medfield.

| 4. John, | born 14 July, | 1652 | 6 Henry, | born 19 Nov | 1657 |
| 5. Moses, | " 26 Oct | 1654 | 7. Samuel, | " 10 Dec. | 1661 |

No. 3 VIII A.   JOSEPH ADAMS,‡

the youngest son of Henry Adams senior, who was born in

---

* "It appears by his last will, (attested by Benjamin Albee and Richard Bracket,) that he had a wife then living, and a daughter Ursula. Of them there is no notice upon the town records. They may have removed with some of the brothers and died in another town."

Henry Adams was buried on the 8 of October, 1646

† "He was the first Town Clerk of Braintree. He soon afterwards removed to Medfield with three of his brothers, Peter, Edward, and Jonathan, and was the first Town Clerk there as he had been at Braintree He had four children born in Medfield."

"His brothers, Samuel and Thomas, settled in Chelmsford, and were among the earliest settlers of that town, which was incorporated in 1655. If any one of the brothers returned to England, as stated by Alden and others, it must have been John, of whom there is no further trace in this country."

‡ Mr. J. Q. Adams says, "He was a Maltster by trade, as I believe the first Henry had been, and as their descendants continued to be till within the memory of my father He bequeathed by his will a considerable estate for those times, to eight children, three sons, Joseph, John, and Peter,

England, in 1626, was admitted freeman in 1653. He married Abigail, daughter of Capt. John Baxter, 26 Nov. 1650, by whom he had twelve children, viz

1. Hannah,	born 13, 9,	1652	7. Mary,	born 9, 8,	1663
2. Joseph,	" 24, 10,	1654		died an infant.	
3. John,	" 12, 11,	1656	8 Samuel, born 6, 7,		1665
———	died 27, 11,	1656	9 Mary, " 25, 12,		1667
4. Abigail,	born 27, 12,	1658	10 Peter, " 7, 12,		1669
5. John and	" 3, 10,	1661	11. Jonathan, " 31, 11,		1671
6 Bethia,			12 Mehitable, bapt. 23, 9,		1678

and five daughters, Hannah Savill, Abigail Bass, Bethiah Webb, Mary Bass, and Mehitable Adams, who afterwards, 21 July, 1697, married Thomas White, Jr. of Braintree The Dwelling House, Malt House, and the bulk of the property were left to Peter, who was also constituted sole Executor of the will. The elder sons, Joseph and John, had doubtless had some provision made for them before To Joseph, the eldest son, the bequest is only of one acre of salt meadow. To John, who was a merchant in Boston, forty pounds sterling, and ten bushels of apples a year from the farm bequeathed to Peter, whenever John should send to fetch them. To Mehitable, twenty pounds sterling, the parlor chamber, feather bed and the furniture belonging to it, and the right to live in the house given to Peter, as long as she should live a Maid " He served at different times in the town offices of Surveyor of Highways and of Selectman. On the 10th of April, 1673, he was associated in this latter office with Edmund Quincy. His son John, who removed to Boston, was the father of Samuel Adams, (See No. 33,) and grandfather of the distinguished Patriot of that name.

Joseph Adams died 6 Dec. 1694, aged 68.
Abigail Adams died 27 Aug. 1692, aged 58.

The following was from the pen of His Excelleny John Quincy Adams, with many of the remarks relating to the genealogy of this family :

The statement in Alden's Collection, that the first Henry Adams came with his family from Devonshire, was received by the Collector of the Epitaphs from my father, but I believe it was not from Devonshire, but from Braintree in the County of Essex, that he came. My father supposed that they formed a part of the company that came with Gov. Winthrop, in 1630, most of whom were from Devonshire, but at the time when my father formed this opinion, Gov. Winthrop's Journal had not been published, and he had never seen it. The evidence upon which my opinion is founded is contained in that book. When Winthrop and his company arrived in June, 1630, Mount Wollaston was in possession of Thomas Morton In Savage's edition of Winthrop's Journal, vol 1, p 34, is the following entry, under date of 30 September, 1630

1630. Thomas Morton adjudged to be imprisoned, till he were sent into England and his house burnt down, for his many injuries offered to the Indians and other misdemeanors.

Governor Dudley's letter to the Countess of Lincoln, dated 28 March, 1631, expresly says that the settlement at Mount Wollaston had vanished away 1. Hist. Collections, 8, 37.

1632, 14 August "The Braintree company, (which had begun to sit down at Mount Wollaston,) by order of Court removed to Newtown. These were Mr. Hooker's Company" Savage's Winthrop's Journal, 1, 37.

Mr Hooker had been a Lecturer at Chelmsford, in the County of Essex, in 1630, he was silenced as a non-conformist, and laid under bonds

No 4 I B   HANNAH ADAMS,

daughter of Joseph and Abigail Adams, was married to
Samuel Savill, 10, 2, 1672, and had by him five children,

1 Hannah,	born 13, 5, 1674	3. William, &	born 19, Feb 1680
2. Abigail,	" 14, Feb. 1678	4 Deborah,	
		5. Bethiah,	" 17, Oct 1684

On the 21 day of August, 1727, Mr. Samuel Savill was
chosen deacon of the Church —[*Church Records.*

to appear before the Court of High Commission He forfeited his bonds
which were paid by a subscription among his flock, and took refuge in Holland, where he preached at Amsterdam and at Rotterdam for the space of
two years He then returned to England, and embarked clandestinely
for New England He arrived in September, 1633 His *Company* from
Chelmsford and the neighboring village of Braintree, had arrived the year
before, and it is of them that Winthrop speaks in the above extract from
his Journal.

They had *begun* it seems to sit down at Mount Wollaston, but by order
of the General Court, were removed to Newtown, where on the 11th of
October, 1633, Mr Hooker was chosen the Pastor. But at the General
Court at Boston, 15 May, 1634, "those of Newtown complained of straitness for want of land, especially meadow, and desired leave of the Court
to look out either for enlargement or removal, which was granted."

[*Journal,* p 132

And in September, 1634, this straitness for want of lands. caused the
first application of Mr Hooker and part of his company to remove to Hart-
ford, which was afterwards effected. In the mean time at the General
Court assembled on this occasion at Newtown, 3 Sept 1634, it was ordered that *Boston* should have enlargement at Mount Wollaston and Rumney
Marsh—Mount Wollaston became thereby a part of the town of Boston.
On the 11 December, 1634, and again on the 18, the inhabitants of Boston
chose seven men to make division of the Town Lands in the Bay.

Journal, 1, 152

1636, 8 Sept. "The inhabitants of Boston who had taken their farms and
" lots at Mount Wollaston, finding it very burdensome to have their bu-
" siness, &c. so far off, desired to gather a Church there—many meetings
" were about it. The great let was in regard it was given to Boston for
" upholding the town and Church there, which end would be frustrated
" by the removal of so many chief men as would go thither For helping
" of this it was propounded that such as dwelt there should pay six pence
" the acre yearly, for such lands as lay within a mile of the water, and
" three pence for that which lay further off." 1639, 17 Sept. a Church
was gathered at the Mount.—[*Journal,* 1, 308.

Mount Wollaston had been formerly laid to Boston, but many poor men
having lots assigned them there, and not able to use those lands and dwell
still in Boston, they petitioned the town first, to have a minister there, and
after to have leave to gather a church there, which the town at length,
(upon some small composition,) gave way unto—so this day they gathered a church after the usual manner, and chose one Mr. Thomson, a very
gracious, sincere man, and Mr. Flint, a godly man also, their ministers

[p 313.

19 Nov. There was now a church gathered at the Mount, and Mr.
Thomson, (a very holy man, who had been an instrument of much good
at Acomenticus,) was ordained the pastor, the 19 of the 9 month.—[p 323.

At a General Court of Elections, held at Boston, May 13, 1640, the pe-

No 5   II B   JOSEPH ADAMS,
son of Joseph and Abigail Adams, married Mary Chapin,
in 1682, by whom he had two daughters. Mrs Adams,
born 27, 6, 1662.

1 Mary, born 6 February, 1683 | 2. Abigail, born 17 February, 1684

Mrs Mary Adams, died 14 June, 1687. His second wife
was Hannah, daughter of John and Ruth Bass, and grand
daughter of the Hon John Alden   (See Alden No 74, and
Bass No 11.)

3 Joseph,	born	1 Jan.	1689	7. Hannah,	born	21 Feb	1698
4 John,	"	8 Feb	1691	8 Ruth,	"	21 March,	1700
5. Samuel,	"	28 Jan	1694	9. Bethiah,	"	13 June,	1702
6 Josiah,	"	8 Feb.	1696	10 Ebenezer,	"	30 Dec.	1701

Mrs Hannah Adams died 24 Oct. 1705   His third wife
was Elizabeth —— by whom he had one child, viz
Caleb, born 26 May, 1710, and died 4 June, 1710.
Joseph Adams died 12 Feb. 1737   He was at the death
of his father 40 years of age, and in 1698—9, was chosen
a Selectman of Braintree
Mrs. Elizabeth Adams died Feb. 1739

No 6. I C   MARY ADAMS,
daughter of Joseph and Mary Adams, was married to Ephraim Jones of Braintree, 1 April, 1714.

No 7 II C.   ABIGAIL ADAMS,
daughter of Joseph and Mary Adams, was married to Seth

tution of the inhabitants of Mount Wollaston was voted, and granted them
to be a town according to the agreement with Boston, and the town *to be
called Braintree*—[Hancock's Sermons, p. 21

Lastly, the Wonder Working Providence, published in London in 1654,
which gives a particular account of the first churches gathered in New
England, and says under date of the year 1640, "About this time there
was a Town and Church planted at Mount Wollaston and named *Braintree*, it was occasioned by some *old planters* and *certain Farmers* belonging
to the great Town of Boston, they had formerly one Mr. Wheelwright to
preach unto them, (till this Government could no longer contain them,)
they many of them in the mean time belonging to the Church of Christ
at Boston, but after his departure, they gathered into a Church themselves,
having some enlargement of land, they began to be well peopled, calling
to office among them the Reverend and Godly Mr. William Thomson,
and Mr Henry Flint, the one to the office of a Pastor, the other of a Teacher.—[*Wonder Working Providence*, Chap 18, p 161

Comparing together these extracts, it appears to me highly probable
that the *Braintree* company mentioned by Winthrop in 1632, as having begun to settle at Mount Wollaston, did not remove to Newtown, or
at least remained, most of them, where they had begun to settle. That
they were the *old planters* mentioned by the Wonder Working Providence,
and that it was at their solicitation that the name Braintree, the place in
England, whence they came, was given to the town.

Chapin, Jr of Mendon. She died before her father, who by his will left a small bequest to her children. The Rev. Dr Chapin, President of Columbia College, in the District of Columbia, is her great grandson.

No. 8. III C. JOSEPH ADAMS,

son of Joseph and Hannah Adams, was graduated at Harvard College, in 1710, and that same year kept the town school in Braintree The 16 Nov. 1715, he was settled in the Ministry at Newington, N H. which station he sustained for 67 years, and died 26 May, 1783, aged 93 years.

Allen's Biographical Dictionary mentions him as a Minister remarkable for longevity—and notices two of his sermons that were published. He was, while he lived, eminent in his profession, and there are respectable descendants from him still residing in New Hampshire

In his father's will, dated 23 July, 1731, he says, "I have given my son Joseph Adams a Liberal Education, and do hereby further give to him, his heirs, &c. five pounds to be paid in money by my Executors, within one year after my decease" The will mentions also the sons Samuel and Josiah, having been provided with portions, and leaves them small bequests He gives most of his estate to the two sons John and Ebenezer, whom he constitutes jointly his Executors.

No. 9 IV C. JOHN ADAMS,*

son of Joseph and Hannah Adams, married Susannah Boylston of Brookline, by whom he had three children, viz.

1. John, born 19 Oct 1735 | 3. Elihu, born 29 May, 1741
2 Peter Boylston, " 16 Oct 1738 |

No 10. I D. JOHN ADAMS,†

son of Deacon John and Susannah Adams, was graduated at Harvard University, in 1755. He married Abigail, daughter of the late Rev William Smith of Weymouth, 24 Feb 1764. Their children were,

1. Abigail, born 14 July, 1765 | 4 Charles, born ———
2. John Quincy, " 11 July, 1767 | 5. Thomas Boylston, " 15 Sept 1772
3 Susannah, " 28 Dec. 1768 |

Susannah was born at Boston, and probably Charles.

*He was chosed Deacon of the Church in Braintree, 11 May, 1747.
[*Church Records.*

† In the History of Quincy, by the Rev. George Whitney, is the following Memoir of this distinguished Patriot of the Revolution:
"John Adams, son of John Adams, senior, a respectable and valued citizen of this place, born 19 Oct. (Old Style,) 1735.
6

No. 11. I E.   ABIGAIL ADAMS,

was married to the Hon. William Smith of New York, by
whom she had three children, viz.

1 William Steuben, | 3. Caroline Amelia,
2. John Adams, |

She died 15 August, 1813, at the age of 48 years. Before her death she removed to Quincy.

His life was one of the most eventful recorded in the annals of history,
and his name will ever be remembered among the benefactors of his
country, and among the glorious asserters of the rights of man   When
quite young he was not distinguished for an ardent love of learning, to
which he afterwards so severely applied himself   Study was rather an irk-
some task to him, and to those acquainted with his youthful spirit, books
seemed but the fetters of a mind, in coming years destined to work won-
ders in the cause of freedom.   It has been most justly observed, that man
is in a great measure the creature of accidental circumstance, and never
perhaps was this remark more clearly illustrated, than in the history of the
early life of John Adams

To those who knew any thing of the last days of this great man, it is
wholly unnecessary to mention how great were his conversational powers,
and that to all who were so fortunate as to listen to him, the fund of anecdote from which he drew for their instruction, no less than entertain-
ment, was inexhaustible.   It was his delight to speak of interesting inci-
dents, which had been connected with himself, not through vanity or os-
tentation, for these were not a part of his nature, but to bring conviction
to the mind, that of much that was considered abstract truth, there were
found sensible illustrations in common life.   The following anecdote, related by him, even to the last days of his life, with all that good humour,
which was so characteristic of him, it is presumed, has not yet passed
away from the minds of many who have heard it from his own lips, a
few only of his strong expressions are remembered

"When I was a boy, I had to study the Latin Grammar, but it was dull
and I hated it   My father was anxious to send me to College, and therefore I studied the Grammar till I could bear with it no longer, and going
to my father, I told him I did not like study, and asked for some other em-
ployment   It was opposing his wishes and he was quick in his answer,
" Well John," said he, " if Latin Grammar does not suit you, you may try
ditching, perhaps that will, my meadow yonder needs a ditch, and you
may put by Latin and try that"   This seemed a delightful change, and to
the meadow I went   But I soon found ditching harder than Latin, and
the first forenoon was the longest I ever experienced.   That day I eat the
bread of labour, and glad was I when night came on.   That night I made
some comparison between Latin Grammar and ditching, but said not a
word about it.   I dug the next forenoon, and wanted to return to Latin at
dinner, but it was humiliating, and I could not do it.   At night, toil conquer-
ed pride, and I told my father, one of the severest trials of my life, that if
he chose, I would go back to Latin Grammar   He was glad of it, and if
I have since gained any distinction, it has been owing to the two days labour in that abominable ditch."

He was prepared for College in the school of Mr Joseph Marsh, then a
distinguished instructer in this place, and was graduated at Harvard University in 1755   After leaving College, he kept a school in the town of
Worcester ; studied law with Col James Putnam of the same place, and

No. 12. II L JOHN QUINCY ADAMS,

married Catharine Louisa Johnson, daughter of Joshua Johnson of Maryland, by whom he had three sons, viz

1 George Washington, | 3 Charles Francis.
2. John, died 23 October, 1834. |

" He was graduated at Harvard University in 1787, and appointed Professor of Rhetoric and Oratory, in the same institution in 1806. He was sent Minister to several of the Courts of Europe, filled other important offices in Government, was made Secretary of State by President Munroe, in 1817, and in 1825 was President of the United States."

[*History of Quincy*, p 53.

No. 13. I F GEORGE WASHINGTON ADAMS,

was graduated at Harvard University in 1821, engaged in the study and practice of law, in Boston, and was chosen a Representative to the General Court from that city, in 1826.

---

while engaged in this study, wrote his famous letter, so prophetical of the greatness of his country

In his profession he became early distinguished, and was appointed Chief Justice of the Supreme Court He was foremost among that band of Patriots, who laid the foundation of the Independence of our Country. His conduct in the cause of Preston, with his friend Josiah Quincy, Jr. would of itself have made his fame enduring

He was a member of the first Congress, in 1774, and was the bold adviser of the Declaration of Independence He was chosen on the committee to draft that paper, and eloquently defended it He was sent Minister Plenipotentiary to the Court of France, the same to the United Provinces, and was many years the American Minister in France and England. In 1789 he was chosen Vice President of the U S and in 1797 was chosen President. In 1817 he was chosen one of the electors for the choice of President. In 1820 he was sent by his native town to the convention for the purpose of amending the Constitution. He was elected President of the American Academy of Arts and Sciences, had been a member of various other societies—filled the most important stations in the gift of the people, and received the highest honours from our Universities and Colleges.

The latter part of his life was spent in private retirement As an orator, he was one of the most powerful his country ever beheld. It was the remark of Thomas Jefferson, that on the subject of the Independence of the Colonies, John Adams, by his eloquence, " moved us from our seats." In learning he was profound, and in religious knowledge surpassed the Theologians of his age. He died at 6 o'clock, P. M. on the 4th of July, 1826, in the XCI year of his age.

The remarkable circumstance of his death, as well as that of his co-patriot and friend, Thomas Jefferson, on the same day, are too well known to need further remark. It may be worth while to mention, that previous to the fourth of July, he had been solicited to give a sentiment for his fellow townsmen at that days' celebration. "I will give," said he, " *Independence forever.*" On being asked if he would add any thing, he answered, " not a syllable. This sentiment was drank amidst the united acclamations of his fellow townsmen, perhaps at the very moment when his spirit was returning to God who gave it.—[*History of Quincy.*

No. 14   III F. CHARLES FRANCIS ADAMS,
was graduated at Harvard University in 1825, engaged in
the study of Law in Washington, D. C

No. 15.   IV E   CHARLES ADAMS,
son of John and Abigail Adams, married Sarah, daughter
of John Smith, Esq. of New York.   Their children were,

1. Susannah Boylston, | 2. Abigail Louisa Smith.

Mr. Adams was graduated at Harvard University in 1789,
engaged in the study and practice of the Law in New York,
and shortly after died there at the age of 30 years.

No. 16.   V E. THOMAS BOYLSTON ADAMS,
brother of the preceding, married Ann, daughter of Joseph
Harrod of Haverhill.   Their children were,

1. Abigail Smith,   4. Isaac Hull,
2 Elizabeth Coombs,   5 John Quincy,
3. Thomas Boylston,   6. Joseph Harrod

He was graduated at Harvard University in 1790, enter-
ed upon the practice of the Law, and was appointed Chief
Justice for the Southern Circuit of the Court of Common
Pleas.   Judge Adams died 12 March, 1832.

No. 17. II D. PETER BOYLSTON ADAMS,
son of Dea. John and Susannah Adams, married Mary
Crosby, 20 August, 1768.   Their children were,

1. Mary,   born 4 March, 1769 | 3 Ann,   born 19 April, 1773
2. Boylston,   "   24 April, 1771 | 4 Susannah,   "   11 Aug   1777

No. 18. III D.   ELIHU ADAMS,
brother of the preceding, married Thankful, daughter of
Joseph White, Jr. 20 Sept. 1765. (See White No. 24,) and
settled in the South precinct of Braintree, (now Randolph)
Their children were,

1. John, | 3. Elisha.
2. Susannah,

Mrs. Adams survived her husband, and was afterwards
married to Aaron Hobart, Esq. of Abington, by whom she
had four children.

No 19   V C.   SAMUEL ADAMS,
son of Joseph and Hannah Adams, married Sarah, daughter of Dea Moses Paine, 6 Oct. 1720.   (See Paine No. 10.)
Their children were,

1. Samuel,	born 15 June,	1723	5. Moses,	born 31 Jan.	1733
2 Sarah,	" 4 March,	1726	6 Aaron,	" 29 July,	1736
3 Mary,	" 4 April,	1728		Died 6 March, 1740.	
	Died 5 July, 1730.		7 Elijah,	born 16 March,	1738
4. Joseph,	born 27 Nov.	1730	8. Nathaniel,	" 19 Jan.	1755

No. 20 I D.   SAMUEL ADAMS, Jr ,

married Submit Crane, 10 Jan 1767, had no children's
names on Record, in Braintree.

No 21   V D   MOSES ADAMS,

brother of the preceding, married Mary —— by whom was
born, 1 Mary, born 6 Aug 1773.
   Moses Adams, died 9 Oct 1778.

No. 22   VI C.   JOSIAH ADAMS,

son of Joseph and Hannah Adams, married Bethiah, daughter of Samuel and Hannah Thompson, 20 Nov 1718.
   Mrs Adams born 20 March, 1693   Their children were,

1. Josiah,	born 30 Sept	1722	3. Joseph,	born 4 July,	1729
	Died 20 Jan 1723			Died 30 July, 1729.	
2. Josiah,	born 6 Sept.	1727	4. Edward,	born 4 May,	1731

   Josiah Adams and his wife were dismissed from the church
in Braintree to the church in Mendon, 6 June, 1735.
                                              [*Church Records.*

No 23. VII C.   HANNAH ADAMS,

sister of the preceding, was married to Benjamin Owen of
Braintree, 4 Feb. 1725

No 24.   VIII C   RUTH ADAMS,

sister of the preceding, was married to the Rev. Nathan
Webb of Uxbridge, Ms. 23 Nov 1731.

No 25   IX C   BETHIAH ADAMS,

another sister of the preceding, was married to Ebenezer
Hunt of Weymouth, 28 April, 1737

No 26   X C   EBENEZER ADAMS,

a brother of the preceding, married Anne, daughter of Peter Boylston of Brookline. Their children were,

1. Peter,	born 11 June,	1730	4 Ebenezer,	born 15 March.	1737
	Died 2 July, 1730.		5 Zabdiel,	" 5 Nov.	1739
2. Anne,	born 24 July,	1731	6 Micajah,	" 6 March,	1741
3. Boylston,	" 28 Feb.	1734			

No 27. III D. BOYLSTON ADAMS,
son of the preceding, married Molly ——. Their children
were,

| 1 Mary, | born 9 Feb. | 1755 | 3 Elizabeth, born 8 Feb. | 1759 |
| 2. Anne, | " 24 Feb. | 1757 | | |

No. 28. I E. MARY ADAMS,
was married to Elkanah Thayer of Braintree, 10 February,
1772.—[See Thayer No 84 12]

No 29 II E ANNE ADAMS,
was married to Josiah Vinton of Braintree, 27 Oct. 1776.
Their children were,

1 Josiah,	born 27 July,	1777	4. Abel,	born 1 Jan	1784
2. Boylston,	" 10 Dec	1779	5 Nancy Adams, " 26 Mar	1786
3 Thomas,	" 5 Sept.	1781	Died 26 Feb 1806, æ. 19 years 11 m

No. 30. IV D Dea EBENEZER ADAMS,
son of Ebenezer and Anne Adams, married Mehitable
Spear, 14 Dec. 1758. Their children were,

1 Joseph,	born 25 Aug.	1759	6 Alles,	born 10 June,	1770
2 Mehitable,	" 21 Dec	1760	7. Thomas,	baptised 2 Aug. 1772
3 Ebenezer,	" 9 May,	1762	8. Anne Boylston, " 23 Nov. 1774
4. Josiah,	" 17 Oct.	1763	9 Elihu,	" 21 Sept. 1777
5. Zabdiel,	" 9 Dec	1767		

No 31. V D. ZABDIEL ADAMS,
brother of the preceding, was one of the students of Mr.
Joseph Marsh, was graduated at Harvard University, in
1759, and ordained Minister of Lunenburgh, on the 5 Sept.
1764 He continued many years an eminent minister of
the gospel, and died 1 March, 1801, aged 62.

No. 32. IV B ABIGAIL ADAMS,
daughter of Joseph and Abigail Adams, was married to
John, son of John and Ruth Bass —[See Bass No 12, I. B]

No. 33. V B JOHN ADAMS,
brother of the preceding, married Hannah ——. Their
children were,

| 1. Hannah, | born 24 June, | 1685 | 3. Samuel, baptised, 12, 3, | 1689 |
| 2. John, | " 28, 7, | 1687 | 4 Abijah, born in Boston. |

Mr Adams was a merchant in Boston, where his youngest son was born, and perhaps Samuel, who was the father of Gov. Samuel Adams.—[See No 3]

No. 34   VI B   BETHIAH ADAMS,
sister of the preceding, was married to John Webb of
Braintree, May, 1680

No. 35.   IX B.   ᵛMARY ADAMS,
a sister of the preceding, was married to Samuel Webb,
16 Dec 1686   Her second husband was Samuel, son of
John and Ruth Bass.—[See Bass No 27]

"Mary and Samuel, her sister and brother, are supposed
to have died in infancy, as they are not named in their
father's will "—[J. Q. Adams

No. 36.   X B.   Capt PETER ADAMS,
a brother of the preceding, married Mary Webb, 12 Feb.
1695.   Their children were,

1. Mary,	born 27 Jan.	1696	6 Mehitable, born 25 Nov	1708
2 Abigail,	" 13 Aug.	1698	7. Jedidah, " 21 Jan	1711
3. Peter,	" 13 Aug.	1700	8. Bethiah, " 3 July,	1713
4 Hannah,	" 12 Oct.	1702	Died 22 April, 1715.	
5. Esther,	" 11 Aug	1707		

On the 21 day of August, 1727, Capt. Peter Adams was
chosen a deacon, in the room of Dea. Belcher, deceased.

Church Records.

No 37.   VII. C.   JEDIDIAH ADAMS,*
a son of the preceding was graduated at Harvard College
in 1733, was settled in the ministry at Stoughton, 19 Feb.
1746, and on the 19 May, the same year, married Mary
Marsh of Braintree.   Their children were,

1. Peter,	born 9 April,	1747	4 Jedidah,	born 29 Dec.	1755
2 Mary,		1750	5. Peter,	" 3 June,	1756
3 Hannah,	" 4 April.	1753	Died Sept. 1832		

*The following sketch of the life and character of the late Rev. Mr
Adams, is taken from the Massachusetts Mercury of March 8th 1799

" Died at Stoughton 25th ult. Rev. Jedidiah Adams, senior pastor of the
church in that town , having just entered the 89th year of his age, and almost completed the 53d of his ministry.

"The memory of this venerable man is too precious to fall into oblivion,
and his character too worthy for the common brevity of newspaper eulogy.

"He was born at Braintree, (now Quincy) on the 21st of Jan O S 1711.
He received the honours of Harvard University in 1733. After making
choice of the clerical profession, he preached for several years, as a candidate, in various places. This gave him an opportunity of travelling, and
forming an extensive acquaintance with the literary and other respectable
characters in New England, and in other parts of the United States Naturally inquisitive, he acquired, in addition to a large fund of academical
knowledge, a correct knowledge of mankind Constitutionally mild and
benevolent, he was easily formed to a candid and liberal mode of thinking.
His manners soft, modest, and unassuming, received the finishing touch of

No. 38. XII B. MEHITABLE ADAMS,

daughter of Joseph and Abigail Adams, was married to Thomas White, Jr. of Braintree, 21 July, 1697 —[See White No. 16]

genuine politeness   It may truly be said of him, that he was learned without pedantry, polite without affectation, moral without austerity, pious without superstition, and devout without enthusiasm

In the year 1145, after receiving several invitations to settle in the work of the ministry, in other places, he accepted one at Stoughton , and was ordained Feb. 19th, O. S 1746   The parish was then new, (Mr Adams being the first minister,) contained but few inhabitants, and was in some respects, an ineligible situation   Two circumstances however, appear to have rendered the place agreeable to his taste , it was a place of retirement, and at the same time in the vicinity of Boston, and the seat of the Muses.

"His good sense, prudence, and exemplary piety endeared him to the people of his charge   He had many friends, and few, perhaps, no enemies, except those who were enemies to virtue

"Relatively to his political opinions, he was like his brethren, the clergy of New England, a friend to *liberty with order*. He advocated American Independence, and was a firm supporter of the Federal Constitution, and the Constitution of this state. In regard to the latter, he took an active part, being a member of the convention by which it was framed.

"During the last seven years of his life, he was called from the duties of his profession, by indisposition of body, and the infirmities usually attendant on old age. With a disposition, however, naturally placid and serene, meliorated by divine grace, old age did not render him querulous , but though burdened with years, and frequently exercised with great pain and distress, he was remarkable for tranquility, the enjoyment of himself and his friends. After a few days of painful illness, which he endured with that christian patience, for which he was always distinguished, he expired. As he lived greatly beloved, so he died greatly lamented. 'Mark the perfect man, and behold the upright; for the end of that man is peace.' "

The town and parish Records of Medfield, Chelmsford, Medway, Milton, Bellingham, Stoughton, Newington, N. H , Mendon and other ancient towns of New England, would probably furnish numerous further notices of births, marriages and deaths in the family.

The Patriarch Henry Adams was not the only one of the name, even in the earliest settlement of the country   There was a John Adams at Plymouth in 1621, a Jeremy Adams at Cambridge in 1632, a William at Cambridge in 1635, a Nathaniel at Weymouth in 1640   Ferdinando (at Dedham whose children were Abigail born 1639, Bethia 1640, Nathaniel 1642) "Christopher, Alexander, all of whom appear in the lists of freemen about the time, and none of whom have left any trace of kindred with Henry or his eight sons   Many of the name, now living, are doubtless descendants from them."—[J Q. Adams.]

THE FAMILY OF ARNOLD.

No 1.   JOSEPH ARNOLD,

was the first of this name among the early settlers of Braintree   " On the 8th day of the 4th month, 1648, he was married to Rebecca Curtis "   Their children were

1 William,	born 16, 1,	1649	4. Samuel,	born 7, 6,	1658
2. John,	" 2, 2,	1650	5. Ephraim,	" 4, 11,	1664
3. Joseph,	" 8, 8,	1652			

Rebecca, wife of Joseph Arnold, died 14 Aug. 1693.

No. 2.   II A.   JOHN ARNOLD,

married Mary ——, lived in Braintree a number of years, and finally settled in Boston. He was a blacksmith. His children, born in Braintree, were

1. William,	born 22 Nov 1678	2. Mary,	born 12 Sept. 1681

Mary was married to Thomas Copeland, 17 May, 1699, for his third wife. [See Copeland, No. 2.]

His father conveyed a piece of land, lying in Braintree, on Monotoquot river, by deed, dated 14 Aug. 1691, to him, then in Boston. [*Suffolk Regr. Deeds.*

No. 3.   V A.   EPHRAIM ARNOLD,

a brother of the preceding, married Mary ——, and settled in Braintree. Their children were

1. Samuel,	born 7 January, 1689	3. Ephraim,	born 21 July, 1695
2 Mary,	" 1 October, 1690		

No. 4.   I B.   SAMUEL ARNOLD,[*]

a son of the preceding, married Sarah Webb, 13 Sept. 1711. Their children were

1. Samuel,	born 16 May, 1713	7. Moses,	born 11 June,	1722
2 Joseph,		8 Abigail,	" 12 Feb.	1725
3. Mary,	" 22 Dec. 1714	9 Nathaniel, "	18 Oct.	1726
4 Sarah,	" 14 Sept. 1716	10 Deborah, "	14 Nov.	1729
5 Joseph,	" 11 Oct 1718	11 David, "	23 July,	1732
6. John,	" 4 Oct. 1720			

* " 1743. March 23. Buried, Samuel Arnold. He was missing Feb 9,

7

No 5 I C SAMUEL ARNOLD,

a son of the preceding, married Bethiah ————. Their children were

1. John,	born	21 Feb	1741	6 Bethiah,	} born 10 Oct 1750	
2 Samuel,	"	5 Nov	1742	7 Abigail,		
3 William,	"	25 Aug.	1744	8 Mary,	" 14 April, 1752	
4. Sarah,	"	11 April,	1746	9 David,	} " 4 Jan. 1756	
5 Betsey,	"	17 July,	1748	10 Jonathan,		

No. 6 II D. SAMUEL ARNOLD,

the second son of the preceding, married Mary Nash, 4 April, 1767. Their children were

1. Alexander,	5 Ruth,
2. Samuel,	6 Mary Nash,
3. Eliphaz,	7. Rhoda,
4. James,	8. Betsey.

Samuel Arnold died in January, 1805

No. 7. III D. WILLIAM ARNOLD,

a brother of the preceding, married for his first wife, Eleanor Daniels, 14 Nov 1772 , for his second, Rebecca Joslyne, 18 Dec 1773 , and for his third, Susan Hunt, 1 March, 1776, by whom he had one daughter

Susanna,h who died of a bilious colic, 15 Oct 1795, aged 15 years.

No 8. IV D. SARAH ARNOLD,

a sister of the preceding, was married to John Delano, of Hanover, Ms., 27 June, 1767.

No. 9. IX D DAVID ARNOLD,

a brother of the preceding, died suddenly, who had been in a delirious state for a number of years and supported by the town, 2 January, 1796. [Records]

No. 10. X D. JONATHAN ARNOLD,

the twin brother of the preceding, married Lydia Allen, 15 July, 1781

and not found till March 22, though much search was made for him He was at length found in Neponset river, below the mills "

[Braintree Ch. Hist Notices]

NOTE —As so many of this family left their native place and were dispersed abroad at an early period, very few, comparatively, were left on the Braintree records.

No. 11. III C   MARY ARNOLD,
daughter of Samuel and Sarah Arnold, was married to
John Spear, 20 Feb. 1736. [See No 4]

No 12. V C.   JOSEPH ARNOLD,
a brother of the preceding, married Mary ———. Their
children were

1 Sherebiah,	4. Joseph, born 23 April, 1751
2 Benjamin,	5 Mary.
3 Moses,	

No. 13. I D   SHEREBIAH ARNOLD,
married Elizabeth, daughter of Abiah and Elizabeth
Thayer, 27 June, 1772. (See Thayer, No. 28) By whom
he had 1 Joseph. His second wife was Deborah, daughter of Uriah and Deborah Thayer. (See second part,
sixth branch, No 27)

No 14. III D   MOSES ARNOLD,
married Sarah, daughter of Capt. John Vinton, 12 Dec.
1773. Their children were

1 John Vinton, born 25 Oct. 1774	3 Samuel Vinton, born 2 Oct. 1780
2 Moses, " 16 Nov. 1777	4 Ralph, " 29 April,1783

No. 15. IV D   JOSEPH ARNOLD,
a brother of the preceding, married Ruth, daughter of
Atherton Thayer, 25 April, 1778. (See Thayer, No. 95.)
Their children were

1 Joseph, born 20 May, 1779	3 Rachel, born 24 Nov. 1784
2. Ruth, " 6 Jan 1782	4. Atherton Thayer, 7 Nov. 1787

No 16. V D.   MARY ARNOLD,
sister of the preceding, was married to Zachariah, son of
Zachariah and Lydia Thayer, 19 Aug. 1775 (See Thayer,
No. 55–9)

No. 17. II B.   MARY ARNOLD,
daughter of Ephraim and Mary Arnold, was married to
Benjamin Hayward, 1 July, 1708. (See No 3.)

No. 18. III B.   EPHRAIM ARNOLD,
brother of the preceding, married Rachel Mekusett, 2
Feb 1721. Their children were

1 William, born 22 Sept 1721	5 Mary, born 8 Feb. 1732
2. Ephraim, " 28 Jan. 1723	6. Susannah, " 2 Feb, 1734
3 Daniel, " 3 Dec. 1725	7. Susannah, " 27 April, 1737
4 Betsey, " 26 July. 1728	

No. 19. II C.   EPHRAIM ARNOLD,

a son of the preceding, married Elizabeth ——, by whom
he had one son,

Peter, born 14 May, 1753
Widow Elizabeth Arnold, died 12 Sept. 1769.

No. 20. III C. Capt. DANIEL ARNOLD,

a brother of the preceding, married Jerusha Glover, of
Dorchester, 30 June, 1763.   Their children were

1 Joseph Neale, born 10 Oct. 1764	4 Jerusha,	born 27 July,	1774
2. Daniel, " 21 Oct. 1766	5. Elisha,	" 28 March,	1778
3. Elizabeth, " 16 Sept 1770			

NOTE.—There were, in the early settlement of New England, the following persons of this name.

BENEDICT ARNOLD, Providence, 1639. Was president of Rhode Island
in 1663, and continued in office 8 years   He died in 1678

EDWARD, Boston, died 8 August, 1657. Son Barachiah, born in 1653

JOHN, Cambridge, freeman 1635, member of the Ar. Co. 1644; was
probably the same who owned an estate in Boston

JOSEPH, Braintree, 1658. Had sons born there. (The patriarch of this
name in Braintree)

RICHARD, Rhode Island, was one of Sir Edmund Andros' council, 1687.
[Hutchinson's Hist. Memoirs, 317.

SAMUEL, the first minister of Rochester, Ms was ordained in 1684, and
died before 1717   [2 Coll. Mass Hist Soc IV. 257, 262.

THOMAS, Watertown, freeman, 1640, had sons Ichabod, born 1640,
.Richard, born 1642.

WILLIAM, Hingham, 1635, perhaps one of the founders of the first
Baptist Church in Rhode Island   [Farmer's Gen. Reg.

SAMUEL ARNOLD, of Marshfield, conveyed land to John Hull, of Boston,
by deed, dated 6 Dec. 1670. [Suffolk Records.

THE FAMILY OF BASS.

No. 1   ' SAMUEL BASS

came to New England, with his wife Anne, and probably
one or two young children, among the first settlers of the
Massachusetts colony, about 1630, or soon after, and settled in Roxbury, near Hog Bridge. Their names were
enrolled among the earliest members of the first church in
that town, which was gathered as early as 1632, where
they may be seen at this day. He was admitted freeman
14 May, 1634, and lived in Roxbury until about 1640, when
he removed with his family to Braintree, (now Quincy.)
He was admitted a member of that church, " having been
dismissed and recommended to them from the church in
Roxbury, 5 July, 1640." (Hancock's Cent. Sermon, 23.)
He was chosen and ordained the first deacon of the church
in Braintree. Deacon Bass was a man of strong and vigorous mind, and was one of the leading men of the town
for many years. (See Hist of Quincy.) In 1641, and
subsequently, he represented the town in the General
Court twelve years. His children were

1. Samuel,	5. Thomas,
2. Hannah,	6 Joseph,
3. Mary,	7. Sarah.
4. John.	

" Deacon Samuel Bass, aged 94, departed this life upon
the 30th day of Dec. 1694 ; who had been a deacon of the
church of Braintree for the space of above 50 years, and
the first deacon of that church ; and was the father and
grandfather and great grandfather of a hundred and sixty
two children, before he died, the youngest whereof was
Benjamin Bass, the son of Joseph Bass and Mary his wife,
born eleven days before his death."—*Town Records.*

" Mrs. Ann Bass, the wife of Deacon Samuel Bass, aged
93, died 5 Sept. 1693."—[*Ibid.*

No 2   I A   SAMUEL BASS,·
the younger, as denominated on the records, married Mary
Howard, by whom he had one child, probably Samuel

No 3   I B   SAMUEL BASS, Sen. †
probably the son of Samuel and Mary Bass, married Rebecca, daughter of Thomas and Deborah Faxon, 30 July,
1678   Their children were

1 Deborah,	born	5, 6,	1679	7 Sarah, baptized 29, 5,		1694
2 Samuel,	"	8 Nov	1681	8 Seth,	" 20, 4,	1697
3 Samuel,	"	26 March, 1684		9 Nathan,	" 30, 4	1700
4 David,	"	15 Nov	1686	10 Anna,	born 21 Feb	1702
5 Rebecca,	"	2 May,	1689	11. Enoch,	" 18 April,	1704
6 Mary,	"	27 Dec	1691	Died 26 Feb 1707.		

This man was denominated Samuel Bass, senior, being
the oldest of the name of this generation.

No 4.   I C   DEBORAH BASS,
was married to Joseph Webb, of Braintree, 29 Nov. 1699.

No. 5   IV C.   DAVID BASS,
married Mary Ruggles, by whom he had three children,
1. Mary,   born   1 Dec.   1715 | 3 Ruth,   born   7 May ——
2 Hannah,   "   26 Jan.   1718 |

Mary, wife of David Bass, died 25 Oct 1723
His second wife was Elizabeth Belcher, married 12 Feb.
1725.

---

  * He died a young man, leaving his widow Mary and this child, to inherit
his estate, the Inventory of which was "dated the 15th day of the 3d
month, called May, 1653," amounting to £201, 18, 5. He died intestate,
accordingly "The Magistrates did also on the widow's relinquishing her
right in the thirds, did judge it meete and determined that the whole estate
shall be equally divided between the Mother (Mary) and the child ; And
that Mr Howard, in behalf of his daughter, shall give in good security's
to deliver the child of the said Samuel Bass, deceased, the one half of the
said estate, at the age of fourteen years."—[Boston Probate Records.

  † "I am led to conclude, that this Samuel Bass was a grandson of Dea.
Bass, and a son of Samuel Bass, deceased, (No 2.) from a bequest in the
will of Dea. Bass, in the following words,—'4th I give Samuel Bass,
carpenter, seven acres of pasture lands in the stony field, with the salt
meadow he hath already in possession, as also a quarter part of my up-
lands in the Farme, after the legacies above specified are paid   Also half
of the wood lot given to my son Joseph, in the Captain's plane, and sixty
pounds out of Joseph's estate, if he have no children, nor spend it. And
I give Joseph Bass, Jr fifty pounds out of Joseph's estate, except he have
children and spend it ; and forty pounds to my grandson, Samuel Bass,
cooper, out of Joseph's estate, except he have children, or have need to
spend it, and all this is to be after my son Joseph Bass' decease.'" (See
Nos 11-2 and 54-2.)

4. Elizabeth, bapt. 4 Feb 1728 | 6 David,   bapt   5 June, 1733
5 Catherine,   "   6 April, 1730 | 7 Gregory,   "   3 Jan   1745
        Died 12 March, 1738.

No. 6   VIII C.   SETH BASS,

a brother of the preceding, married Eunice Allen, 18 Nov.
1735. Their children were

1 Jeriah,   born   4 Nov   1736 | 2 Samuel, born 3 Nov. 1737
    His second wife was Bathsheba Crosby, married 9 Dec.
1746

No 7.   II D   SAMUEL BASS,

son of the preceding, married Alice Spear, 21 Sept 1758.
Their children were

1 Jeriah,   bapt.   6 Jan.   1760 | 2 Seth,   bapt. 8 March, 1761

No. 8   } Jeriah Bass married Lucretia Savil, about 1783
        { Seth Bass married Mary Jones, about 1779.

No 9.   II A.   HANNAH BASS,

daughter of deacon Samuel and Anne Bass, was married
to Stephen Paine, 15, 9, 1651   (See Paine, No. 2)

No. 10. III A.   MARY BASS,

a sister of the preceding, was married to Capt John Capen,
of Dorchester, in 1647, (See Capen, No 2.)

No. 11 IV A   JOHN BASS,

a brother of the preceding, was probably born in Roxbury
about the year 1632   "On the 12 month, 3, 1657, John
Bass and Ruth Aulden were married by Mr John Aulden,
of Duxbury " (Records of Braintree) Their children
were

1 John,   born   26, 9,   1658 | 5 Hannah,   born 22 4,   1667
2. Samuel,   "   25, 1,   1660 | 6 Mary,   "   11, 12, 1669
3. Ruth,   "   28, 11, 1662 | 7. Sarah, _ "   29, 1,   1672
4 Joseph,   "   5, 10, 1665 |

    Ruth, wife of John Bass, died 12, 8, 1674.
    His second wife was Hannah Sturtephant, of Plymouth,
married 21, 7, 1675
    John Bass died 12 Sept. 1716, in the 84th year of his age.
    "Ann Bass, the wife of John Bass, was dismissed from
the church of Plymouth, and admitted to the church of
Braintree, 30, 8, 1676.—[Church Records.
    Ann and Hannah were synonymous names, at that age

No. 12. I B. JOHN BASS,
son of the preceding, married Abigail, daughter of Joseph
and Abigail Adams (See Adams, Nos. 3–4 and 32) Their
children were

1. John, born 3 June, 1688 | 2. Samuel, born 17 June, 1691.

Abigail, wife of John Bass, Jr. died 26 Oct. 1696, aged
37

His second wife was Rebecca Savil, married 17, 3, 1698.

3. Ebenezer, bapt. 11, 8, 1702 | (ch. records)

John Bass died 30 Sept. 1724

No. 13. I C. JOHN BASS,
son of the preceding, married Lydia Savil, 18 Feb. 1713,
who died in childbed with her infant, 4 Feb. 1715.

His second wife was Hannah Neale, married 21 June,
1716.

Mrs. Bass born 15 March, 1692. Their children were

1 John, born 26 March, 1717 | 4. Joseph, born 29 Feb 1723
2. Benjamin, " 17 Sept. 1719 | 5 Jonathan, " 23 April 1729
3. Jedidiah, " 29 April, 1721 | 6 Hannah, " 12 March 1732

Hannah, wife of John Bass, died 15 May, 1761, aged 69
years, 2 months

No. 14 I D. JOHN BASS,
a son of the preceding, was graduated at Harvard University in 1737 He was a man of great mathematical genius.
(Hist of Quincy.) He was settled in the ministry at Ashford, Ct. 7 Sept 1743, which he afterwards relinquished,
and entered the Medical profession, and died at Providence,
R. I. about 1762, aged 45 years

No. 15 II D. Dea BENJAMIN BASS,
a brother of the preceding, married Mary Brackett, 1 Jan.
1755

Mrs. Bass born 20 July, 1723 Their children were

1 John, born 19 Jan 1756 | 3. Hannah, born 16 June, 1760
2. Mary, " 19 Sept. 1758 | Died 7 July, 1822, aged 62 years.

Mary, wife of Dea Benjamin Bass, died 8 July, 1760,
aged 37.

His second wife was Hannah Jones, of Nantasket, born
10 Dec 1731 ; married 21 July, 1764, and she died 25
April, 1810, aged 78 years, 4 months.

Deacon Benjamin Bass died 24 Sept. 1808, aged 89

No. 16. III D   JEDIDIAH BASS,

a brother of the preceding, married Hannah Tolman, by whom he had two sons,

1. Jedidiah, born 9 June, 1750 | 2. Joseph, born 28 Dec 1751

His second wife was Sarah Hall, of Grafton, married 30 Sept. 1763, by whom

3 Hezekiah, born 1772.

Jedidiah Bass died 12 March, 1806, aged 85, years 10 months. He was blind 16 years before his death.

No. 17. IV D   JOSEPH BASS,

a brother of the preceding, married Hannah Banks, of Boston

He died 23 Sept. 1800, aged 77 years 7 months, leaving no issue.

No 18 V D.   JONATHAN BASS,

a brother of the preceding, married Hannah Hayward, 5 May, 1762. Their children were

1. Jonathan, born | 3. Susannah, bapt. 22 May, 1768
2 Hannah, bapt. 4 Aug. 1765 |

Jonathan Bass died 20 July, 1778, aged 49 years 3 mo

No. 19 VI D   HANNAH BASS,

the sister of the preceding, was married to Josiah Rawson, of Braintree, 28 Aug 1750.

No. 20 II C.   SAMUEL BASS,

son of John and Abigail Bass, married Sarah Savil, 15 Aug. 1723, by whom he had one son,

1. Samuel, born 29 Dec. 1724.

Sarah, wife of Samuel Bass, died 28 Jan. 1725.

His second wife was Hannah Gould, who had one child,

2. Abigail, born 31 Jan. 1728.

No. 21 I D.   SAMUEL BASS, Jr.

son of the preceding, married Anna Rawson, 30 Oct. 1746, by whom he had four children

1. Samuel, born 22 Aug. 1747 | 3. Mary, born 21 Oct. 1750
2. Edward, "   1749 | 4. William, " 19 July, 1755
                                 | Died 21 Aug. 1755

His second wife was Abigail Turner, widow, formerly Crosby.

8

5. Abigail,   born   1758 | 7. Esther,   born   1766
6. Elizabeth,   "   1762 | 8 Josiah,   "   1768
    Samuel Bass died about April, 1807, aged 82.

No. 22. I E.   SAMUEL BASS, 4th

son of the preceding, married Elizabeth Brackett, 29 Sept.
1772. He removed to Braintree, Vermont, where he is
still living. His children were

1. William, bapt. 3 Oct. 1773 | 4 Peter,
2. Samuel, born 2 June, 1775 | 5. Seth,
3. Moses,   " | 6. Hiram

No. 23. II E.   EDWARD BASS,

son of Samuel and Anna Bass, married Bathsheba Keith,
of Bridgewater, daughter of Abiah Keith, 9 Nov. 1771.
1. Isaac, born 5 Nov. 1772 | 2 Ziba, born 28 May, 1774

No 24. *Isaac Bass*, settled in Braintree, Vermont, where
he died, leaving children

No 25. *Ziba Bass*, is the subject of the following Memoir:
    After having completed his professional studies under
the tuition of Dr Ebenezer Alden, of Randolph, he commenced the practice of Medicine in the North parish of
Bridgewater, under the most favorable auspices, with the
fairest prospects of usefulness to his fellow men. His
pleasing address, his affectionate and amiable disposition,
his unwearied attention to the welfare of his patients ; his
assiduity in search of knowledge, and his constant and
undeviating fidelity in all the duties of his profession, won
the affections and established the confidence of a numerous
class of the community in the circle of his acquaintance.
But soon and suddenly he was called away from his earthly
labors, leaving a weeping multitude to deplore his loss
    At his interment, the Rev Dr. Strong, of Randolph,
delivered a funeral sermon, from which the following
extract is made :
    " There we behold the ruins of mortality ! There are the
lifeless remains of one of our fellow creatures, who but a
few days since was numbered among the living, and under
circumstances of health and prosperity ! Where is the
person, who two weeks since, would have marked *him* out
as an earlier victim for the grave than any of his neighbors, friends or acquaintance ? He had, for aught we
knew to the contrary, as fair prospects of long life as any
one of this numerous assembly. But alas ! He is gone !

His work on earth is finished ! How uncertain is life ! How true the observation, that the grave is '*without any order.*' How mysterious are the ways of Providence ! Why should such a fixed enemy to all vice, such a friend to morality, order and regularity in society, such an industrious, economical, useful, prudent, faithful, modest, friendly, amiable, and we hope truly pious man, as was Dr. Bass, be cut down in the midst of his days and usefulness, while so many of a totally different character are spared Such dispensations of Providence are involved in clouds and darkness. But it becomes short sighted mortals to be still, to know and rejoice that the Lord God omnipotent reigneth ; who is infinite in every possible perfection, is under no temptation to do wrong ; who has adopted the wisest and best system of government ; who will bring order out of disorder, regularity out of confusion, and good out of evil, and will not only overrule all things for the highest good of the moral system, but for the best good of every one, who makes him the supreme object of his affection and confidence "

ERECTED TO THE MEMORY
OF
DOCTOR ZIBA BASS,
who died September 23, A D 1804, and in the 31st year of his age.
Giving full proof that usefulness was his grand object in life
He was a pattern of Modesty, Temperance, Fidelity, Prudence, Economy,
and Uprightness, and died in hope of eternal rest and glory.
Hence the following appropriation :
" Blessed are the dead who die in the Lord, from henceforth, yea,
saith the Spirit, that they may rest from their labors,
and their works do follow them "

No. 26   III C   EBENEZER BASS,
son of John and Rebecca Bass, married Sarah Mosely, (Maudsley) of Dorchester, 3 July, 1733, and had one son,
1 Ebenezer, born 11 Dec. 1741.

No. 27   II B.   SAMUEL BASS,
son of John and Ruth Bass, married Mary, daughter of Joseph and Abigail Adams, and widow of Samuel Webb, deceased. (See Adams, No. 35—9 B.) Their children were

1 Jonathan,	bapt 3, 8, 1697	4. Samuel, born 26 July, 1700
2. Abigail,		5. Bethiah, " 2 Feb 1704
3 Mary,	" 14, 6, 1698	

Mary, wife of Samuel Bass, died 9 March, 1706.
He afterwards had a second wife and one child, viz.
Bathsheba. bapt 29 March, 1711.

(as appears by the records of the second church, where he is called Deacon,) who was the wife of Naphtali Thayer. (See 2d part, 10 branch, No. 1.)

No. 28. I C.   JONATHAN BASS,
son of the preceding, married Susannah ————, by whom he had two children.

1. Jonathan, born 19 July, 1720 | 2. Susannah, born 9 Nov. 1722

✗ No. 29. III C   'MARY BASS,
a sister of the preceding, was married to William Bowditch, 2 April, 1720

No. 30. IV C   Dea. SAMUEL BASS,
a brother of the preceding, married Hannah White, 4 Dec 1723 (See White, No 21—2) Their children were

1. Hannah, born 18 Aug. 1725 | 4 Jonathan, born 14 Nov. 1733
2. Abigail,   "   1 Feb. 1728 | 5 Daniel,   "   9 May, 1736
3 Samuel,   "   5 Aug. 1731 | 6 a child,   "   11 Sept 1740
     Died 12 March, 1733 | Died 22 Sept. 1740

Mary, wife of Dea Samuel Bass, died 6 June, 1743. His second wife was Jerusha Webb, married 10 Jan 1744
Dea. Samuel Bass died 3 April, 1768, in his 68th year.

No. 31. I D.   HANNAH BASS,
daughter of the preceding, was married to Dea. Jonathan Wild, 25 Sept. 1744

1. Joshua, born 4 Nov.   1748 | 5 Sarah, born 10 Sept   1757
2. John,   "   3 June,   1751 | 6 Eunice,   "   28 Feb. 1760
3. Jonathan, "   20 April, 1753 | 7. Daniel, "
4. Hannah,   "   26 April, 1755 |

No 32. IV D.   Col. JONATHAN BASS,
a brother of the preceding, married Susannah Belcher, 24 Dec. 1756, and settled in Randolph, (then Braintree.)

1. Samuel, born 15 May, 1757 | 2. Sarah,   born 24 Jan. 1759
Col. Bass died 12 May, 1790, aged 57 years.

No. 33. I E   SAMUEL BASS, Esq.
son of the preceding, married Sally Lawrence, of Lincoln, in 1783, by whom he had

1. Jonathan, born 29 Oct. 1784 | 3 Samuel,
2. Sally,   " | 4 Henry.
Mrs. Sally Bass died
His second wife was Abigail, daughter of Dr. Baylies, of Randolph, Vermont, by whom he has two children.

No. 34. II E.   SARAH BASS,

daughter of Jonathan and Susannah Bass, was married to
Dr. Ebenezer Alden.   (See Alden, No. 40)

1. Ebenezer, born 17 March, 1788 | 3 Susannah.
2. Henry Bass, " 7 June, 1791 |

Mrs. Sarah Alden died 2 Dec. 1833, aged 74.

No 35. V D.   DANIEL BASS,

son of Samuel and Hannah Bass, married Molly Wales.
Their children were

1. Thomas, born 1 Feb 1759 | 2 Molly, born 16 Jan. 1761

Daniel Bass died 19 Jan 1761.

No. 36. III B.   RUTH BASS,

daughter of John and Ruth Bass, was married, and had
issue, but there is no record of her marriage, or of children, in Braintree, but from a clause in her father's will,
it appears that she died before said will was made, leaving
one or more daughters, to wit "I give to my grand
daughters, that are the children of my two deceased
daughters, viz. Ruth and Hannah, 10 s. apiece, to be paid
to each of them by my executor in convenient time after
my decease, to such as are of age, and the rest as they
come of age " Proved 10 Feb 1717. Also, her grandfather, Dea. Samuel Bass, in his last will has the following
bequest "7thly. I give to my grand daughters, except-
ing Sarah Biling, (Billings) all my moveable household
goods ; and HANNAH WALSBEY,' is to share with them, to
be equally divided amongst them, after my decease, &c.
(Will proved Jan. 1695) Was not Hannah Walsbey the
orphan daughter of said Ruth, deceased ? If so, perhaps
her husband was Samuel Walsbey, born 9, 2, 1651, or
David Walsbee, born 29, 7, 1655, (children of David and
Hannah Walsbee.)

No. 37. IV B.   JOSEPH BASS,

a brother of the preceding, married Mary Belcher, 5 June,
1688.

1. Mary, born 22 June, 1690 | 6 John, born 19 Jan. 1702
- 2 Joseph, " 1 July, 1692 | Died 31 Jan. 1702
3 Benjamin, " 19 Dec 1694 | 7. Elizabeth, born 2 Feb. 1703
4. Moses, " 23 Oct. 1696 | 8. Alden, " 28 Oct. 1705
5 Ruth, " 21 March, 1699 |

* Hannah Walsbee, wife of David Walsbee, died 2, 12, 1655 His
second wife was Ruth Ball, married 24, 7, 1656, by whom he had one
child, Ruth, born 22, 7, 1659.—Ruth, wife of David Walsbee, died 1, 1,
1660

Mary, wife of Joseph Bass, died 2 Nov. 1707.
His second wife was Lois Rogers, married 23 Feb. 1708.

No. 38   II C.   JOSEPH BASS,
son of the preceding, married Elizabeth Breck, 14 Sept
1715, and settled in Dorchester

1. Elizabeth, born	15 Nov.	1719	7. William,	born	8 Jan.	1731
Died in infancy			8. Susannah,	"	18 Feb.	1733
2. Elizabeth, born	5 May,	1721	9. Benjamin,	"	24 Oct.	1734
3. Joseph,	",	28 Sept	1723	10 John,		
4. Edward,	"	23 Nov	1726	11 Hannah,		1741
5 Mary,	"	10 Sept.	1728			
6 William,	"	12 Nov	1729			
Died in infancy.						

Capt. Joseph Bass died 9 Jan. 1752
Mrs Elizabeth Bass died 21 June, 1751.
                              [*Dorchester Records*

No. 39.   II D.   ELIZABETH BASS,*
daughter of the preceding, was married to the Rev. Philip
Curtis, of Stoughton, (now Sharon) 6 Sept. 1744.

1. Samuel,	born	11 May,	1746	4 Elizabeth, born	13 Aug. 1750
Died 22 Jan	1747			5 Mary, and ⎞	
2 Samuel,	born	1 Sept	1747	6 Susan. ⎠	
3. Hannah,	"	21 Nov.	1748		

Rev. Philip Curtis married Eliza Randall, 31 Dec 1754,
(2d wife.)—[*Stoughton Records.*

Samuel Curtis, son of the Rev. Philip and Elizabeth
Curtis, was graduated at Harvard College, in 1766 ; en-
tered the study and practice of Medicine, and settled at
Amherst, N. H

Hannah Curtis, was married to James Porter, of Peterborough, N. H.

Elizabeth Curtis, was married to Capt Nathaniel Curtis,
of Boston.

Mary Curtis was married to George Ferguson, of Easton.

Susan Curtis was married to Daniel Coney, Judge of
Probate for the County of Kennebeck, Augusta, Maine.

No 40   III D.   JOSEPH BASS,
son of Joseph and Elizabeth Bass, (No. 38,) married Lydia
Searle, and lived in Dorchester, where seven of his chil-

---

* Here lies the remains of Mrs Elizabeth Curtis, consort of the Rev.
Mr Philip Curtis. She departed this life May the 29th, 1752, aged 31
years.

dren were born ; he afterwards removed to Annapolis, in
Nova Scotia, where his two youngest children were born,

1	Sarah,	born	14 Aug	1748,	Died young
2	Alden,	"	12 July,	1750,	Deceased
3	Sarah,	"	12 Nov.	1751,	Living at Annapolis.
4.	Elizabeth,	"	8 May,	1753,	Living at Minot
5	William,	"	23 Nov.	1755,	Living at Annapolis.
6.	Lydia,	"	11 Oct.	1757,	Deceased.
7	Edward,	"	26 Feb.	1760,	Living at Newburyport.
8	Thankful,	"	24 July,	1762,	Born & living at Annapolis.
9	Joseph,	"	7 July,	1767,	Born and died at Annapolis.

Mrs. Lydia Bass died in 1789.

Mr. Joseph Bass died a few years afterwards.

No. 41   IV D   EDWARD BASS,[*] D D.

son of Joseph and Elizabeth Bass, the first Bishop of the
Protestant Episcopal Church in the Eastern Diocese, was
graduated at Harvard College, in 1744   He married, for
his first wife, Sarah Beck.

His second wife was Mercy Bass, a grand daughter of
his uncle Alden Bass, and settled at Newburyport.

[*] At his decease, the following character appeared in the newspapers of
that date, printed in that town.

"Edward Bass, D D was born at Dorchester, near Boston, on the 23d
day of November, 1726   At the early age of 13 he entered Harvard
College, and commenced Bachelor of Arts at that seminary, in 1744.
From this period until he received the degree of Master of Arts, he was
engaged in instructing a school, occupying his leisure hours in such
studies as were suitable to the profession for which he was intended.
From 1747 to 1751, he resided at the college, making progress in theological studies, and occasionally supplying vacant pulpits in the congregational churches. In 1752, at the invitation of the Episcopal Society in
this place, he went to England, and on the 24th day of May, was ordained
by the excellent Dr. Thomas Sherlock, then Bishop of London, in his
chapel at Fulham.   In the autumn of the same year he returned to New
England, and soon after took charge of the Church in Newbury, at that
time vacant by the death of the Reverend Matthias Plant

"In July, 1789, the University of Pennsylvania conferred on him the
degree of Doctor in Divinity. In 1796, he was unanimously elected by
the Convention of the Protestant Episcopal Churches of the Commonwealth of Massachusetts to the office of Bishop of that Church, and was
accordingly consecrated in Christ Church, on the 7th day of May, 1797,
by the Bishops of Pennsylvania, New York and Maryland   On the 27th
day of the same month he was received and acknowledged in the most
affectionate and respectful manner, by the Clergy of his Diocese, then
assembled in Trinity Church, Boston. Some time after, the Episcopal
churches in the state of Rhode Island, elected him their Bishop, and the
last summer, a convention of the churches in New Hampshire, also put
themselves under his jurisdiction

" Bishop Bass was a sound divine, a critical scholar, an accomplished
gentleman and an exemplary Christian. His manners were polished, his
disposition amiable, his temper mild, his conversation improving, his be-

No 42 IX D   BENJAMIN BASS,
a brother of the preceding, lived in Boston, and died a few years since

No 43 X D   JOHN BASS,
a brother of the preceding, was graduated at Harvard College, in 1761 He went to Nova Scotia and kept a school, where he spent his days and died. He was never married

nevolence warm, his piety uniform, his charity unlimited. For more than fifty years, he sacredly devoted all his talents to his great Lord and Master, in the affectionate and diligent cultivation of that portion of the gospel-vineyard committed to his care Seriously impressed with a sense of the duties of his station, nothing short of necessity formed in his mind an apology for the omission of them. In his public discourses, he aimed at plainness and usefulness From subjects the least connected with practical topics, he rarely failed to draw something calculated to mend the hearts or the manners of his hearers He had nothing of that new-fangled candor, which looks with equal indifference on all opinions, even on the most important subjects. With the most scrupulous respect for the rights of conscience and of private judgment in others, he united a firm and unshaken adherence to that system of christian doctrine and discipline, which he had adopted from conviction. In his devotions, he led his people with the winning example of piety, chastened in its manner with the most temperate gravity, never relaxing into formality, nor strained into enthusiasm Although from principle, as well as habit, he was zealously attached to the forms prescribed by the church, yet on occasions out of the ordinary course, he exhibited in his devotional compositions, a talent rarely equalled, and never excelled, by those whose mode of worship authorizes and requires extemporaneous addresses to the Deity

"In private life, Dr Bass was uniformly amiable and respectable, and this inspired all his associates with affection and reverence ; keeping always in view the decorum of his station in society, he did not morosely abstain from the innocent relaxations of life, but by cheerfully joining in decent and moderate festivity, he taught others how far it was safe to indulge and prudent to restrain.

"But it was in the elevated station of a diocesan, that the character of this excellent man was most fully displayed. Anxious above all things to approve himself to the great Head of the Church, his humility grew with the honors conferred upon him by his brethren. So far was he from claiming the distinctions appertaining to his rank, that he did not receive them without sensible pain, and constantly exhibited a winning example of meekness and gentleness, which gave lustre to all his virtues. Though at some periods of his life he was severely tried, he maintained a moderation and forbearance, which checked the rage of party, and fortified him against sufferings, which a mind less correct must have undergone, in similar situations

"Blest by nature with a vigorous constitution, which he judiciously preserved by temperance and exercise, he enjoyed an uncommon share of health, through the greatest part of his life. On the 10th inst. after an illness of but two days, he died as he had lived, full of piety, resignation and humility ; and is doubtless now receiving the rewards of a long and diligent life, spent in the service of his God and his fellow men."

[*Dr. Morss's Cent. Sermon, p.* 24.

No 44   XI D   HANNAH BASS,

the youngest sister of the preceding, was married to Capt.
Amos Turner, of Medway, 30 Oct 1759

1. Amos,	born	7 Sept	1760	Died	4 Dec.	1820, aged 60.
2. Charles,	"	29 Dec.	1764	"	1 May,	1766.
3 Polly,	"	22 Oct.	1767	"	Oct.	1821.
4. Vesta,	"	26 Sept	1772.			
5. Hannah,	"	27 Aug.	1775	"	10 July,	1821.
6 Charles,	"	14 Sept.	1778.	"	31 March,	1799.

Captain Amos Turner died 1 Aug 1780, aged 50 years.
Her second husband was Henry Mellen, of Hopkinton,
married 1 Sept. 1785
Henry Mellen died 17 March, 1813
Mrs. Hannah Mellen died 12 Aug 1828, aged 87 years

EPITAPH.

Decay, ye tenements of dust,	A nobler mansion waits the just,
Pillars of earthly pride decay,	And Jesus has prepared the way.

No. 45.   III C.   BENJAMIN BASS,

son of Joseph and Mary Bass, was graduated at Harvard
College in 1715, settled in the ministry at Hanover, (Ms)
11 Dec. 1728, and died in 1756, aged 63.

No. 46.   V B.   HANNAH BASS,

daughter of John and Ruth Bass, was married to Joseph,
son of Joseph and Abigail Adams.   (See Adams, No. 5.)

No. 47.   VI B.   MARY BASS,

a sister of the preceding, was married to Christopher
Webb, Jr. 24, 3, 1686, by whom she had,

1 Hannah,	born 16 Dec. 1686	3 Christopher,	born 19 Aug 1690
2. Sarah,	" 10, 10, 1688		

Christopher Webb, Jr. died of the smallpox, in March,
1690.
Her second husband was William Copeland, married 13
April, 1694.   (See Copeland, No. 9)

No. 48.   VII B.   SARAH BASS,

the youngest sister of the preceding, was married to
Ephraim Thayer, 7 Jan. 1692   (See Second Part, No. 1.)

No. 49.   IV A.   THOMAS BASS,

son of Dea. Samuel and Ann Bass, married Sarah Wood,
of Medfield, 4 October, 1660   (Married by Mr. Ralph
Wheelock.)   There children were,

9

1. Abigail,   born   2 Jan   1667 | 4. John,   born 26, 1,   1675
2. Samuel,   "   20 Dec   1669 | 5. Mehitable, "   18 Sept   1678
3. Mary,   "   20, 2,   1672 | Died 24 Jan. 1679.

Sarah, wife of Thomas Bass, died 2½ Dec 1678

His second wife was Susannah Blanchard, of Weymouth, married 1680.

Mr. Thomas Bass lived in Medfield awhile after his marriage, and two of his children were born there; he then removed to Braintree, was chosen a deacon of the church, where he spent the remainder of his days

No. 50. II B.   SAMUEL BASS,

son of Dea. Thomas and Sarah Bass, married Mercy Marsh, 29, 9, 1689 He died with the smallpox on board a vessel, and was thrown overboard with several others, at Nantasket, in August 1690   (See Copeland, No. 74)

No. 51. IV B.   JOHN BASS,

the brother of the preceding, married Elizabeth Neale, 7 March, 1695.

1. Elizabeth, born 5 Sept. 1696 | 4 Henry,   born 20 May, 1704
2 Sarah,   "   19 Sept 1699 | 5 John,   "   7 May,   1706
3. Thomas,   "   7 Oct. 1701 |

No. 52. V A.   JOSEPH BASS,

son of Dea. Samuel and Ann Bass, married Mary ———, who died 15 March, 1678, without issue

His second wife was Deborah ———, by whom he had one child, Deborah, baptized 22, 10, 1700.

Joseph Bass died about 16 Jan. 1714

No. 53. VII A   SARAH BASS,

daughter of Dea. Samuel and Ann Bass, was married to Dea. John Stone, of Watertown, and had one daughter,
Sarah,   born   8, 1,   1663.

Her second husband was Joseph Penniman, married 10 May, 1693. Dea Joseph Penniman died 5 Nov 1705. She survived many years, and was living in Sept. 1739.

[*Hancock's Cent. Sermon.*

THE FAMILY OF BILLINGS.

No 1.   ROGER BILLINGS,

of Dorchester, was a member of the church in 1640, admitted freeman, 1643. (Farmer) By his wife Mary he had one child   1. Mary, born 10, 5, 1643, who died 4, 10, the same year   His second wife Hannah had by him,

2 Mary,		6. Elizabeth, born	27, 8, 1659
3 Hannah,		7. Zipporah, "	21, 3, 1662
4 Ebenezer,		Died 8 Oct 1676.	
5. Roger, born 18, 9,	1657	8 Jonathan, who died 14 Jan. 1677	

Hannah, wife of Roger Billings, died 25, 3, 1662.

No. 2. II A.   MARY BILLINGS,

was married to Samuel Belcher of Braintree, 15, 10, 1663.

No. 3. III A.   HANNAH BILLINGS,

was married to John Penniman of Braintree, 24, 12, 1664.

No 4. IV A. EBENEZER BILLINGS,

married Hannah ————. Their children were,

1. Richard,	born 21 Sept. 1675	8 Benjamin, born 31 May, 1689
2. Ebenezer,	" 13 July, 1677	9 Samuel, " 30 April, 1691
3. Zipporah,	" 20 March, 1679	10. Beriah, } " 21 Dec. 1692
4. Jonathan,	" 24 April, 1681	11 Bezaleel, }
5. Elizabeth,	" 8 March, 1683	12. Hannah, " 3 Jan. 1697
6. Hepzibah,	" 11 May, 1685	13 Elkanah, " Jan. 1698
7. Mary,	" 22 June, 1687	

Hannah, widow of Capt Ebenezer Billings, died 19 Oct. 1732.

No. 5. I B.   RICHARD BILLINGS,

was graduated at Harvard College, in 1698. He was settled in the Ministry at Compton, in the State of Rhode Island.—[*Hist. Coll.* 9, 183

Nov 1, 1704 William Pabodie and Thomas Gray, wrote to Rev. Peter Thatcher and Rev. John Danforth, with others, who on the 29 of the same month, came and ordained

Rev. Richard Billings, Pastor of the church   Ten other members signed the church covenant.

He was a facetious companion, spent much of his time among his parishoners, and being fond of Medical studies, ministered to their bodily as well as spiritual health.

Hist Coll 206.

Mr. Billings instructed the Indians at a Meeting House of their own once a month on the Lord's day —[*Ib.*

No 6. II B   EBENEZER BILLINGS,-
a brother of the preceding, married Jerusha ——.   Their children were,
1. Jerusha,   born 7 August, 1705 | 2 Ebenezer, and perhaps others.
                                       [*Dorchester Records.*

No 7. I C.   JERUSHA BILLINGS,
was married to Cornelius Kollock, 26 Sept. 1723

No 8   II C. EBENEZER BILLINGS, Jr.
married Susannah Hartshorn of Walpole, about 1744, and settled in Stoughton.   Their children were,
1 Timothy,   born 26 March, 1745 | 3 Hepzibah, born 10 April, 1761
2. Sarah,   "   19 June, 1748 | 4. Eunice,   "   13 Sept   1763
        Died 18 Feb 1754. | [*Stoughton Records*

No. 9. V B.   ELIZABETH BILLINGS,
daughter of Ebenezer and Hannah Billings, was married to Stephen Badlam of Weymouth, 17 June, 1719.
                                       Dorchester Records.

No 10. IX B. SAMUEL BILLINGS,
a brother of the preceding, married Sarah Bates, 14 Nov. 1716, whose children were, 1 Samuel. 2. Elijah.

Sarah, wife of Capt. Samuel Billings, died 21 Oct. 1732. His second wife was Hannah Fisher of Dedham, married in 1736   Their children were,
3. Benjamin   born 8 Feb. 1738 | 4. Sarah,   born 23 Aug 1744
                                | Died 4 Dec. 1745 —[*Ib.*

No. 11   I C.   SAMUEL BILLINGS, Jr.
married Keziah Hartshorn of Walpole, about 1743.   Their children were,

---

* Ebenezer Billings, and Ebenezer Billings, Jr. were among the Proprietors of Stoughton Lands, set off to them 20 Sept. 1713, and in 1717, and to Roger Billings the same year, to Elkanah Billings and John Billings, 7 Dec. 1712.

1. Elkanah,	born	4 Oct.	1744	4 Samuel,	born 21 April,	1751
2. Molly,	"	25 Jan.	1747	5 Jacob,	" 19 Aug.	1755
3. Levitt,	"	8 Feb.	1749	6 Spencer,	" 23 Sept	1759

[*Stoughton Records*

No. 12. II C.   ELIJAH BILLINGS,

a brother of the preceding, married Elizabeth Hartshorn of Walpole, about 1746. Their children were,

1. Elkanah,	born 17 April, 1747	3 Elijah,	born 26 Feb. 1750
2 Elijah,	" 5 June, 1749	4 Sarah,	" 14 Feb. 1753
Died 5 Sept. the same year			[*Ib.*

No. 13. III C. BENJAMIN BILLINGS,

son of Samuel and Hannah Billings, married Rachel Pratt of Norton, about 1759 Their children were,

1. Benjamin, born 25 Aug. 1760 | 2 Sarah, born 4 March, 1764 – [*Ib.*

No. 14 X B.   BERIAH BILLINGS,

son of Ebenezer and Hannah Billings, married Mary ——.
Their children were,

1. Hannah, born 23 Aug. 1732 | 2. Beriah, born 16 May, 1739. – [*Ib.*

No. 15. XIII B. ELKANAH BILLINGS,

a brother of the preceding, married Mary Crehore of Dorchester, 26 Sept. 1723. Their children were,

| 1. Elkanah, | born about 1726 | 2 William, | born 5 Aug 1731 |
| Died 16 May, 1743 | | 3 Rebecca, born 19 Sept 1734. – [*Ib.* |

No. 16. V A.   ROGER BILLINGS,

son of Roger and Hannah Billings, married Sarah, daughter of Stephen and Hannah Paine of Braintree, 22 Jan. 1678. (See Paine No. 2, 4) Their children were,

1. Hannah,	born 21 Jan.	1679	7. Stephen,	born 27 Aug.	1691
2. Joseph,	" 27 May,	1681	8 Moses,	" 20 Nov.	1696
3. John,	" 10 March,	1683	9 Ann,	" 4 Aug.	1698
4 Roger,	" 9 Jan	1684	10 Abigail,	" 15 Feb.	1700
5. William,	" 27 July,	1686	11. Elizabeth,	" 11 June,	1702
6. Sarah,	" 27 Feb.	1688	12 Isaac,	" 9 July,	1703

[*Dorchester Records.*

No 17. II B.   JOSEPH BILLINGS,

son of the preceding, married Ruhami ———, and settled in Milton. Their children were,

1. Hannah,	born 25 Feb.	1707	6 William,	born 21 Sept	1717
2 Joseph,	" 17 June,	1709	7. Ebenezer,	" 19 Sept.	1719
3 Benjamin,	" 6 Sept.	1711	8 John,	" 29 May,	1722
4. Sarah,	" 6 Nov.	1712	9. Ruhami,	" 19 Feb.	1725
5. Patience,	" 21 March, 1715			

Ruhami, wife of Joseph Billings, died 2 Feb. 1740, aged 54   Joseph Billings died 18 Jan. 1765.—[*Milton Records.*

No. 18. II C.   JOSEPH BILLINGS,

son of the preceding, married Anna, daughter of Col. John Holman of Milton, 23 June, 1730, (Milton Records,) and settled in Stoughton.   Their children were,

1. Samuel,	born 8 June,	1731	3. Anna,	born 1 Nov. 1736
2. Sarah,	" 6 Feb.	1735	4 Joseph,	" 15 June, 1739
Died 23 Aug. same year.			Died 16 July, same year.	

Anna, wife of Joseph Billings, died 17 Oct N S. 1753, in the 45th year of her age.—[*Stoughton Records.*

No. 19. V C   PATIENCE BILLINGS,

a sister of the preceding, was married to Thomas Vose of Milton, 4 March 1740 —[*Milton Records.*

No. 20. VI C   WILLIAM BILLINGS, 3d.

a brother of the preceding, married Sarah Nason, 22 Dec. 1757, and settled in Stoughton, (now Canton.) Their children were 1. Oliver, born 21 Sept. 1758, and two other sons.

No. 21. VII C.   EBENEZER BILLINGS,

a brother of the preceding, married Jerusha Vose of Milton, about 1744, and settled in Milton. Their children were,
1 Jerusha, who died 12 Feb 1745 | 2 Jerusha, born 29 Oct. 1746
Jerusha, wife of Ebenezer Billings, died 5 Nov. 1746. His second wife was Miriam Davenport of Stoughton, married 23 Feb. 1749, whose children were, -

3 Mary,	born 24 April,	1750	7 Lydia,	born 21 March, 1760
4 Hannah,	" 5 Nov	1752	8 Miriam,	" 10 April, 1763
5. Joseph,	" 12 March,	1755	9. Benjamin,	" 26 Oct. 1765
6. Lemuel,	" 26 March,	1757		

Ebenezer Billings died 16 Sept. 1766.—[*Milton Records.*
2 Jerusha, was married to Roger Sumner of Stoughton, in 1764
3 Mary, was married to Adam Davenport of Milton.
4. Hannah, was married to Henry Vose of Milton.
7. Lydia, was married to William Crehore of Milton.
8. Miriam, was married to Samuel Vose of Milton.

No 22. VIII C   JOHN BILLINGS,

a brother of Ebenezer, last named, married Sarah Spear of

Braintree, about 1744, and settled in Stoughton. Their children were,

1 John,	born	1 Sept.	1745	3 Sarah,	born 15 Aug.	1749
2 Joseph,	"	13 Dec.	1747	4. Frederick,	" 9 Nov.	1752
	Died 22 Feb. 1749.				[*Stoughton Records.*	

No. 23. V B. WILLIAM BILLINGS,

a son of Roger and Sarah Billings, married Ruth Crehore of Milton, 17 June, 1719, and afterwards settled in Stoughton Their children were,

1. William,	2. Ruth, who died 19 Aug. 1736.

No. 24. I C. WILLIAM BILLINGS, Jr.

married Mary Badlam of Weymouth, about 1741–2, and settled it Stoughton. Their children were,

1. William,	born 14 Nov	1742	4. Daniel,	born 11 Feb.	1749
2 Hannah,	" 21 Dec.	1744	5 Sarah,	" 22 Sept.	1751
3 Mary,	" 29 Jan. 1746–7				

No. 25. I D. WILLIAM BILLINGS,

married Mary Leonard of Stoughton, 13 Dec. 1764. He afterwards settled in Boston, and was said to be the first author and publisher of Musick in this country, and his productions in that science are too well known to need even a passing notice. His second wife was Lucy, daughter of Major Robert Swan of Stoughton, married 26 July, 1774.

No. 26. VII B. STEPHEN BILLINGS,

a son of Roger and Sarah Billings, married Elizabeth Fenno, and settled in Stoughton, (now Canton) Their children were,

1 Stephen,	born 23 Feb	1725	7. Amariah,	born 27 Oct.	1738
2 Seth,	" 1 Feb.	1728	8 Abraham, }	" 14 July,	1745
3 Roger,	" 15 March,	1730	9 Isaac. }		
4. Jacob,	" 1 July,	1732	10 Elijah,	" 9 March, 1748
5 Thomas, }	" 14 Oct.	1735	11 Sarah,	" 28 May,	1751
6. Elizabeth, }					

Elizabeth, wife of Stephen Billings, died 17 Oct 1783.

No. 27. I C. STEPHEN BILLINGS, Jr.

married Betty Kenney, about 1751–2, and settled in Stoughton, (now Canton.) Their children were,

1. Nathaniel,	born ————	3. Stephen,	born ————
2 Nathan,	" 14 Nov. 1756	4 John,	" 7 June, 1763

No. 28. II C. SETH BILLINGS,

a brother of the preceding, married Jerusha Redman about

1750, and settled in Stoughton. Their children were,

1 Jerusha,	born 3 Aug.	1750		3. Robert,	born 29 Dec.	1759
2 Seth,	" 30 May,	1756		4 Zemah,	" 15 Aug.	1762
	Died 12 Aug. 1769.					

Seth Billings died 7 Aug. 1766

No 29. III C   ROGER BILLINGS,

a brother of the preceding, married Susannah Wiswall of Dorchester, about 1753. Their children were,

1. Enoch,	born 27 Oct	1754		6 Jesse,	born 8 May,	1765
2 Jonathan,	" 29 Oct.	1756		7 Ruth,	" 7 Aug.	1767
3 Hannah,	" 1 Aug	1759		8 Timothy,	" 16 Aug	1770
4 Elizabeth,	" 24 Aug.	1761		9 Susannah,	" 7 June,	1773
5 Rhoda,	" 19 March,	1763		10. Sally,	" 17 July,	1776

No. 30 IV C.   JACOB BILLINGS,

a brother of the preceding, married Rachel, a daughter of Philip and Mary White of Milton, 3 April, 1760 She was born 29 April, 1739 Their children were,

1. Joseph,	born 10 March,	1763		2. Peter,	born 18 May,	1767
	Died 28 Jan. 1828.					

No. 31. II D.   PETER BILLINGS,

married Rebecca, daughter of Comfort and Grace Whiting* (Whyton) 2 Dec 1784, and settled in Canton. Their children were,

1. Rebecca,	born 4 Oct.	1787		6 Clarissa,	
2 Mary,	" 1 Dec	1789		7 Catharine,	
3 Rachel,	" 8 May,	1792		8 Sarah White, }	Died in infancy.
4. Nancy,	" 11 Oct.	1794		9 Sarah White, }	
5. Hannah,	" 21 July,	1797			

Peter Billings died 26 June 1807.

No. 32. VI C. ELIZABETH BILLINGS,

daughter of Stephen and Elizabeth Billings, was married to Samuel Dwelley, about 1751.

---

* Grace, the wife of Comfort Whyton, was a daughter of John and Joanna Lyscom, and was born 14 Aug O S. 1732, her mother was a Leonard She was married to John Fadden, a Mariner, 12 April, 1751, by whom she had two sons, viz. John, who married Mary Billings, 6 March, 1775. James, who married Mehitable Wentworth, 13 Aug 1772. Her second husband was Comfort Whiting before named, a native of Hingham, by whom she had,

1. Joanna,	born 27 April,	1759		7. Nathaniel,	born 24 Dec.	1768
2. Nathaniel, }	" 28 Jan.	1761		8. Abigail,	" 1 March,	1771
3 Philip, }				9 Lemuel,	"	1773
4 Mary,	" 1 Dec.	1762		10. Grace,	" July,	1775
5 Ruth,	" 6 Nov.	1764		11. Comfort,	" March,	1777
6. Rebecca,	" 6 March,	1767				

No. 33 IX C. ISAAC BILLINGS,

a brother of the preceding, married Mary McKendry of Canton, 7 Sept. 1769. Their children were 1. Mary. 2. Isaac.

No 34 XII B. ISAAC BILLINGS,

a son of Roger and Sarah Billings, was graduated at Harvard College in 1724, and in 1737 or 38, married Beulah Vose of Milton, where he spent his days. Their children were,

1 Sarah, born 14 Jan 1739, the wife of John Daniels, Jr.
2. Elizabeth, " 18 June, 1740, the wife of Joseph Shepard
3. Ruth, " 11 Aug. 1742, the wife of Vern Daniels.
4 Abigail, " 29 July, 1749.

No. 35. C' JONATHAN BILLINGS, Jr.

son of Jonathan Billings of Dorchester, and grandson of Ebenezer and Hannah Billings, (No 4-4) married Sarah, daughter of Nathaniel and Mehitable Guild of Dedham, in 1748. She was born 18 April, 1723. Their children were,

1 Jonathan, born 16 Aug 1749
2 Sarah,
3 Richard,
4. Mary,
5 Mehitable,
6 Hannah,
7. Nathaniel,
8 Susannah,

No 36. JOSEPH BILLINGS,

probably a son of Roger and Hannah Billings of Dorchester, lived in Braintree, who by his wife Hannah had three children born there, viz :

1 Elizabeth, born 13 July, 1691
2 Hannah, " 23 March, 1693
3. Joseph, born 17 May, 1695
[Braintree Records.

There was a JOHN BILLINGS, Portsmouth, 1640, Belknap 1 Hist. N. H. 47. NATHANIEL, Concord, was admitted freeman 1641, and died 24 Aug. 1673, leaving sons Nathaniel, and John, who married Elizabeth Hastings, 1661, and died 1704, Shattuck, M. S Hist. Concord. (ROGER, Dorchester, the progenitor of the foregoing numbered families.) WILLIAM, one of the proprietors of Lancaster.—(Farmer.)

10

THE FAMILY OF CAPEN.

No 1.   **BERNARD CAPEN,**

with his wife Jane were among the early settlers of Dorchester, and are supposed to be the Progenitors of all of the name of Capen in New England, if not in the United States. "He was admitted freeman 1636, died 8 Nov. 1638, aged 76 His widow Jane Capen, died 26 March, 1653, aged 75."—[*Dorchester Sexton's Monitor*, 13. *Farmer*.

No. 2. A.   **Capt JOHN CAPEN,** *

was the only son of Bernard Capen, of whom we have any record. He came to this country with his aged parents, and settled in Dorchester, from which records it appears he had two children by his first wife Rœdegon.

1 Joanna,   born 3, 8, 1638 | 2. John,   born 21, 8, 1639
       Died 19, 9, 1638. |

His second wife was Mary Bass of Braintree. Their children were,

3. Samuel,	7. Joseph,	born 29, 10,	1658
4. Mary,	8. Hannah,	" 1, 8,	1662
5. Bernard,	9 Elizabeth,	" 29, 10,	1666
6. Preserved, born 4, 1, 1656-7			

Capt. John Capen died 4 April, 1692, aged 80.

---

* "John Capen son of Bernard and Jane Capen, born in England in 1612, admitted freeman 1634, married Mary, the daughter of Goodman Bass, deacon of the first Church in Braintree in the year 1647, as appears of three letters of courtship written by him to her; the first dated 15, 2—the second the 5, 3, and the third 1, 5 mo 1647. He was ordained deacon of the Church in Dorchester, Feb. 13, 1658, and died April 4, 1692, aged 80 ; having been deacon 33 years and 2 months, Selectman 16 years, Representative of the town 6 years, Recorder (town clerk) 13 years, a Military Officer 50 years, the last rank he held was that of Captain of the whole militia of the town. Mary, his widow, died June 29, 1704, aged 73 years.
                            [*Rev Dr Harris.*

No 3. II B.   JOHN CAPEN, Jr.,
married Susannah Barsham, 19, 9, 1663, and spent his days
in Dorchester. Their children were,

1 Susannah,	born 16, 7,	1664	7. Dorothy,	born 16, 7,	1673
2. John,	who died 7 Aug.	1681	8 Purchase,	" 14 Nov.	1675
3 Samuel,	born 28, 8,	1667	9. Nathaniel,	" 1 Oct.	1677
4 Thankful,	" 22, 2,	1669	Died 29 Nov. 1682.		
5 Sarah,	" 9, 10,	1670	10 Elizabeth, who died 17 Apr. 1680		
6. Dorothy,	" 13, 8,	1672	11. Elizabeth, born 21 March, 1682		
Died 27, 9, 1672.			12 Hannah,	" 21 Oct.	1684

No. 4. III C   SAMUEL CAPEN,
son of the preceding, married Ann —— and lived in Dorchester. Their children were,

| 1. Hannah, | born 1 March, 1696 | 3. John, | born 21 March, 1702 |
| 2. Samuel, | " 6 July, 1698 | 4 Purchase, | " 17 Aug. 1703 |

No. 5. I D.   HANNAH CAPEN,
was married to John Glover of Dorchester, 15 Feb. 1714.

No. 6. III D.   JOHN CAPEN,
married Elizabeth Hall of Dorchester, 5 Jan. 1727.

No. 7. IV C.   SARAH CAPEN,
daughter of John and Susannah Capen, was married to
Jonathan Clap of Dorchester, 23 June 1703

No. 8. IX C. ELIZABETH CAPEN,
a sister of the preceding, was married to Samuel Lyon of
Roxbury, 1 Dec. 1703.

No. 9 III B.   SAMUEL CAPEN,
son of Capt. John and Mary Capen, married Susannah
Payson, 9, 2, 1673. Their children were,

1. Samuel,	born 1, 12,	1673	6. Edward,	born 24 Sept.	1683
Died 5, 4, 1674.			7. Samuel,	" 1 March,	1686
2. Samuel,	born 4 Nov.	1675	8 Susannah,	" 10 Nov.	1688
Died 6 Jan 1676			9. Jabish,	" 3 March,	1690
3 Hopestill,	born 13 Oct	1677	10 Jonathan,	" 17 March,	1691
4. Mary,	" 23 Sept	1679	11 Susannah,	" 5 Sept.	1693
5 Ebenezer,	" 30 April,	1682	12. John,	" 19 June,	1696
Died 1 Nov 1682.			13. Elizabeth,	" 28 Sept.	1698

No. 10 III C. HOPESTILL CAPEN,
married Thankful Baker of Dorchester, 14 Aug. 1702.
    Their children were,

| 1. Hopestill, | born 31 July, | 1704 | 2. Thankful, | born 30 Dec. | 1706 |

Thankful Capen was married to Jacob Humphrey, 26 Nov. 1730.

No. 11. IV C.   MARY CAPEN,
daughter of Samuel and Susannah Capen, was married to John Preston of Dorchester, 21 May, 1701.

No. 12. VI C.   EDWARD CAPEN,
a brother of the preceding, married Patience Tolman. Their children were, 1. Edward, who died young. 2. John, who married a Davis of Roxbury, and had five sons, John, Edward, Lemuel, Aaron, Joel, and four daughters, one of whom was the wife of Abraham, son of Edward and Susannah Capen, (No. 21)

No. 13. VII C   SAMUEL CAPEN,
a brother of the preceding, lived in Dorchester and had two sons, and perhaps other children 1. Josiah, 2. Robert.

No. 14. I D.   JOSIAH CAPEN,
married Charity Dwelley of Dorchester, 1 Jan 1744, by whom he had four sons, Josiah, Samuel, Benjamin, Lemuel, and one daughter The two oldest sons died young, the other two settled in Watertown.

No. 15. II D   ROBERT CAPEN,
married Jane Lyon of Dorchester, 1 Nov 1744. He lived near the Meeting House in Stoughton Their children were

1 Samuel,	born		Died 7 May, 1755.		
2 Lydia,	" 27 Feb.	1747	6 Robert,	born 2 Aug	1752
3. Robert,	" 28 Feb.	1749	7 Waitstill,	" 25 Sept.	1753
Died 9 Feb 1750.			8 Bethiah,	" 19 Sept.	1756
4. Robert,	born 11 Aug.	1750	9 Andrew,		
Died — August, 1752.			10. Hannah.		
5. Sarah,	born 12 April,	1751			

No. 16 I E.   SAMUEL CAPEN,
son of the preceding, married Elizabeth Withington about 1767. Their children were,

1. Robert,	born 1 May,	1768	3. Olive,	born 28 Sept.	1772
2. John,	" 11 March,	1770	4. Samuel,	" 27 May,	1777

Samuel Capen, Gent died in Dec. 1809, leaving a widow Elizabeth, two children, Samuel and Olive Wentworth and one grand-daughter Eliza, daughter of John Capen, deceased

No. 17. IX E ANDREW CAPEN,

a brother of the preceding, married Hannah Richards
Their children were Robert, Andrew, Nahum, a bookseller
in Boston of the firm of Marsh, Capen & Lyon, Benjamin
and John.

No. 18. X C JONATHAN CAPEN,

son of Samuel and Susannah Capen, married Jane, daughter of Dea Ebenezer Houghton of Milton, 22 Feb. 1722.
Their children were,

1 Elizabeth,	4 Edward,
2. Jonathan,	5 Joseph,
3. Samuel,	6 Jane

No. 19 II D. JONATHAN CAPEN, Jr

married Jerusha Talbot, 20 Nov 1746 and settled in Stoughton. Their children were,
1. Rebecca, born 3 July, 1748, the wife of Elijah Wentworth. 2. Jerusha, born 16 May, 1750, the wife of Jacob Leonard. 3 Jonathan, born 20 Sept. 1752, married Hannah Glover, and had a number of daughters and two sons, Jonathan, who died young, and Thomas who is now living in Stoughton with his father 4. John, born 13 Feb. 1755, married Patience Drake, and had five sons, John, Nathan, Adam, Peter and George, who are all now living. 5. Melatiah, born 10 Sept. 1757, the wife of Jos Porter, Jr. 6 Theophilus, born 5 June, 1760, married Rachel Lambert, and moved into the State of Vermont He had a number of sons and daughters. 7. Eleanor, born 18 June, 1763, the wife of David Wadsworth 8 Azubah, born 20 March, 1766, the wife of David Clap
Jonathan Capen died in August, 1813

No 20 III D. SAMUEL CAPEN,

a brother of the preceding, married Sarah Bailey of Dorchester, about 1756. Their children were,
1. Elisha, born 20 March, 1757, his wife was Mille Gay, and his children were Elisha, Samuel, Avery, and three daughters. 2 Rachel, born 11 Sept. 1759, was the wife of Col. Robert Swan 3. William, born 13 June, 1763, his wife was Rebecca Swan, had one son William, who lives in Boston, and one daughter. 4 Elijah, born 5 May, 1768, who probably died young.

No 21. IV D EDWARD CAPEN,

a brother of the preceding, married Susannah, daughter of

Benjamin Clap   Their children were,

1 James, born 13 Dec 1756, married Elizabeth Cummings. Their children were James, Asa, Samuel, Susannah, Betsey, Azel, Ansel, Zilpah   Their grand-children are very numerous

2 Hannah.		7. Jane,	
3 Susannah,		8 Benjamin, born 13 Sept. 1772	
4 Edward,	born 12 April, 1762	9 Abraham, } " 1 June, 1774	
5 Lemuel,	"	10 Sarah, }	
6. Uriah,	" 24 May, 1767	11 Joseph.	

Abraham, married Elizabeth, daughter of Capt Isaac Thayer (See Thayer, No 48, 1)   He afterwards married a daughter of John Capen   (See Capen, No 12)

Joseph, died in March, 1813, leaving his widow Lydia, and two children, Elizabeth and Mary   Lydia his widow was afterwards married to Samuel, son of John Capen (See No 22)

No 22 XII C   JOHN CAPEN,

son of Samuel and Susannah Capen, married a Miss Bugbee of Roxbury   Their children were,

1 *Samuel*, whose wife was Lydia, widow of Joseph Capen, by whom he had one son, named Samuel John (See No 21, 11) 2 *John*, who is now living in Dorchester

No 23 IV B   MARY CAPEN,

daughter of Capt John and Mary Capen, was married to James Foster, 22 Sept. 1674 —[*Dorchester Records*

No 24 V B   BERNARD CAPEN,

a brother of the preceding, married Sarah Trott of Dorchester, 2 June, 1675   Their children were,

1 Bernard,	born 26 March, 1676	4 Joseph,	born 28 Nov.	1681
2 John,	" 18 Feb 1677	Died 5 Sept 1691.		
	Died the same day.	5 James,	born 8, 2,	1684
3 Sarah,	born 5 Jan. 1678	Died the same day.		
		6 John,	born 1 July,	1685

No 25   BERNARD CAPEN, Jr.

married Sarah Clap of Dorchester, 14 Dec 1704.   Their children were,

1. Bernard, born 5 Feb. 1706 | 2 Joseph, born 27 Oct. 1707

No. 26 VI B PRESERVED CAPEN,

son of Capt. John and Mary Capen, married Mary Payson of Dorchester, 16 May, 1682   Their children were,

1 Mary,	born 28 March,	1683	5 John,	born 16 Oct	1691
2 Preserved,	" 10 April,	1686	6 Ebenezer,	" 6 Sept.	1698
3. Elizabeth,	" 1 March,	1690	7 Ebenezer,	" 8 Jan	1700
4 Anne,	" 12 Nov.	1692	8 Anne,	" 9 May,	1703

No 27   II C   PRESERVED CAPEN, Jr.

married Susannah Withington of Dorchester, 11 Aug 1708, and afterwards settled in Stoughton   Their children were,

1 Preserved,	born 12 May,	1710	4 David,	born 3 April,	1720
2 Ebenezer,	" 15 April,	1716	5 Elijah,	" 6 June,	1724
3. Susannah,	" 20 Jan.	1718	6 Mary,	" 16 July,	1729
				Died 19 May, 1746, aged 17	

Preserved Capen died 18 Oct 1757, aged 71 years 6 months. Susannah, widow of Preserved Capen, died 14 Oct 1762, in the 74th year of her age

No 28   II D.   EBENEZER CAPEN,

a son of the preceding, married Elizabeth ————, and settled in Stoughton. Their children were,

1. Ezekiel,	born 28 July,	1745	4. Susannah,	born 18 Sept	1751
2 Lemuel,	" 6 Dec.	1747	5 Samuel,	" 17 Nov.	1754
3. Susannah,	" 18 Feb.	1750			

He married Abigail Kingsbury of Dedham, in 1763, his second wife, by whom he had one son Nathaniel, now living in Dedham.

He married Mrs Jerusha Leonard, a widow, 25 Dec. 1771, who had by him two sons, Oliver and William.

No 29.   IV D.   DAVID CAPEN,

son of Preserved and Susannah Capen, married Relief —— and settled in Stoughton. Their children were,

1 David,	born 28 July,	1747	4 Susannah,	born 19 April,	1751
2. Thomas,	" 30 July,	1748	5 Sarah,	" 22 Oct.	1753
3 David,	" 7 Jan.	1750	6 Molly,	" 10 May,	1755

No. 30   V D.   ELIJAH CAPEN,

a brother of the preceding, married Elizabeth Bird, about 1743, and settled in Stoughton. Mrs. Capen was born in 1716. Their children were,

1. Elijah,	born 25 June,	1744	4. Elijah,	born 5 June,	1749
	Died 5 Sept 1744.		5 Sarah,	" 14 Feb N S	1753
2. Damaris,	born 26 June,	1745	6. Samuel,	" 20 May,	1757
3 Mary,	" 8 March,	1747			

Elizabeth, wife of Elijah Capen, died 10 February, 1786, aged 71 years

No 31.　VII B　　JOSEPH CAPEN,
a son of Capt John and Mary Capen, was graduated at
Harvard College in 1677, ordained at Topsfield, 11 June,
1684　He married Priscilla Appleton, (Felt's Hist. of Ipswich, p 171,) died 30 June, 1725, aged 67　His widow
Mrs Priscilla Capen, died 18 Oct. 1743. Their children were

1　Priscilla, born 1 Sept 1685, married 21 Sept. 1708,
Caleb Thomas of Marshfield.

2. John, born 15 June 1687, died 26 April, 1732　(It appears that he had a daughter baptized 1 Feb. 1715-16.)

3. Mary, bapt 17 Feb 1688-9—married 5 Jan. 1709-10
Thomas Baker of Topsfield

4. Elizabeth, bapt. 26 April, 1691—married 12 Oct. 1711
Simon Bradstreet of Topsfield　Mrs Bradstreet died 22
March, 1781.　Simon Bradstreet, born 14 April, 1682. He
was a son of John and Sarah Bradstreet, and a grandson
of Gov Simon Bradstreet

5 Joseph, bapt 6 Aug 1693, died in youth.

6. Nathaniel, born 13 July, 1695, died 16 Feb. 1749-50,
unmarried

7.　Sarah, born 2 April, 1699, married 9 May, 1717 John
Bradford of Boston

No. 32　　　　JOHN CAPEN,
supposed to be a son of Preserved and Mary Capen, (No.
26-5,) married Ruth, daughter of Ephraim and Sarah Thayer, 20 Sept 1722, and settled in Braintree.　(See second
part, 8 Branch, No 1)

NOTE.—Rev. Joseph Capen delivered a funeral sermon occasioned by
the death of Rev Joseph Green, minister of Salem Village, now Danvers,
North Parish, which sermon was printed with a prefatory epistle, by Dr.
Increase Mather.—*Town Clerk of Topsfield.*

THE FAMILY OF COPELAND.

No. 1.   "LAWRENCE COPELAND,

was married to Lydia Townsend, the twelfth day of the tenth month 1651, by Mr. Hibbins of Boston." There children were,

1. Thomas,	born 3, 10,	1652	5 Lydia,	born 31, 3,	1661
	Died 4, 11, 1652.		6 Ephraim,	" 17, 11,	1665
2. Thomas,	born 8, 12,	1654	7. Hannah,	" 25, 12,	1668
3 William,	" 15, 9,	1656	8. Richard,	" 11, 5,	1672
4. John,	" 10, 12,	1658	9 Abigail,	"	1674

" Lawrence Copeland, a very aged man, born in the Reigne of our gracious Sovereign Queen Elizabeth, of blessed memory, dyed December, ye. 30, 1699.

"Lydia, wife of Lawrence Copeland, dyed 8 Jan. 1688."

[*Braintree Records.*

No. 2. II A.   THOMAS COPELAND,

a son of the above Lawrence, married Mehitable Atwood, widow, 3 Feb 1692, by whom he had

1. Mary, born 24 Nov. 1692.   Mehitable, wife of Thomas Copeland, died 2 Nov. 1695, aged about 30 years.   His second wife was Mercy ———, who died 20 Feb 1699. His third wife was Mary daughter of John Arnold. (See Arnold, No. 2, 2,) married 17 May, 1699.   Their children were,

2. Thomas,	born 10 April, 1700	4 Nathaniel,	born 30 April, 1704
3 Sarah,	" 23 Dec. 1700		Died 11 May, 1706.
		5. Elizabeth,	born 18 June, 1706

Thomas Copeland died 6 June, 1706.

No. 3. I B.   MARY COPELAND,

daughter of the preceding, was married to Ephraim Thayer, Jr. 1 April, 1718. (See second part, 2. Branch, No. 1.)

No. 4. II B. THOMAS COPELAND, Jr.

married Susannah ———.   Their children were,

11

1. Susannah,	born	8 May,	1724	6. Elizabeth,	born	7 Feb	1735
2 Jane,	"	14 Oct	1725	7 Gershom Collier,			1738
3 Thomas,	"	20 April,	1729	8 Thomas,	born	19 Jan.	1741
4 Jacob,	"	Jan	1731	9. Josiah,	"		1743
5. Mary,	"	23 Feb.	1733				

No. 5.   IV C   JACOB COPELAND,

of Boston, son of the preceding, married Rachel Adams of Stoughton, about 1765, and settled in Stoughton. By her he had 1. Rachel, born 10 Aug 1766
  Rachel, wife of Jacob Copeland, died 10 Nov 1766.

No 6.   VII C.   GERSHOM C. COPELAND,

a brother of the preceding, married Betsey Collier of Hull, 7 April, 1764   Gershom Copeland, Jr of Weymouth, died in Oct. 1807, leaving a widow Hannah Copeland, who died in March, 1814.

No. 7   III B.   SARAH COPELAND,

daughter of Thomas and Mary Copeland, was married to Jonathan Hayden of Braintree, 22 Dec 1719.

No. 8.   V B.   ELIZABETH COPELAND,

sister of the preceding, was married to Benjamin Paine, May, 1725. (See Paine, No. 15)

No. 9.   III A.   WILLIAM COPELAND,

a son of Lawrence and Lydia Copeland, married Mary, widow of Cristopher Webb, Jr. and daughter of John and Ruth Bass, 13 April, 1694. (See Bass, No. 47.) Their children were,

1. William,	born	7 March,	1695	6 Joseph,	born	18 May,	1706
2. Ephraim,	"	1 Feb	1697	7. Benjamin,	"	5 Oct.	1708
3. Ebenezer,	"	16 Feb.	1698	8. Moses,	"	28 May,	1710
4. Jonathan,	"	31 Aug	1701	9. Mary,	"	28 May,	1713
5. David,	"	15 April	1701				

No. 10.   I B.   WILLIAM COPELAND, Jr.

married Mary, daughter of Richard and Rebecca Thayer, 15 June, 1718. (See Thayer, Nos. 3 and 31.) Their children were,

1. Rebecca,	born	16 March,	1718	4. James,	born	19 March,	1724
2. Lydia,	"	25 Oct.	1720	5. Mary,	"	31 May,	1726
3. William,	"	19 Aug.	1722	6. Anna,	"	4 Aug.	1728
	Died 29 June, 1727.			7. William,	"	6 Dec.	1730

No 11. III B. EBENEZER COPELAND,
a brother of the preceding, married Deborah, daughter of
Samuel and Deborah White, 17 Feb. 1726. (See White,
No 21) Their children were,
  1. Deborah, 2. Abigail, 3. Mary, 4. Hannah.

No. 12. *Deborah*, was married to Uriah Thayer. (Second
        part, 6 Branch, No 2)
No. 13   *Abigail*, was married to Daniel Kingman of
        Bridgewater.
No 14.   *Mary*, was married to Thomas Belcher, 6 Aug
        1768.
No 15   *Hannah*, was married to Ezra Shaw of Abington,
        18 Sept. 1767.

No 16   IV B   JONATHAN COPELAND,
a brother of the preceding, married Betty Snell, who was
born in 1705, and settled in West Bridgewater. Their
children were,
  1 Abigail, born in 1724—2 Betty, 1726—3 Jonathan,
1728—4. Mary, 1731—5 Joseph,1734—6. Hannah, 1737—
7 Elijah, 1739—8 Daniel, 1741—9 Sarah, 1744—10. Ebenezer, 1744—11 Betty, 1750.
Jonathan Copeland died at the age of 90 years

No. 17. I C.   ABIGAIL COPELAND,
was married to George Howard of West Bridgewater.

No. 18   II C.   BETTY COPELAND,
died unmarried in the year 1750, at the age of 24 years.

No. 19. III C. JONATHAN COPELAND, Jr.
married Mehitable Dunbar, lived and died in West Bridgewater. Their children were,
  1. Jonathan—2. Mehitable—3. Sarah—4. Asa—5. Caleb
—6. Ephraim—7. Polly—8. Martha.
Jonathan Copeland died at the age of 92 years.

No. 20. I D. JONATHAN COPELAND,
a son of the preceding, married Deborah Otis. Their children were, Jonathan, Charles, George, William, Mehitable, Samuel, Deborah

No. 21. II D. *Mehitable*, was married to Daniel Hartwell.

No 22 IV D. *Asa*, married Persis Howard. Their children were, Albert, Azel, Asa, Francis.

No. 23. V D. *Caleb*, married Sally Biram. Their children were Lawrence, Temperance, Caleb, Seth, Vesta, Sally, Elizabeth, Almira, Ephraim, Mary.

No 24. VI D *Ephraim*, married Lucy Keith, settled in Leicester, and had three children.

No 25. VII D. *Polly*, was married to John Burr, and went to Virginia. *Sarah* and *Martha* have no families.

No. 26. IV C. MARY COPELAND,

daughter of Jonathan and Betty Copeland, was married to Benjamin Gannett of Sharon

No. 27. V C. JOSEPH COPELAND,

a brother of the preceding, married Rebecca Hooper. Their children were, 1 Rebecca—2. Joseph—3. Salmon—4 Hannah—5 Polly—6 Sarah—7. Winslow—8. Huldah—9. Hezekiah—10. Lucy. Joseph Copeland died aged 77 years.

No. 28. I D. *Rebecca*, daughter of the preceding, was married to a Dunbar.

No. 29. II D. *Joseph*, died without issue.

No 30. III D. *Salmon*, married Kelly Snell. Their children were, Lyman, Pardon, Nathan.

No. 31. V D. *Polly*, was married to a Mr. Hall.

No. 32. VII D. *Winslow*, went to New Hampshire.

No. 33. VIII D. *Huldah*, was married to a Mr. Holmes.

No. 34. IX D. *Hezekiah*, also went to New Hampshire.

No. 35. X D. *Lucy*, was married to a Mr. Holmes.

No. 36. VI C. HANNAH COPELAND,

daughter of Jonathan and Betty Copeland, was married to Jonathan Kingman of West Bridgewater.

No. 37. VII C. ELIJAH COPELAND,

a brother of the preceding, married Rhoda Snell, and settled in Easton. Their children were, 1. Elijah—2. Josiah —3. Luther—4. Rhoda—5. Abigail—6. Martin—7. Polly. Elijah Copeland died aged 78 years.

No. 38. I D. *Elijah*, son of the preceding, settled in Weston.

No. 39. II D. *Josiah*, married a Miss Howard. Their children were Horatio, Susannah, Hiram.

No. 40. III D. *Luther*, settled in Vermont.

No. 41. VI D. *Martin*, has a family in Easton.

No 42. VIII C. DANIEL COPELAND,

a son of Jonathan and Betty Copeland, married Susannah Ames, and lived in Bridgewater. Their children were, 1. Azel—2 Daniel—3. Susannah—4. Cyrus—5. Martin—6. Shalat—7. Matilda—8. Alfred—9 Betsey—10. Clara—11. Ralph. Daniel Copeland died aged 86.

No. 43. IX C. SARAH COPELAND,

a sister of the preceding, was married to David Keith of Easton.

No. 44. X C. EBENEZER COPELAND,

a brother of the preceding, married Abby Godfrey for his first wife. Their children were, 1 Ebenezer—2 James— 3. Betty—4. Abby—5. Lydia—6. Rachel—7 Ruth—8. Molly, who died in infancy—9. Molly—10. Oakes, who now lives on the homestead of his father in Foxborough.

In the year 1800, his family was sick, and James, Betty, Mrs. Copeland, Rachel, Ruth and Molly died. His second wife was a widow Bridget Wood of Foxborough, whence he removed and spent the remainder of his days.

Ebenezer Copeland died in April, 1829, aged 83 years.

No. 45. I D. *Ebenezer*, the oldest son of the preceding, married Mehitable Snell, and settled in West Bridgewater, by whom he had one daughter. His wife died in 1800.— His second wife was Hannah Godfrey. Their children are, James, Rachel, Mary, Abby, Ruth, Hannah, Betsey, Lawrence.

No. 46. IV D. *Abby*, was married to Elijah Snell, and settled at Winthrop, Maine.

No. 47. V D. *Lydia*, was married to Nathan Howard, and settled at Winthrop.

No. 48. XI C BETTY COPELAND,

daughter of Jonathan and Betty Copeland, was married to a Mr. Belcher of Sharon, and had three children, all of whom with their father and mother are dead.

No 49.　V B.　　DAVID COPELAND,

son of William and Mary Copeland, married Elizabeth (Newcomb ?) and settled in Milton. Their children were,

1 Rachel,	born 20 Aug.	1729	5. Moses,	born	6 April,	1741
	Died 5 Oct. 1745.		6. Newcomb,	"	about	1743–4
2. Mary,	born 19 Feb.	1731–2	7 Joseph,	"	19 March,	1747
3 Hannah,	" 3 Nov	1733–4	8. Rachel,	"	12 Feb	1750
4 David,	" 14 May,	1738				

David Copeland died 15 April, 1750.

No. 50　II C.　Mary, was married to Joseph Crane, 29 Nov. 1750.

No 51.　III C　Hannah, was married to Seth Crane in 1756.

No. 52.　IV C.　David, married Elizabeth Clap about 1759.

No 53.　V C.　Moses, married Patience Sweet, in 1761, by whom he had Nathaniel, born 29 March, 1762.

[Milton Records

No 54.　VI C.　Newcomb, was living in Mansfield in 1833, aged about 90.

No. 55.　VI B　JOSEPH COPELAND,

a son of William and Mary Copeland, married Elizabeth Tolman and settled in Scituate. Their children were,

1. Elizabeth, born 1736, died in 1828—2 Ruth, born 1738—3 Mary, 1740—4. Hannah, 1743, was living in 1833 —5 Rhoda, 1745—6 Lydia, 1747—7 Joseph, 1749—8. William, 1751—9. Ebenezer, 1753, died 1810—10. Rebecca, born 1755—11. Sarah, 1758—12. Elisha, 1759, lived in Fairhaven. Joseph settled in Turner, Maine, the rest in Scituate and Hanover.—[Ebenezer Copeland, M. S

No. 56.　VII B　BENJAMIN COPELAND,

a brother of the preceding, married Sarah Allen, 21 Nov. 1734, and had one son born in Braintree, viz: Benjamin, born 7 June, 1736 —[Braintree Records

He afterwards settled in Norton, and had four sons and five daughters . William, Moses, now living, Samuel, Asa dead, and some of his daughters are still living

[Ebenezer Copeland, M S

No 57　IX B　MARY COPELAND,

a sister of the preceding, was married to Ephraim Jones of Braintree, 2 Dec. 1731. Their children were,

1. Abraham,	born 4 Sept	1732	7 Joseph,		born 27 Feb	1746
2 Moses,	" 27 Sept.	1734	8 Mary,			
3. Abraham,	" 13 March,	1738	9 Ephraim,	"	1 Sept.	1751
4. Hannah,	" 8 March,	1739	10 Hannah,	"	19 Feb	1755
5. Ephraim,	" 12 Sept.	1742	11. Betty,	"	13 June,	1758
6 John,	" 29 Jan.	1744				

No 58   IV A.   JOHN COPELAND,

a son of Lawrence and Lydia Copeland, married Ruth ——
and settled in Braintree   Their children were,

1. John,	born Sept.	1683	5 Lydia,	born 24 April,	1692
2. Samuel,	" 20 Sept.	1686	6 Bethiah,	" 19 March,	1694
3. William,	" 5 April,	1689	7 Seth,	" 22 Jan.	1698
4. Ruth,			8. Mercy,	" 10 Dec	1700

No 59.   II B   SAMUEL COPELAND,

a son of the preceding, married Mary ——.   Their children were,

1. Samuel,	born 28 Oct	1711	7 Susannah,	born 22 Feb.	1724
2 Mary,	" 7 July,	1713	8 Isaac,	" 27 March,	1726
3. Desire,	" 22 Oct.	1715	9 Hannah,	" 29 Feb.	1728
4 John,	" 27 May,	1718	10 Bethiah,	" 27 July,	1729
5. Abigail,	" 6 Aug.	1720	11. Seth,	" 21 April,	1731
6 Ruth,	" 21 March,	1722	12. Daniel,	" 30 July,	1733

No. 60   I C   SAMUEL COPELAND,

a son of the preceding, married Mary Owen, 2 April, 1736.
Their children were,

1. Abraham,	born 25 June,	1737	5. Isaac,	born 11 April,	1744
2. Hannah,	" 12 July,	1740	6 Jacob,	" 10 July,	1746
3 Ruth,	" 26 April,	1742	7. Sarah,	" 20 Sept	1748
4 Sarah,					

No 61.   II C.   MARY COPELAND,

a sister of the preceding, was married to Caleb Dunham,
30 March, 1732.

No 62   III C   DESIRE COPELAND,

a sister of the preceding, was married to Peter Hobart of
Braintree   (See Hobart, No 20)

No. 63.   VI C.   RUTH COPELAND,

a sister of the preceding, was married to Daniel Spear, 11
Aug. 1743.

No 64   VIII C.   ISAAC COPELAND,

a brother of the preceding, married Lydia, daughter of John
and Lydia Thayer.   (See Thayer, Nos. 84 and 87)   Their

children were, 1 John—2 Abigail—3 John—4. Abigail—
5 Isaac, born 17 Oct 1753—6. Seth—7. Samuel—8. Lydia
—9. Elkanah—10 Lawrence—11. Mary.

Isaac Copeland died 19 June, 1795. Lydia, widow of
Isaac Copeland, died March, 1799.—[*Braintree Records.*

No 65. V D. ISAAC COPELAND,
a son of the preceding, married Rebecca Pierce, and settled in Milton. Their children were,

1 Elizabeth,	born 24 Sept	1780	6. Elisha,	born 17 Aug.	1791
2. Charles,	" 13 Feb.	1782	7 Thomas,	" 28 June,	1794
3. Rebecca,	" 19 March,	1784	8. Lewis,	" 10 Dec.	1795
4. Mehitable,	" 24 Oct.	1786	9 Mary,		
5. Isaac,	" 14 June,	1789	10. Joseph Warren,	born 12 Jan.	1802

[*Milton Records.*

No. 66. *Isaac*, married Nancy Miller, daughter of Jonathan
Cobb, Esq. of Sharon. She was born 18 Feb 1801. Their
children were, Frederick, Richard, Gridley, Isaac Richard.
Isaac Copeland died in 1827

No. 67. VII D. SAMUEL COPELAND,
a son of Isaac and Lydia Copeland, married Ruth Whitmarsh, 10 Dec. 1783.—[*Braintree Records.*

No 68 VIII D. LYDIA COPELAND,
a sister of the preceding, was married to Jackson Field, 19
Feb. 1777.—[*Ib.*

No. 69. IX C. HANNAH COPELAND,
a daughter of Samuel and Mary Copeland, was married to
John White.

No 70. X C. BETHIAH COPELAND,
a sister of the preceding, was married to Eben'r Newcomb.

No. 71 XI C. SETH COPELAND,
a brother of the preceding, married Lydia Kingman, 3
April, 1755. Their children were,

1. Asa,	born 18 March,	1756	4. Frances,	born 18 Jan.	1764
2. Lydia,	" 8 March,	1758	5. Seth,	" 30 June,	1771
3. Aletheah,	" 12 Sept.	1761	6. Daniel,	" 1 Jan.	1775

No. 72. VII B. SETH COPELAND,
a son of John and Ruth Copeland, married Mary Holbrook,

12 Dec. 1722, by whom he had one son Seth, born 19 June, 1723. His second wife was Abigail White, married 7 March, 1734.—(See White, No. 20.)

No. 73.   VIII B.   MERCY COPELAND,
a sister of the preceding, was married to Josiah Hobart, about 1719.   (See Hobart, No. 8.)

No 74.   VI A.   EPHRAIM COPELAND,
a son of Lawrence and Lydia Copeland, died with the small pox on board a vessel, and was thrown overboard with several others at Nantasket, in 1690.   (See Bass, No. 50.)

No. 75.   IX A.   ABIGAIL COPELAND,
a sister of the preceding, was married to Eleazer Isgale, 23 Nov. 1715.

No. 76.   LYDIA COPELAND,
probably a daughter of John and Ruth Copeland, was married to the Rev Ebenezer Thayer of Roxbury, 4 June, 1719.   (See No. 58, and Thayer, No. 78)

No. 77   There was a LYDIA COPELAND of Mendon, married to Benjamin Fassett of Pomfret, 27 Oct 1740   Perhaps she was a daughter of William and Mary Copeland, No. 10, 2.

12

THE FAMILY OF FRENCH.

No. 1.   〃JOHN FRENCH,

of Dorchester, was the progenitor of the family commemorated in this Memorial. He was admitted freeman in 1639. His children were, 1. John, born 28 Feb. 1641, in Dorchester 2 Thomas, born 10 July, 1643, in Dorchester. Died in Braintree, 28, 8, 1656. He removed to Braintree, where he spent his days, and where

3. Dependence was born 7, 1, 1648	6. Elizabeth,	born 20, 7, 1655
4. Temperence,	" 30, 1, 1651	7. Thomas,	" 10, 1, 1657
5. William,	" 31, 1, 1653	8 Samuel,	" 22, 12, 1659

Children of John and Grace French. John French died 6 Aug. 1692, aged about 80 years. Grace, wife of John French, died 1 Feb. 1680.

No. 2. I A.   JOHN FRENCH, Jr.,

married Experience, daughter of Thomas Thayer. (See Thayer, No. 80.) Their children were,

1. John,	born 20 Sept. 1686	5 Deborah,	born 2 Aug. 1694
2. Anna,	" 15 Jan 1688	6 William,	" 16 Jan. 1696
3 Thomas,	" 23 June, 1690	7. John,	" 16 April, 1699
4. Grace,	" 22 Feb 1692		

Experience, wife of John French, died 29 Sept. 1719, in the 61 year of her age.

No. 3. III B.   THOMAS FRENCH,

a son of the preceding, married Mary Allen, 18 Aug. 1714. Their children were,

1. Joseph,	born 21 July, 1716	4 Thomas,	baptized in 1723
2. David,	" 1 May, 1718	5 Samuel,	born 23 Oct. 1724
3 Micah,	" 3 Nov. 1720	6. Micah,	" 9 Sept. 1726
	Died 27 March, 1722.		

No. 4 II C.   DAVID FRENCH,

a son of the preceding, married Mehitable ——. Their children were,

1 Nathaniel, born 19 July, 1756 | 3. Joseph, born 27 Sept. 1763
2. Silas, " 13 Feb. 1761 |

No. 5.   IV C.   THOMAS FRENCH, 3d.,

a brother of the preceding, married Silence Wild of Braintree Their children were,

1. Silence, born 22 Aug. 1750 | 7. Jotham, born 23 Sept 1760
2. Thomas, " 23 March, 1751 | 8 Luther, " 21 March, 1762
3 Joseph, " 2 Oct. 1753 | 9. Polly, wife of Silas Alden. (See
4 Sarah, " 20 Feb. 1755 | Alden, No 59.)
5 Timothy, " 9 Feb 1757 | 10. Calvin, who died young.
6. Susannah, " 30 Aug. 1758 | 11. William, born 28 Jan. 1770

No. 6   VI C.   MICAH FRENCH,

a brother of the preceding, married Ruth ——, and settled in Stoughton. Their children were,

1. Barzillai, born 2 Aug. 1762 | 2 Alpheus, born 1 Jan. 1767

No. 7.   VII B   JOHN FRENCH,

probably a son of John and Experience French, settled in Mendon, with his wife Margaret. Their children were,

1. Jesse, born 9 Oct. 1723 | 4. Hannah, born 25 Aug. 1733
2. John, " 14 March, 1728 | 5 William, " 28 May, 1737
3. Margaret, " 10 June, 1729 |

No. 8.   { JOHN, married Hannah Thayer, about 1750.
{ WILLIAM, married Sarah Alexander, 13 July,
1758. Their children were,

1 Margaret, born 13 Jan. 1759 | 4. Daughter, born 13 Sept. 1764
2. Nathan, " 26 Feb. 1761 | 5. Daughter, " 25 Feb. 1767
3. Royal, " 19 July, 1762 |

No. 9.   III A   DEPENDENCE FRENCH,

son of John and Grace French, married Mary ——, by whom he had one child, 1. Mary, born 30 March, 1684. His second wife was Rebecca ——. Their children were,

2. John, born 10 March, 1689 | 5. David, } born 4 Mar. 1699
3. Dependence, " 15 April, 1691 | 6 Elizabeth, }
4 Rebecca, " 13 May, 1694 |

No. 10.   I B.   MARY FRENCH,

a daughter of the preceding, was married to Samuel Savil, 25 April, 1707.

No. 11.   II B.   JOHN FRENCH,

a son of Dependence and Rebecca French, married Mary Vinton. Their children were,

1. Mary,	born about	1713	6 Abigail,	born	6 Dec.	1725
2. John,			7. Mehitable,	"	14 Oct.	1727
3 Dependence,	" 25 Dec.	1714	8. Rebecca,	"	11 June,	1728
4. Hannah,	" 17 Sept.	1718	9. Abiathar,	"	7 April,	1732
5. Elizabeth,	" 1 Jan.	1722	10. Joshua,			1734

No. 12.   I C.   MARY FRENCH,

a daughter of the preceding, was married to Josiah, son of Samuel and Hannah French.   (See No. 44.)

No. 13.   II C.   JOHN FRENCH,

a brother of the preceding, married Mary Fenno of Stoughton, 19 Jan. 1748, and settled in Stoughton.   His second wife was Christian Holbrook, widow, married about 1753. His children were,

| 1. Rebecca, | born 14 July, | 1754 | 3 John, | born 13 June, | 1763 |
| 2. Ruhamah, | " 12 July, | 1757 | | | |

No. 14.   III C.   DEPENDENCE FRENCH,

the twin brother of the preceding, married Mary Linfield, 28 May, 1738, and settled in that part of Braintree which is now Randolph.   Their children were,

1. Dependence,	born 21 April,	1739	7 William,	born	2 Nov.	1751
2. Levi,	" 27 April,	1740	8 Elizabeth,	"		
3. Deliverance,	" 31 Jan.	1742	9. Silence,	"	14 Nov	1756
4. Mary,	" 7 Oct.	1744	10 Martha,	"	14 Feb	1759
5. Martha,	" 24 July,	1747	11. Olive,	"	5 April,	1761
6. John,	" 26 Jan.	1749				

Dependence French died in 1803, aged 89 years.

No. 15.   V C.   ELIZABETH FRENCH,

a sister of the preceding, was married to Caleb Hobart, Jr. 15 March, 1743.   (See Hobart, No. 5.)

No. 16.   VII C.   MEHITABLE FRENCH,

a sister of the preceding, was married to Micah Thayer, 14 Jan. 1748.   (See Thayer, No. 26.)

No 17.   IX C.   ABIATHAR FRENCH,

a brother of the preceding, removed to Northampton, and he has descendants now living in West Hampton, Mass. and vicinity.

No. 18.   X C.   JOSHUA FRENCH,

the youngest brother of the preceding, married Esther, daughter of Joseph Wales.   (See Wales, No. 15.)   Their children were,

1. Esther, born 1 Nov 1756, wife of David Linfield, married 26 March, 1774.

2. Joshua, born 9 March, 1758, married Lucy Thayer, 21 Feb. 1782.

3 Prudence, born 29 March, 1759, wife of Simeon Curtis, married about 1779.

4 Sarah, born 14 Dec 1760, wife of Eleazer Beals, married about 1778

5. John, born 26 March, 1762, married Hannah Wales, · about 1783.

6. Hannah, born 13 Oct. 1763, wife of Luther French, married about 1782

7 Rachel, born 30 June 1765, wife of Simeon Alden, _ married about 1785.

8. Charlotte, born 5 July, 1767, wife of Ezra Thayer, and 2d of Silas Alden.

9. Jedidiah, born 20 Dec 1770, married Phebe Wales, 20 Sept. 1792.

10 Mehitable, born 9 Sept. 1772, wife of Benjamin Linfield.

11. Elizabeth, born 10 Sept. 1779, wife of Theophilus Wentworth.

12 Wales, born 10 Dec 1782, married Mehitable Niles Joshua French died 11 Sept. 1791, aged 57 years.

Esther, widow of Joshua French, died 1 Dec. 1810, aged 73 years.

No. 19. III B. DEPENDENCE FRENCH,

son of Dependence and Rebecca French, (No 9,) married Anna, daughter of Richard and Rebecca Thayer, 10 July, 1718. (See Thayer, Nos 3 and 33) Their children were,

1. Rebecca,	born 1 May, 1721	3. Anna,	born 18 Oct. 1728
2. Gideon,	" 11 Sept. 1726	4. Elizabeth,	" 27 Oct. 1730

No. 20. I C. REBECCA FRENCH,

daughter of the preceding, was married to Clement Crane, 14 April, 1742.

No. 21. II C. GIDEON FRENCH,

brother of the preceding, married Elizabeth ——. Their children were,

1. Elizabeth,	born 15 June, 1751	5. Ebenezer,	born 15 Feb 1761
2. Rachel,	" 19 April, 1753	6 Mary,	" 4 Aug. 1763
3. Gedeon,	" 1 Oct. 1755	7. Arodi,	" 21 Aug. 1766
4. Joanna,	" 11 Aug. 1758	8. Rhoda,	" 4 May, 1772

Gideon French died 22 March 1794.

No 22   VI B.   ELIZABETH FRENCH,

a daughter of Dependence and Rebecca French, (No. 9)
was married to Samuel Vinton, and settled in Woburn, afterwards removed to Braintree.   Their children were,

1 Samuel,	born 1 Feb.	1722	5 Rebecca,	born 15 Aug.	1729
2. Elizabeth,	" 8 Dec.	1723	6. Hannah,	" 12 June,	1732
3 David,	" 17 March,	1726	7. John,	" 11 Feb.	1735
4. Rebecca,	" 11 July,	1728	8. William,	" 22 Jan.	1739

These were born at Woburn, and the rest at Braintree.

Died 6 Feb 1741

9. William,   died 7 Feb.   1747

Samuel Vinton died 17 July, 1756, aged 61 years.

Elizabeth, widow of Samuel Vinton, died 31 March, 1770,
aged 71 years.

No 23.   IV A.   TEMPERANCE FRENCH,

daughter of John and Grace French, was married to John
Bowditch of Braintree   Their children were,

1 William,	born 20 June,	1683	3 John,	born 11 Oct. 1693
2. Mary,	" 17 Feb.	1687		

Temperance, wife of John Bowditch, died 12 Aug 1720.

No 24.   V A   WILLIAM FRENCH,

a brother of the preceding, married Rachel Twells in 1689,
by whom he had one son, 1 William, born about 1690.

Rachel, wife of William French, died 14 Feb. 1691.

William French died 22 Feb. 1691

No. 25   I B.   WILLIAM FRENCH,

only son of the preceding, married Sarah ———.   Their
children were,

1 William,	born 13 Feb.	1714	3. Sarah,	born 28 Jan. 1722
2. David,	" 28 Sept.	1719		

No 26   VII A.   THOMAS FRENCH,

a son of John and Grace French, married Elizabeth ———.
Their children were,

1 Elizabeth,	born 16 Dec.	1696	6. Samuel,	born Sept.	1706
2. Thomas,	" 5 Aug.	1698	7. Abijah,	" 25 May,	1709
3 Moses,	" 16 Feb.	1700	8. Ebenezer,	" 9 Sept	1711
4 Jonathan,	" 20 June,	1702	9. Sarah,	" 16 Feb.	1714
5. Rachel,	" 26 March,	1704	10 Seth,	" 25 Oct.	1716

Thomas French died 22 Sept. 1717.   Elizabeth, widow
of Thomas French, died 23 Dec. 1718.

No 27.   I B   ELIZABETH FRENCH,

a daughter of the preceding, was married to Edward Dorr,
9 Nov. 1720.

No 28. II B. THOMAS FRENCH, Jr,

a brother of the preceding, married Rebecca ———, by whom he had one son, 1 Jonathan, born 1 July, 1723. His second wife was Mary Owen, married 5 Nov 1723 Their children were,

2 Samuel,	born 23 Oct.	1724		Died 5 July, 1735	
3 Elijah,	" 23 Nov	1726	9 Sarah,	born 18 Nov.	1739
4 Mary,	" 29 Oct.	1728	10 Eunice,	" 14 Aug.	1741
5 Elizabeth,	" 1 Nov.	1730		Died 8 Feb 1754	
6. Timothy,	" 22 March,	1732	11. Thomas,	born 3 April,	1743
7. Rachel,	" 27 Jan	1733	12 Jerusha,	" 29 July,	1746
8. Sarah,	" 26 June,	1735			

No. 29. II C. SAMUEL FRENCH,

a son of the preceding, married Mary ———, by whom he had one son, 1 Elijah, born 10 Feb 1755

No. 30. III C. ELIJAH FRENCH,

a brother of the preceding, married Mary Clark, 13 July, 1750. Their children were,

1. Samuel born 13 Oct 1753 | 2. Elijah.
       Died 22 Nov. 1753 |

Mary, wife of Elijah French, died 18 Aug 1747. His second wife was Molly ———, by whom he had
3. Molly,   born 15 July, 1761 | 4. Abraham,   born 12 Aug. 1763

No. 31 III B. MOSES FRENCH,

a son of Thomas and Elizabeth French, married Esther, daughter of Ephraim and Sarah Thayer, 24 Dec. 1730
(See 9th Branch, second part, No. 1)

No. 32 IV B. JONATHAN FRENCH,

a brother of the preceding, married Rebecca ———. He was a member of the Episcopal Church in Braintree, (now Quincy,) where all his children were baptized Their children were,

1. Jonathan,	born 1 July,	1723	4. Ruth,	born 31 Dec.	1727
2 Ephraim,	" 20 Jan.	1725	5. Elizabeth, bapt 9 March, 1728-9		
3. Jacob,	" 8 March, 1727				

No 33. III C. JACOB FRENCH,

a son of the preceding, married Miriam Downs of Stoughton, 22 Nov. 1751, and settled in Stoughton. There children were,

1. Samuel,	born 20 July,	1752	4 Edward,	born 23 Sept	1761
2. Jacob,	" 15 July,	1754	5. Rebecca,	" 27 Jan.	1763
3 Lemuel,	" 15 Sept.	1757			

No 34. V B.   RACHEL FRENCH,
a daughter of Thomas and Elizabeth French, was married
to Eleazer Thayer of Braintree, 28 April, 1730. (See
Thayer, No. 96.)

No. 35. VII B.   ABIJAH FRENCH,
a brother of the preceding, married Joanna ——, and settled in Mendon, Mass   Their children were,

1. Mary,	born 22 July,	1736	6 Sarah.	born 13 Oct.	1748
2. Jesse,	" 15 Dec.	1737	7. Lois, }	" 2 June,	1750
Died 29 Sept 1741			8 Eunice, }		
3 Abijah,	born 14 Feb.	1741	9 Joanna,	" 28 Aug.	1752
4 Samuel,	" 10 April,	1744	10. David,	born 26 Nov 1755 O. S	
5 Abijah,	" 20 March,	1746		7 Dec N S.	

[*Mendon Records.*

No 36. IV C   SAMUEL FRENCH,
a son of the preceding, married Ruth Daniels of Holliston,
in 1767, and settled in Mendon.   Their children were,

1. Jotham,	born 21 May,	1768	5 Abijah,	born 11 Aug.	1773
2 Ruth,	" 31 Dec	1769	6. Perley,	" 14 June,	1775
3 Elizabeth, }	" 20 Aug.	1771	7. Adams,	" 1 July,	1777
4. Mary, }					[*Ibid.*

No 37. VIII B.   EBENEZER FRENCH,
son of Thomas and Elizabeth French, married Mary Fuller of Stoughton, and settled in Milton. Their children were,

1 Ebenezer,	born 6 Sept.	1738	5. Mary,	born 26 Sept.	1744
2 Joshua,	" 4 March,	1740	6 Esther,	" 10 Nov.	1747
3 Thomas, }	" 2 Oct	1742	7. Benjamin,	" 23 March,	1750
4. Samuel, }			8 Samuel,	" 8 July,	1752
Died 6 Dec. 1750.			9. Sarah,	" 8 April,	1756

THOMAS, married Salome Babcock of Milton.   Their
children were, Lemuel, born 16 May, 1770, Jason, born 6
Jan 1772, Sally, Samuel, Thomas, Rufus, Azel, Alexander,
Avis, Nathaniel, Ansel, who graduated at Brown University, in 1814.   Thomas French died in April, 1820.
    BENJAMIN, married Mary Dean for his first wife, and
Hannah Glover for his second, and settled in W. Dedham
    SAMUEL, married Mary Morse, and settled in West Ded-
ham.   Their children were, Mary, Moses, Samuel, Hannah, Rufus, Lucy.   Samuel French died in Dec. 1822.

No. 38. X B.   SETH FRENCH,
the youngest son of Thomas and Elizabeth French, married Patience Stevens, 7 Feb 1745, by whom he had one
son Seth, born 30 Sept. 1745

Patience, wife of Seth French, died 1 April, 1754, who by reason of sores had not lain down in bed nor stood without help above three years.—[*Braintree Records*.

No. 39. VIII A. SAMUEL FRENCH,

a son of John and Grace French, married Anna ————, (Hannah, the same name formerly) Their children were,

1. Samuel,	born 17 Nov.	1680		5. Alexander,	born 13 Dec.		1695
2. Samuel,	" 13, 7,	1688		6. Josiah,	" 20 March,		1700
3. Hannah,	" 15 Jan.	1690		7. Nathaniel,	" 1 April,		1702
4. Mary,	" 20 Sept.	1691		8. Benjamin.			

Hannah, wife of Samuel French, died 4 Feb. 1712.
Samuel French died 13 Oct. 1718.

No. 40. II B. SAMUEL FRENCH,

a son of the preceding, died 11 Jan. 1770, it is supposed unmarried.

No. 41. V B. ALEXANDER FRENCH,

a brother of the preceding, married Mary, daughter of Thomas and Mehitable White, 6 June, 1723. (See White No. 19.) Their children were,

1. Alexander,	born 28 Feb.	1724		3 Isaac,	born 13 Nov.	1729
2. Samuel,	" 5 Sept.	1725		4. Benoni,	" 30 May,	1732
					Died 2 June, 1732.	

Mary, wife of Alexander French, died 30 May, 1732.
His second wife was Rebecca Staples, married 14 May, 1734, by whom he had,

5. Elizabeth,	born 13 Aug.	1735		8. Jacob,	born 19 Sept.	1739
6. Jacob,	" 11 June,	1736		9. Experience,	" 23 April,	1742
	Died 20 June, 1736			10 Job,	" 16 June,	1744
7. Asa,	born 7 May,	1737			Died 19 June, 1744.	

No. 42. I C. ALEXANDER FRENCH,

son of the preceding, married Susannah Crane, 22 Oct. 1747. Their children were,

1. Susannah,	born 1 June,	1748		3 Alexander,	born 9 Aug.	1756
2. Daniel,	" 1 July,	1753				

DANIEL, married Rebecca, daughter of Micah and Mehitable Thayer, 1 April, 1775. (See Thayer, No. 26, 4.) His second wife was Mary Damon, married about 1787. She died 18 Dec. 1812.

No. 43. II C. SAMUEL FRENCH,

a brother of the preceding, married Mary ————. Their children were,

13

1. Mary,	born 21 Jan.	1718		Died 2 Nov. 1753.	
Died 17 April, 1748.			3. Samuel,	born 18 Jan	1755
2. Mary,	born Oct.	1750	4 Asa,	" 3 May,	1757

No 44. VI B   JOSIAH FRENCH,

a son of Samuel and Hannah French, married Mary, a daughter of John and Mary French   (See Nos. 11 and 12.) Their children were,

1. Josiah,	born 22 Jan.	1736	4 Ahaz,	born 31 Oct.	1746
2. Nathaniel,	" 13 Oct.	1737	5. Josiah,	" 8 July,	1750
3. Mary,	" 26 Aug.	1742			

Josiah French died 15 Nov. 1760. Mary, widow of Josiah French, who had been discomposed many years, died 5 March, 1770.

No. 45. II C. NATHANIEL FRENCH,

a son of the preceding, married Silence, daughter of Peter and Dorothy Dyer, 21 Aug. 1762. Their children were,

1. Ahaz,	born 12 Dec	1762	5 Silence,	born 3 Nov.	1771
2. Samuel,	" 9 Jan.	1765	6. Mary,		
3. Nathaniel,	" 12 Jan	1767	7. Josiah.		
4. James,	" 6 April,	1769			

Ahaz, married Judith French, about 1782.
Samuel, married Susannah Penniman, 14 June, 1789.
Nathaniel, married Eunice Spear, about 1790.
James, married Lydia Hollis, 27 June, 1778.
Mary, was married to Barzilla Penniman, 15 Jan. 1795.
Josiah, married Rachel Penniman, 23 April, 1801.

No. 46. V C.   JOSIAH FRENCH,

a brother of the preceding, married Anna, another daughter of Peter Dyer before named, 26 May, 1769. Their children were, Anna, born 26 Dec. 1769, the wife of John V. Arnold.   Rhoda, born 3 April, 1773, Rebecca, Sally, wife of William Thayer, Mary, wife of Moses Hunt, Josiah.
Josiah French died in Oct. 1823.

No. 47. VII B. NATHANIEL FRENCH,

a son of Samuel and Hannah French, married Susannah Blanchard, 17 Aug 1725. Their children were,

| 1. Nehemiah, | born 15 Jan. 1726 | 2. Susannah, | born 4 March, 1727 |

Nathaniel French died of nervous fever, sick only 4 days, 24 Sept. 1791, aged 54 years.

No. 48. I C.   NEHEMIAH FRENCH,

married Joanna Whitmarsh Their children were, Reu-

ben, Joanna, Nathaniel, Betsey, Adonijah, Sally, wife of William French, (No 5, 11,) Stephen.
Joanna, wife of Nehemiah French, died 7 April, 1804.

No 49. VIII B   BENJAMIN FRENCH,

son of Samuel and Hannah French, married Hepzibah, daughter of Samuel White, Jr 17 Sept. 1730. (See White No 21, 4) Their children were,

1 Benjamin, } baptised in 1735
2. Hepzibah, }
3 Samuel,   born 3 March, 1737

4. Adam,   born 6 Feb.   1741
   Died 29 Jan 1761.
5. Paul,   baptised in   1744
6 Sarah,   "   "   1746

No 50. I C.   BENJAMIN FRENCH, Jr.

married Judith Baxter   Their children were,

1. Benjamin,   born 27 March, 1760
2. Judith,   "   5 April,   1762
3. Samuel,   "   7 Oct.   1764

4. Adam,   born 10 Nov.   1766
5. Polly, the wife of John Hollis.

No. 51 III C.   SAMUEL FRENCH,

son of Benjamin and Hepzibah French, married Elizabeth Allen, by whom he had one daughter Elizabeth, born 8 Nov. 1761, and died unmarried in Oct 1825 Her father died soon after her birth, and her mother was afterwards married to Robert Hayden, Esq. by whom she had,

1. Mary,   born 21 March, 1765
2. Susannah,   "   3 May,   1767
3 Robert,   "   29 Jan.   1769
4. Charles,   "   19 Sept.   1770
5. Priscilla,   "   10 July,   1772

6. Samuel,   born 2 Dec. 1774
7. Thomas Allen,   "   10 Feb. 1777
8. Mehitable,   "   1 July, 1779
9. Josiah,   "   31 May, 1781

Mr. Farmer enumerates a large number of this name, as EDWARD FRENCH, Ipswich, 1636, probably removed to Salisbury, and a proprietor there in 1640. Ten of the name of French had graduated at Harvard and the other N. E. Colleges, in 1826. JACOB, Weymouth, admitted freeman 1652 JOHN, Cambridge, freeman 1644, whose children were Sarah, born Oct. 1637, Joseph, born 4 April, 1640, married Experience Foster, and settled in Billerica, from whence he removed ; Nathaniel, born 7 June, 1643 Joanna, his wife, died 20 Jan. 1646 , his housekeeper died in Feb. 1646, and he died soon after. JOHN, Dorchester, the Progenitor of all of the above numbered families. JOHN, Ipswich, 1648 STEPHEN, Weymouth, freeman 1634, Representative in 1638, was perhaps father of Jacob, freeman 1652. THOMAS, Boston, admitted freeman 1632, member of the church from whence he was dismissed 27 Jan 1639, to Ipswich, where he appears to have resided as early as 1634 He may have been the ensign of the Artillery Company in 1650. THOMAS, Guilford, 1650 WILLIAM, brother of John French of Cambridge, came to New England as early as 1635, was admitted freeman 1636, and settled at Cambridge, from whence he went to Billerica with the first settlers ; was a Lieutenant, appointed to solemnize marriages, and was the first Representative in 1660, and again in 1663. He died 20 Nov. 1681, aged 78. His children were,

THE FAMILY OF HOBART.

No. 1.   EDMUND HOBART,

who was admitted freeman 1634, came from Hingham, in England, in 1633, and settled at Charlestown, from thence to Hingham in 1635, which he represented from 1639 to 1642 four years. He died 8 March, 1646, leaving sons, 1 Edmund—2. Thomas—3. Peter—4 Joshua, and 2 daughters.

No 2.   I A.   EDMUND HOBART,

Hingham, 1635, son of the preceding, died in 1686, aged 82. His children were, 1 Daniel—2. Samuel—3. John.

No. 3.   II A.   THOMAS HOBART,

a brother of the preceding, was admitted freeman 1634, settled in Hingham, 1635, and had sons, 1. Caleb—2. Joshua, and 3. Thomas.—[*Lincoln's Hist. Hingham*, 156.

No. 4.   I B   CALEB HOBART,

probably a son of the preceding, married Mary ———, and settled in Braintree. Their children were,

1. Mary,	born 11, 12,	1663	4 Hannah,	born 11, 10,	1668
2. Caleb,	" 23, 3,	1665	5. Josiah,	" 11, 10,	1670
3. Elizabeth,	" 12, 4,	1666			

Elizabeth and Mary, born in England, John, born in Cambridge, and settled with his father in Billerica, had a large family, and died Oct. 1712, aged about 78; Sarah, born March, 1638; Jacob, born 16 Jan. 1640, settled in Billerica, had a large family, and died 20 May, 1713, aged 73; Hannah, born 21 Feb. 1641; Samuel, born 3 Dec. 1645, the five last born in Cambridge. He had other children by a second wife. His posterity have been numerous in Billerica, and still remain so —[*Farmer Gen. Reg.*

JOHN, son of John French, 1st of Rehoboth, came to that town about 1710, married Martha Williams, had five children, John, (6 in Rehoboth,) Ephraim and Martha, twins, (died infants,) Hannah, Samuel, 1709, 1714. His second wife was Abigail White, married 23 May, 1728, by whom he had two children, John, born 1729, Thomas, born 1730. THOMAS, brother of the preceding, also came from Rehoboth, married Mary Brown, 5 Jan. 1720-1, had 6 children, Thomas, Christopher, Mary, Joseph, Elizabeth, Bridget, Sarah, Hannah, 1722, 1738.

[*Daggett's Hist. of Attleborough* p. 91.

Mary, wife of Caleb Hobart, died 22, 5, 1675 His second wife was Elizabeth Faxon, widow, married 15, 11, 1676. 6. Benjamin, born 13, 2, 1677. Caleb Hobart died 4 Sept. 1711, aged 89 years —[*Braintree Records*

NOTE.—Caleb Hobart, Senior was dismissed from the church in Hingham, and received to full communion in the church at Braintree, Fast Day, 12, 3, 1697 —[*Ch. Records.*

No. 5. II C.   CALEB HOBART, Jr.,

married Hannah Saunders of Braintree, widow, 15, 9, 1704. Had no children on record. ⁑

No. 6. IV C.   HANNAH HOBART,

a sister of the preceding, was married to Jonathan Hayward, 17 Feb. 1692.

No. 7. V C   JOSIAH HOBART,

a brother of the preceding, married Mary Cleverly of Braintree, 21 March, 1695. Their children were,

1. Caleb,	born 14 Jan	1696	3. Mary,	born 28 Feb, 1701
Died 1 March, 1696, aged 7 weeks			4. John,	" 14 April, 1701
2. Josiah,	born 24 May,	1697		

Mary wife of Josiah Hobart, died 18 Oct. 1718. His second wife was Sarah Savil, married 23 Dec 1719. 5 Susannah, born 25 March, 1724. Josiah Hobart died 2 Sept. 1725.

No. 8. II D.   JOSIAH HOBART, Jr ,

married Mercy Copeland. (See Copeland, No 73.) Their children were,

1. Josiah,	born 9 July,	1720		Died 16 Dec 1726.
2. Mercy,	" 1 Oct.	1721	3. Mary,	born 6 Feb. 1721

His second wife was Esther Thayer, married 4 Nov 1736. 4 Nathaniel, born 10 Feb. 1738.

No. 9. IV D.   JOHN HOBART,

a brother of the preceding, married Elizabeth, daughter of Ebenezer and Ruth Thayer, 24 Nov. 1726. (See Thayer No. 90, 11. Their children were,

1. Mary,	born 26 Aug	1732	3. Hannah,	born 8 April, 1717
2. Ruth,	" 1 Oct.	1734		

No. 10. VI C. BENJAMIN HOBART,

son of Caleb and Elizabeth Hobart, married Susannah Newcomb, 5 April, 1699 Their children were,

1. Ann,	born	4 July,	1699	4. Peter,	born	3 April,	1709
2. Benjamin,	"	6 Sept	1701	5. Israel,	"	15 April,	1713
3. Caleb,	"	9 Feb	1704	6. Joshua,	"	5 May,	1716

Susannah, wife of Benjamin Hobart, died 23 Dec. 1725.

No. 11. II D. BENJAMIN HOBART, Jr.,

married Rebecca ———. Their children were,

1. Benjamin,	born 29 Aug	1723	3. Sylvanus,	born 6 Aug.	1732
2. Thomas,	"	17 Feb. 1729			

No. 12. III D. CALEB HOBART,

a brother of the preceding, married Elizabeth Hollis of Braintree. Their children were,

1. Caleb,	born 18 Aug	1725	6. Elizabeth,	born 19 Aug.	1736
2 Elizabeth,	"	6 July,	1727		Died Oct. 1737.
3. Susannah, }	"	11 Sept.	1730	7. Elizabeth,	born 1 May, 1739
4. Elizabeth, }				8. Adam,	" 9 June, 1743
	Died 16 June, 1734.			9. Joshua,	" 1 Aug. 1747
5. Joshua,	born 8 Feb.	1734			

Elizabeth, wife of Caleb Hobart, died in May, 1790.

No 13. I E. CALEB HOBART, Jr,

married Elizabeth French, 15 March, 1743. (See French No. 15.) Their children were,

1. Caleb,	born 20 Jan.	1744	3. John,	born 26 April,	1755
2. Elizabeth,	"	16 May,	1747	4. Rebecca.		

Caleb Hobart, Jr. died 5 June, 1795, aged 70 years.
Elizabeth, widow of Caleb Hobart, died 6 Jan. 1803, aged 81 years.

No 14. II F. ELIZABETH HOBART,

a daughter of the preceding, was married to Nehemiah Holbrook of Braintree, 25 May, 1765.

No. 15 III F. JOHN HOBART,

a brother of the preceding, married Deborah, daughter of Thomas White, 17 Sept. 1777. She was born 4 March, 1756. Their children were,

1. John,	born 2 Aug	1779	6. Caleb,	born 3 June,	1793
2. Augustus,	"	11 Nov.	1781	7. Susannah,	" 4 March, 1796
3. Lydia,	"	4 May,	1784	8. Deborah,	" Feb 1799
4 Charlotte,	"	3 May,	1787	9. Solomon,	" 3 Oct. 1802
5. Betsey,	"	23 April,	1790			

John Hobart died.
Deborah, wife of John Hobart, died

No 16   IV F.   REBECCA HOBART,

a sister of the preceding, was married to Nathaniel Hollis of Braintree.

No 17.   VII E.   ELIZABETH HOBART,

daughter of Caleb and Elizabeth Hobart, (No. 12, 7,) was married to Deacon Moses French. (See second part, 9th Branch, No. 2.)

No. 18.   VIII E.   ADAM HOBART,

a brother of the preceding, married Mary Thayer, 29 Feb. 1763.   (See Thayer, No. 46)   Their children were,

1 Caleb,   born 8 May,   1765 | 3. Relief,   born 29 April, 1769
2. Mary,   "   4 Dec.   1766 |

His second wife was Avis Thayer, married 7 Nov. 1772. (See Thayer, No. 48, 5)   Their children were,

4. Avis,   born 8 July,   1774 | 6. Abraham,   born 21 Aug.   1779
5. Adam,   "   18 March,   1776 | 7. Elisha

Adam Hobart was a deacon of the church at Braintree many years before his death.

No. 19.   IX E.   JOSHUA HOBART,

the youngest brother of the preceding, married Sarah Thayer, 30 Aug. 1766.   (See Thayer, No. 48, 4.)   Their children were,

1. Joshua,   born 13 Sept.   1767 | 2. Sarah,   born 14 Sept   1769

No 20.   IV D.   PETER HOBART,

a son of Benjamin and Susannah Hobart, married Desire Copeland   (See Copeland, No. 62.)   Their children were,

1. Mercy,   born 15 Nov.   1733 | 3 Daniel,   born 7 Feb.   1737
2. Benjamin,   "   14 Feb.   1735 | 4. Elisha,   "   28 April,   1752

No. 21.   V D.   ISRAEL HOBART,

a brother of the preceding, married Priscilla Gregory, 23 Sept. 1736.   Their children were,

1. Abigail,   born 20 Sept.   1738 | 3 Anne,   born 5 April, 1744
2. Bethiah,   "   18 June,   1741 |

No. 22.   II B.   JOSHUA HOBART,

probably a son of Thomas Hobart, (No. 3.) died in Braintree, 28 Dec. 1713, probably without issue.

No 23.   III A.   PETER HOBART,

the first minister of Hingham, was the son of Edmund Ho-

bort, and born at Hingham, England, in 1604, was educated at the University of Cambridge, came to New England
8 June, 1635, and admitted freeman same year.   He settled at Hingham in Sept. 1635, and there died 20 Jan. 1679,
in his 75th year   Lincoln gives the names of his children.
1. Joshua—2. Jeremiah—3 Gershom—4 Japhet—5. Nehemiah—6. David—7 Josiah—8. Israel, and 3 daughters.

No. 24.   I B   JOSHUA HOBART,
the minister of Southold, L I. a son of the preceding, was
born in England, graduated at Harvard College, 1650, died
in Feb or March, 1717, aged 89, having been settled there
45 years.—[*Savage*, II. *Winthrop*, 222.

Wood, (Hist Sketch,) says, "The Rev. Joshua Hobart
succeeded Mr Youngs at Southold, 1674.   He was a son
of the Rev. Peter Hobart, who was educated at Cambridge
and preached at Haverhill and other places in England,
till 1635, when he with his children came over to Massachusetts, and settled in the town of Hingham, where he
gathered a church and continued " a faithful pastor and an
able preacher" until his death, 1679. He had four sons,
who became preachers   Joshua was born in 1628 graduated at Harvard College 1650.   He settled at Southold, in
1674 and continued there during his life time.   He died in
1717 aged 89 years "

" The church and congregation at Southold, after the
death of Mr Youngs, sent a messenger to Boston to seek
" an honest and godly minister," and in procuring Mr Hobart, their wishes seem to have been realized, and they
had the happiness to enjoy his labours during a long life."

Rev N. B. Cook, pastor of the same church says, " Some
of the posterity of Mr Hobart in the female line recently resided in the town of Southold, and were respectable, but
it is not known that he has any descendants now living."
                                    [*Southold L I.* 24 *Dec.* 1834.

No 25.   II B.   JEREMIAH HOBART,
a brother of the preceding, graduated at Harvard College,
1650, was ordained at Topsfield, 2 Oct. 1672, dismissed
21 Sept. 1680 ; went to Hempstead, L. I. ; was there settled, 1682 ; removed to Haddam, Conn , and re-installed
there 14 Nov. 1700, died in March, 1717, aged 87.   He
married Dorothy, daughter of the Rev. Samuel Whiting of
Lynn.—[*Farmer's Gen Reg.*

No. 26. III B.   GERSHOM HOBART,

a brother of the preceding, graduated at Harvard College, 1667, was admitted freeman 1673, was ordained at Groton, Mass, 26 Nov. 1679, dismissed by the town, Dec. 1685, died 19 Dec. 1717, aged 62.—[*Farmer's Gen. Reg.*

No. 27. IV B.   JAPHET HOBART,

a brother of the preceding, was born in April, 1647, graduated at Harvard College, 1667, went to England before 1670, in the capacity of a surgeon of a ship, with a design to go from thence to the East Indies, but was never heard of afterwards.   [*Lincoln's Hist. Hingham*, 115.   *Ibid.*

No. 28.   V B.   NEHEMIAH HOBART,

second minister of Newton, Mass. was son of Rev. Peter Hobart, was born 21 Nov. 1648 ; graduated at Harvard College, of which he was fellow from 1707 to 1712 ; was ordained 23 Dec. 1674, freeman 1675, died 12 Aug. 1712, aged 64   His wife was Sarah, daughter of Edward Jackson, Sen.   (See Jackson, No. 4.)—[*Ibid.*

Epitaph on the Tomb Stone of the Rev. Nehemiah Hobart, Pastor of the Church in Newton.

" In this Tomb are deposited the remains of the Reverend and very learned Teacher of Divinity, Nehemiah Hobart, an estimable fellow of Harvard College, a highly faithful and watchful pastor of the Church of Newton for forty years.   His singular gravity, humility, piety, and learning, rendered him the object of deep veneration and ardent esteem to men of science and religion.   He was born Nov 21, 1648, and died Aug. 25, 12, 1712, in the 64th year of his age.—[*Hist. Coll. 5, 269.*

No. 29. IV A.   JOSHUA HOBART,

a Captain, son of Edmund Hobart, lived in Hingham, was admitted freeman 1634, member of the Artillery Company 1641, Representative 1643, twenty-five years, Speaker of the House 1674, died 28 July, 1682.   His children were 1. Joshua, 2 Enoch, born 1654, and probably 3. Solomon and two daughters —[*Lincoln's Hist. Hingham   Farmer.*

No. 30. II B.   ENOCH HOBART,

a son of Capt. Joshua Hobart, married Hannah, daughter of Thomas Harris, 7 Aug. 1676, and settled in Hingham. Their children were,

14

1. Hannah, born 12 Aug. 1677	4. Thomas, born 31 March, 1683
Died 26 Aug. 1677	5 Deborah, " 4 Nov. 1685
2 Ruth, born 1678	Died 25 Feb 1687–8.
3. Hannah, " 8 Dec 1680	

No. 31.   NOAH HOBART,

minister of Fairfield Conn was a man of great talents and extensive acquirements , he wrote in favor of presbyterian ordination, and died in 1773 —[*Universal Biog Dictionary*.

He graduated at Harvard College, in 1724. A page of interesting particulars respecting him may be found in Allen's Dictionary

No. 32.   NEHEMIAH HOBART,

a native of Hingham, graduated at Harvard College in 1714, was ordained at Cohasset, 13 Dec 1721, died 31 May, 1740, aged 43.—[*Rev Dr Pierce*

No. 33.   JOHN SLOSS HOBART, LL D.

Judge of the District Court of New York, and Senator of the United States, graduated at Yale College in 1757   He died in 1805.—[*Univ Biog Dict*

No. 34   "JOHN HENRY HOBART,

the second son of Enoch and Hannah Hobart, (whose original name was Pratt,) was born in Philadelphia, the 14 Sept 1775 "

" He commenced his Collegiate education in the University of Pennsylvania, in 1788 or 89, which he left in 1791, and it was decided by his family and approved by himself, that he should finish it at Princeton "   " He graduated in 1793 "   " He resided at Princeton until the spring of 1798, when he returned to Philadelphia and was ordained in the month of June, by Bishop White."   " He accepted the charge of Trinity Church Oxford, and All Saints, Pequestau "   " He accepted an invitation to Christ Church, New Brunswick, in 1799 "   " He afterwards settled at Hempstead on Long Island   In the spring of 1800, he married Mary Goodin Chandler, daughter of the Rev. Dr Chandler, formerly Rector of St John's Church, Elizabethtown, N. J."   " In the month of Dec the same year, he received an invitation as an assistant Minister to Trinity Church, New York, which he accepted."

"The Rt. Rev John Henry Hobart, D. D of New York, was consecrated in Trinity Church, New York, on Wednesday, 29 May, 1811, by Bishop White, Bishops Provoost and Jarvis present and assisting "

[*Memoir of Bishop Hobart Extracts*

"The strong attachment of Mr Hobart to the distinctive principles of the Episcopal Church, and his bold, active and persevering defence of them, at all times, through good and through evil report, were striking peculiarities in his character and life He was constantly endeavouring to rouse others to a sense of their importance, and by his indefatigable labours, his noble enthusiasm, even in the cause of soberness and truth, and the influence of his talents, character, and station, he revived the languid zeal of Episcopalians, gave a new tone to their sentiments in this diocese, and stamped the impress of his own mind and feelings on thousands throughout the Church at large. " *Pro Ecclesia Dei*, he adopted in as full a sense as the "venerable prelate, (Whitgift,) by whom these words were first chosen, as the standard of his wishes, his duties, his labours, his dying prayers "

"There are no means of ascertaining what gave this strong bent to his mind in regard to the distinguishing principles of the Church : he was nurtured in her bosom indeed, but at a very early period of his life he was removed to a Presbyterian College, withdrawn for many years from the services of his own communion, and evidently estranged in a measure from his "first love," though it was never entirely discarded or forgotten While acting as a tutor at Princeton, he performed in his turn the prescribed services in the chapel, according to the Presbyterian mode , but he was always apprehensive of the dangerous influence of his residence at that institution, on his attachment to the Church, and with a view, perhaps, of fortifying himself in her principles, he often entered into discussions on these points, with Dr Smith, and Mr Kollock, in which he was aided and sustained by some of his Episcopal friends Perhaps this very circumstance of contending with the President, who was so greatly his superior in age and attainments, may have led him to a stricter examination of the subject, than he would have otherwise made, with a view to a more able and successful defence But his warm, decided and unchangeable attachment to the Church, in her peculiar and distinctive character, must, no doubt, be chiefly attributed to the course of his reading in the further progress of his ecclesiastical studies "—[*Ibid*, 88

1830, 12 Sept Bishop Hobart of New York, died at Auburn, Cayuga County, on a visitation of his diocese

[*Churchman's Almanac*

The last four named gentlemen were undoubtedly descendants from the family of Hobart of Hingham, but the
author of this Memorial has no means of ascertaining to
which branches of the family they respectively belonged.
                                                [*Editor.*

Besides the foregoing, "William Hobart, graduated at
Harvard, 1774—Peter, 1775—Nathaniel, 1784—James, at
Dartmouth, 1794—Benjamin, at Brown, 1804—Aaron, 1805
—Caleb, at Dartmouth, 1815—Benjamin, at Waterville,
1825.—[*Farmer.*

THE FAMILY OF JACKSON.

No. 1.   EDWARD JACKSON,

was born in 1602. He came from White Chapel, a parish in London, where he had prosecuted the business of a Nailer, to New England, took the freeman's oath in May, 1645; purchased a farm of 500 acres for £140, of Gov. Bradstreet, in Cambridge, (now Newton) in 1646, and increased the same by subsequent purchases to about 1800 acres. He married Elizabeth, widow of John Oliver,* deceased, and daughter of John Newgate of Boston, merchant, in 1649. Their children were,

1. Sarah,	bapt.	21, 2, 1650	5. Lydia,	born		1656
2. Edward,	born	15, 10, 1652	6 Elizabeth,	"	28 April,	1658
3. Jonathan,			7. Hannah,	"		
4. Sebas,			8. Ruth,	"	16 Jan.	1661

He was a Representative from Cambridge 16 years, commencing in 1647 and ending in 1676 ; was a member of the Rev. Mr. Mitchell's Church, and died 17 July, 1681, aged 79 years.†

---

*JOHN OLIVER, the first husband of Edward Jackson's wife, had by her five children, viz : 1 John, born 21, 9, 1638, died 27, 1, 1639 ; 2. Elizabeth, 28, 12, 1639 ; 3. Hannah, 3, 1, 1641, she died 11, 9, 1653 ; 4. John, 12, 2, 1644 ; 5. Thomas, 12, 12, 1645. John Oliver died 12 April, 1646, aged 30, nearly.

Elizabeth, was married to Enoch Wiswall of Dorchester, 25, 9, 1657.— Their children were, 1. John, born 10, 10, 1658, 2, Oliver ; 3. Samuel

John, married Susannah ———, and settled in Boston, was a member of the Artillery Company, and had five sons—1 Sweet—2. John—3. William—4. Samuel—5. Hammond, and four daughters.

Thomas, married Grace Prentiss, 27, 9, 1667, and settled in Cambridge Village. His second wife was Mary Wilson, married 19, 2, 1682, had five sons and four daughters ; was Representative from Cambridge, in 1692, and died 1 Nov. 1715, aged 70.

†Mr. Jackson left an estate appraised at £2477 19s 0d. of which he bequeathed 400 acres of land in Billerica, to Cambridge College, appraised at £80, together with some books, and all the debts due to him in England. He also bequeathed 25 acres of land in Newton, for the use of the ministry in that town forever.

It appears that Mr. Jackson had three children by a former wife, born in England, viz : 1. Hannah, born in 1631 —2 Rebecca—3. Francis, died 5 Oct. 1648.

No 2.   HANNAH JACKSON,
was married to John Ward of Newton, (then Newtown,) by whom she had,

1. John,	born 26, 11,	1653	7. Richard,	born 15, 11,	1666
	Died 1654		8 Mercy,	" 27 Jan.	1668
2. Rebecca,	born 15, 4,	1655	9. Edward,	" 13 March,	1671
3. John,	" 8, 1,	1658	10. Eleazer,	" 26 Feb	1672
4 Elizabeth,	" 18 June.	1660	11 Jonathan,	" 22, 2,	1674
5. Deborah,	" 19, 8,	1662	12. Joseph,	" 15, 9,	1677
6 William,	" 19 Nov.	1664	13 Mary, died		1685

Hannah, wife of John Ward, died 21 April, 1704, aged 73. John Ward represented the town from 1689 onward, about 15 years.

No. 3.   REBECCA JACKSON,
sister of the preceding, was married to Thomas, son of Capt. Thomas Prentice * He died previous to 1689, leaving one son John, who is named in his brother John's Will

No. 4.   I A.   SARAH JACKSON,
daughter of Edward and Elizabeth Jackson, was married to the Rev Nehemiah Hobart, 21, 1, 1678   (See Hobart, No. 28.)   Their children were,

---

* Capt. Thomas Prentice of Newtown, that renowned partizan Commander of horse, was one among others, whom the Divine Providence raised up and qualified for distinguished usefulness in the Phillipic war, in 1675. Capt. Prentice was active and eminently serviceable in every period of the war ; his name was a terror to the hostile tribes of Indians, by his suddenly collecting and marching his cavalry at the shortest notice, fighting on horseback or on foot, as the nature of the ground or the situation of the enemy required. * * * *

The gallant Prentice, who at the age of 54 began his military career, survived until 7 July, 1709, when he died aged 89, by a similar casualty with his brave companion in arms, Col. Church, in consequence of a fall from his horse, upon his return from public worship Lord's day, 7 May. He was buried with the respect due to so good a man, as well as brave defender of his country, by the troop under arms.

On the footstone of his grave are inscribed the following lines, which the teeth of time have almost effaced :—

He that's here interred needs no versifying—
A virtuous life will keep the name from dying ;
He'll live though poets cease their scribbling rhime,
When that this stone shall mouldered be by time

1 Elizabeth,	born 27 June,	1679	4 Abigail,	born 22 Jan.	1684
2. Rebecca,	" 13 Feb.	1680	5 Sarah,	" 13 March,	1687
3 Mary,	" 16 Jan.	1682	6 Hannah,	" 19 Jan	1689

Mrs. Sarah Hobart, died 23 Feb 1711. Rev. Nehemiah Hobart died 12 Aug 1712.

No. 5.   II A.   Deacon EDWARD JACKSON,

a brother of the preceding, married Abigail ——. Their children were,

1. Elizabeth,	born 23 Feb.	1687	5. Allice,	born	
2. Abigail,	" 13 May,	1690	6 Edward,	" 3 April,	1700
3. Samuel,		1694		Died 1 July, 1708, aged 8.	
4. Hannah,			7 Abigail,	born 11 Sept.	1705

He was ordained deacon in 1707 ; was Representative in 1702 ; Selectman in 1688, and Town Clerk, and died 30 Sept 1727, aged 75

No. 6.   I B.   ELIZABETH JACKSON,

a daughter of the preceding, was married to Thomas Prentice. She died 19 Oct 1757, aged 67.

No. 7   III B   SAMUEL JACKSON, Esq ,

a brother of the preceding, was a Justice of the Peace, and Town Clerk, and died 3 Dec. 1742, aged 48.

No 8   IV B.   HANNAH JACKSON,

a sister of the preceding, was married to a Mr Loring.

No 9.   III A   JONATHAN JACKSON,

a son of Edward and Elizabeth Jackson, married Elizabeth —— and settled in Boston. Their children were,

| 1. Elizabeth, | born 16 Feb | 1668 | 3 Jonathan, | born 28 Dec. | 1672 |
| 2 Mary, | " 3 Dec. | 1670 | 4 Sarah, | " 9 Oct. | 1679 |

No. 10.   IV A   SEBAS JACKSON,

a brother of the preceding, married Sarah Baker, 19, 2, 1671. Their children were,

1 Edward,	born 12 Sept.	1672	5 John,	born 15 March,	1685
2. John,	" 21, 1,	1675	6 Jonathan,	" 10 Sept	1686
	Died in childhood.			Lost at sea in 1714 or 15	
3 Sarah,	born 10 Nov.	1680	7. Mary,	born 26 Dec.	1687
4. Elizabeth,	" 2 March,	1683	8. Joseph,	" 6 March,	1690

Sebas Jackson died 6 Dec. 1690.

No. 11.   III B   SARAH JACKSON,

a daughter of the preceding, was married to a Mr. Draper.

No. 12.   IV B   ELIZABETH JACKSON,
a sister of the preceding, was married to a Mr. Grant.

No. 13.   VIII B.   JOSEPH JACKSON,
the youngest brother of the preceding, married Patience
Hyde, 28 Nov. 1717.   Their children were,

1 Lydia,	born 20 Sept.	1718	3. Joseph,	born 2 Aug	1729
2. Timothy,	" 20 April,	1726	4. Patience,	" 21 April,	1734

No. 14.   I C.   LYDIA JACKSON,
a daughter of the preceding, was married to a Mr. Upham,
and settled at Weston

No 15.   II C.   TIMOTHY JACKSON,
a brother of the preceding, married Sarah Smith, and settled in Newton.   Their children were,

1. Lucy,	born 22 June,	1753	4. Polly,	born 22 June,	1760
2. Sarah,	" 9 Nov.	1754	5. Abigail,	" 10 June,	1763
3. Timothy,	" 3 Aug.	1756			

Timothy Jackson died in 1774.

No 16.   I D.   LUCY JACKSON,
was married to Moses Souther, and settled in Marlborough.

No. 17.   II D.   SARAH JACKSON,
died unmarried, 6 July, 1788.

No. 18.   III D.   TIMOTHY JACKSON,
married Sarah Winchester, and settled in Newton.   Their
children were,

1 William,	born 2 Sept.	1783	4. Francis,	born 7 March,	1789
2. Lucretia,	" 16 Aug.	1785	5. George,	" 22 April,	1792
Died 27 Dec. 1812.			6. Edmund,	" 9 Jan.	1795
3. Stephen W. born 19 March, 1787					

No. 19.   IV D   POLLY JACKSON,
was married to Caleb Gardner of Brookline.

No. 20.   V D.   ABIGAIL JACKSON,
is living in Boston ; for the last 30 years unmarried.

No. 21.   V A.   LYDIA JACKSON,
a daughter of Edward and Elizabeth Jackson, was married
to Joseph Fuller, 13, 12, 1679   Their, children were,

1. John,	born 15, 10,	1680	4. Lydia,	born 15 Feb.	1691
2 Joseph,	" 4 July,	1685	5 Edward,	" 1 March,	1694
3. Jonathan,	" 7 Jan.	1686-7	6. Isaac,	" 16 March,	1698

No. 22. VI A. ELIZABETH JACKSON,

a sister of the preceding, was married to John, son of Capt. Thomas Prentice, 28, 4, 1677. He died 14 March, 1689, leaving no son, and bequeathed some of his estate to John Prentice, son of his brother Thomas, in his will.

No. 23. VII A. HANNAH or ANNE JACKSON,

a sister of the preceding, was married to Nathaniel, son of Nathaniel Wilson of Brookline Their children were,

1. Nathaniel,	born 4 Nov.	1682	4. Susannah,	born 6 Nov.	1688
2 Elizabeth,	" 9 Nov	1684	5 Edward,	" 3 Oct.	1689
3. Hannah,	" 18 Oct.	1686			

No 24. VIII A. RUTH JACKSON,

the youngest sister of the preceding, died unmarried in 1692, aged 28 years.

Dea JOHN JACKSON,

a brother of Edward Jackson, married Margaret ————. Mrs. Jackson was born in 1624 Their children were,

1. John,	born in	1639	7 Abigail,	born 14 Aug	1648
2 Grace,	"		8 Margaret,	" 20 June,	1649
3 Theodosia,	"		9 Edward,	" 11 Jan.	1650
4. Caleb,	" 10 Oct	1645	10. Abraham,	" 14 Aug.	1655
5 Hannah,	" 7 June,	1646	11 Deliverence,	" 9 Nov.	1657
6. Anne,	" 1 Aug	1647	12. Joshua,	" 15 Sept.	1659

Dea John Jackson died 30 Jan 1674. Margaret, widow of Dea. John Jackson, died in 1684, aged 60.

1. A. *John*, died unmarried, 14 Oct. 1675, aged 36 years.

5. A. *Hannah*, was married to Elijah Kenricke, who died 4, 10, 1680, aged 37 years, leaving one son John.

8 A. *Margaret*, was married to James Trowbridge, and died 17, 6, 1672.

9. A *Edward*, married Grace ————, who died in 1685, aged 30, and he died in 1677, aged 27, leaving one son Edward, who died 20 Aug 1691.

10 A. *Abraham*, married Elizabeth ————, in 1681. Their children were, 1 John, born 25, 2, 1682, died 9 Sept 1755 —Thomas, who died 24 Jan. 1703—Abraham, who died in 1694, aged 1 year—Abigail, born 2 Feb 1690, died in 1702, aged 12—Elizabeth, born 8, 8, 1680 ?—Mary, born 2 Dec. 1686

15

1. B. *John*, son of Abraham and Elizabeth Jackson, married and had two sons, John and Thomas.

1. C. *John*, son of John Jackson, married and had one son Thomas.

1. D. *Thomas*, son of John Jackson, married and had one son John, who died in Newton, leaving a son John now living.

This name is very numerous in New England, 34 having graduated at the New England Colleges.

[*See Farmer's Gen. Reg.*

THE FAMILY OF PAINE.

MOSES PAINE,

one of the early settlers of Braintree, and probably the progenitor of the families of this name in that town, was buried there on the 21, 4, 1643, leaving probably three children, viz : Moses, Elizabeth, the wife of Henry Adams, Jr. (See Adams, No. 2,) and Stephen.

No. 1.   MOSES PAINE,

probably a son of the preceding, a member of the Artillery Company, 1644 ; freeman 1647 ; a Lieutenant, Representative, 1666 and 1668, with his wife Elizabeth, had nine children, viz :

1. Moses,	born 16, 5,	1646	5. Mary,	born 12, 1,	1655
Died 2, 12, 1648.			6. William,	" 1, 2,	1657
2 Elizabeth,	born 5, 6,	1648	7. John,	" 12, 8,	1659
3. Sarah,	" 30, 11,	1650	Died 1, 2, 1660.		
Died 10, 6, 1651.			8. Sarah,	born 2, 3,	1662
4. Moses,	born 26, 4,	1652	9. Margaret,	" 20, 10,	1664
Died 10, 6, 1657.					

No 2.   STEPHEN PAINE,

probably a brother of the preceding, married Hannah, a daughter of Dea. Samuel Bass, 15, 9, 1651. (See Bass, No. 9,) by whom he had seven children, who lived to a great age.—[See Hancock's Cent. Sermon, p. 26.

1. Stephen,	born 8, 1,	1652	5. Moses,	born 26, 1,	1660
2. Samuel,	" 10, 4,	1654	6. John,	" 21, 7,	1666
3. Hannah,	" 28, 11,	1655	7. Lydia,	" 20, 7,	1670
4. Sarah,	" 1, 9,	1657			

Seargent Stephen Paine died 29 July, 1691.

No. 3.   I A.   STEPHEN PAINE, Jr.,

married Ellen Veasey, 20 Feb. 1681. Their children were,

1. Stephen,	born 7 Nov.	1682	3. Samuel,	born 13 Feb.	1686
2. Ellen,	bapt. 12, 8,	1684	Died 13 Feb. 1688.		
			4. Samuel,	bapt. 14, 2,	1689

Stephen Paine, a devout christian, a cunning artificer,

and ingenious to admiration, died in the flower of his age, of the small pox, 24 May, 1690   His widow was afterwards married to Joseph Crosby, 5, 8, 1693

No. 4   II B   ELLEN PAINE,

daughter of the preceding, was married to Samuel Penniman of Braintree, 14 May, 1707.

No. 5.   IV B   SAMUEL PAINE, 3d.,

a brother of the preceding, was a member of the Episcopal Church in Braintree, (now Quincy.) He married Susannah Ruggles, 5 Nov. 1728.   Their children were,

1. Susannah,	bapt. 16 Oct.	1729	4 Joseph Ruggles, b. 30 June, 1735		
2. Eleanor,	born 23 March,	1731	Died 16 Oct 1735.		
3 Jos. Ruggles,	" 3 Dec.	1732	5 Sarah,	born 12 Nov.	1736
Died in infancy.			6. Ebenezer,	" 14 March,	1738
			Died 26 March, 1739.		

No 6. II A.   SAMUEL PAINE,

a son of Stephen and Hannah Paine, married Mary Penniman of Braintree, 4 April 1678   Their children were,

1 Mary,	born 27 Oct	1680	5. Joseph,	born 3 Aug.	1689
2. Lydia,	" 6 Jan	1681-2	6. Mehitable,	" 8 Dec.	1693
3. Samuel,	" 26 Nov.	1684	7. Benjamin,	" 28 Dec	1696
4. Hannah,	" 1 Feb	1687			

Samuel Paine, died 10 Dec. 1739, in his 86 year.

II B. *Lydia*, was married to Joseph Sawin of Braintree, 17 Dec. 1714, probably the father of Capt Eliphalet Sawin. (See second part, 6 Branch, No 126)

No. 7. III B.   SAMUEL PAINE, Jr.,

married Rachel ——.   Their children were,

1. Rachel,	born 22 Dec.	1712	Died 31 Aug 1739.		
Died the same day.			6 Peter,-	bapt. in	1723
2. Rachel,	born 21 Sept.	1713	7. Ebenezer,	born 22 Dec.	1724
Died 20 July, 1739.			8 Enoch,	"	
3. Samuel,	born 26 Aug.	1714	Died 31 July, 1739.		
Died 20 June, 1739.			9. Jacob,	born 18 Aug.	1728
4. Stephen,	born 8 Jan	1717	10. Susannah,	" 16 Oct	1729
Died 18 July, 1739			11. Hannah,	" 8 Feb.	1730
5. Nehemiah,	born 6 May,	1721			

Rachel, wife of Samuel Paine, Jr., died 3 Oct. 1739.

IX C. *Jacob*, and Rachel Paine, his wife, had one son Samuel, born 18 Nov. 1753

Note.—There appears to have been some malignant disease among children during the summer of 1739, which proved mortal to a large number in Braintree, and the adjacent towns.

No. 8   V B   JOSEPH PAINE,

a son of Samuel and Mary Paine, married Sarah Powell, 28 March, 1717.   Their children were,

1. Bathsheba, born 9 Dec. 1718 | 3 Mary,   } born 16 July, 1723
2. Sarah,   " 25 Dec. 1720 | 4 Abigail,   }
                                 | 5 Lydia,   " 9 Jan.   1726

No. 9.   III A.   HANNAH PAINE,

a daughter of Stephen and Hannah Paine, was married to Shadrach Wilber of Taunton, 14, 7, 1692.

No. 10.   IV A.   SARAH PAINE,

a sister of the preceding, was married to Roger Billings of Dorchester   (See Billings, No 16)

No. 11.   V A   MOSES PAINE,

a brother of the preceding, married Mary ———.   Their children were,

1. Mary,   born 4 May, 1689 | 4 Sarah,   born 3 July, 1697
2 Hannah,   " 2 April, 1692 | 5 Moses,   " 13 June, 1700
3. Moses,   " 21 Oct. 1694 | 6 Aaron,   " 8 Nov. 1703
        Died 12 Sept 1697. | Died 24 Feb 1710

Dea. Moses Paine died 22 June, 1746.

No. 12.   V B.   MOSES PAINE,

a son of the preceding, married Abigail, daughter of Capt. Peter Adams, 31 Oct. 1723.   (See Adams, No 36, 2)
    Their children were,

1 Abigail, born 11 Dec. 1728 | 3 Moses,   born 30 Nov. 1732
2. Mary,   " 30 Jan. 1730 | 4 Hannah,   " 17 Oct. 1731

No. 13   VI A.   JOHN PAINE,

a son of Stephen and Hannah Paine, married Deborah Neale, 20 Jan, 1689.   Their children were,

1. John,   born 13 Aug. 1690 | Died 6 Dec 1697
2. Deborah,   " 28 Sept. 1692 | 6. Benjamin, born 6 March, 1700
        Died 19 July, 1703. | 7 Seth,   " 16 Jan.   1702
3. Stephen, born 19 Jan. 1694 | 8. James,   } " 27 July, 1704
4. Joseph,   " 26 Oct. 1695 | 9 Deborah, }
5. Moses,   " 7 Nov 1697 |

I B.   *John*, son of John Paine, died an untimely death, accidentally shooting himself about the year 1706 —[*Records*

III B   *Stephen*, a brother of the preceding, married Mary
Littlefield, 23 Nov 1738, by whom he had one son Stephen
born 6 Sept. 1739.

No. 14. IV B.   JOSEPH PAINE,
of Boston, probably a son of John and Deborah Paine,
married Mrs. Mary Babcock of Milton, 27 Jan. 1732, (perhaps a second wife,) and settled in Milton.   Their children were,

| 1 Joseph, | born | 4 Feb. | 1733 | 3. Annah, | born | 6 Nov. | 1736 |
| 2 John, | " | 14 Oct. | 1734 | 4. Mary, | " | 7 Jan. | 1739 |

Milton Records.

No. 15. VI B.   BENJAMIN PAINE,
a son of John and Deborah Paine, married Elizabeth,
daughter of Thomas and Mary. Copeland, May, 1725. (See
Copeland, No. 8.)   Their children were,

| 1. Nathaniel, | born | 30 April, | 1727 | 3. Phebe, | born | 26 July, | 1737 |
| 2. Mary, | " | 8 May, | 1730 | 4. Phinehas, | " | 6 Aug. | 1742 |

No. 16   I C.   NATHANIEL PAINE,
a son of the preceding, married Hannah, daughter of Joseph and Hannah Wales   (See Wales, No. 15.)   Their
children were, 1. SILAS, who married Lydia White, 22
April, 1790. (See White, No 25, 9)   2. BENJAMIN, who
married Mary Thayer, 19 Jan. 1782. (See Thayer, No.
26, 6)   3. ZEBA, who married the daughter of Col. Barnabas Clark.

No. 17. IV C   PHINEHAS PAINE,
a son of Benjamin and Elizabeth Paine, married Mrs. Nancy Babcock of Milton, 9 July, 1771, and settled in Milton.
Their children were,

| 1. Wm. Babcock, b. | 5 April, | 1772 | 3. Hannah, | born 29 Dec. | 1774 |
| 2 Benjamin, | " 26 April, | 1773 | | |

No. 18   VII A.   LYDIA PAINE,
the youngest daughter of Stephen and Hannah Paine, was
married to Benjamin Neale, 20 Jan. 1689.

This name is very numerous in New England, there being thirty-six who have graduated in the New England
Colleges.—[See *Farmer's Gen. Reg.*

THE FAMILY OF THAYER.

No. 1.   RICHARD THAYER,*

of Boston, appears to be the first of this name in New England. He was admitted freeman in 1640. His three sons who were probably born in England, and came to this country with him were, 1. RICHARD—2. ZACHARIAH—3. Nathaniel, and Jael, Deborah, Sarah, Hannah and Abigail, who died 6 Aug. 1727, aged 66, were probably his daughters, who settled in Braintree. Richard Thayer Sen. died in Braintree 27 Aug. 1695.

No. 2. I A.   RICHARD THAYER, Jr.,

married Dorothy Pray of Braintree, 24, 10, 1651, and settled in that town. Their children were,

1. Dorothy,	born 30. 6,	1653	3. Nathaniel,	born 1 Jan.	1658
2. Richard,	" 31, 6,	1665	4. Cornelius,	" 18, 7,	1670

Richard Thayer died 4 Dec. 1705. Dorothy, widow of Richard Thayer, died 11 Dec. 1705.

No. 3. II B.   RICHARD THAYER,

a son of the preceding, married Rebecca Micall, 16 July, 1679. She was born 22, 11, 1658. Their children were,

1. Rebecca,	born 16 Aug.	1680	7. Deborah,	bapt. 11, 2,	1697
2. Benjamin,	" 6 Oct.	1683	8. Anna,	" 14, 9,	1697
3. Richard,	" 26 Jan.	1685	9. Gideon,	born 26 July,	1700
4. John,	" 12 Jan.	1688	10. Obadiah	" 1 May,	1703
5. Mary,	Feb.	1689		Died 5 April 1721.	
6. James,	" 16 Nov.	1691			

Richard Thayer died 11 Sept. 1729.

---

*This name has been spelled in various ways, as *Thaire*. Palmer's Reports 109, (17 James 1st.) *Thayer*, item 112. *Theyar*, Popham's Reports 178, (2 Charles 1st). *Thair*, Latch's Reports 212, (3 Charles 1st.) *Theyer*, 4th Barrow's Reports, 2032, (1767.)—[*T. Metcalf Esq. Dedham, Ms.*

Mr Arodi Thayer, late of Dorchester, (No. 15, 2) once stated to a friend that the ancestors of his family came from the West of England.

No 4. I C. REBECCA THAYER,

a daughter of the preceding, was married to Thomas Bolter, of Weymouth, a weaver, 12, 12, 1701

No. 5. II C. BENJAMIN THAYER,

a brother of the preceding, married Margaret Curtis, 17 Aug. 1704   Their children were,

1 Margaret,	born 26 June,	1705	3. Zebulon, born 29 Aug.	1711
2. Benjamin,	" 23 Feb	1708		

Benjamin Thayer died 4 May, 1712   His widow Margaret, was married to John Hayden, 26 Feb. 1713.

No. 6. I D. MARGARET THAYER,

daughter of the preceding, was married to Amos Stetson of Braintree, 9 May, 1728

No. 7 II D. BENJAMIN THAYER,

a brother of the preceding, married Hannah Vinton, 8 Nov 1728.   Their children were,

1. Benjamin,	born 6 Oct.	1729	4 Benjamin,	born 11 Dec.	1738	
	Died 1 Feb. 1730.		5 Anne,	" 11 Aug.	1741	
2. Benjamin,	born 3 Feb.	1731	6. Adam,	" 4 July,	1744	
3. Adam	" 7 March, 1735		7. Vashti	" 20 Feb.	1745	

No. 8. IV E. BENJAMIN THAYER,

a son of the preceding, married Hannah Howland of Pembroke, 29 Jan 1763, and had several children. By his second wife Chloe, his children were,

1. Jane,	born 12 Dec.	1783	4. Melvin,	born 4 Oct	1791
2 Luther,	" 25 March,	1786	5. Benjamin,	" 8 Jan.	1794
3 William,	" 15 Nov.	1788			

Benjamin Thayer died 1 March, 1802, aged 64.

No. 9. III D. ZEBULON THAYER,

a son of Benjamin and Margaret Thayer, married Mary ——.   Their children were,

1. Mary,	born 25 Aug	1729	5. Joshua	born 1 March, 1745
2 Zebulon,	" 17 Aug.	1731	His second wife was Sarah ——.	
3. Mary,	" 15 May,	1735	6 Lucy,	born 29 Oct	1747
4. Caleb,	" 27 Feb.	1743	7 Asa,	" Jan.	1749
			8. Elias,	" 18 May,	1752

No 10. II E ZEBULON THAYER,

a son of the preceding, married Abigail ——.   Their children were,

1 Abigail,	born	6 June,	1752	4 Naomi,		
2. Mary	"	12 Oct.	1754	5. Ruth,	} born 5 July,	1761
3. Caleb,	"	23 May	1757			

No. 11.   III C   Lieut. RICHARD THAYER,

a son of Richard and Rebecca Thayer, married Mary, a daughter of Samuel and Anna White, 6 Feb 1711. (See White, No. 14; 2.) He was blind for many years. Their children were,

1. Isaiah,	born	5 Nov.	1711	5. Obadiah,	born 26 Dec.	1720
2. Mary,	"	26 Sept.	1713	6. Anna,	" 31 Jan.	1722
3. James,	"	4 Oct.	1716	7. Obadiah,	" 29 March,	1724
4 Gideon,	"	16 Jan.	1718			

His second wife was Sarah Ford.

| 8. Richard, | born 18 March, | 1731 | 10. Ruth, | born 1 Aug. | 1734 |
| 9. Sarah, | baptised in | 1733 | 11. Jerusha, | " 18 Jan. | 1737 |

Sarah, wife of Lieut. Richard Thayer, died 14 Feb. 1742. His third wife was Lydia Pray.

No 12.   I D.   ISAIAH THAYER,

married Sarah, daughter of Benjamin White, 17 Sept. 1741 (See White, No. 22.) Their children were,

1. Eleanor, born 15 Nov. 1742, second wife of Elijah Thayer, No. 30.
2. Sarah,   " 14 Sept. 1744—3 Lois, baptised in 1748   [Branch.
4. Eliphaz,   " 11 Mar. 1762, married Deliverance Thayer, 2d part, 13

No. 13.   II D.   MARY THAYER,

was married to John Ludden, 25 Oct 1733 Their children were,

1. Sylvanus,	born 23 Aug.	1734	6. Sarah,		
	Died 5 July, 1741 *		7 Elizabeth,	} born 1 Dec 1744	
2. Mary,	born 4 May,	1737	8 Anne,	" 14 Nov 1746	
3. Silas,	"	1739		Died 12 March, 1753	
	Died 29 Oct. 1756.		9 Ezra,	born 3 Oct 1748	
4. Elisha,	born 12 Dec.	1740	10 Simeon,	" in 1750	
	Died Aug. 1750.			Died 11 March, 1753	
5. Timothy,	born 3 Dec.	1742	11 John, who died in infancy		
	Died 21 March, 1743.		12 Sylvanus,	born 21 June, 1754	

John Ludden died about 1789 or 1790. Widow Mary Ludden died 2 Oct. 1803, aged 90 years, wanting 5 days.

---

*1741, July 6. "Buried a child of John Ludden—an early instance of the Grace of God operating on some children, for he appeared more sober and thoughtful than is common for one of his age; and in his sickness was under a lively sense of death, and yet undaunted; prayed for the pardon of sin, and the salvation of his soul, and gave religious counsel to his sister, younger than himself, though he was not quite seven years old "
                                            [Hist. Notices. 1 Cong. Ch. Br.

No. 14. III D. JAMES THAYER,

married Esther, daughter of Nathaniel Wales. (See Wales, No. 5) Their children were,

1. Nath'l Wales, born 21 Aug 1748
2. Esther, " 21 May, 1750
3. James, " 15 July, 1753
4. Barnabas, born 13 March, 1755
5. Mary, " 29 March, 1757
Married to Daniel Loring, in 1778.
Died in 1834.

No. 15. IV D. GIDEON THAYER,

married Rachel ——, (probably a sister of Gideon French's wife Elizabeth.) (See French, No 21.) Their children were,

1. Zepheon, born 6 Nov. 1741
Died in May, 1804.
2. Arodi, born 19 Feb. 1743
Died 5 May, 1831.
3 Rachel, born 20 Dec. 1744
Died in Sept. 1819.
4 Mary, born 24 June, 1746
5. Nathaniel,
6 Francis.

No. 16. VI D. ANNA THAYER,

was married to Jonathan Wild, by whom she had one daughter. 1. Anna, born in Aug 1749, the wife of Col. John Holbrook, married 30 Aug 1766, by whom she had ten children, viz :—*John*, who died unmarried—*Anna*, the first wife of Caleb Thayer—*Susannah*, whose first husband was Caleb Holbrook, and second Seth Turner, Esq.—*Elisha*, who married Sarah Thayer—*Joseph*, who married Ruth Linfield—*Mary*, the second wife of Caleb Thayer—*Sarah*, wife of Samuel Dyer—*Abia*, who married Mary Thayer—*Charlotte*, wife of James Adams—*Clarissa*, wife of Barnabas Lothrop

Mrs. Anna Wild was married to Elisha, a son of the Rev. Samuel Niles, 7 Dec. 1752. He was born 30 July, 1719 ; died about 1774.

No. 17. VII D. OBADIAH THAYER,

married Joanna ——, afterwards settled in Boston. Their children born in Braintree were,

1. Lydia, born 21 March, 1752
2 Susannah, " 29 May, 1754
3. Joanna, " 10 Sept. 1756
4. Rachel, " 3 Sept 1760
5 Andrew, born 15 May, 1763
Died 17 July, 1765.
6. Obadiah, born 24 May, 1766

No. 18. VIII D. RICHARD THAYER,

married Esther, a daughter of Moses and Esther French. (See second part, 9 Branch, No. 1, 3.)

No. 19. IX D. SARAH THAYER,

was an invalid from her childhood, and died unmarried.

No. 20. X D. RUTH THAYER,

was married to Capt. Silas Wild, and had four children.

| 1. Sarah, | born 23 Feb, | 1758 | 3 Paul, | } | born 13 Jan. | 1762 |
| 2. Jonathan, | " 4 Dec. | 1759 | 4 Silas, | } | | |

Ruth, wife of Capt. Silas Wild, died 29 Dec. 1793 His second wife was Sarah Kingman of Weymouth, married 1794 Capt. Silas Wild was born 8 March, 1736 ; died 30 Sept 1807, aged 71.

No. 21. XI D. JERUSHA THAYER,

was married to Randall Wild. Their children were,

1. Asa, born 25 Feb. 1757, married Anna Wales, settled in Fairlee, Vt.
2 Levi, b 23 Aug 1758, married Rhoda Capen, settled in Braintree
3. Randall, b. 14 June, 1760, married Sarah Hunt, settled in Fairlee, Vt.
4 Esther, b. 5 Sept. 1762, married Isaac Horton, settled in N. Bridgewater.
5. Elisha, b 4 April, 1764, married Abigail Faxon, settled in Fairlee, Vt.
6 Richard, b 4 Sept 1765, settled in Easton, Ms.
7. Sarah, b 26 April, 1772, married Nehemiah Holbrook, Braintree.

Randall Wild was born 9 May, 1732. Widow Jerusha Wild died 31 May, 1809, aged 72.

No. 22. IV C. JOHN THAYER,

a son of Richard and Rebecca Thayer, married Rebecca, daughter of Dependence French, 26 May, 1715. (See French, No 9, 4) Their children were,

1. John,	born 18 Feb	1716	6. Richard,	born 15 Dec.	1725
	Died 15 April, 1716.			Died 30 Jan. 1726	
2 John,	born 27 July,	1717	7. Richard,	born 26 Jan.	1727
3. Benjamin,	" 11 Jan	1720	8. Abiah,	" 25 June,	1729
4. Obadiah,	" 31 Dec.	1721	9 Simeon,	" 22 May,	1732
5. Micah,	" 31 Oct	1723	10. Elijah,	" 16 July,	1736

John Thayer died 9 Feb. 1768. Rebecca, wife of John Thayer, died 30 Oct 1762.

No. 23. II D. JOHN THAYER, Jr.,

married Abigail ——, by whom he had one son, 1. John, born 26 Nov. 1745. John Thayer, Jr. died 10 Sept. 1745.

John, son of John and Abigail Thayer, married Elizabeth Hollis, 12 July, 1771, for his first wife, and Eunice West in 1781, for his second, and settled in East Bridgewater, had two children, John, born 29 May, 1783, and Molly, born 22 Dec. 1784.

No. 24. III D. BENJAMIN THAYER,

married Ruth, daughter of John and Ruth Capen, 17 Jan. 1741. (See second part, 8 Branch, No 1, 4) His second wife was Bethiah, daughter of Naphtali Thayer. (See second part, 10 Branch, No. 1, 2) Benjamin Thayer died in Oct. 1807, in his 88 year.   Bethiah, widow of Benjamin Thayer, died in Oct. 1816.

No. 25.   IV D.   OBADIAH THAYER,
settled in South Weymouth, and spent his days there.

No. 26.   V D.   MICAH THAYER,
married Mehitable French, 14 Jan. 1748. (See French, No. 16.)   Their children were,

1. Micah, born 9 Oct 1749, married Abigail Wales, 27 Feb. 1779.
2. Mehitable, b 3 June, 1751, m. John Tower, 23 Feb. 1776
3. Zerviah, b. 5 March, 1753, m Edward Faxon, 16 June, 1770.
4. Rebecca, b. 28 April, 1755, m. Daniel French, 1 April, 1775.
5. Alexander, b. 17 Sept 1756, m. Lucy Edson, Bridgewater, in 1788.
6. Mary, b. 27 Dec. 1758, m. Benjamin Paine.
7 Lucy, b 27 Oct 1760, m. Joshua French, 21 Feb 1782.
8. Ezra, b. 21 Dec. 1762, m Charlotte French, about 1784.
9. Thaddeus, born 19 Oct 1765 , 10. Alpheus, born 5 April, 1768.

   Mehitable, wife of Micah Thayer, died 12 Jan. 1773.
   Micah Thayer died in 1802.

No. 27.   VII D.   RICHARD THAYER,
married Susannah (Randall ') and settled in Weymouth. Their children were,

1. Randall,   born 8 June,   1753
2. Susannah,   "   19 June,   1754
3 Rhoda,   "   9 Sept.   1755
4. Richard,   "   13 Sept.   1757
5. Barnabas,   "   23 Oct.   1759
      Died 12 Jan. 1833
6. Rebecca, born 1 April,   1761

7. Jonathan,   born 1 Sept. 1763
8 Sarah,
9 Anna,
10. Phinehas,
11. Beza, died 5 Mar. 1812 aged 44.
12. Luther.

No. 28   VIII D.   ABIAH THAYER,
married Elizabeth ——." Their children were,

1. Oliver,   born 27 May,   1753
2. Elizabeth,   " 12 April,   1754
3. Phebe,
4. Anna,

5. Amasa,   born 26 March, 1764
6. Eliphalet,   "   14 March, 1766
7. Sylva,   "   18 April, 1768
8. Adonijah,   "   29 Oct.   1770

No. 29.   IX D.   SIMEON THAYER,
married Martha Blanchard of Weymouth, by whom he had
1. Simeon, born March, 1757 ; who married Olive Braman of Norton, about 1778. She was born 25 May, 1761 ; and he died 5 Nov. 1805. 2 an infant who died.

No. 30. X D.   ELIJAH THAYER,
married for his first wife, Hannah Hayden, 18 May, 1765;
and for his second, Eleanor Thayer, 11 May, 1790. (See
No. 12, 1.)

No. 31. V C.   MARY THAYER,
a daughter of Richard and Rebecca Thayer, was married
to William Copeland, Jr. (See Copeland, No. 10)

No. 32. VII C.   DEBORAH THAYER,
a sister of the preceding, was married to Josiah Faxon, 13
Jan. 1718.

No 33. VIII C.   ANNA THAYER,
another sister of the preceding, was married to Dependence French. (See French, No. 19)

No. 34. IX C.   GIDEON THAYER,
a brother of the preceding, married Hannah Hollis, 3 June,
1723. Their children were,

1. Abigail,	born 15 Nov.	1723	5 Gideon,	born 2 Oct	1732
2 Mercy,	" 1 Nov.	1725	6. Eunice,	" 20 Dec.	1735
3. Hannah,	" 5 April,	1728	7. Job,	" 15 Aug	1738
4 Eunice,	" 10 Oct	1730		Died 9 May, 1751.	
	Died 16 Aug. 1732.		8. Elidealh,	born Aug.	1741

1742, 17 Feb. "Gideon Thayer was drowned in our river,
(Monoquot,) when coming to meeting on the Sabbath day
morning, by falling through the ice."—[Records.

No. 35. V D.   GIDEON THAYER,
the son of the preceding, married Susannah ——. Their
children were, 1. *Job*, who married Mary Wade of Weymouth, about 1785—2 *Gideon*, who married Jemima Vinton, 24 April, 1800, for his first wife; she died 11 March,
1801, aged 33 years; and for his second, Hannah Belcher
in 1802—3. *Sylvanus*, who married Abigail, daughter of Asa
Copeland—4. *Rachel*, who was married to William Wild, Jr.
Their children were, John, Rachel, Calvin, Daniel, Ludo-
vicus —5. *Naomi*, who was married to Lot Wade, 4 March,
1791—6. *Zephorah*, who was married to Reuel Harris, 20
June, 1802. Their children were, Daniel, Susannah.—7.
Leah, who died young
  Gideon Thayer, died 27 Nov. 1800, aged 68 Widow
Susannah Thayer died 6 June, 1806, aged 61.

No. 36. III B. NATHANIEL THAYER,

a son of Richard and Dorothy Thayer, married Hannah Hayden, 27 May, 1679. Their children were,

1. Nathaniel,	born about	1680	5. Ruth,	born 17, 5,	1689
2. Richard,	" "	1683	6. Dorothy, }	baptized in	1715
3. Hannah,	" 17 Feb.	1686	7. Lydia, }		
4. Zachariah,	" 16 Mar.	1687	8. Daniel.		

Nathaniel Thayer died 28 March, 1728.

No. 37. I C. NATHANIEL THAYER, Jr.,

married Sarah, daughter of Elder Nathaniel Wales, 25, 11, 1704. (See Wales, No. 3.) Their children were,

| 1. Sarah, baptized 1, 2, | 1705 | 2 Joanna, baptized 18, 6, | 1706 |

His second wife was Relief Hyde, married 13 Jan. 1709.

3. Nathaniel,	born 7 Oct.	1709	7. Abraham,	born in	1717
4. Elizabeth,	" 11 Sept.	1711	8. Hannah,	" 2 Dec.	1720
5. Josiah,	" 30 Nov.	1713	9. Relief,	" 11 March,	1723
6. Caleb,	" 10 Feb.	1716	10. Lydia,	baptized in	1726

Nathaniel Thayer died 3 Jan. 1752.

No 38. III D. NATHANIEL THAYER, .

married Mary, daughter of Capt Richard Faxon, 3 April, 1735. She was born 8 March, 1713. Their children were,

1. Mary,	born 19 Aug.	1735		Died Nov. 1748.	
	Died 29 Jan. 1753.		6. Nathaniel,	born 15 Aug.	1745
2. Elihu,	born 9 Aug.	1737		Died 24 Nov 1748	
	Died Aug. 1738.		7. Elihu,	born 18 March,	1746
3. Nathaniel,	born 2 Sept.	1739	8. Sarah,	" 14 Sept.	1749
	Died March, 1740.		9. Nathaniel,	" 18 April,	1754
4. Relief,	born 25 Oct.	1741	10 Calvin,	" 15 July,	1756
5. Anna,	" 17 Sept.	1743			

No. 39. RELIEF, was married to Samuel Spear, 15 Nov. 1766, and had one son Calvin.

No 40 ELIHU THAYER, D. D. " was educated at New Jersey College, the honours of which he received in 1769. His ordination at Kingston in New Hampshire, took place 18 Dec 1776. From the time of the organization of the N. H. Missionary Society in 1801, Dr. Thayer was annually elected the President of that institution till 1811, when his feeble state of health obliged him to decline a re-election. He finished his christian course on the 3d of April, 1812, at the age of 65 years. He was distinguished for his meekness and humility, piety and learning, and was an eminent minister of the gospel of Jesus Christ."

[*Alden's Collection*, 3, 207.

No. 41. Sarah, died unmarried 10 July, 1795, aged 45 years 10 months.

No. 42. Nathaniel Thayer, Esq , married Hannah Penniman of Braintree, and had 3 sons, Nathaniel, James, and Thomas P. who all died before their father, who died in 1829.

No. 43. Calvin, married Sarah Penniman, 14 Feb 1792, and had two sons, Calvin and Elihu. She died 13 Feb. 1800, aged 34. His second wife was Hannah Nash, who had by him one daughter Sarah.

No. 44. IV D. ELIZABETH THAYER,

daughter of Nathaniel and Relief Thayer, was married to Capt. Theophilus Curtis, 28 Feb. 1734, and settled in the corner of Stoughton, afterwards incorporated with North Bridgewater ; had three sons, Theophilus, Jesse, and Moses, and three daughters, Eunice, Elizabeth, and Relief.

Eunice, married *Edmund Soper—Elizabeth*, married Capt. Simeon Leach—*Relief*, married Peter Dunbar.

Capt. Theophilus Curtis died in 1795, aged 85.

No. 45. *Theophilus*, married a Keith, and had two sons, Josiah and Theophilus. *Jesse* and *Moses* died in youth.

[*Cary's Genealogy*, 39.

No 46. V D   JOSIAH THAYER,

a son of Nathaniel and Relief Thayer, married Mary Veasey, 20 April, 1743. Their children were,

1 Mary,	born 6 Feb. 1744	5. Josiah,	born 28 Jan.	1752
2. Elizabeth,	" 18 Sept. 1745	6. Lydia,	" 5 Oct.	1754
	Died 2 Dec 1748	7 Timothy,	" 8 June,	1757
3 Relief,	born 21 March, 1748	8. John,	" 8 Aug.	1759
4. Elizabeth,	" 7 April, 1750			

His second wife was Rebecca Hunt, married 3 July, 1762.

No. 47. VI D.   CALEB THAYER,

a brother of the preceding, married Abigail, daughter of Capt. Richard Faxon. She was born 26 July, 1715 Their children were,

1. Abigail,	born June, 1746	3. Nathaniel,	born 11 April,	1752
2 Caleb,	" 2 June, 1748	4. Allice,	" 18 Aug	1755

Abigail, was married to Capt Isaac Thayer, 3 May, 1764. (See No 48) *Nathaniel*, married Dorcas, daughter of Azariah Faxon, 28 Nov. 1776. Their children were, Dorcas,

Mehitable, Nathaniel, Luc, Sylvanus, Abigail, Livia. *Caleb* and *Allice* died young.

No. 48. VII D. ABRAHAM THAYER,

a brother of the preceding, married Sarah Hunt of Braintree. Their children were,

1 Isaac,	born 9 May,	1712	5 Avis,	born	March,	1751
2. Prudence, bapt.		1746	6 Elizabeth,	"	28 July,	1753
Died 21 Dec. 1748.			7. Abraham,	"	30 April,	1757
3 Avis,	bapt.	1747	8. Relief,	"	18 April,	1759
Died 26 Dec 1748.			9. Hannah, died in infancy.			
4. Sarah,	born 3 June,	1750	10 Hannah.			

Abraham Thayer died 4 June, 1794, aged 77.

1. Isaac, married Abigail Thayer, (No 47, 1) Their children were, Caleb, who married Anna Holbrook in 1790, and Mary Holbrook in 1797. Allice, who married Jonathan Spear in 1790. Luther, who married Olive Turner, and 2d Elizabeth Davis. Abigail, who married Jonathan Belcher in 1792. Relief, who married Stephen Penniman, Jr. in 1792. Sarah, who married Elisha Holbrook in 1793. Isaac, who married Polly French Rebecca, who married Silas Spear in 1796 Elizabeth, who married Abraham Capen in 1802. Mary, who married Capt. Abia Holbrook. Hannah, who married Luther French, Jr.

4. *Sarah*, was married to Joshua Hobart, 30 Aug. 1766. (See Hobart, No. 19)

5. *Avis*, was married to Adam Hobart, 7 Nov. 1772 (See Hobart, No 18.)

6. *Elizabeth*, was married to Solomon Thayer, Esq. 12 Sept. 1785. (See 2d part, 13 Branch, No 1, 5.)

7. *Abraham*, married Lydia Thayer, 18 Feb 1787. (See 6 Branch, 2d part, No 75)

8. *Relief*, was married to Zenas French, 18 April, 1782. (See 2d part, 9 Branch, No. 3.)

10. *Hannah*, was married to Sylvanus French, 19 Oct. 1786 (See 2d part, 9 Branch, No. 17.)

No. 49. II C. RICHARD THAYER,

a son of Nathaniel and Hannah Thayer, married Susannah, daughter of Samuel and Anna White, 18 May, 1708. (See White, No 14, 1,) and settled in Braintree, afterwards removed to West Bridgewater. Their children were,

1. Susannah,	born 26 March,	1710	5. Seth,	born 17 Aug.	1721
2. Jeremiah,	" 22 June,	1713	6. Micah,	" 24 April,	1724
Died 29 June, 1729			7. Abijah,	" 9 Oct.	1726
3 Enos,	born 30 Jan.	1716	8. Jeremiah,	" 18 June,	1729
4. Anna,	" 23 May,	1718	9. Thankful,	" 20 June,	1731

No. 50. I D. SUSANNAH THAYER,

was married to Joseph Lovell of Braintree, and settled in East Stoughton. Their children were, 1. Rachel—2 Sally—3. Hannah, wife of Jesse Richards of Dedham—4. Susannah, wife of Noah Kingsbury of Dedham—5. Mehitable, wife of Thomas Oliver of Stoughton.

No. 51. IV D. ANNA or HANNAH THAYER,

was married to Ephraim Thompson of West Bridgewater, and settled in Halifax, Mass

No. 52. V D. SETH THAYER,

married a Pray, had three sons, Enos, Micah, and Seth, and three daughters, Hannah, Susannah, and Mary. Hannah married Daniel Cary ; Mary married Silas Howard. Seth Thayer died 1798, aged 72. Enos married a widow Reynolds ; had no children. Micah died in youth. Seth, 2d married a Thayer, had eight sons, Enos Micah, Seth, Eliphalet, Zachariah, Zebah, Samuel, and Charles, and one daughter Hannah, who married Thomas Dunbar, Enos, 2d married a Damon ; Micah and Seth live in Springfield ; Eliphalet married a Stone ; Zachariah lives in the State of Maine ; Zebah married a Stone.—[*Cary's Genealogy*, 36.

No. 53. VIII D. JEREMIAH THAYER,

married a Leavitt, and settled in West Bridgewater. Their children were, 1. Jeremiah—2. Richard—3 Leavitt—4 Abijah—5. Susannah—6 Polly—7. Betsey—8 Amy—9 Anna.

1. JEREMIAH, married Catharine Pratt* of Westshires, N. Bridgewater, and had children, Solomon, Psylvina, Thankful, Daniel, Solomon, 2d, Omer, Barnabas, Friend.

They moved from N Bridgewater in 1802, to Sidney, Me. and died within a week of each other in March, 1831, both aged 75. Psylvina, married Timothy Reynolds, now lives in Sidney, and has about a dozen children. Daniel lives in Sidney, and has four children *Solomon* graduated at Brown University in 1815 ; studied Law with Benjamin Orr, Esq. and moved to Lubec in 1818 ; married in 1821 to Lydia Eliza, only daughter of John Faxon, a native of

*The father of Mrs. Thayer was Barnabas Pratt, and her mother's original name was Isabel Downey, who was born in Glasgow, Scotland, and died in 1830 at the age of 103 years. They had children, Barnabas, *Catharine*, Isabel and Susan. Isabel married Levi Bronnock and lives in Vermont; Susan married Simeon Davy, and lives in Hebron, Me They have large families

17

Braintree, and son of Azariah and Dorcas Faxon. (See Thayer, No 47) Omer lives in Sidney, and unmarried ; Barnabas is dead, but left five sons , Friend is dead.

2 RICHARD, has three children, Earle and Hiram living in E. Bridgewater, and married. Huldah, living with her father and unmarried.

3. LEAVITT, has one child Sally, first married to a Mr. Howard of W. Bridgewater, and now to a Mr. Berry of N. Bridgewater.

4. ABIJAH, has several children.

5. SUSANNAH, married a Mr. Dyer, and died leaving two children living in Leeds, Me.

6. POLLY, married George Lothrop of Leeds, and died leaving six children.

7. BETSEY, married Paul Borley, and died leaving four children living in Sidney.

9 ANNA, married Jonathan Reynolds, and died leaving two children living in Sidney.

No. 54. IV C. ZACHARIAH THAYER,

a son of Richard and Hannah Thayer, married Elizabeth Curtis, 4 Feb. 1718   Their children were,

1. Zachariah,	born 26 Feb.	1719	6. Abel,	born 28 Feb.	1741
2 Elizabeth,	" 12 April,	1721	7. Joshua,	" 11 Feb.	1742
3. Amy,	" 1 Aug.	1726	8 Silence,	" 11 Feb	1744
His second wife was Abigail ——			9. Silence,	" 12 Feb	1745
4. Ruhamiah,	born 4 March,	1735	10. Enoch,	" 8 Feb	1747
5. Abigail,	" 20 June,	1739	11. Bethiah,	" 22 April,	1748

No. 55. I D.   ZACHARIAH THAYER,

married Lydia Pray. Their children were,

1. Abraham,	born 10 July,	1739	8 Asa,	born 9 Feb	1752
2 Isaac,	" 23 Nov.	1741	9 Zachariah,	" 9 March,	1754
3 Lydia,	" 23 June,	1743	10. Thankful,	" 11 May,	1756
4. Phebe,	" 11 Feb.	1745	11 Rachel,	" 13 July,	1758
5. Zachariah,	" 6 Jan.	1746	12. Mary, } 13. a son, }	" 13 Aug.	1761
Died 23 April, 1751.					
6 Amy,	born 20 Oct.	1748	14. Zeba,	" 8 April,	1764
7. Elizabeth,	" 28 May,	1750			

Lydia, wife of Zachariah Thayer, died with the numb palsey, 22 Dec 1801. Zachariah Thayer died in Jan. 1812.

---

*In Westhampton, Mrs. Miriam, relict of *Mr. Asa Thayer*, 83. Mr. Thayer was a native of Braintree. By his last will he ordered $1000 to be put into the hands of the Selectmen of Westhampton, to pay his widow the interest as long as she lived, and after her decease the interest was to be annually appropriated for the sole purpose of reimbursing the minister and school tax of such persons as in the judgment of said Selectmen shall stand in the greatest need of it —*Norfolk Advertiser, Feb.* 28, 1835.

                                        (See also, No. 9, 7.)

No. 56.   VII D.   JOSHUA THAYER,

a brother of the preceding, married Sarah Hunt of Braintree, 25 Aug. 1764, and had one son Ambrose, born 9 Feb. 1766 ; married Sarah Hollis, and settled at Williamsburgh.

No. 57.   VIII D.   SILENCE THAYER,

a sister of the preceding, was married to Silas Hunt, 10 Dec. 1762.

No. 58.
{
III C.   HANNAH THAYER,
a daughter of Nathaniel and Hannah Thayer, was married to Thomas Vinton, 10 Aug. 1708.

VI C.   DOROTHY THAYER,
a sister of the preceding, was married to Joseph Ludden of Braintree, 9. Jan. 1717.   Their children were, 1. Benjamin, born 24 Nov. 1719 ; 2. Dorothy, born 28 June, 1723; 3. Hezekiah, born 15 April, 1726 ; 4. Nathaniel, born 28 July, 1728.
}

No. 59.   VIII C.   DANIEL THAYER,

a son of Nathaniel and Hannah Thayer, married Elizabeth Thompson, 2 June 1719.   Their children were,

1. Patience,	born 29 Aug.	1719	5. Jaazaniah,	born 11 Dec.	1733
2. Daniel,	" 3 Aug.	1721	6. Mary,	" 29 June	1736
3. Jacob,	" 27 Feb.	1730	7. Nathaniel	" 6 Feb.	1738
4. Elizabeth,	" 11 Sept.	1730			

Mr Daniel Thayer died at the age of about CIV. years.

No. 60.   II. D.   DANIEL THAYER, Jr.

married Ruth Clark, of Braintree, 15 April 1741.   Their children were,

1. Mercy,	born 27 Feb.	1743	4. Avis,	born 28 April,	1751
2. William,	" 26 Aug.	1745	5. Nathaniel,	" 4 March	1754
3. Aletheah,	" 20 April,	1748	6. Daniel,	" 9 Sept.	1756

William, married Susannah Dunham, 21 Dec. 1765.

Aletheah, married Samuel Stowel Jr. of Abington, 22 Aug. 1772.

Avis, married William Clark of Norton 2 May, 1771.

3. JACOB, married Molly Pratt of Weymouth, 5 April, 1766.

4. ELIZABETH, daughter of Daniel and Elizabeth Thayer, was married to Bliss Tolman, 30 July, 1768.

No 61. IV B. CORNELIUS THAYER,

the youngest son of Richard and Dorothy Thayer, married Abigail ————. Their children were,

1. Cornelius,	born about*	1695-6	6 Eliakim,	born about		1706
2. Moses,	" "	1698	7. Hezekiah,	" "		1708
3. Gideon,	" 1 March,	1700	8. Jeremiah,	died	9 Nov.	1711
4. David,	" about	1702	9. Abigail,	" 11 Jan.		1712
5. Ezekiel,	" "	1704	10. Jeremiah,	born 20 Aug.		1716

Abigail wife of Cornelius Thayer died 1 Jan. 1731.

No. 62. I C. CORNELIUS THAYER, Jr.

married Rachel Spear of Braintree, 19 July 1717, in Dorchester, as appears by the Records. Their children were,

1. Eleazer—2. Jeremiah, both baptized in Braintree in 1730.

No 63. II C.   MOSES THAYER,

a brother of the preceeding, married Christian Aspinwall 6 Aug. 1723. Their children were,

1. Christian, born 14 May, 1724 | 2. Christian, born 12 April, 1726

No. 64 II D CHRISTIAN THAYER,

daughter of the preceding, was married to Nehemiah Holbrook, 10 May, 1744. Her second husband was John French. (See French No 13)

No. 65. IV C.   DAVID THAYER,

a son of Cornelius and Abigail Thayer, married Dorothy, a daughter of Nathaniel and Dorothy Blanchard, 17 Dec. 1724. Their children were,

1. David,	born 29 March,	1725	4. Abigail,	born 8 Dec.	1731
2. Cornelius	" 6 Sept	1726	5. Dorothy,	" 11 Jan.	1733
3 Ruth	" 1 Dec.	1729			

Ruth, was married to Capt. John White, (See White, No. 25.)

Dorothy, was married to Dea. Samuel Blanchard of Weymouth.

No. 66. V C. EZEKIEL THAYER,

a brother of the preceding, married Mehitable White, 4 March 1725. (See White No 18.) Their children were

*The Records of this branch of the family are so deficient, that it is not improbable there may be some errors, although no pains have been spared to avoid them.

1. Elijah,	born 17 May,	1726	4 Micah,	born 7 March,	1730
2. Moses, }	" 7 Nov.	1728	5. Mehitable,	" 25 May,	1734
3. Enoch, }					

1. *Elijah*, married Mercy Burrill of Abington, 12 Jan. 1765 for his second wife. He had one son *Elijah*, probably by his first wife, who married Phebe Thayer 5 May1774.

2. Moses, married and had three daughters, the wives of Stephen Hollis, of John Thayer and of Asa Copeland.

Moses Thayer died 26 Jan. 1800 aged about 69 years.

No. 67. VI C. ELIAKIM THAYER,

a brother of the preceding, married Deborah Hearsey of Milton, 12 Aug. 1729. (Dorchester Records.) Their children were,

1. Eliakim,	born 25 Oct.	1731	5. Solomon,	born 23 Sept.	1744
2. Jesse,	" 18 April,	1733	6 Betty,	" 10 April	1749
3. Cornelius,	" 10 Feb.	1738	7. Abigail,	" 16 Oct.	1751
4. Gideon,	" about	1740			

2. *Jesse*, married Deborah Niles, 28 May 1763.

4. *Gideon*, married Betty Wild, 12 March 1768 and had children.

5. *Solomon*, married Susannah, daughter of Peter Dyer, 12 Oct. 1771 and had one daughter, Susannah. His second wife was Aletheah Hayden, who had two daughters, Beulah and Amelia. Solomon Thayer died 27 Feb. 1801

No. 68. VII C. HEZEKIAH THAYER,

a brother of the preceding, married Christian, widow of Moses Thayer, deceased, 3 Nov. 1729, [No. 63.] Their children were,

1 Hezekiah,	born Sept.	1730	4 Silas,	born 20 July,	1742
2. Thankful,	" 11 Sept.	1732	5. Noah	" 11 July,	1745
3. Dorcas,	" 20 Aug.	1734			

No. 69. I D. HEZEKIAH THAYER, Jr.

married Mary Stetson in May 1751. Their children were,

1 *Levi*, who married Hannah Curtis—2 *Rufus*, who married Esther Mann—3 *Reuben*, who married 1, Rachel Stetson, 2 Betsey Howard—4 *Samuel*, who married Sarah Stetson—5 *Nancy*, wife of Gideon Stetson—6 *Dorcas*, wife of Jonathan Thayer of Weymouth, [No. 27-7]—7 *Ames*, who married Mille Holbrook—8 *Thankful*, died unmarried.

No. 70. X C. JEREMIAH THAYER,

a son of Cornelius and Abigail Thayer, married Joanna ———— Their children were,

1. Susannah, born 16 Oct. 1737 | 3 Paul.
2. Jeremiah, " 20 Aug 1739 |

2. *Jeremiah*, married Elizabeth, daughter of Peter Dyer, in 1777.

3. *Paul*, married Prudence Dyer, a sister of the above, 6 May, 1769.

No 71. II A ZACHARIAH THAYER,

a son of Richard Thayer, Sen. [No 1.] died at Braintree, 29 July, 1693, and his brother Richard was appointed Administrator on his estate, by the Court of Probate, as recorded in the Boston Probate Records. Probably unmarried.

No. 72. III A. NATHANIEL THAYER,

a brother of the preceding, married Deborah ————, and settled in Boston   Their children were,

1. Nathaniel, born 28 Aug 1671 | 5. John, 2, born 2 July, 1688
2. Zachariah, " 29 May, 1683 | 6 Ebenezer, " 1 Feb 1689
3. Cornelius, " 14 Nov. 1684 | 7. Deborah, " 14 Oct 1691
4. John, " 2 April, 1687 | And probably other children.

No 73. II B. ZACHARIAH THAYER,

a son of the preceding, married Lydia ————, and settled in Boston. They had one child Mary, born 14 Jan. 1707.

No. 74. III B. CORNELIUS THAYER,

a brother of the preceding, married Lydia ————, and settled in Boston. Their children were,

1. Lydia, born 6 March, 1707 | 4. Deborah, born 27 Jan 1714
2. Nathaniel, " 17 July, 1710 | 5. Cornelius, "
3. Samuel, " 30 Dec. 1712 | 6. Tuzell, " 13 March, 1725

[*Boston Records.*

No. 75 II C NATHANIEL THAYER,

a son of the preceding, married Ruth Eliot, a sister of the late Rev. Andrew Eliot, D D. of Boston. Their children were, 1. Ebenezer, born July, 1734—2 Catharine—3. Ruth—4. Lydia—5. Deborah.

No. 76. I D Rev. EBENEZER THAYER,

son of the preceding, graduated at Harvard College, in 1753. He married Martha, daughter of Rev. John Cotton of Newton, Mass. Their children were,

1. Ebenezer, born 16 July, 1767 | 4 John, born July, 1773
2 Nathaniel, " 11 July, 1769 | 5 Catharine, " Sept. 1775
3. Martha, " April, 1771 | 6. Andrew Eliot, " Nov 1784

Rev. Nathaniel Thayer, D. D. MS.

HIS EPITAPH.

In memory of the Rev. EBENEZER THAYER, who for nearly 26 years, dispensed the bread of life to the society in this place, (Hampton, N. H) and on the 6 Sept. 1792, fell asleep in Jesus, supported by the christian hope of a resurrection to eternal life, aged 58.

> While o'er this modest stone religion weeps,
> Beneath, a humble, cheerful, christian sleeps;
> Sober, learned, prudent, free from care and strife,
> He filled the useful offices of life.
> Admired, endeared, as husband, father, friend,
> Peace blessed his days and innocence his end
> Blameless throughout, his worth by all approved,
> True to his charge and by his people loved.
> He lived to make his hearers' faith abound,
> And died, that his own virtues might be crowned.

Mrs. Thayer survived her consort till 1809, when she died in Boston, leaving that good name which is better than precious ointment —[*Alden's Coll.* 2, 65.

No. 77.   Rev. JOHN THAYER,

a son of Cornelius Thayer, and grandson of Cornelius and Lydia Thayer, (No. 74,) "a native of Boston, converted to the Catholic faith 1783, and who received Priest's orders at Rome, began his mission here, (in a small brick church in School Street, Boston, built by some French Protestants, and afterwards sold to one or more individuals who had separated from other churches,) June 10, 1790."
[*Hist. Coll.* 9, 196.

Rev. Dr. Thayer of Lancaster, Mass, says he died at Rome, and bequeathed his estate to the propagation of the faith he had embraced.

No 78.   VI B   Rev. EBENEZER THAYER,

a son of Nathaniel and Deborah Thayer of Boston, was graduated at Harvard College in 1710. "He was ordained pastor of the second church in Roxbury, 26 Nov 1712."
[*Hist. Coll.* 9, 196

He married Lydia Copeland, 4 June, 1719. (See Copeland, No 76) His wife Sarah, (probably a second wife,) died at Roxbury, 8 Feb. 1730   Mr Thayer died 6 March, 1733 *

---

*Mr. Farmer says, "He must have been a respectable minister, as he preached the Election Sermon in 1725, which was printed "
"In his own hand writing is the following Memorandum among the Church Records:
March 13, 1729–30. "This day was set apart by our people for solemn

No. 79 THOMAS THAYER,

the progenitor of a numerous offspring, (distinct from the foregoing family, although there have been many intermarriages between them,) came to New England at an early period of its settlement, with his wife Margery, and three sons, THOMAS, FERDINANDO, and SHADRACH. He was admitted freeman in 1647. They lived in Braintree, near the Monotoquot River, on a farm owned by the late Solomon Thayer, Esq. and which has been owned and occupied by their descendants to the present day.

"Old Thomas Thayer dyed 2 d. 4 mo. 1665. Margery Thayer dyed 11 d. 12 mo. 1672.—[*Braintree Records.*

No. 80.   I A.   THOMAS THAYER, Jr.,

was probably married in England to Hannah or Anna ——. Their children were,

1. Thomas, probably b. in England.
2. Elizabeth, born 23, 1, 1647
3. Isaac, " 7 Sept 1654
   Died 30, 5, 1658.
4. John, born 25 Dec 1656
5. Experience, born 15 Mar. 1658
6. Isaac, " 30 May, 1661
7. Ebenezer, " 7 July, 1665
8. Deborah, died in 1677

Thomas Thayer, aged more than 70 years, died 9 Aug. 1693. Anna, wife of Thomas Thayer, died 7 Feb. 1698, aged about 73 years.

No. 81.   I B.   THOMAS THAYER,

a son of the preceding, married Abigail Veasey, 25 March 1680. Their children were,

1. Thomas, born 14 Jan. 1681
   Died 13 Sept 1704
2. William, born 15 Aug. 1682
   Died 17 Sept. 1701.
3. Abigail, born 13 July, 1685

Thomas Thayer died an untimely death, 7 Dec. 1705. Abigail Thayer died 11 Jan. 1712.

No. 82   III C   ABIGAIL THAYER,

the only surviving daughter of the preceding, was married to James Penniman of Braintree, 12, 5, 1705.

NOTE.—"1752, July 3, James Penniman, (perhaps a grandson of the above,) a youth, was struck with lightning while sitting in a chair, his posture not being altered by the stroke, and not being known to be dead, for some time by those about him.—[*Church Records*

supplication and prayer, on ye. account of ye. threatning maladies I am and have been long visited with Mr. Webb of Boston began in the morning with prayer. Mr. Waller preached from Psalms, 34, 12. Mr. Cotton concluded P. M. Mr Sewall began with prayer. Mr. Foxcroft preached from Psalms, 102, 24. Mr Abbot concluded with prayer. The good Lord give an answer of Peace to the prayers of his servants and People."
[*Rev. Geo. Whitney, pastor of the same church.*

No. 83.   IV B.   JOHN THAYER,

a son of Thomas and Hannah Thayer, married Mary ——.
Their children were,

| 1. John, | born 30 June, | 1686 | 2. Henry, | born 1 Aug. | 1688 |
| | | | | Died 2 March, 1689. | |

"1724, July 6, was buried the wife of John Thayer, who
had been under distraction more than 35 years, and was
in the woods without any common or ordinary food for
mankind, fifty-three days, without coming into any house.
She was found in a wilderness swamp, almost naked, and
in a very weak and sad condition, and died soon after"

"1746, Dec. 19, buried John Thayer, wanting about five
days to complete his 90th year. He was visited with a
palsy 56 years before"—[*Ibid*

No 84   I C.   JOHN THAYER, Jr.,

married Mary, a daughter of Elder Nathaniel Wales, 8
April, 1714 (See Wales, No. 8.) Their children were,

1. Thomas,	born 2 April,	1715	2. Joanna,	born 1 Dec.	1716
	Died 14 April, 1715.			Died 14 Dec. 1716	
			3 Thomas,	born 7 April,	1718

His second wife was Lydia ——.

4. Lydia,	died 15 June,	1728	9. Judith,	born 25 Dec	1731
5. Mary,	born 27 Feb	1720	10. Elkanah,	" 1 Jan.	1733
6. Lemuel,	" 3 April	1721	11 Judith,	" 25 Dec.	1734
7. John,	" 1 March,	1723	12. Elkanah,	" 13 Aug.	1737
8. Lydia,	" 12 Aug	1730			

No. 85.   III D.   THOMAS THAYER,

a son of John and Mary Thayer, married Lydia ——.
Their children were,

1. Thomas,	born 26 Jan.	1741		Died 7 Feb. 1755.	
2. Gaius,	" 20 Nov.	1744	5 Susannah,	born	1752
3. Elkanah,	"	1746	6. Mary Wales,	" 30 May,	1756
4. Thomas,	" 10 Jan.	1749	7. Lydia,	" 10 May,	1759

His second wife was Anne Savil, married in 1776.

No. 86.   VI D.   LEMUEL THAYER,

a son of Thomas and Lydia Thayer, married Anne ——.
Their children were,

| 1. Lemuel, | born 14 July, | 1744 | 3 Lydia, | born 15 Feb. | 1752 |
| 2. Anne, | " 2 Aug. | 1747 | Lemuel Thayer died 18 Nov. 1793 | | |

No. 87.   VIII D.   LYDIA THAYER,

a sister of the preceding, was married to Isaac Copeland
of Braintree. [See Copeland, No. 64.]

18

No. 88. V B. EXPERIENCE THAYER,

a daughter of Thomas and Hannah Thayer, was married to John French. (See French, No 2.)

No 89. VI B.   ISAAC THAYER,

a brother of the preceding, probably died unmarried, as there is no record of any descent. The following is the record of his death, with several others " Upon the 9th day of August, there went out afloat, soldiers to Canada in the year 1690, and the small pox was aboard, and there died six of it, four were thrown overboard at Cape Ann. Corporal John Palmer, *Isaac Thayer*, *Ephraim Copeland*, Ebenezer Owen, *Samuel Bass*, and John Chency, were thrown overboard at Nantasket." (See Copeland, No. 74, and Bass, No. 50)

No. 90. VII B. EBENEZER THAYER,

a brother of the preceding, married Ruth ————. Their children were,

1. Ruth,	born 25 July,	1690	6. Eleazer, born 17 Jan.	1701
	Died 19 Aug 1704.		Died 13 April, 1704	
2. Ebenezer,	born 3 May,	1692	7. Deborah, born 16 March,	1702
3. Hannah,	" 16 Oct.	1693	8. Eleazer, " 28 Jan.	1704
4. Thomas,	" 19 Feb.	1698	9. Ruth, bapt. 26, 6,	1705
	Died 16 April, 1698.		10 Ruth, born 26 June,	1707
5. Rachel,	born 3 April,	1699	11 Elizabeth, " 12 Oct	1709

Ebenezer Thayer died 11 June, 1720

No. 91. II C. Capt. EBENEZER THAYER,

a son of the preceding, married Rachel, a daughter of Elder Nathaniel Wales, 12 Nov. 1719. (See Wales, No. 18.) Their children were,

1. Ebenezer,	born 18 June,	1720	7 Jacob, born 7 July,	1730
	Died 25 June, 1720.		8. Nathaniel, " 2 March,	1733
2. Ebenezer,	born 31 July,	1721	9 Atherton, " 20 June,	1735
3. Rachel,	" 10 Oct.	1723	10. Zephaniah, " 13 June,	1737
4. Ruth,	" 18 Jan.	1726	11 Jedidiah, " 14 April,	1740
5. Joanna, }	" 10 May,	1728	Died 10 Nov 1740.	
6. Elizabeth, }			12 Jedidiah, bapt.	1743

His second wife was Sarah Neale, widow, (formerly Mills,) married 18 Oct. 1763 Capt. Ebenezer Thayer died 2 Nov 1777.

"Mrs. Sarah Thayer, wife of the late Capt. Ebenezer Thayer, died at Randolph, 20 Nov. 1800, and was deposited in the family tomb of the late Hon Ebenezer Thayer, Esq. of Braintree, deceased. She was CII years old "

[*Braintree Records.*

Note —Sarah, daughter of John and Hannah Mills, was born 8 Sept 1698 —[*Ibid.*

No. 92. II D. Hon. EBENEZER THAYER,
a son of the preceding, married Susannah, a daughter of
Rev. Samuel Niles of Braintree, 3 April, 1746 ; who was
born 30 July, 1719. Their children were,

1. Ebenezer,	born 21 Aug. 1746	3. John Coddington, d. 4 Dec. 1753
2. Elisha,	" 4 Dec. 1748	4 An infant, died 9 May, 1754

Mrs Susannah Thayer died in childbed, and her infant
also, 9 May, 1754   His second wife was Rebecca Miller
of Milton, married in 1755   Their children were,

5 Sam'l Miller, born 27 Nov 1756 Died 7 Feb 1757.	9 Atherton, born 9 Feb. 1766
6 Rebecca, born 6 Aug 1758	10. Rachel, " 13 Feb. 1768
7. Sam'l Miller, " 9 April, 1761	11 Stephen, " 2 Jan. 1770
8. Susannah, " 8 Jan. 1764	12. Minot, " 25 Dec. 1771

" Rebecca, wife of Hon Ebenezer Thayer, died 3 Dec.
1784." " The Hon. Ebenezer Thayer, Esq. died 7 Feb
1794, in the 73d year of his age, after a confinement of 16
years. He served the town in the office of Selectman 18
years, and was chosen Representative to the General
Court 17 years successively, and chosen one of the council in 1776."*

No. 93. I E. EBENEZER THAYER, Esq.,
a son of the preceding, married Rachel, a daughter of Gideon and Rachel Thayer of Boston, 19 Dec 1772. (See
No. 15 3.) Their children were,

---

*The following tribute of respect to the memory of a worthy character,
was prepared by the Rev. Ezra Weld of Braintree, for the Massachusetts
Magazine :—

13 Feb. (7) 1794, aged 73, after a sore conflict for many years, deeply
depressed, in the arms of his affectionate offspring, and other condoling
friends, fell asleep, the Hon EBENEZER THAYER, some time of the council board, and for many years a Representative of the ancient town of
Braintree. His person and aspect was pleasing to the eye, while a con-
descending affability touched the heart, and gained the esteem of a numerous acquaintance ; gentle and graceful were his manners, his affection
tender and flowing, naturally hospitable and generous, many tasted the
fruits of his bounty Friendly to religion and virtue, he contributed to
their support with cheerfulness, and while health remained, the house of
God, sacred to worship, witnessed his presence, with such as keep holy
day, an example honorable in all to imitate. He lived to see and lament
the vanity of worldly parade and the increasing dissipation of the present age.

He now sleeps where the weary are at rest, waiting the final summons
of the last trump, when the breath of God shall reanimate his humble
dust! Hush, then, the filial flowing tear, nor call him back, again the
galling shafts of envy to sustain, or drink anew the bitter cup of time, or
over human woes to shed more tears! Adieu, thou friendly sleeping
shade, adieu !—[Alden's Coll. 3, 27.

1. Elisha,   born 22 Nov.   1773 | Died 22 Dec. 1805.
       Died 24 Oct 1805 | 4 Gideon Latimer, b. 24 Sept. 1777
2 Eben'r Coddington, b. 1 Ap. 1775 | 5 Nathaniel,   born 10 Aug   1779
       Died 25 Aug. 1775 | 6. Eben'r Francis, b. 12 June, 1783
3 Eben'r Coddington, 31 May, 1776 | 7. Samuel Niles, born 25 Nov. 1786

Hon. Ebenezer Thayer, Esq died aged 62 years 8 months
and 30 days   He served the town many years as Selectman, Town Clerk and Treasurer ; was chosen their Representative — years ; was Senator of this County, (Norfolk)
several years ; chosen and served as a Counsellor, and was
appointed the first Sheriff of the County of Norfolk, Justice
of the Peace throughout the Commonwealth, &c.   All
which offices he filled with integrity, and with no less usefulness to the public than honour to himself He rose from
grade to grade in the Militia, to Brigadier General.   He
left a fair reputation, one which even his enemies respected and envied.

His children were seven in number, four of whom survived him.   He died of a general debility consequent on
the stopping of a severe cough, with which he was exercised nearly twenty years His death, though somewhat
sudden, was easy , his senses unimpaired, his mind calm
and unruffled   He died like a real disciple of that pure religion, of which he for many years was a professor, 30
May, 1809.

Reveremini virtutes, et œmulamini ejus exemplum.
                              [*Braintree Records.*

No. 94. II E   ELISHA THAYER,
a brother of the preceding, was graduated at Harvard College in 1767.   The Records give the following account of
his death.
   "ELISHA THAYER, a young gentleman, greatly esteemed,
in company with a lady, to Barbadoes, to whose family he
had been Preceptor, died at Barbadoes, 1 Feb 1774."

No. 95. IX D ATHERTON THAYER,
a son of Ebenezer and Rachel Thayer, married Ruth Hobart, about 1756. (See Hobart, No. 9, 2.)   Their children
were, 1 Ruth, born 11 July, 1758, wife of Joseph Arnold.
(See Arnold, No. 15) 2 Rachel, born 27 Oct. 1760, wife
of Paul Wild   (See No. 20, 3.)

No. 96. VIII C. ELEAZER THAYER,
a son of Ebenezer and Ruth Thayer, married Rachel

French, 28 April, 1730. (See French, No. 34) Their children were,

| 1. Richard, | born 31 May, | 1731 | 3. Eleazer, | born 29 Feb. | 1739 |
| 2. Patience, | " 29 Feb. | 1736 | 4. Comfort, | " | 1741 |

No. 97. 1 D.   RICHARD THAYER,

a son of the preceding, married Elizabeth ——. Their children were, 1. Patience, born 25 Nov 1752—2 Rachel —3. Elizabeth—4 Zeba—5. Lot—6. Richard.

No. 98   FERDINANDO THAYER,

the second son of Thomas and Margery Thayer, married Huldah Hayward of Braintree, 14 Jan. 1652. He lived in Braintree until after his father's death, when he removed to Mendon, Mass. with a colony from Braintree and Weymouth, where many of his descendants are living at this day. Their children born in Braintree were,

1. Sarah,	born 12, 3,	1654	4. David,	born 20, 4,	1660
2. Huldah,	" 16, 4,	1657		Died 1, 6, 1671.	
3. Jonathan,	" 18, 1,	1658	5. Naomi,	born 28, 11,	1662

Those born in Mendon were,

6. Thomas,	9. Josiah,
7. Samuel,	10 Ebenezer,
8. Isaac,	11. Benjamin.

12 David, was baptized, (if not born) in Braintree, 17 April, 1677. Died 29 Aug. 1678.

Huldah, wife of Ferdinando Thayer, died at Mendon, 1 Sept. 1690 Ferdinando Thayer died in Mendon, 28 March, 1713.

No. 99. 1 A   SARAH THAYER,

a daughter of the preceding, was married to Joseph Stevens of Mendon, who died in a short time after their marriage, probably before the birth of her child which she named Tryall, born 16, 10, 1677, at Braintree

In the church records of Braintree is the following account of her baptism .—" Tryall, daughter to widow Stevens, Ferdinando Thear's daughter of Mendon, baptized 10, 12, 1677."

"Mendon was first settled by the *whites* as a *plantation*, in 1662, and continued in that form of union until 1667, when it was invested by the General Court with town privileges, and so remained until the breaking out of Indian hostilities in 1675, when the settlement was broken up, the settlers fleeing to Braintree and Weymouth, where they stand till 1679 or 80 —there being a *hiatus* in the record of town meetings from May 1, 1675, to Jan. 3, 1780, after which date there is no interruption up to the present time."—[*Alexander H. Allen, Town Clerk of Mendon.*]

No. 100. III A. JONATHAN THAYER, *French*,
a brother of the preceding, married Elizabeth ——,* and
settled in Mendon. Their children were,

1. Huldah,	born 11 May,	1682	3 Deborah,	born 4 Nov.	1687
2. Grace,	" 20 Dec.	1684	4. Jonathan,	" 8 Sept.	1690
	Died 3, Oct. 1703				

*Perhaps she was a daughter of John and Grace French.
(See French, No. 1, 6)

No 101. I B. HULDAH THAYER,
a daughter of the preceding, was married to Benjamin
Wheelock of Mendon, 9 Dec. 1700.

No. 102. III B. DEBORAH THAYER,
a sister of the preceding, was married to John Albee of
Mendon, 6 June, 1705

No. 103. IV B. JONATHAN THAYER,
a brother of the preceding, married Sarah ——, by whom
he had one child, 1 Sarah, born 9 Jan. 1711. His second
wife was Bethiah ——, by whom he had,

2 Grace,	born 31 Aug	1715	8 Dependence, born	1 Feb.	1731
3 Jonathan,	" 27 Feb.	1717	9. Deborah,	" 15 April,	1732
4. Bethiah,	" 5 March,	1719	10 Experience,	" 22 Oct.	1733
5 Deborah,	" 5 Aug.	1720	His third wife was Rachel ——.		
6. Seth,	" 29 Jan.	1726	11 Asael,	born 17 Oct.	1737
7. Huldah,	" 26 March,	1729	12. Bethiah,	" 28 June,	1742

No. 104. III C. JONATHAN THAYER,
a son of the preceding, married Mary Wharfield of Mendon, 12 July, 1738. Probably removed to some other town,
perhaps Bellingham

There lived in Bellingham about the middle of the last century, and
some years after, Dr Jonathan Thayer, reputed to be a man of science,
and of high standing in his profession. He died about 70 or 75 years ago.
He left one son, whose name was Micah, who married a Howard of Mendon, and moved to Ware. He was alive and visited Mendon with his wife
about 40 years since There was one incident in the life of this Dr. Thayer, which has often been related by the aged people of Bellingham, which
was believed and reported by them to be true, which was very extraordi-
nary. In the summer season he was called to visit a patient in an urgent
case, which he declined to visit, and assigned as a reason for not going,
that some great misfortune was about to befal some one of his family, before he could return However, at the repeated solicitations of the messenger he reluctantly consented to attend his professional call, but hasten-
ed with much speed to return, he immediately inquired for his absent son,
and exclaimed "he is drowned," which after a long search, was found to
be a fact. The boy had wandered with another boy to a deep place in
Charles River, surrounded with wood, where they ventured to bathe
some time, at length young Thayer sunk and rose no more.
[*Daniel Thurber, M D. Mendon.*

No. 105. VI C.   SETH THAYER,

a brother of the preceding, married Judith ——.   Their children were,

1. Elizabeth,	born 31 Dec.	1752	6. Experience, born		5 March,	1763
2. Hannah,	" 10 April,	1754	7. Seth,	"	27 July,	1765
3. Judith,	" 4 July,	1756	8. Abigail,	"	8 Sept.	1767
4. Joshua,	"		9. Uel,	"	7 May,	1770
5. Jotham,	" 12 Feb.	1761				

No. 106. VII C.   HULDAH THAYER,

a sister of the preceding, was married to Job Wharfield of Mendon, 12 June, 1751.

No. 107. IX C.   DEBORAH THAYER,

a sister of the preceding, was married to John Rockwood of Mendon, 11 March, 1750.

No. 108. X C.   EXPERIENCE THAYER,

a sister of the preceding, was married to Israel Brown of Mendon, about 1753.

No. 109. XI C.   ASAEL THAYER,

son of Jonathan and Rachel Thayer, married Esther Daniels, 25 April, 1759.   Their children were,

1. Olive,	born 28 Jan.	1760	2. Eli,	born 5 March, 1762

No. 110. XII C.   BETHIAH THAYER,

sister of the preceding, was married to Nathaniel Perry, 26 May, 1763.

No. 111. VI A.   THOMAS THAYER,

a son of Ferdinando and Huldah Thayer, married Mary Adams, and settled in Mendon.   Their children were,

1. Mary,	born 19 Jan	1689	6. Elizabeth,	born 2 March,	1703
2. Thomas,	" 14 Jan.	1694	7 John,	" 17 Sept	1706
3. Samuel,	" 28 March,	1696	8. William,	" 22 Jan.	1708
4. Temperance,	" 7 July,	1698	9. Margaret,	" 12 Dec.	1710
5. David,	" 8 Feb.	1701	10 Jemima,	" 13 Feb.	1712

Capt Thomas Thayer died 1 May, 1738.

No. 112. II B.   THOMAS THAYER, Jr.,

married Ruth Darling of Dedham, 5 Jan. 1715.   Their children were,

1. Priscilla,	born 6 June,	1717	4. Thomas,	born 23 Jan.	1722
2 Elizabeth,	" 29 Jan.	1719	5. Elizabeth,	" 18 Feb.	1724
3. Peter,	" 16 April,	1720			

His second wife was Hannah Holbrook, married 16 July, 1729

6. Oliver,	born 15 March, 1730	8. Joseph,	born 10 March, 1734
7. Stephen,	" 31 Dec. 1732	9. Hannah,	" 8 July, 1736

No 113　III C.　PETER THAYER,

a son of the preceding, married Sarah Holbrook of Uxbridge, 12 June, 1740. Their children were,

1. Nancy,	born 4 July, 1751	4 Oliver,	born 9 July, 1758
2 Reuben,	" 27 June, 1753	5 Sylvanus,	" 4 Sept. 1762
3. Peter,	" 2 Oct 1755	6. Hannah,	" 28 July, 1764

No 114.　VII C.　STEPHEN THAYER,

a brother of the preceding, married Rachel Davis, 5 Aug. 1762. Their children were,

1. Philadelphia, born 10 Nov. 1763		5 Dolenda,	born 13 April, 1774
2. Stephen,	' 29 Dec. 1765	6 Windsor,	" 21 June, 1778
3 Nancy,	" 24 May, 1771	7 Aaron,	" 29 June, 1780
4 Limon Alanson, b 27 Oct. 1772		8 Lucinda,	" 1 Jan. 1782

No. 115.　III B.　SAMUEL THAYER,

a son of Thomas and Mary Thayer, married Mary ——. Their children were,

1 Abigail,	born 22 Aug. 1718	6. Comfort,	born 28 July, 1728
2. Samuel,	" 10 June, 1721	7 Margaret,	" 20 March, 1730
3. Zilpah,	" 14 Sept. 1722	8 Susannah,	" 14 Sept. 1731
4. Mary,	" 12 Feb 1724	9. Stephen,	" 26 Sept. 1733
5 Thankful,	" 4 Aug. 1725		

No 116.　I C.　ABIGAIL THAYER,

was married to John Partridge of Wrentham, about 1737.

No. 117.　V C.　THANKFUL THAYER,

was married to Sylvanus Holbrook of Uxbridge, 25 Oct. 1748.

No. 118.　VI C　COMFORT THAYER,

was married to Samuel Fish of Upton, 1 Nov. 1750.

No 119　VII C.　MARGARET THAYER,

was married to Jonathan Farnum of Uxbridge, 16 Nov. 1752.

No. 120.　VIII C　SUSANNAH THAYER,

was married to Elisha Hail, about 1752

No. 121　IV B.　TEMPERANCE THAYER,

a daughter of Thomas and Mary Thayer, was married to John Legg of Mendon, 1 June, 1719.

No. 122. V B. DAVID THAYER,

a brother of the preceding, married Jean Keith, 31 Dec. 1729. Their children were,

1. Jean,	born 20 Dec	1730	6. Faithful,	born 18 June	1744
2. David,	" 13 Feb	1734	7. Jemima,	" 27 July	1746
3 Susannah,	" 18 March	1736	8. Mary,	" 14 Jan	1750
4. Simeon,	" 3 April	1737	9. Elizabeth,	" 11 May	1752
5. George,	" 1 March	1742			

No. 123. I. Jean, was married to Benjamin Staples, 24 Aug. 1749.

III Susannah, was married to Henry Benson, about 1763.

IV. "General Simeon Thayer, (probably this individual,) bravely distinguished himself in the war of the revolution. He was a native of Mendon, and died suddenly on the road from Providence to Cumberland, about 40 years ago."—[Dr. Thurber

No. 124. VII B. JOHN THAYER,

a son of Thomas and Mary Thayer, married Abigail Darling, 27 July, 1729. He probably removed away.

No. 125. VIII B. WILLIAM THAYER,

a brother of the preceding, married Abigail Sumner, 13 Nov. 1729. Their children were,

1. Hepzibah	born 28 Feb	1731	6. Abigail	born	10 May	1748
2. Beulah	" 10 May	1733	7. Increase	"	23 Sept	1750
3. Beriah	" 28 April	1735	8. Amasa	"	2 March	1754
4. Silence	" 4 Oct.	1741	9. Beriah,	"	28 May	1758
5 Alexander	" 25 Jan.	1744				

I. Hepzibah, was married to Elisha Ballou of Cumberland, 30 Nov. 1748.

IV. Silence, was married to Abner Thayer of Providence, in 1759.

V. Alexander, was graduated at New Jersey College, in 1765.

No. 126. VII A. SAMUEL THAYER,

a son of Ferdinando and Huldah Thayer, married Mary ——. Their children were,

1 Samuel,	born 1 Dec	1691	4. Mary,	born 11 Feb	1701
2. Sarah,	" 11 Feb	1695	5. Joseph,	" July	1707
3. Huldah,	" 30 Nov	1698	6 Benjamin,	" 11 Sept	1709

Lieut. Samuel Thayer died 19 Dec. 1721.

18

No. 127. I B. SAMUEL THAYER, Jr.,
married Mary Sampson, 1 Aug 1716. He probably removed, perhaps to Milford or Uxbridge.

No. 128. II B. SARAH THAYER,
a sister of the preceding, was married to David Hill of
Sherburne, 17 Dec. 1716

No. 129. IV B. MARY THAYER,
a sister of the preceding, was married to Benjamin White,
23 May, 1720. (See White, No. 11.)

No. 130. V B. JOSEPH THAYER,
a brother of the preceding, married Hannah Hayward, 30
Aug 1729. Their children were,

1. Joseph, born 3 Dec 1727 | 3. Samuel, 2, born 20 Feb 1732
2. Samuel, " 24 Jan 1730 |

Joseph Thayer died 14 Feb 1734.

No. 131. I C. JOSEPH THAYER, Jr.,
married Abigail —— Their children were,

1. Provided, born 20 Aug 1752 | 5. Abigail, born 27 June 1760
    Died 8 Sept 1753 | 6. Reuben, " 10 Jan 1763
2. Joseph, born 16 June 1754 | Died 12 Jan same year.
3. Benjamin, " 3 Jan 1756 | 7 Nahum, born 6 April 1768
4. Nicholas, " 7 March 1758 |

No. 132. III C. Ensign SAMUEL THAYER,
a brother of the preceding, married Sarah Robinson, 30
Aug. 1759. Their children were,

1. Samuel, born 6 Sept 1762 | 2. Simeon, born 25 May 1765

No. 133 VI B BENJAMIN THAYER,
a son of Samuel and Mary Thayer, was married to Marcy
Wilkinson of Providence, R I (by James Arnold, Esq.
Justice Peace,) 24 Aug. 1727 Their children were,

1. Patience, born 3 Jan 1730 | 5. Benjamin, died 7 July 1740
2. Huldah, " 5 Nov 1730 | 6. Patience, born 25 May 1740 -
3. Gideon, " 12 Jan 1733 | 7. Hope, } " 1 Aug 1742
4. Samuel, " 5 Dec 1734 | 8. Marcy, }
    PATIENCE, was married to Abraham Thayer, 8 April, 1757.

No. 134. IV C SAMUEL THAYER, 3d ,
a son of the preceding, married Mary ——. Their children were,

1. Ferdinando, born 14 Jan 1764 | 2. Bill Turpin, born 1 Sept 1771

No. 135. VIII A. ISAAC THAYER,

a son of Ferdinando and Huldah Thayer, married Mercy
——. Their children were,

1. Mercy,	born	2 Nov	1693	3. Ebenezer,	born 6 Sept	1697
2. Isaac,	"	24 Sept	1695	4. Comfort,	" 19 Feb	1700

Mercy, wife of Isaac Thayer, died 18 Dec 1700.
His second wife was Mary ——. Their children were,

5 Mary,	born 22 Dec	1704	7. Nathaniel,	born 20 April	1708
6. John,	" 9 May	1706	8. Moses,	" May	1710

No. 136 II B. ISAAC THAYER, Jr,

married Miriam Thayer, 18 May, 1716 (See No. 155.)
Their children were,

1. Susannah,	born 4 July 1719	2. Ichabod,	born 31 March 1721

His second wife was Mary ——.

3. Bathsheba,	born 1 April 1741	4. Levi,	born 1 June 1743

No. 137 I C. SUSANNAH THAYER,

was married to Aaron White of Uxbridge, 25 Dec 1739.

No. 138. II C. ICHABOD THAYER,

married Mrs. Hannah Cheeney, formerly Bigelow of Weston, and settled in Milford. Their children were,

1. Hannah,	born 10 March 1742	2. Ichabod,	born 6 March 1745
	Died in childhood.	3. Elijah,	" 4 June 1747

No. 139. II D. ICHABOD THAYER, Jr,

married Mary Marsh, about 1765, and settled in Milford.
Their children were,

1. Hannah,	born 12 Dec	1765	5. Adah,	born 9 July	1773
2 Asa,	" 30 Oct	1767	6 Ziba,	" 23 April	1775
3 Charlotte,	" 20 Aug	1769	7. Rufus,	" 11 June	1777
4. Alexander,	" 15 March	1771			

His second wife was Eunice ——. Their children, were,

8. Laban,	born 7 Dec	1792	9 Davis,	born 9 Feb	1795

No. 140. III D. ELIJAH THAYER,

a brother of the preceding, married Sarah Robinson in 1768,
and settled in Milford. Their children were,

1. Phebe,	born 17 Aug	1769	7. Libby,
2. Olive,	" 11 Oct	1771	8 Sarah,
3. Artemas,			9. Amasa,
4. Joel,			10. Elijah,
5 Jonathan,			11. Ruby,
6 Nathan,			12 Hollis.

No 141. III B. EBENEZER THAYER,

a son of Isaac and Mercy Thayer, married Mary Wheelock,
9 Aug. 1721, and settled in Bellingham Their children
were, 1. Elizabeth—2. Ebenezer—3 Lydia—4 Isaac, and
perhaps Micah

I. *Elizabeth*, was married to Josiah Nelson of Mendon, 25
April, 1754.

III *Lydia*, was married to Warfield Hayward of Mendon,
in 1761.

IV. *Isaac*, married Margaret Atwood of Mendon, 23 Oct.
1760.

No. 142 II C. Capt EBENEZER THAYER,

a son of the preceding, married a Miss Green, and settled
in Bellingham Their children were, 1 Elias—2 Ebenezer
—3. Silas—4 Hannah, the wife of a Mr. Blake of Wrentham—5. Huldah, the wife of a Mr. Thayer of Bellingham.
He married Martha Thayer of Mendon, 2 May, 1759. (See
No. 165.)

No. 143. I D. Lieut. ELIAS THAYER,

a son of the preceding, married Hannah Ellis of Medway,
and settled in Bellingham. Their children were,

1. Alpheus, born Dec. 1764, now living.
2. Martha, who died at the age of 15 years.
3. Elizabeth, who died in 1823
4. Elias, born in 1773, died in June, 1833.
5. Hannah, born Nov. 1776.
6 Abigail,   "   1778.
7. Ebenezer, "   1781, died 1787, aged 6 years

Lieut. Elias Thayer died Sept. 1806, aged 66. Mrs.
Hannah Thayer died in 1822, aged 78.

No. 144. II D. EBENEZER THAYER, Jr.,

settled in Bellingham, and had five sons, viz .—Calvin,
Thaddeus, Luther, Ebenezer, and Philo. Ebenezer Thayer, Jr. died before his father.—[*Dr. Thurber, MS.*

No. 145. III D.   SILAS THAYER,

a brother of the preceding, married Perley Pond, about
1767. Their children were,

1. Charlotte, born 19 Feb   1768 | 3. Sabra,   born 5 April, 1772
2. Jarvis,   "   24 Nov. 1770 | 4. Olive,   "   11 April, 1774

No 146. VI B.   JOHN THAYER,

a son of Isaac and Mary Thayer, married Ruhamah ——.
Their children were,

1. Pelatiah,	born 13 Oct	1739	3 Desire,	born 11 Oct	1745
2. Ruhamah,	" 13 Jan	1742	4. Robert,	" 26 Nov	1747

No. 147. I C. PELATIAH THAYER,

a son of the preceding, married Hannah Thayer, 26 May, 1762. (See No. 152, 1.) Their children were,

1. Robert,	born 22 Nov	1763	4 Smith,	born 15 Dec	1770
2 Artemas,	" 20 Feb	1766	5. Laban,	" 19 March	1773
3. Henry,	" 19 Sept	1768	6. Putnam,	" 15 Aug	1775
	Died 23 Feb 1776.			Died 14 Nov 1776.	

No. 148. VII B. NATHANIEL THAYER,

a son of Isaac and Mary Thayer, married Anna Partridge of Wrentham, 19 Jan. 1731. Their children were,

1. Nathaniel,	born 17 Sept	1733	3. Abner,	born 20 Oct	1737
2. Jemima,	" 21 Dec	1735			

No. 149. I C. NATHANIEL THAYER, Jr,

married Hannah ——. Their children were,

1. Nathaniel,	born 19 Feb	1753	3. Hannah,	born 5 Feb	1757
2. Nathan,	" 13 April	1755			

No. 150. II C. JEMIMA THAYER,

sister of the preceding, was married to Uriah Thayer, 8 May, 1751. (See No. 163.)

No. 151. III C ABNER THAYER,

married Silence Thayer, 29 Nov. 1759, and settled in Providence, R. I. (See No. 125, 4.)

No. 152. VIII B. MOSES THAYER,

a son of Isaac and Mary Thayer, married Hannah ———. Their children were,

1. Hannah,	born 6 Feb	1738	4 Rhoda,	born 11 Nov	1746
2. Moses,	" 7 March	1741	5. Chloe,	" 26 Feb	1748
3. Lois,	" 7 July	1744			

Moses Thayer died 24 May, 1769.

No. 153. II C. MOSES THAYER, Jr.,

married Rachel ——. Their children born in Mendon were,

1. Ezra,	born 22 Aug	1768	2. Rachel,	born 21 Aug	1769

III C. LOIS THAYER,

was married to Micah Thayer of Bellingham, 17 Nov. 1763. Perhaps a son of Ebenezer Thayer, (No 141.)

No. 154.   IX A.   JOSIAH THAYER,

a son of Ferdinando and Huldah Thayer, married Sarah
——.   Their children were,

1. Sarah,	born 25 May	1691	5. Jonathan,	born 28 Feb	1702
2. Josiah,	" 4 June	1694	6. Rebecca,	" 29 July	1704
3. Susannah,	" 13 Sept	1696	7. Bathsheba,	" 10 Sept	1706
4. Miriam, v	" 3 June	1699	8. David,	" 6 March	1710

No. 155.   IV B.   MIRIAM THAYER,

was married to Isaac Thayer, 18 May, 1716. (See No. 136.)

No. 156.   V B.   JONATHAN THAYER,

a brother of the preceding, married Elizabeth ——. Their
children were,

1. Cornelius,	born 14 Dec	1723	3. Mercy,	born 26 Sept	1726
2. Sarah,	" 3 May	1725			

No. 157.   VI B.   REBECCA THAYER,

was married to Charles Sherlock of Providence, R. I   25
Feb. 1719.

No. 158   VIII B.   DAVID THAYER,

married Hannah ——.   Their children were,

1. Rebecca,	born 8 April	1731	6. David,	born 7 Aug	1737
2. Hannah,	" 19 Dec	1731	7. David,	" 1 May	1739
3. Dinah,	" 20 Oct	1733	8 Dinah,	" 19 Dec	1740
4 Mary,	" 26 June	1735	9. Elijah,	" 14 May	1744
5. Susannah,	" 18 March	1736	10. Elizabeth,	" 6 Dec	1749

His second wife was Rebecca Williams of Scituate, R. I.
married 1752.

No. 159.   X A.   EBENEZER THAYER,

a son of Ferdinando and Huldah Thayer, married Martha
——.   Their children were,

1. Deborah,	born 13 Oct	1696	4. Hannah,	born 15 Sept	1704
2. Ebenezer,	" 12 April	1699	5 Uriah,	" 10 Sept	1706
3. Abigail,	" 3 Sept	1701	6. David,	" 5 May	1715

No. 160.   II B.   EBENEZER THAYER, Jr.,

married Sarah ——.   Their children were,

1. Jeremiah,	born 11 March 1725	5. Jerusha,	born 27 Feb	1736
2 Sarah,	" 22 Feb 1726		Died 22 Aug 1740.	
3 Noah,	" 4 May 1730	6. Patience,	born 16 April	1739
4. Ebenezer,	" 16 Jan 1732	7. Jerusha,	" 26 March	1741
	Died 14 July 1736.	8. Nehemiah,	" 13 Oct	1747

His second wife was Huldah Thompson of Bellingham,

married 11 July, 1754, by whom 9 Ruth was born 21 Sept. 1755.

No. 161. I C. JEREMIAH THAYER,

married Allice ———. Their children were,

1. Caleb,	born 7 Jan	1748	4. Nehemiah,	born 4 March 1755	
2. Jeremiah,	" 3 Sept	1750	5 Sylvia,	" 12 March 1757	
3. Allice,	" 10 Sept	1752	6. Rhoda,	" 27 Aug 1759	

No. 162. III C. NOAH THAYER,

married Abigail ———. Their children were,

1. Enoch,	born 15 May	1748	4. Daniel,	born 8 Feb	1759
2. Elijah,	" 24 April	1753	5. Shadrach,	" 6 Jan	1767
3. Noah,	" 3 Nov	1755			

VI C. PATIENCE THAYER,

was married to Abraham Thayer, 8 April, 1757.

No. 163. V B URIAH THAYER,

a son of Ebenezer and Martha Thayer, married Rachel ———. Their children were,

1. Ebenezer,	born 22 Nov	1731	4. Martha,	born 8 Oct	1737
2. Eleazer,	" 22 March	1733	5 Simeon,	" 20 Oct	1739
3. Rachel,	" 19 June	1735	6. Grindel,	" 14 June	1744

His second wife was Jemima Thayer. (See No. 150.)

His third wife was Sarah Hadaway of Warwick, married about 1752. His fourth wife was Abigail White of Uxbridge, married about 1768.

No. 164. I C. EBENEZER THAYER,

married Lydia Hayward, 9 July, 1766, by whom he had one child Phinehas, born 17 Jan. 1767.

No. 165. IV C. MARTHA THAYER,

was married to Ebenezer Thayer of Bellingham, 2 May, 1759. (See No. 142.)

No. 166. VI C GRINDEL THAYER,

married Sarah Parker, about 1767.

No. 167. XI A. BENJAMIN THAYER,

the youngest son of Ferdinando and Huldah Thayer, married Sarah Hayward, 15 Sept. 1699. Their children were,

1. Rachel,	born 1 March	1700	5. Benjamin,	born 23 Sept	1707
2. Margaret,	" 17 Dec	1701		Died 23 Feb 1708.	
3. Grace,	" 6 May	1704	6. Lydia,	born 24 April	1709
4. Sarah,	" 23 March	1706			

Sarah, wife of Benjamin Thayer, died 18 Dec. 1711.
His second wife was Hannah Hayward, married 20
Dec. 1712.

7. Benjamin, born 13 July   1713 | 8 Aaron,   born 11 Nov   1715

No. 168. I B. RACHEL THAYER,
was married to Eleazer Taft, 15 Dec. 1720.

No. 169. II B. MARGARET THAYER,
was married to Jonathan Wood, 15 Dec 1720.

No. 170. IV B SARAH THAYER,
was married to John Hayward, 21 April, 1726.

No 171. VI B. LYDIA THAYER,
was married to John Gage, 4 Jan 1729

No 172. VII B. BENJAMIN THAYER, Jr.,
married Silence Sumner, 19 Dec. 1734, and died 7 July,
1739. His widow was married to Alexander Sessions of
Pomfret, 20 May, 1740

No 173. VIII B. AARON THAYER,
married Jemima *Cook*. Their children were,

1 Hannah,	born 12 March 1739		9. Elona,	born 19 May	1754
2 Elizabeth,	" 29 Oct 1740		10. Lavina,	" 30 Jan	1756
3 Jemima,	" 14 Sept 1742		Died 19 May 1758.		
4. Benjamin,	" 16 April 1744		11. Aaron,	born 26 Feb	1758
5. Susannah,	" 23 April 1746		12 Elijah,	" 12 Aug	1760
6. Rachel,	" 26 March 1748		Died 20 Sept 1764.		
7. Joanna,	" 16 Feb 1750		13 Phebe,	born 17 Aug	1762
8. Urana,	" 12 Aug 1752				

No. 174. IV C. BENJAMIN THAYER,
a son of the preceding, married Sarah Bosworth of Bellingham, about 1767. Their children were,

1. Elijah,	born 21 Aug 1768		5. Benjamin,	born 29 July	1781
2. Caleb,	" 31 Jan 1770		6 Sarah,	" 5 Aug	1783
3. Philaty,	" 7 June 1772		7. Zilpha,	" 28 May	1785
4 Amos,	" 7 May 1774				

NOTE —The foregoing embraces nearly all the families of this name
born in Mendon and married there, previous to about the middle of the
last century, and will enable most of their descendants of the present generation to trace their genealogy back to the first settlers of New England.
   There have been 28 of this name who have graduated at the New England Colleges, viz —

Ebenezer, graduated at Harvard, 1708. See No 78.

No. 175.   SHADRACH THAYER,

the youngest son of Thomas and Margery Thayer, married Mary Barrett, 1, 11, 1654, and settled in Braintree, Mass. Their children were,

1. Rachel,   born 9, 8,   1655 | 2. Tryall,   born 7, 12,   1657
      Died 23, 9, 1656.

Mary, wife of Shadrach Thayer, died 2, 2, 1658.
His second wife was Deliverance Priest.

3. Freelove,   born 30 4,   1662 | 7. Ephraim,   born 17, 11,   1669
      Died 5, 6, 1662. | 8. Hannah,   "   8, 2,   1672
4. Mary,   born 1, 2,   1663 | Died 5, 12, 1677.
5. Timothy,   " 3, 7,   1666 | 9. William,   born 1, 6,   1675
6. Samuel,   " 7 Sept   1667 |

Shadrach Thayer died 19 Oct. 1678. Deliverence, widow of Shadrach Thayer, died 17 Jan. 1723, aged about 79 years.

Ebenezer,	grad	at Harv.	1753, See No 76.
Ezra,	"	at "	1754.
Alexander,	"	at N. Jers.	1765, See No. 125, 5.
Elisha,	"	at Harv	1767, See No 94.
Elihu, D. D.	"	at N. Jers.	1769, See No. 40.
Jabez,	"	at Brown,	1776.
Nathaniel, D. D.	"	at Harv.	1789 See No. 76, 2.
Eben'r Coddington,	"	at "	1795. See No. 93, 3.
Gideon Latimer,	"	at "	1798. See No. 93, 4.
Andrew,	"	at "	1803.
Jonathan,	"	at Brown,	1803. See No 140, 5.
John Goulding,	"	at "	1804. See No. 125, 5.
Sylvanus,	"	at Dart.	1807. See No. 47, 5.
Willard,	"	at "	1810.
Amasa,	"	at Harv.	1810. See No. 140, 9.
Alexander, received degree M. D. Dartmouth, 1812.			
James,	grad.	at Brown,	1814.
Joseph,	"	at "	1815.
Solomon,	"	at Bowdoin	1815. See No. 53.
Zebina,	"	at Dart.	1817.
Elijah,	"	at Wm's	1820.
Christopher Tappan,	"	at Harv.	1824.
John Holbrook,	"	at "	1826. See No. 48.
Henry W. M. D.	"	at Harv.	1831.
Foster,	"	at Wm's	1828.
Albert C.	"	at Waterville, 1828.	
Norton,	"	at Harv.	1828. See No. 48.

[*Farmer.*

√ No. 176.   IV A.   MARY THAYER,

was married to Samuel Bagley. Their children were,

1. James,	baptized	8, 5,	1688	3. Abigail,	baptised 2, 8,	1699
2. Sarah,	"	17, 3,	1696	4. Mary,	" 5, 5,	1702

No 177.   I B.   JAMES BAGLEY,

married Jane ——. Their children were,

1. James,	born 1 March 1714	3. John,	born 18 Aug 1725
2. Anne,	" 9 Aug 1718		

No. 178.   VI A   SAMUEL THAYER,

married Susannah Scant of Braintree, 18 Jan. 1694. She was born 30, 11, 1663. Their children were,

1. Samuel,	born 8 March 1695		Lydia died 9 March, 1721.
2. Susannah,	" 23 May 1697	4. Timothy,	born 31 Dec	1701
3 Lydia,	" 25 Dec 1699	5. Hannah,	" 27 Jan	1704

No. 179.   I B.   SAMUEL THAYER, Jr.,

married Jane Mortimon, 25 Oct. 1722. Their children were,

1. Samuel,	born 14 Jan 1726	2. Nathan,	born 26 July 1729
			Died 12 March 1755.

No. 180.   I C.   SAMUEL THAYER, 3d ,

married Mary Wells of Braintree, 6 April, 1749.

No. 181.   VII A.   EPHRAIM THAYER,

a son of Shadrach and Deliverance Thayer, married Sarah Bass of Braintree, 7 Jan. 1692. (See Bass, No. 48, and second part, No. 1.)

No. 182.   IX A.   WILLIAM THAYER,

the youngest brother of the preceding, married Hannah Hayward, a widow, 22 Sept. 1699 Their children were,

1. Bethiah,	baptized 18, 6, 1700	3. William,	born 11 May 1705
2. Jonathan,	" 2, 3, 1703		

Note.—"In Anthony Wood's Athenæ Oxoniensis, vol. ii. p. 519, is a sketch of John Thelter, Gent. who was born of genteel parents at Cowper's-hill, in the parish of Brockworth, in the County of Glocester, England He was an author, and his works are enumerated by Wood. He died 25 Aug. 1673, leaving a Library, in which were about 800 manuscripts collected principally by himself.—[*Farmer.*]

THE FAMILY OF WALES.

No. 1.   NATHANEL WALES,

Dorchester, 1636, perhaps the same who died in Boston 4 Dec 1661, leaving a son NATHANIEL, who died there 10 May, 1662.—[*Farmer.*

There were two of this name, probably brothers, and sons of the preceding, first named, who settled in Dorchester, viz. TIMOTHY and JOHN.

No. 2. 1 A.   NATHANIEL WALES,

of Braintree, was probably a son of Nathaniel Wales, Jr., who died in Boston in 1662, as aforesaid. He settled in Braintree with his wife Joanna, about the year 1675. Their children were,

1. Elizabeth,	born 10 Feb	1675		Died 22 Feb 1690			
2. Joanna,	" 18 April	1679	9. Mary,	born	1 April	1691
	Died 25 April 1679		10. Samuel,	"	23 June	1693
3. Sarah,	born 11 March	1680	11. Thomas,	"	19 April	1695
4. Nathaniel,	" 29 Dec	1681	12 Joseph,	"	29 April	1697
5. Joanna,	" 19 Dec	1683	13 John,	"	25 May	1699
6. Elkanah,	" 1 Dec	1685	14. Rachel,	"	15 Oct	1701
7. Deborah,	" 16 Oct	1687	15. Atherton,	"	8 March	1704
8. Thomas,	" 6 Oct	1689				

Mrs Joanna, wife of Elder Wales, died 11 May, 1704. Elder Nathaniel Wales died 23 March, 1718.

Mr. Nathaniel Wales was a deacon in the church at Braintree, and "afterwards ordained ruling-elder, viz. Feb. 27, 1700, by Mr. Fiske. The Rev. Peter Thatcher of Milton, and elder John Rogers of Weymouth, joining in the laying on of hands."—[*Hancock's Cent. Sermon,* p. 23.

No 3. III B.   SARAH WALES,

a daughter of the preceding, was married to Nathaniel Thayer, 25, 11, 1704. (See Thayer, No. 37.)

No. 4. IV B. NATHANIEL WALES,

a brother of the preceding, married Esther Ashley. Their children were,

1. Nathaniel, born 10 Dec   1709 | 3. Esther,   born 17 Dec   1717
        Died 6 Feb 1710. | 4. Nathaniel,   " 10 May   1728
2. Joanna,   born 5 April   1711 | Died 10 Feb 1738.

No. 5. III C.   ESTHER WALES,

a daughter of the preceding, was married to James Thayer of Braintree. (See Thayer, No. 14.)

No. 6. VI B.   Capt. ELKANAH WALES,

a son of Elder Wales, married Elizabeth ——. Their children were,

1. Elizabeth, born 31 Aug   1709 | 3 Samuel,   born 7 June   1714
       Died 16 Sept 1709. | Died 19 June 1714.
2 Elkanah,   born 19 Oct   1711 | 4. Nathaniel, born 11 April   1717
       Died 11 Feb 1712.

Elizabeth, wife of Capt. Elkanah Wales, died 27 Feb. 1763. Capt. Elkanah Wales died 12 Dec. 1763.

No. 7. IV C.   Capt. NATHANIEL WALES,

the son of the preceding, married Anna ——. Their children were,

1. Asaph,   born 1 Aug   1745 | 4 Elkanah,   born 6 Feb   1751
2. Elizabeth, " 22 April   1747 | 5 Elizabeth, born 13 April 1754
       Died 29 June 1750 | 6 Nathaniel,   " 8 Feb   1757
3. Acksak,   born 30 May   1749 | 7. Benjamin,   " 5 June   1759

Anna, wife of Capt. Nathaniel Wales, died 14 May, 1763. Capt. Nathaniel Wales, died 26 June, 1790, aged 73 years 1 month 15 days.

No. 8. IX B.   MARY WALES,

a daughter of Elder Wales, was married to John Thayer, 8 April, 1714. (See Thayer, No 84.)

No. 9. XI B.   THOMAS WALES,

a brother of the preceding, married Mary Belcher, 13 Jan. 1719. (He was a deacon in the church.) Their children were,

1. Samuel,   born 3 Nov   1719 | 8. Deborah, born 27 March 1731
2. Atherton,   " 11 Feb   1721 | 9. Thomas,   " 24 Aug   1733
3. Mary,   " 21 Nov   1722 | Died 3 July 1736.
       Died 13 July 1731. | 10. Mary,   born 27 Feb   1736
4. Ephraim, born Oct   1725 | 11. Thomas, " 20 Feb   1738
5. Ephraim,   " 3 Nov   1727 | Died 9 Nov 1759.
       Died 6 Oct 1744. | 12. John,   born 3 March 1739
6. Moses,   born 20 Dec   1728 | Died 23 March 1740.
7. Nathaniel, " 26 Oct   1729 |

Mary, wife of Dea. Thomas Wales, died 30 Jan. 1741.

His second wife was Sarah, widow of Samuel Belcher, deceased, married 7 Sept. 1742. Their children were,

13. Joanna,   born 13 Jan   1741 | 15. John,   born 14 Feb   1717
14. Ephraim,   "   9 May   1746 | Died 7 March 1747.

No. 10. II C. ATHERTON WALES,

a son of the preceding, married Sarah Belcher of Braintree, 4 Dec. 1744. She was born 12 Dec. 1729. Their children were,

1. Jonathan,   born 28 March 1746 | 2. Atherton, who died in youth.

Atherton Wales died 31 May, 1801. Sarah, widow of Atherton Wales, died in 1816.

No. 11. I D. JONATHAN WALES,

the son of the preceding, married Abigail Penniman of Braintree, 17 May, 1766. She was born 15 Aug 1745.

Their children were, 1. Sarah—2. Abigail—3 Atherton —4. Jonathan. Mr Jonathan Wales died 16 Dec. 1832. Mrs. Abigail Wales died 25 June, 1833.

1. SARAH, born 21 May, 1767, married Thomas Tolman of Stoughton. Their children were,

Thomas W. born   5 April 1793, married Sarah Alden of Randolph.
James P   "   22 June 1795, married Sarah Alden of E. Bridgewater.
Johnson,   "   14 Nov 1796, married Polly S. Briggs of Stoughton.
Samuel,   "   21 Aug 1800, married Sarah Packard of Stoughton
Abigail,   "   12 July 1802, died 23 Jan 1803
Sarah,   "   5 March 1804, died 28 Nov 1805.

Mrs Sarah Tolman died 6 March, 1826.

2 ABIGAIL, born 3 Feb. 1769, married Seth Turner, Esq. of Randolph. Their children were,

Sarah W. born 6 Oct 1788, married John King, Esq Randolph
Royal,*   "   6 Dec 1792, married Maria White, Weymouth, who was born 27 June 1800.

Mrs. Abigail Turner died 21 March, 1823.

3. ATHERTON, born 8 Aug. 1772, married Sally Damon of Dedham. She was born 8 Aug. 1772. Their children were, *Ephraim*, born 10 Jan. 1796, married Deborah Copeland, West Bridgewater—*Clarissa*, born 8 Oct. 1797, died 1816—*Hiram*, born 21 Aug. 1799, married Sally Whitcomb, Randolph—*Avis*, born 2 Aug. 1801—*Atherton*, born 12 Dec. 1805, married Mehitable French, Randolph—*Sarah*, born 17 Dec. 1803, married Edward A. Child, Roxbury—*Mary A.* born 23 July, 1810, married Leonard French, Randolph —*John*, born 13 July, 1812—*Jonathan*, born 5 Jan 1815— *Rebecca*, born 18 Feb. 1817—*Elizabeth*, born 31 Dec 1821.

* Graduated at Harvard University in 1813

4. JONATHAN, born 5 April, 1779, married Fanny Cobb, Taunton. She was born 24 Aug 1786. Their children were, *Bradford Leonard,* born 1 May, 1804, married Elizabeth Howard, Boston, who was born 12 March, 1814—*Fanny Wales,* born 2 April, 1809, married John J. Soren—*Jane,* born 7 Aug. 1814, died 27 Feb 1817—*George Whitfield,* born 27 June, 1819, died 14 Sept. 1822—*Ann Maria,* born 8 Aug. 1823, died 14 July, 1825.

No. 12.   VI C.   MOSES WALES,

a son of Dea Thomas Wales, married Elizabeth ——, and settled in Stoughton.   Their children were,

1. Joanna,	born 14 Sept	1754	5. Thomas,	born 4 April	1763
2 Elizabeth,	" 16 June	1757	6. Susannah,	" 20 June	1765
3 Sarah,	" 13 July	1759	7. Moses,	" 3 Oct	1768
4. Mary,	" 20 Feb	1761			

No 13   VII C.   NATHANIEL WALES, 3d ᵤₖₑ⟩

a brother of the preceding, married Sarah ——, and settled in Stoughton, and was a deacon in the church.   Their children were,

1. Sarah,	born 30 Oct	1747	7. Eunice,	born 28 Jan	1758
2. Mary,	" 17 Feb	1749	8 John,†	"	
3. Nathaniel,	" 30 May	1750	9. Theodore,	" 25 Dec	1767
4 Joshua,	" 21 Feb	1752	10 Deborah,	" 23 Sept	1769
5 Thomas,†	" 30 March	1754	11. Hannah,	" 16 Oct	1771
6. Elizabeth,	" 20 March	1756			

† See Cary's Genealogy of North Bridgewater.

VIII C.   DEBORAH WALES,

a daughter of Dea Thomas Wales, was married to William Curtis of Stoughton, about 1751.

No. 14.   XIV C.   Doct. EPHRAIM WALES,

a son of Dea. Thomas Wales, (by his second wife,) was graduated at Harvard College in 1768. He married a Miss Beale, for his first wife, by whom he had two sons, *Thomas Beale,* who graduated at Harvard College in 1795, and lives in Boston—*Ephraim,* who received his Medical education at Dartmouth College—married Mary, daughter of Silas Alden, (See Alden, No 59, 3,) and had one daughter, the wife of —— Whiting, Esq and by his second wife he had one daughter *Emily,* the wife of Aaron Littlefield, Randolph.

Dr. Wales was a man of science, and eminent in his profession.

*Graduated at Middlebury College, and received his Medical degree at Harvard, in 1828.

No. 15. XII B. JOSEPH WALES,

a son of Elder Wales, married Hannah Allen of Braintree. Their children were,

1. William,	born	3 Feb	1723	7. Sarah,	born 7 Sept	1731
2. Abigail,	"	10 Feb	1724	8 John,	" 7 July	1736
3 Hannah,				9. Esther,	" 7 Nov	1738
4. Joseph,	"	22 March	1726	10 Nathaniel,	" 20 Oct	1740
5 Samuel,	"	12 Jan	1728	11. Lemuel,	" 20 June	1742
6. Daniel,	"	26 Feb	1730	12. Jacob,	" 19 Feb	1748
	Died 13 March 1730.					

3. Hannah Wales, married Nathaniel Paine. (See Paine, No. 16.)

No. 16. IV C. JOSEPH WALES, Jr ,

married Abigail ———. Their children were, 1 Abigail, born 13 Oct. 1750—2. Elisha, born 14 May, 1753, who married Lydia, daughter of Josiah Thayer. (See Thayer, No 46, 6) Her second husband was Capt Isaac Thayer. (See Thayer, No 48, 1.)

9. Esther Wales, married Joshua French. (See French, No. 18.)

11. Lemuel Wales, married Silence French about 1778. (See French, No. 5, 1.)

No. 17. XIII B. "JOHN WALES,

a son of Elder Wales, was graduated at Harvard College in 1728. His wife was the second daughter of Samuel Leonard, and grand-daughter of Thomas Leonard, and great-grand-daughter of James Leonard, the progenitor of this family."*—[*Hist Coll.* 3, 174

"He was ordained at Raynham in the month of October, 1731. The first meeting house in Raynham was built the year preceding the incorporation of the town, which then contained about thirty families "

"He was blessed with talents which rendered him very amiable and interesting in social life."

"In public prayer, his performances were eminent, and on some occasions almost unequalled. He was a faithful, plain preacher ; and having served in the gospel ministry thirty-four years, he died 23 Feb 1765, in the sixty-sixth year of his age "—[*Ibid*, 3, 168.

He was father of the Rev. Samuel Wales, late Professor of Divinity at Yale College in Conn. He died in 1794 —[*Ib*

*Of the family of Leonard, the following genealogical sketch is intended to show that longevity, promotion to public office, and a kind of hered-

No. 18. XIV B. RACHEL WALES,

the youngest daughter of Elder Wales, was married to Capt. Ebenezer Thayer, 12 Nov 1719. (See Thayer, No 91.)

itary attachment to the iron manufacture, are all circumstances remarkably characteristic of the name and family of Leonard

The great progenitor JAMES LEONARD, lived to be more than seventy years old. He had three brothers, five sons, and three daughters Of his sons, four lived to be more than eighty, and all his daughters above seventy-five.

THOMAS, the oldest son of James, was a distinguished character. He held the office of a Justice of the Peace, a Judge of the Court, a Physician, a Field Officer, and was eminent for piety. Sacred to his memory, an eulogy was printed in 1713, by the Rev. Samuel Danforth of Taunton, one of the most learned and eminent ministers of his day. This THOMAS had five sons of whom four lived above seventy years

His son George was a Justice of the Peace, and a Military Officer. In Norton, in a poem published by a character of eminence, on occasion of his death in 1716, he is styled, "the prudent, pious, worthy, and worshipful Major George Leonard, Esq" He had four sons and three daughters.

His oldest son George was a Colonel and a Judge, both of the Probate and Common Pleas; he lived to be more than eighty. He had one son and two daughters.

His son is the Hon George Leonard, Esq., late member of Congress. His oldest daughter is the wife of the Rev. David Barnes, and the mother of David Barnes, Esq. Attorney at Law The other daughter was the wife of the late Col. Chandler of Worcester.

The second son of Major George Leonard was Nathaniel, a pious, worthy minister, who settled in Plymouth. He lived more than seventy years; and he had a son Abiel, who was a minister in Connecticut, and a Chaplain in the American Army, in the revolution war.

The third son of Major George Leonard was Ephraim; he was a Col. a Judge of the Court, and a man of eminent piety; he lived to be more than eighty. He had one child only, viz: Daniel, who is now Chief Justice of the Islands of Bermuda. He also has but one son, Charles, now a student at Cambridge College, (1793) Two of the daughters of Major George Leonard lived to be aged One was the wife of Colonel Thomas Clap, formerly a minister of Taunton; the other was the wife of a respectable Clergyman.

Samuel Leonard, the fourth son of THOMAS LEONARD, was a man of distinguished piety He held the office of a Deacon, a Captain, and Justice of the Peace. He had four sons and five daughters. Two of his sons Captains, one a Justice of the Peace, and all of them Deacons. Three are yet alive, one above eighty and two above seventy. His third son Elijah has a son of his own name, lately settled in the ministry. His oldest daughter was the parent of Dr Simeon Howard of Boston. His second daughter was the wife of the Rev. John Wales of this town, (See Wales, No. 17,) and the mother of Rev. Dr. Samuel Wales, Professor of Divinity at Yale College. The other daughters were the wives of respectable characters and all in public offices.

Elkanah, the fifth son of THOMAS LEONARD, had three sons, two of whom lived to see more than seventy. One was a Captain the other a Major, a Lawyer, and one of the most distinguished geniuses of his name and day. He left two sons, both Captains, and above sixty; one of them, viz: Zebulon, has an only child, that is now the wife of Dr. Samuel Shaw.

No. 19. XV B ATHERTON WALES,

the youngest son of Elder Wales, was graduated at Harvard College in 1726. He was settled in the ministry at Marshfield, Mass

No 20. TIMOTHY WALES,

probably a son of Nathaniel Wales of Dorchester, (No 1,) was one of the early settlers of that town   He had one son Eleazer, born 25, 10, 1657 , and perhaps other children born before

---

John was another son of THOMAS LEONARD   He had four sons and three daughters, who all lived to be above eighty. A daughter of the oldest son was the wife of the Rev Ehab Byram, and the parent of the present wife of Josiah Dean, Esq of this town, who himself is also a lineal descendant, and the present owner of the forge first built by his great ancestor.

JAMES, the second son of JAMES, bore his own name   He had four sons and three daughters, three of his sons lived to be near eighty, and two of the daughters above ninety. One of them was the wife of Dr Ezra Dean, and the other was the parent of Gershom Crane, Esq who lived to be almost an hundred years old, and was the father of the present Dr. Jonathan Crane, Esq   The oldest son of JAMES, was Capt James Leonard, who had three sons and five daughters. Two of his sons were Military Officers, and all of them lived to nearly the age of seventy. His oldest daughter was the wife of Thomas Cobb, Esq and the mother of the Hon. David Cobb, Esq. Speaker of the House, Member of Congress, &c. (She was the grand-mother of the wife of Dr Jonathan Wales, Randolph. See No. 11, 4)

The second son of JAMES, was Stephen Leonard , he was a Justice of the Peace, and a Judge of the Court of Common Pleas He had four sons, three of whom lived to be aged , one was the Rev. Silas Leonard of New York ; the oldest was Major Zephaniah Leonard, Esq. and Judge of the Court. He had five sons of whom four are yet alive, three of them had a public education at Yale College. The oldest is Capt Joshua, who now inhabits the ancient paternal building, and is nearly seventy , he has a son of his own name, who at the age of twenty-two, was an ordained minister in Connecticut. The second son is Col Zephaniah Leonard. He has held the offices of an Attorney at Law, a Justice of the Peace, and is now Sheriff of the County. He has three sons, two of whom are now members of College. The third son is Apollos Leonard, Esq one of the Special Justices of the County. The youngest son is Samuel Leonard, lately appointed a Justice of the Peace   He is a respectable, opulent merchant, and has a number of promising sons, that wait only for the proper age, to receive such an education as will add still greater honour to the ancient, honourable family and name they bear. Such has been the longevity and promotion to public offices in two branches of this family only.

The circumstance of a family attachment to the *iron manufacture* is so well known as to render it a common observation in this part of the country, viz · *where you can find iron works, there you will find a* LEONARD.

Henry, the brother of James, went from this place to the Jerseys, and was one of the first who set up iron works in that State   He was the progenitor of a numerous and respectable posterity in that part of America.

[*Hist. Coll.* 3, 173, 6 *Feb* 1793.

No. 21.   JOHN WALES,

probably a brother of the preceding, also settled in Dorchester, and had children born there, viz :

1. Content,   born 14, 3,   1659 | 3 Elkanah,   born 16, 4,   1665
2. Elizabeth,   "   1, 5,   1662 | 4. John, who died   18 June   1683
          Died 3, 4, 1673.

Content was married to John Mason, 15 Oct. 1679.

No. 22. A.   SAMUEL WALES,

perhaps a son of John Wales, born prior to 1657,* in Dorchester, had children,

1. Jerijah,   born 26 Feb   1678 | 5. John,   born 5 April 1688
2. Elizabeth,   "   9 Jan   1680 | 6. Jonathan,   "   29 Dec   1700
3. Sarah,   "   5 May   1683 | 7. Hannah,   "   14 Jan   1703
4. Samuel,   "   15 July   1685 |

The two last were the children of Samuel and Hannah
Wales, and probably the former.

No. 23. I B.   JERIJAH WALES,

married Sarah Parson of Dorchester, 24, 11, 1704. Their
children were,

1. Sarah,   born 7 Nov   1705 | 3 Mary,   born 25 Feb   1710
2. Mary,   "   30 May   1708 | And probably others.

No. 24. II B.   ELIZABETH WALES,

was married to Samuel Leeds of Dorchester, 18 Nov. 1702.

No. 25. V B.   JOHN WALES,

married Ruth Parson of Dorchester, 29 May, 1716.

No. 26. VII B.   HANNAH WALES,

was married to James Bird, Jr. of Dorchester, 2 Jan. 1728.
                              [*Dorchester Records.*

---

*In consequence of the loss of the town records of Dorchester, by fire,
prior to 1657, it is difficult, if not impossible to indentify the families to
which many of its inhabitants belonged, as in this case, whether Samuel
was a son of Timothy, No. 20, or John, No. 21, is uncertain. He may have
been a brother of Elder Wales of Braintree ; and the same remark will
apply to Mary Wales, married to Nicholas George, 4 June, 1684.

THE FAMILY OF WHITE.*

No. 1. THOMAS WHITE,

of Weymouth, was Representative 1636 and 1637 ; died Aug. 1679, leaving children, 1. Joseph of Mendon—2. Samuel, born 1642—3. Thomas of Braintree—4. Hannah, who married John Baxter, (See Adams, No. 3,)—5. Ebenezer, born 1648 ; died 24 Aug. 1703, who was father of Ebenezer White, H. C. 1692, minister of Bridge Hampton, L. I. who died 1756, aged 84.—[*Shattuck. Farmer.*

No. 2. I A. Capt. JOSEPH WHITE,

a son of the preceding, with his wife Lydia, had one child born in Weymouth, 1. Joseph, born 17 Dec 1662 ; died young. He afterwards removed to Mendon with a colony from Braintree and Weymouth, where they continued till the breaking out of the Indian war in 1675, when they returned and remained among their friends until about 1679 or 1680. . (See Thayer, No. 98. Note) Their children born in Mendon were,

2. Experience,	born	1 Dec	1680	8. Abigail,	born 10 Nov	1693
3. Hannah,	"	29 Nov	1681	9 William,	"	1696
4. Joseph,	"	19 Oct	1683	10. Samuel,	" 21 Sept	1700
5. Lydia,	"	10 May	1686	11. Benjamin,	" 28 May	1701
6. Thomas,	"	26 Nov	1688	12 Ebenezer, who died 24 Aug 1726.		
7. Hannah,	"	9 Dec	1691			

Capt. Joseph White died 23 March, 1706. Lydia, wife of Joseph White, died 8 May, 1729.

No. 3. II B. EXPERIENCE WHITE,

was married to Ephraim Miller of Mendon, 10 Feb. 1701.

---

*Mr. Farmer says, "The name of White prevails in every State, and nearly every County in New England. No less than 70 had graduated at the various colleges in 1826, 22 of whom have been clergymen."

This Memorial is limited almost exclusively to the family of Thomas White of Weymouth, and even this is very deficient, from the want of official records ; most of which, in this town, prior to the commencement of the last century, being lost.

No 4. IV B. JOSEPH WHITE, Jr ,

married Prudence ——, and settled in Mendon. Their children were,

1 Joseph,	born 22 Sept	1712	3. Aaron,	born 22 May	1717
2. Peter,	" 6 Dec	1714	4 Moses,	" 31 Aug	1721

No. 5. V B. LYDIA WHITE,

a sister of the preceding, was married to Michael, a son of Michael and Elizabeth Metcalf of Dedham, 21 March, 1705. He was born in Dedham, 9, 3, 1674.

No. 6. VI B. THOMAS WHITE,

a brother of the preceding, married Deborah ——. Their children were,

1. Peregrine,	born 11 Jan	1711	6. Deborah,	born 16 Feb	1722
2. Seth,	" 22 Sept	1713	7. Josiah,	" 29 April	1723
3. Lydia,	" 16 Jan	1716	8 Nathan,	" 31 Jan	1732
4 Hopestill,	" 15 July	1717	9 Phebe,	died 23 July	1734
5. Samuel,	" 17 May	1719	10. Asa,	born 11 May	1735

No. 7 V C. SAMUEL WHITE,

a son of the preceding, married Abigail Adams, in 1744. Their children were,

1. Adams,	born 17 Feb	1745	5 Margery,	born 16 Oct	1754
2 Samuel,	" 21 March	1747	6 Artemas,	" 3 March	1757
3 Nathan,	" 27 June	1750	7. Antipas,	" 12 March	1760
4. Barach,	" 3 May	1752			

No. 8. IX B WILLIAM WHITE,

a son of Capt. Joseph and Lydia White, married Huldah, probably a daughter of Samuel and Mary Thayer, (See Thayer, No. 126,) and had 1. William, born 22 Aug. 1720, who died young She died 26 Aug 1720. His second wife was Elizabeth, daughter of Capt Thomas Thayer. (See Thayer, No. 111, 6,) married 3 Aug. 1721. Their children were,

2. Huldah,	born 27 Aug	1722	7. William,	born 22 Nov	1732
3. Elizabeth,	" 28 Feb	1724	8. a Son,	" 8 March	1735
Died 17 Sept 1740.			9. Mary,	" 31 Aug	1737
4. Lydia,	born 1 March	1726	10. Elizabeth,	" 5 Oct	1740
5. Ruth,	" 10 April	1728	11 Elisha,	" 16 Jan	1743
6. Jemima,	" 26 July	1730	Died young.		

His third wife was Elizabeth Brummell, widow, (formerly Harper,) married 16 Nov. 1749 Their children were,

12 Elizabeth,	born 20 July	1750	14. Elisha,	born 8 March	1753
13 Abigail,	" 28 Dec	1751	15 Gideon,	" 20 March	1755

No. 9.   X B.   SAMUEL WHITE,

a brother of the preceding, married Triall ———.   Their children were,

1. Samuel,   born 2 March 1723 | 3. Johannah,   born 12 Oct   1729
2. Hannah,   "   11 April 1727 |

His second wife was Comfort Tyler married 26 Nov. 1739.

No. 10   III C.   JOHANNAH WHITE,

was married to Solomon Chapin of Mendon, 28 May, 1754.

No. 11.   XI B.   BENJAMIN WHITE,

son of Capt. Joseph and Lydia White, married Mary Thayer, 23 May, 1720. (See Thayer, No. 129) Their children were,

1. Benjamin,   born 7 Jan   1723 | 5 Huldah,   born 5 Nov   1730
2 Mercy,   " 8 Oct   1728 | 6. Gideon,   "   12 Jan   1733
3. Joseph,   " 8 March   1729 | 7. Samuel,   "   5 Dec   1731
4. Patience,   " 3 Jan   1730 |

No. 12.   III C.   JOSEPH WHITE,

a son of the preceding, married Margery Aldrich of Mendon, 11 April, 1751. Their children were,

1 Mary,   born 19 Oct   1751 | 3 Benjamin,   born 5 Oct   1755
2. Jacob,   " 10 Aug   1753 | 4. Marcy,   "   21 March 1757

Joseph White died 28 Oct. 1757. Margery White died 11 May, 1759.

No. 13.   II A.   SAMUEL WHITE,

of Weymouth, son of Thomas White, was born 1642 ; admitted freeman 1666 , representative 1679. He married Mary Dyer, and died without issue.—[Shattuck. Farmer.

No. 14.   SAMUEL WHITE,*

also of Weymouth, married Anna Bingley.* Their children were,

1. Susannah,   born 12 March 1689 | 7. Elisha,   born 16 June 1702
2. Mary,   " 12 Sept   1690 | Died 1 July 1702.
3. Lydia,   "   4 Sept   1693 | 8. Rachel,   born 20 March 1703
4. Anna,   " 14 Oct   1696 | 9. Matthew,   "   17 April 1704
5 Ebenezer,   " 22 Feb   1699 | 10. Samuel,   "   4 May   1706
6. Thankful,   " 17 April 1700 | 11 Experience, "   1 Jan   1707
                                   | 12. Samuel, 2d. "   2 April 1710

*The family tradition is, that the parents of *Anna Bingley*, both died soon after her birth ; and that the parents of *Samuel White* adopted her as then own, a year or two before this *Samuel* was born, when they had no child of their own, and that in process of time, his adopted sister became his wife. Who his father was, is uncertain, on account of the loss of the early records of Weymouth.

1. *Susannah*, was married to Richard **Thayer**. (See Thayer, No 49.) 2. *Mary*, was married to Lieut. Richard Thayer. (See Thayer, No 11.) 3. *Lydia*, was married to Joseph Pray, 5 Dec. 1715. 4. *Anna*, was married to William Wild, 2 Dec. 1717. 6. *Thankful*, was married to Isaac Newcomb, 9 April, 1722. 8. *Rachel*, was married to Shadrach Thayer. (See 2d part 6 Branch.) 11. *Experience*, was married to Abijah Neale, 4 Dec. 1733.

No. 15. III A.   THOMAS WHITE,

a son of Thomas White of Weymouth, married Mary ——, and afterwards settled in Braintree. Their children were, 1. Thomas—2. Samuel, born 19 Sept. 1676, and probably 3. Benjamin—4. Joseph, and 5. Ebenezer.

Thomas White and Deborah Penniman were married 4, 10, 1701. Thomas White died 11 April, 1706.

No. 16. I B.   THOMAS WHITE, Jr.,

married Mehitable, a daughter of Joseph and Abigail Adams, 21 July, 1697. (See Adams, No. 38) Their children were,

1 Thomas,	born 2 Oct	1698	3 Mary,	born 21 Aug	'1703
2. Mehitable,	" 15 Feb	1701	4. Abigail,	" 23 Feb	1707

Mehitable, wife of Thomas White, Jr. died 2 Oct. 1713. He married, for his second wife, Mary Bowditch, 29 April, 1714. (See French, No. 23, 2.) Their children were,

5. Ruth,	born 17 Feb	1715	8. Sarah,	born 20 May	1720
6. Rachel,	" 14 April	1716	9. Micah,	" 10 Dec	1721
7. Josiah,	" 1 April	1718			

No. 17. I C.   THOMAS WHITE,

a son of the preceding, married Abigail Penniman, 17 June, 1725.

No. 18. II C. MEHITABLE WHITE,

a sister of the preceding, was married to Ezekiel Thayer of Braintree, 1. Nov. 1725. (See Thayer, No. 66.)

No. 19. III C.   MARY THAYER,

a sister of the preceding, was married to Alexander French. (See French, No. 41.)

No. 20. IV C.   ABIGAIL WHITE,

a sister of the preceding, was married to Seth Copeland, 7 March, 1734. (See Copeland, No. 72.)

Micah White, the youngest son of Thomas White, Jr., married and had five children, viz : *Susannah, Anna, Lot,* who married a Tower, and had one son John, who lives in Boston. *Micah,* born 10 March, 1758, who married Sarah Mann and settled in Randolph. Their children were, Sally, born 6 Oct. 1784—Calvin, born 5 Sept 1786—Charlotte, born 5 Sept. 1788—Caleb, Nathan, Phebe, Livingston, Warren, Eliza. *Ebenezer,* who married a Patridge, and settled in Braintree, Vt.

No. 21. II B.   SAMUEL WHITE,

a son of Thomas and Mary White, married Deborah Penniman of Braintree. 5 Dec. 1701. Their children were,

1. Deborah,	born	5 April 1703	4. Hephzibah,	born	28 Mar 1709
2. Hannah,	"	11 Dec 1704	5. Samuel,	"	22 July 1710
3. Samuel,	"	4 Dec 1706	6. Samuel,	"	26 Aug 1712

Samuel White of Braintree, was chosen deacon of the church 28 April, 1719.

1. *Deborah,* was married to Ebenezer Copeland. (See Copeland, No. 11.) 2. *Hannah,* was married to Samuel Bass. (See Bass, No. 30.) 4. *Hephzibah,* was married to Benjamin French. (See French, No. 49) 6. *Samuel,* married Susannah Allen, 21 Nov. 1734.

No. 22. III B.   BENJAMIN WHITE,

probably a son of Thomas and Mary White, married Mary ——. Their children were,

1. Joseph,	born 12 Aug	1704	2. Mary,	born 14 Feb.	1706
	Died 6 Jan 1712.		3. Sarah,	" 18 March	1709

He married Lydia Sacan, a second wife, 17 Jan 1716.

3. *Sarah,* was married to Isaiah Thayer. (See Thayer, No. 12.)

No. 23. IV B.   JOSEPH WHITE,

probably a brother of the preceding, married Sarah Bayley, 6 Dec. 1704 or 5. Their children were,

1. Joseph,	born 1 Oct	1706	5. Daniel,	born 18 April	1714
2. Benjamin,	" 18 March	1709	6. Benjamin,	" 7 July	1716
	Died 3 Oct 1715.		7. David,	" 12 Aug	1719
3. John,	born 28 Feb	1710	8. Sarah,	" 12 Jan	1721
4. Sarah,	" 17 Feb	1712	9. Hannah,	" 28 Jan	1724
	Died 7 Oct 1715.		10. Mary,	" 11 June	1727

No. 24. I C.   JOSEPH WHITE, Jr ,

married Ruth Nash, 21 March, 1734. Their children were,

1. Ruth,	born 15 July	1738	4. Thankful,	born 25 May	1747
2 Joseph,	" 22 Nov	1712	5. Mary,	" 1 Aug	1751
3. David,	" 19 May	1745			

1. *Ruth*, was married to Adam Kingman, and had one son Joseph 2. *Joseph*, married Ruth Porter, 16 June, 1766. Their children were, Ruth, born 12 April, 1769, 2d wife of Zenas French, (2d part, 9 Branch) Relief, born 7 Jan. 1772, the wife of Bailey White (No. 25, 11.) 3. *David*, married Relief Thayer, 5 Jan. 1771. (See Thayer, No 46, 3 4. *Thankful*, was married to Elihu Adams. (See Adams, No. 18.) Her second husband was Aaron Hobart, Esq of Abington, by whom she had Benjamin, Solama, Mary, Thankful 5. *Mary*, was married to Dea. William Linfield, 6 Oct 1771. Their children were, Samuel, who married Relief Wales—Mary, wife of Robert Whitcomb—Sarah, wife of Col. Simeon White, (No. 25, 12,)—Ruth, wife of Joseph Holbrook—Thankful, wife of William Alden—Nancy, late wife of Dr. Jonathan Wild—Olive, wife of John White of Thetford, Vt —Joseph, who married Nancy Adams. Dea. William Linfield died in 1823.

No 25 III C. Capt JOHN WHITE,

a son of Joseph and Sarah White, married Ruth, daughter of David and Dorothy Thayer (See Thayer, No. 65.)
Their children were,

1 John,	born 4 Jan	1749	8 Caleb,	born 17 March	1762
	Died 4 July 1750		9. Lydia,	" 25 March	1764
2. John,	born 7 May	1751	10 Bailey,	" 1 Jan	1766
3. Cornelius,	" 8 Oct	1752		Died 9 Aug 1766.	
4 Solomon,	" 30 Aug	1754	11. Bailey,	born 27 Aug	1767
	Died 1 April 1755.		12. Simeon,	" 11 July	1769
5 John,	born 6 May	1756	13 Levi,	" 4 March	1771
6 Ruth,	" 20 May	1758	14. Isaac,	" 5 Feb	1774
7. Solomon,	" 18 March	1760			

3 Cornelius, married Abigail Thayer of Weymouth, in 1773 5 John, married Hannah Thayer (See 2d part 6 branch.) 7. Solomon, married 1st Bathsheba Wales in 1785 —2d Lurancy Loud of Weymouth 8 Caleb, married Mehitable Randall, 13 June, 1790. 9 Lydia, married Dea. Silas Paine (See Paine, No. 16.) 11. Bailey, married Relief White in 1792. (See No. 24.) 12. Simeon, married Sarah Linfield (See No. 24.) 13. Levi, was graduated at —— College, and is settled in the Ministry. 14. Isaac, married Mary Whitcomb. She died 10 Nov. 1732. He died 26 May, 1833.

No. 26. V C. DANIEL WHITE,

a son of Joseph and Sarah White, married Elizabeth Mills,

12 June, 1737, had one child, 1. Elizabeth, born 2 Dec.
1738. His second wife was Mary Shaw, married 25 Dec.
1740. He married Betty Orcutt for his third wife, and
had one child, Daniel, born 27 Dec. 1750, who married
Betty (Elizabeth) Thayer.

No. 27. VI C.   BENJAMIN WHITE,

a brother of the preceding, married Mercy, daughter of
Gideon and Hannah Thayer. (See Thayer, No. 34, 2.)
  Their children were,

1. Benjamin,	born 12 Aug	1748	3 Sarah,	born 14 Feb	1753
2. Hannah,	" 22 Nov	1750	4 Silence.		

  Benjamin was drowned 15 July, 1801. Hannah was the
wife of Zeba Thayer. (See Thayer, No. 97, 4)

No. 28. V B.   EBENEZER WHITE,

supposed to be a son of Thomas and Mary White, married
Lydia ——. Their children were,

1. Lydia,	born 2 Sept	1710	5. William,	born 8 Feb	1718
2. Elizabeth,	" 20 April	1713	6 Anne,	" 28 May	1720
3. Ebenezer,	" 16 July	1714	7. Thomas,	" 15 Sept	1731
4. William,	" 1 Sept	1716			

No. 29. V C.   WILLIAM WHITE,

a son of the preceding, married Sarah ——. Their children were,

1. Ebenezer,	born 25 Feb	1742	4. William,	born 21 May	1752
2 Betty,	" 22 Nov	1747	5 Job,	" 23 June	1758
3. Sarah,	" 28 Feb	1750			

  Ebenezer, married Alethea Hollis of Braintree, 2 May,
1767. Betty, married Salter Soper, 8 Nov. 1765.

No. 30. V A.   Capt. EBENEZER WHITE,

the youngest son of Thomas White of Weymouth, (No 1)
married Hannah, perhaps a daughter of Peregrine White.
(See Alden, No. 62, and Note.) Their children were,

1. Ebenezer, born in 1672, graduated at Harv. College in 1692. (See No. 1.)
2. Hannah, born 5 May 1681, the wife of John Alden. (See as above.)

3. Abigail,	born 3 March	1682	5 Experience,	born 1 July	1687
4. Benjamin,	" 21 Feb	1684	6. Elizabeth,	" 9 Nov	1688

No. 31. There was a PEREGRINE WHITE, with his wife

Susannah, who lived in Weymouth, and had one son Be-
noni, born 26 Jan. 1685.

No. 32. There was a THOMAS WHITE, with his wife Mary

22

who also lived in Weymouth, and had children, 1. Jonathan, born 21 Oct. 1702—2. John, born 26 Sept. 1704—3. Thomas, born 5 May, 1707—4 Ebenezer, born 21 Dec. 1709.

No. 33.   There was a THOMAS WHITE of Mendon, with his wife Mehitable, who were probably natives of Weymouth. Their children were, 1. *Mehitable*, born 20 Jan 1689—2. *Thomas*, born 15 April, 1691—3 *Thankful*, born 13 Aug. 1693—4 *Joseph*, born 28 Aug 1695—5. *John*, born 12 Mar. 1698—6. *Ebenezer*, 4 Feb. 1704.   Mehitable, wife of Thomas White, died 27 Sept. 1704.   His children by his second wife Mary, were 7 Daniel, born 18 June, 1708—8. Mary, born 29 Nov. 1711.

1. *Mehitable*, was married to Benjamin Darling, 11 June, 1708.   2. *Thomas*, married Margaret —— Their children were, Dinah, born 19 Dec. 1713—Mehitable, born 16 Dec. 1717—Mehitable, born 20 Nov. 1718—Abigail, born 14 Sept. 1723—Margaret, born 15 April 1726—Joseph, born 2 June, 1729—Susannah, born 19 Sept. 1732.

Dinah, was married to Samuel Leland of Holliston, 30 Dec. 1736   Joseph, married Anna Coleson of Holliston, 26 Sept. 1751.

4. *Joseph*, married Abigail Skinner of Oxford, 15 April, 1718. 5. *John*, married Sarah Cheney, 28 April, 1720.   Their children were, Rachel, born 4 April, 1721—Sarah, born 17 March, 1729—William, 7 Feb. 1731—Mary, born 25 Aug. 1734.

No. 34.   There was also a John White, with his wife Sarah, who lived in Mendon, probably a brother of Thomas. Their children were, 1. Sarah, born 5 July, 1700—2. John, 13 March 1702—3. Edward, born 18 July, 1704—4 Ezekiel, born 11 Aug. 1707—5. David, born 28 April, 1810—6. Hester, born 16 Aug. 1711.

JOHN WHITE, 1698, native of Brookline, was ordained in Gloucester, 21 April, 1703, and died 16 Jan. 1760, aged 83.

EBENEZER WHITE, 1704, native of Dorchester, was ordained in Attleborough, 17 Oct. 1716, and died 4 Sept. 1726.

EBENEZER WHITE, 1733, native of Brookline, born 29 March, 1713, and ordained in Norton, now Mansfield.

[*Rev Dr. Pierce, Brookline.*

" As to William White, the Plymouth pilgrim, who died 21 Feb. 1621," says Mr. Farmer, " I could never learn that he had more than two children, one born in Europe, when he had *resolved* to embark for the shores of America, and

whom he named RESOLVED, and the other born after he
had become a pilgrim and *peregrinator* on those shores, whom
he named PEREGRINE. Mr. White was probably *a young
man* when he died, as his children were so young at the
time of his death, and as his widow was the mother of
children by a subsequent husband. But this however is
conjecture."

No. 35.   EDWARD WHITE,

was one of the early settlers of Dorchester, a distinct family from that commemorated in the foregoing pages. He
was admitted freeman in 1636. His children were,

1. JAMES—2. JOHN—3 HENRY, and probably 4 PETER,
of Milton.

No. 36.   I   JAMES WHITE,

married Sarah Baker of Dorchester, 22, 12, 1664. Their
children were,

1. Sarah,	born 8, 9,	1665	5 Martha,	born 28 Aug	1675
	Died 2, 11, 1665.		6 James,	" 29 May	1679
2 Thankful, born 18, 6,		1667	7. Richard,	" 2 March	1681
3. Ichabod,	" 26 April	1669	8. Edward,	" 4 Aug	1683
	Died 12 May 1669.		9. Ebenezer,	" 3 July	1685
4. John,	born 7, 4,	1670			

He married Elizabeth Wilkinson, (a second wife) 13 Feb.
1696.

No. 37. VIII A. EDWARD WHITE,

a son of the preceding, settled in Dorchester, had one child
Sarah, born 1 March, 1708, and probably others.

No. 38. IX A.   EBENEZER WHITE,

a brother of the preceding, was graduated at Harvard College in 1704; ordained in Attleborough, Mass. 17 Oct. 1716,
and died 4 Sept. 1726.—[*Rev. Dr. Pierce, Brookline.*

No. 39. II   JOHN WHITE,

a son of Edward White, married Mary Swift of Dorchester,
11, 11, 1663. Their children were,

1. Susannah, who died 18 June 1678		3. Thankful,	born 18 Jan	1677
2. Mary,	born 8, 8,	1666		

No. 40 III   HENRY WHITE,

a brother of the preceding, married Mary ——. Their
children were,

1. Return,	who died Dec	1680	6 Josiah,	born 30 Dec	1692
2 Josiah,	born 14 June	1680	7. Sarah,	" 11 Oct	1693
3. William.	" 7 Feb	1684	8. Annah,	" 6 June	1695
4 Submit,	" 9 Dec	1688	9 Rebecca,	" 10 Dec	1696
5. Jerusha,	" 19 Feb	1690	10 Abigail,	" 25 March	1698

No 41. IV A.   SUBMIT WHITE,
was married to Samuel Bullard, 24 May, 1710.

No. 42. V A.   JERUSHA WHITE,
was married to James White Jr. 29 Ap 1719. (See No 36,6.)
[*Dorchester Records.*

No. 43. IV.   PETER WHITE,
of Milton, probably a son of Edward White Senr. married
Rachel ——. Their children were,

1. John,	born 3 Sept	1683	Paul died 13 Jan 1695.		
2 Peter,	" 20, 12,	1684	6 Paul,	born 24 July	1699
3. George,	" 5 Oct	1686	7. Benjamin,	" 6 Feb	1701
4. Sarah,	" 21, 10,	1693	Died 15 Feb 1719.		
5. Paul,	" 20 Feb	1694	8. Philip,	born 26 July	1705

Rachel, wife of Peter White died 20 Oct. 1732. Peter
White died 7 May, 1743.

No. 44. VIII A.   PHILIP WHITE,
a son of the preceding, married Mary —— Their children were,

| 1. Rachel, | born 29 April | 1739 | 3 Mary, | born 10 Oct | 1750 |
| 2. Eliphalet, | " 12 Feb | 1746 | | | |

Philip White died 8 April 1752. Mary his widow died 6
Jan. 1753 —[*Milton Records.*

No. 45.   JOSEPH WHITE,
(the grandfather of Mr. Joseph White of Charlestown, Ms)
was said to have been a Captain of a ship of war in the
English service. He married for his second wife Catharine
Andrews of Boston, and settled in Boston. Their children were, 1. Josiah—2. Benjamin—3. Sarah—4. Abigail.

No 46   JOSIAH WHITE
a son of the above, married Sarah Holbrook of Braintree
in the year 1744, settled in Boston. Their children were,

1. Sarah, born 6 June 1745, died 13 Oct 1751.
2. Elizabeth, b. 27 July 1747 died in 1818.
3. Abigail, b 14 Sept 1749, married Jeremiah Niles, son of Judge Niles of
Braintree, 3 Nov 1770
4. Sarah, b 19 Oct 1752, living in Weymouth
5. Joseph, b. 27 Feb. 1755, living in Charlestown
6. Lucy, b. 20 June, 1758, died ——.
7. Mary, b. 12 Jan 1760, wife of Samuel Richards, living in Dedham
    Josiah White and his wife died 1776, six weeks apart

APPENDIX

FAMILY MEMORIAL.

ALDEN.

Martin Alden, "whose wife was Mary Kingman. Their children were, Albert, a bookbinder and an engraver on wood, of Lancaster, Caleb Holmes, Mary Kingman, a lovely daughter, who died at the age of thirteen years. Timothy, Isaiah, and Martin Luther. (See Alden, No. 52.)—[*Rev. T. Alden, MS.*

ADAMS.

William Adams of Braintree, with his wife Ruth had children,

1. William,	born 13 May	1744	5. Benjamin,	born 25 Oct.	1754
2 Anna,	" 26 Aug	1745	6. Mary,	" 25 Nov	1756
3. Elisha,	" 25 Feb	1751	7 Joanna,	" 25 June	1761
4. Jonathan,	" 27 Nov	1753	8. Sarah,	" 26 July	1762

He was not a descendant of Henry Adams, (No. 1.)

Edward Adams,

of Milton, married Rachel Saunders of Braintree, 11 Sept. 1706, and settled in Milton. Their children,

1 Edward,	born ——		6. Samuel,	" 5 March 1718
2. John,	" 26 Feb.	1709		Died 10 April, 1718.
3 Rachel,	" 17 June	1711	7. Patience,	born 7 Aug.	1720
4 Seth,	" 30 Sept	1713		Died 30 Aug. 1720.
5. Nathan,	" 28 March	1716	His wife Rachel died 14 Nov. 1727

He married Sarah Bracket, a second wife, 5 Feb. 1729 Edward Adams died 22 Sept. 1743.

Edward Adams, Jr married Deliverance ——, and settled in Milton Their children,

1. John,	born 17 June,	1727	Anne died 5 July 1739.
2 Rachel,	" 18 Aug	1729	6. Seth, born 14 Sept 1737
	Died 2 May 1731.		Died 10 July 1739.
3. Ruth,	born 15 July	1731	7. Deborah, born 12 June 1740
4. Nathan,	" 20 July	1733	8. Deliverance, " 25 Jan 1744
	Died 7 July 1739.		9. Patience, " 16 Dec 1745
5. Anne,	born 29 May	1735	

JOHN ADAMS, a brother of the preceding, married Sarah Swift, 18 May, 1730, and settled in Milton. Their children,

1. Samuel,	born 30 Jan	1731	Eliphalet died 5 Feb 1748
	Died 18 Feb 1731		8 Judith, born 24 Nov 1746
2, Rachel,	born 6 Jan	1732	9. Eliphalet, " 5 Feb 1748
3. John,	died 12 Aug	1735	10 Lemuel, " 1 Dec 1748
4. Andrew,	born 12 Aug	1735	Died Dec 1833.
5 Annah,	" 20 May	1737	11 Sarah, born 31 March 1752
6 Seth,	" 3 Dec	1740	Died 28 Jan 1766.
7. Eliphalet,	" 23 Feb	1743	12. Mary, born 21 Dec 1753

ANDREW ADAMS, a son of the preceding, married Ruth Wadsworth, daughter of a Clergyman in that vicinity, and settled first in Milton. Their children,

1. Andrew,	born	4 Ruth,	born 1 July 1763
2 Lucy,	" 18 Feb 1759	5 Lemuel,	" 15 April 1769
3 John,	" 23 July 1761	6 Benjamin,	"

They afterwards removed to Pelham, N. H. and had one son Lewis, born there, from thence they removed to Lancaster, N. H His wife died about 1818 or 19

In Lancaster, N. H. 14 April, 1833, died Andrew Adams, Esq aged 98, an officer of the revolution, formerly of Milton, Mass Mr Adams held a Commission under George III. dated 1761, Coroner "for the County of Suffolk, in our Province of Massachusetts Bay."—[*Norfolk Advertiser, May* 4, 1833. ·

" *John Adams*, son of the first Henry Adams, went with his brother Thomas to Concord, and when the latter removed to Chelmsford, John probably accompanied him, as we find him there in 1654, but after this period I have not been able to trace him "—[*Adams, No 2 Note*

" *John Bass*, the graduate of Harvard College in 1737, and the minister of Ashford, Conn. published a "True Narrative of an unhappy contention in the church at Ashford, and the several methods to bring it to a period " 4 to pp. 28, 1751." (Bass, No 14)

"The late Bishop Hobart of New York, was a descendant from Capt Joshua Hobart." (Hobart, No 29.) [*Farmer.*

Errata —Copeland, No 23, for *Lawrance*, read Lurancy. Thayer, No 2—2 Richard, born 31, 6, 1655, not 1665

THAYER
COPY OF THE LAST WILL AND TESTAMENT OF
THOMAS THAYER.
(See Thayer, No 79)

I Thomas Thayer of Braintree in the County of Suffolk, in the Massachusetts colony of New England, Shoe Maker, being in perfect health and memory praysed be God, this 21 of June, A. D 1664 doe make this my last Will and Testament as followeth:

IMPRIMIS. I give unto my wife Margery, that now is all my lands, goods and estate whatsoever, situated, lying and being in Braintree aforesaid, during the term and time of her natural life; and after her decease, I give and bequeath unto my Sonne Thomas Thayer, his heirs and assigns all that my ground lying and being over Monotoquott River within the limits of the said town of Braintree with the timber or other wood growing or fallen upon the same with other the appurtenances, part of which ground he hath already in his possession.

ITEM I give and bequeath unto Ferdinando Thayer my Sonne, his heirs and assigns, next and immediately after the decease of Margery, my said wife, my house and orchard thereunto belonging, lying and being in Braintree aforesaid, with all the planting ground and pasture lying between the highway and River called Monotoquott River aforesaid and on the other side of the highway from the South side of the barne to the end of the lot

Further my Will and Mind is that the said Ferdinando my sonne shall have free liberty to cutt, fall and carry away fire wood for his and his now wife's own burning of and from my lott called 20 acre lott for his and his said wife's life

ITEM., I give and bequeath unto my Sonne Sydrach Thayer his heirs and assigns, next and immediately after the decease of my said wife Margery a parcell of ground in Braintree aforesaid, which shall begin at the corner of the Barne, next his Dwelling house and shall runne with a straight line to the upper end of the lott.

ITEM. I give and bequeath 20 acres of land more unto the said Sydrach, my sonne, his heirs and assigns, next and immediately after the decease of my said wife Margery, which land lyeth in Braintree aforesaid, next unto the ground of Henry Neale, provided, He, his heirs and assigns permit and suffer my sonne Ferdinando and his now wife to take wood thereof for their own burning during their natural lives according as is before expressed.

ITEM. I give and bequeath all my goods and chattels, unto my Grand children to be equally divided among them.

AND LASTLY, If any of my said children shall appear to be discontented and murmur at this my last Will and Testament, Then my Will and mind is that any such child one or more of them shall have but 5s. for their Portion, and the Portion or Portions of any such child or children so murmuring and discontented as aforesaid shall be equally divided amongst the rest of my children and grand children

And I do nominate and appoint my said wife Margery and my sonne Ferdinando to be my Executors of this my last Will and Testament; and all other former Wills, Testaments and Bequests, I do hereby utterly revoke and make void forever by these Presents.

In witness whereof I have hereunto set my hand and seal the day and yeare above written.

his mark
THOMAS ✕ THAYER.
and seal

Read, Sealed and Published in presence of us.

The mark of Sadrach
The mark of R. B.
Margery Flint.
Sarah Saville.
Ruth Basse

At a meeting of the Magistrates and Recorder in Boston 13 Sept. 1665, Sarah Saville and Ruth Basse deposed before the Magistrates and Recorder, that having subscribed their names to this Instrument were present on the date thereof and did both see and hear the above mentioned Thomas Thayer, to sign, seal and publish the same to be his last Will and Testament, that when hee so did hee was of a sound and disposing mind to your best knowledge.

EDWARD RAWSON, Recorder

[*Suffolk Probate Office*, vol 1, page 458.

of   and

narried   and settled in
                    (Sec   No.   .)
Their children were,

of   and

married   and settled in
                    (See   No.   )

Their children were,

 of   and

married   and settled in

(See   No.   )

Their children were,

of   and
married   and settled in
                    (See   No   .)
Their children were,

FAMILY MEMORIAL.

PART II.

GENEALOGY

OF

EPHRAIM AND SARAH THAYER,

WITH THEIR

FOURTEEN CHILDREN;

ROM THE TIME OF THEIR MARRIAGE TO 1835, WITH
NOTES OF REFERENCE, &c. AS IN PART FIRST.

BY ELISHA THAYER,
DEDHAM, MASS

"Quos omnis, Deus omnipotens prounigeniti filii sui
Ac Salvatoris nostri meritis, vita æterna dignetur."
Dr. Benjamin Thompson.

HINGHAM:
J FARMER ..PRINTER
1835.

GENEALOGY.

.

No 1.　　　EPHRAIM THAYER, *[handwritten]* a son of Shadrach and Deliverance Thayer, was born in Braintree, Mass. 17, 11, 1669. (See Part 1, No 175, 7.) He married Sarah, the youngest daughter of John and Ruth Bass, 7 Jan. 1692. (See Bass, No. 11, and Thayer, No. 181.)　Their children were,

1 Sarah,	born	5 Feb	1693	8. Ruth,	born	1 April	1704
2 Ephraim,	"	8 July	1694	9. Esther,	"	24 July	1705
3 Philip,	"	14 April	1696	10. Naphtali,	"	30 Jan	1707
4. Hannah,	"	13 Jan	1698	11. Peter,	"	12 July	1708
5 Joseph,	"	28 July	1699	12 Priscilla,	"	7 March	1710
6 Shadrach,	"	18 April	1701	13. James,	"	16 March	1712
7. Christopher,	"	4 March	1703	14. Abigail,	"	15 Nov	1713

Sarah, wife of Ephraim Thayer, died 19 Aug. 1751, aged 79 years and 5 months.

"1757, June 15.　Died Ephraim Thayer, suddenly, in the 88 year of his age—occasioned, as is supposed by a violent blow in his forehead, with the sharp end of a rail, at the barn door, where he was found dead.　A great concourse of people attended his funeral."—[*Church Records.*

When Mr. Thayer was 84 years of age, he married a second wife, (Mrs. Mary Kingman, widow.)　She was a pious, good christian, and the tradition is, that his children provided for her comfort, in her old age, with dutiful attention.

VERSES, on the death of Mrs. SARAH THAYER, written in the year 1751.　By Edward Chesman, Braintree.

Good people all I pray attend,
　To what I've got to say,
Concerning one that's dead and gone,
　Death summon'd her away.

An ancient handmaid of the Lord,
　The wife of Ephraim Thayer,
Who lately from us has deceased;
　Her praise I will declare.

No. 2.   SARAH THAYER,
the oldest child of Ephraim and Sarah Thayer, married

This person now of whom I write,
  Is worthy of our praise ;   [died,
With God she walked, in Christ she
  She sprung from goodly race.

Her grand-father, he was a man
  Who did the truth reveal,
And to defend Christ's kingdom great,
  He burned with holy zeal.

Like holy Abraham of old,
  Left land and kindred all,
And wandering up and down, he went
  Wherever God did call

From old England he did come o'er,
  Where heathen did possess,
For to enjoy religion pure,
  And God this man did bless —

And made him once a ruler here,
  Let's not forget his fame
He lived above the age of man,
  JOHN ALDEN was his name.

Her other grand-father, elder was,*
  In Braintree church of old ,
He lived an holy, honest life,
  To his praise let it be told.

Also her father was a man
  Who lived to good estate ;
He lived an honest, holy life,
  And died a hopeful saint.

She wedded was in youthful days,
  To Mr. Ephraim Thayer,
He lived a good religious life,
  This truth I can declare.

They lovingly together lived,
  And never did provoke—
But like two lambs they did agree,
  And both pulled in one yoke.

The time she lived a married life,
  Was fifty-nine years and more—
The whole time of her pilgrimage,
  Lack'd some months of four-score.

Also she was a fruitful vine,
  The truth I may relate—
Fourteen was of her body born,
  And lived to man's estate

From those did spring a numerous race
  One hundred thirty-two—
Sixty and six each sex alike,
  As I declare to you

And many of them went to war,
  The enemy to suppress,
And all returned safe home again,
  The Lord this race did bless.

And one thing more remarkable
  Which here I shall record—
She'd fourteen children with her
  At the table of the Lord

Now the time comes that she must die,
  God calls his handmaid home—
She obeys his voice most cheerfully,
  Saying Blessed Lord I come.

Then sending for her children all,
  And counsel'd them aright,
For to obey Jehovah's call,
  And serve the Lord of might.

And having ended thus her work,
  Her breath she did resign—
Into thy hands I do commend
  This spirit, Lord of mine.

Her weeping friends stood round her bed
  Closed up her eyes of clay—
Then for her funeral did prepare—
  In dust they did her lay.

Could you have seen the numerous race
  That did for her lament—
In number more than Jacob had,
  When down to Egypt went.

Good people all, both far and near,
  Count it a heavy frown,
When God sends his messenger death,
  To cut the righteous down.

The nineteenth of August she did die,
  Seventeen hundred fifty-one—
Her body here in dust doth lie,
  Her soul to rest has gone.

Good people all, attend the call,
  In her decease of late—
And walk with God as she hath done,
  And he will bless your state.

*Dea. Samuel Bass was indeed a candidate for the office of ruling elder,
and votes were given for him, for Dea. Brackett, and for Mr. Kinsley, but
Mr. Hancock, in his cent. sermon, page 23, says, "I suppose Mr. Brackett
and Mr. Bass refusing, the lot fell upon Mr. Kinsley." (See Bass, No 1)

Seth Dorman, 4 Aug 1715, and settled in Norton. Their children were,

1 Micaiah,	born 5 March 1717	4 Ruth,
2. Sarah,		5. Judith,
3 Mercy,		6 Phœbe.

The widow Sarah Dorman died at Braintree 12 June, 1753.

No. 3.   1 A.   MICAIAH DORMAN,

the only son of the preceding, married Mary, daughter of Jonathan Smith of Sudbury, Mass , by whom he had one son, 1. Jonathan, born in Mansfield, a non compos mentis, who died in Willington, Ct. about 1804.

His second wife was Charity,* a daughter of Edward and Elizabeth White, by whom he had one son, 2. Jabez, born 26 April, 1773, who married Eunice Calkins of Mansfield, Ct 19 Feb 1795. She was born 28 Oct. 1772. They lived in Willington till after the death of his father, when he removed to Caroline, County of Tompkins, New York, where they are still living. They have no child. Mrs. Charity Dorman died in Willington about 1783, in the fortieth year of her age.

His third wife was Eunice Kingsley of Lebanon, Ct. (her mother was a Bass) She died about 1833, at the age, it is supposed, of nearly one hundred years Mr. Dorman died 15 Jan. 1809, aged nearly 92 years.

No. 4.   II A.   SARAH DORMAN,

a sister of the preceding, was married very young to a Mr Peabody, and settled in the vicinity of Mansfield, Ct. and had by him two sons, John and Isaac, who both afterwards had families.   They lived very happily together, enjoying

---

O strive to live religious lives,	So fare you well her numerous race,
And not like Balaam vile,	These few lines I do pen,
Desire to die a righteous death,	That you may seek Jehovah's face,
And live a life defiled.	And serve the Lord Amen.

These lines are here perpetuated, more on account of the historical facts therein contained, than the style in which they are composed

*She was a true descendant of Mr William White, and from the first born son of New England.   Her grandfather was Edward, a son of Peregrine White, according to the family tradition.   Her father was Edward White, whose wife was Elizabeth Castel   Their children were, 1 Henry, who settled in Colebrook, Ct. where his sons are still living   He had one by the name of Peregrine.   2 Edward, who had a son Edward, a grandson Edward, and an Edward of the next generation.   3 Abijah—4 Royal— 5. Charity—6. Eunice, whose husband was Samuel Perry   Jabez Dorman's wife had an uncle James Dunham, whose wife was Experience White, of the same descent

the Love of God and of each other. They both died in one
hour and were buried in one grave.—[*J Dorman, MS.*

No 5   III A   MERCY DORMAN,

a sister of the preceding, was married to Benjamin Porter
of Braintree, 20 Nov 1744, where they lived a number of
years. They afterwards removed to Wendell, Mass
    Their children were,

1. Micaiah,	born 26 April	1745	6. Seth,	born 6 Feb 1755
2. Eli,	" 25 March	1747		Died 27 April same year.
3. Ruth,	" 26 Oct	1748	7. Daniel,	born 21 Oct 1757
4. William,	" 15 Aug	1750	8. Noah,	" 21 July 1760
5. Job,	" 24 April	1753		

    Mr. Benjamin Porter died at Wendell, in 1793.

No. 6.   I B.   MICAIAH PORTER,

a son of the preceding, was graduated at Brown Universi-
ty in 1775 He married Elizabeth, the eldest daughter of
Capt. Isaac Gallup of Voluntown, Ct. (part of which is now
Sterling,) Nov. 1781, the evening after his ordination. She
was descended from Capt. John Gallup,* killed in the
" Naraganset swamp fight," of 1675 —[*Goodrich's Hist. U.
S.* 41, 35 edit. She is now living at Plainfield, N. H.
    Their children were,

1. Isaac,	born 11 Oct	1783	5 An Infant,	born Feb 1791
2 William,	" 11 Feb	1785		Died same month.
	Died 13 Nov 1816		6 John,	born 25 Jan 1795
3 Benjamin,	born 11 May	1788	7 Jabez,	" Dec 1797
4 Phebe,	" 11 March	1790	8. Martha,	" Feb 1799

    Rev. Micaiah Porter died 4 Sept. 1829.
    After completing his theological studies with the Rev.
Dr Levi Hunt of Preston, Ct Mr Porter travelled through
the Southern States as a preacher, and occasionally preached to the army in Virginia. He was settled in the ministry at Voluntown in 1781, where he remained the pastor
of the first church and society until Aug. 1800, when that
relation was dissolved After supplying vacant places for a
few years, he was installed pastor of the first church and
society in Plainfield, 17 July, 1805. He was able to per-
form ministerial labours till within four or five years of
his death
    Mr. Porter possessed a mind well stored with various in-
formation—easy and affable in his manners—of great conversational powers, and was endowed with an ardent evan-

*The murder of Mr John Oldham, by the Indians, was avenged by Mr.
John Gallup, in Aug. 1636.—[*Hist. of U S.*

gelical spirit, with an easy flow of speech, well adapted to extemporaneous speaking.

No. 7.   I C.   ISAAC PORTER, M. D.

graduated at Brown University 1808, and at Dartmouth received a Medical degree in 1814, commenced the practice of Medicine at Lebanon, N. H in 1816, removed to Charlton, Mass where he continued till 1825, when he removed to Boston, where he still resides.

He married Amey, daughter of Capt. William Potter of Cranston, R. I. 11 June, 1817. She was descended from one who received the Charter from Charles II. with Roger Williams and others. Their children are, 1. William Micaiah, born 18 March, 1818—2 Joseph Kennicutt Potter, born 25 July, 1819—3 Phebe Rebecca, born 5 April, 1824 —4. Isaac Gallup, born 21 Aug. 1827.

No. 8.   II C.   WILLIAM PORTER,

was an Instructer of youth, in which he spent four years in Freetown and vicinity, until his health declined, in which state he continued four years and died at his father's house in Plainfield, in the 32 year of his age

No. 9.   III C.   Dr BENJAMIN PORTER,

commenced the practice of Medicine at Northfield, Vt. in 1816.   He married Sophia K Fulerton, 9 June 1822 Mrs. Porter was born 3 July, 1801   Their children are,

1. Elizabeth P. born 17 March 1823 | 3. Ewen,   born 21 April 1826
2. Edward,   " 24 April 1826 | 4 Benjamin F. " 20 April 1833

No. 10   IV C.   PHEBE PORTER,

an eminent and devout christian died unmarried, 24 June, 1819, in the 29 year of her age.

No. 11.   VI C.   JOHN PORTER, M. D.

received his Medical Degree at Dartmouth College in 1820, and settled at Duxbury, Mass He married Ann, the youngest daughter of John and Lucy Thomas of Marshfield, 19 July, 1829.   Their children are,

1. John Thomas, born 27 Aug 1830 | 2 George K.   born 9 Feb   1833

No. 12.   VII C.   JABEZ PORTER,

lives in Plainfield with his surviving parent, "following the directions of St. Paul, preferring a single state "

No. 13.   VIII C.   MARTHA PORTER,

was married to the Rev. Charles Walker, 8 Aug. 1827.
Rev. Charles Walker was born at Ringe, N. H. 21 Nov.
1795, was graduated at Dartmouth College, Aug. 1823,
was ordained at New Ipswich, 28 Feb 1827   Their children were,

1. Charles Porter, born 12 Nov 1828 | Henry L   died 11 June   1833
2. Henry Lankton, " 29 Apr 1830 | 3. Henry Lankton, b 23 Mar 1833

Mrs Walker died 30 July, 1834, leaving her friends to
mourn her premature departure, in the 36th year of her
age.   She had made a profession of religion in 1817.

No. 14.   IV A.   RUTH DORMAN,

a daughter of Seth and Sarah Dorman, married David
Vinton, (See French, No. 22, 3,) and lived in Braintree
and Stoughton, and afterwards removed to Willington,
Conn where they spent their days   Their children were,

1 Mary,   born 27 Oct   1748 | 7. Ruth,   born 21 Sept   1761
2. Samuel,   "   9 Oct   1750 | 8. Sarah,   "   6 July   1763
       Died 14 Dec. 1751. | 9. Naomi,   " 17 March   1765
3. Elizabeth, born 27 Feb   1752 | 10 William,   " 21 Jan   1767
4 Samuel,   "   7 Sept   1754 | 11. Azubah,   "   1 April   1769
5 Seth,   "   6 June   1756 | 12. Phebe,   "   3 Feb   1772
6 David,   " 18 March 1759 |

No 15.   I B.   MARY VINTON,

a daughter of the preceding, married John Howard of
Braintree, about 1767   They afterwards lived in Stoughton and had two children. 1 Mary—2. Zilpah.

No. 16.   I C.   MARY HOWARD,

married William Hall, and settled in Stoughton. Their
children were, 1. William—2. John—3 Nathan—4. Joseph
—5 Benjamin.

Her second husband was William Page, and their children, 6 Mary—7. Catharine.

No. 17.   II B.   ZILPAH HOWARD.

married William Linfield 3d of Randolph about 1789.
Their children were, 1. William—2 Zeno—3. Ephraim—4.
Noble—5. a daughter—6. Jefferson. William and Ephraim
died young

No. 18.   II C.   ZENO LINFIELD,

married Angelina, daughter of Simeon Thayer, late of
Randolph. (See Thayer No 29, 1) Their children are,

1. Angelina,   born 7 May 1819 | 3. Henry Thayer, born 25 Aug 1831
2. Isaac Newton, " 17 Aug 1821 |

No. 19.   VI C. JEFFERSON LINFIELD,
married Eliza Sprague, and settled in Randolph.   Their children are 1 William—2 Mary Zilpah.

No. 20   III B.   ELIZABETH VINTON,
a daughter of David and Ruth Vinton, married James Niles of Braintree, about 1771.

No 21.   IV B   SAMUEL VINTON, .
a brother of the preceding, married Hannah Allen of Stoughton, about 1775   They removed to Stafford, Ct. and afterwards to the County of Onondago, N. Y.

No 22.   V B   SETH VINTON,
a brother of the preceding settled at Willington, Ct.

No. 23   VI B.   DAVID VINTON,
a brother of the preceding, settled at Stafford, Ct where he spent his days, and was buried.

No. 24.   VII B   RUTH VINTON,
a sister of the preceding, married Shadrach Thayer, and settled at Monson, Mass. (See Sixth Branch, No. 111.)

No. 25.   VIII B.   SARAH VINTON,
a sister of the preceding, married Stephen Cross.   Their children were,

1. Hannah,   born 26 Aug   1779
2 a Son,   " 10 March   1782
   Died same year.
3. a Daughter, born 7 March   1783
   Died same year.
4 Polly,   born 26 Feb   1784
5. Stephen,   " 26 Jan   1787
   Died 2 April 1833
6. Amos,   born 29 Oct   1787

Died May 1791.
7 Sally,   born 16 Feb   1792
8 Lyman,   " 9 Nov   1794
9 Cyrus,   " 16 April   1797
10. Lucinda,   " 17 Jan   1800
   Died March 1802.
11 Eli,   born 8 Aug   1803
12 Porter,   " 15 July   1807

No 26   IX B.   NAOMI VINTON,
married Nathan Lilly, and settled in Mansfield, Ct.

No. 27.   XI B.   AZUBAH VINTON,
married John Fuller, and settled in Willington, Ct.

No 28.   XII B   PHEBE VINTON,
married a Mr. Root, and removed to Ohio.

24

No 29   V A.   JUDITH DORMAN,
a daughter of Seth and Sarah Dorman, married Isaac Lovell of Weymouth, 12 Jan 1738, and settled in Mansfield, Ct. They had three sons, Isaac, Seth and David. Isaac was a deacon of the Baptist Church.

No. 30.   PHEBE DORMAN,
a daughter of Seth and Sarah Dorman, married Martin Dorsent, and settled in Keene, N. H.

SECOND BRANCH.

No. 1.   EPHRAIM THAYER, Jr.,
married Mary, daughter of Thomas Copeland, 1 April, 1718. (See Copeland, No. 2,) and settled in Braintree.
   Their children were,

1. Ephraim,   born 29 March 1720
       Died 22 May 1720
2. Mehitable,   born 17 April   1722
       Died 9 June 1731.
3. Mary,   born 27 April   1725

4. William,   born 9 July   1727
       Died 25 June 1731.
5 Ephraim,   born 6 Oct   1730
       Died 30 June 1731.

No. 2.   III A.   MARY THAYER,
the only surviving child of the above, married James Packard of North Bridgewater. (Cary says his father was "James Packard, who married a Keith, was one of the first deacons in the North Parish, had two sons, *James* and Reuben, and three daughters, Kezia, Jemima, and Rebecca. Kezia married Nehemiah Lincoln—Jemima married Ichabod Edson—Rebecca married Ensign Luke Perkins. Dea. James Packard died 1765, aged 75.

   1. *James*, married a *Thayer*, (as above,) they went to the westward   2. Reuben, married a Perkins ; they removed to Hebrom, Me." p. 25.)
   The children of James and Mary Packard, were,

1. Luke,
2 James,
3. Israel,
4. Ephraim,

5. Eve,
6. Contentment,
7. Mary.

No. 3.   I B.   LUKE PACKARD,
married, but where he settled is not known

No. 4. II B.   JAMES PACKARD,
married a Churchill, and had one daughter Keziah, and perhaps other children.

No. 5. IV B.   EPHRAIM PACKARD,
married Charity, oldest daughter of Capt. David Packard.
[*Cary*, p. 21.
It has been said, they had nine children. They removed from Bridgewater, probably with the rest of the family.

No. 6. V B.   EVE PACKARD,
married Benjamin Robinson of East Bridgewater. Their children were,

1. Anna,
2. Deborah,
3. Susannah,
4. Benjamin,
5. Kilbourne,
6 May,
7. Hodijah.

No. 7. I C.   ANNA ROBINSON,
married Uriah Brett, and settled in E. Bridgewater. Their children were, 1. Diana—2. Sidney—3. Royal—4. Sarah.

No. 8. II C.   DEBORAH ROBINSON,
married John Alden, and settled in Minot, Me. Their children were, 1. Benjamin—2. Mary—3. Alvina—4. Charles.

No. 9. III C.   SUSANNAH ROBINSON,
married Ichabod Keith, and settled in E. Bridgewater.
Their children were, 1. Edwin—2. Eleanor—3. Francis—4. Ralph—5. Mary.

No. 10. IV C.   BENJAMIN ROBINSON,
married Mary Packard. Their children were, 1. Benjamin R.—2. James L.—3. Elijah P.—4. Mary.

No. 11. V C.   KILBOURN ROBINSON,
lives in East Bridgewater, unmarried.

No. 12. VI C.   MARY ROBINSON,
married a Mr. Bradbury, and settled in the State of Maine. Their children were, 1. Edward—2. Malinda—3. Jane.
She has since married a man by the name of Kerrick.

No. 13. VII C.   HODIJAH ROBINSON,
married Sylvia Orr. Their children were, 1. Lucy Ann—2. Herbert.

No 14 VI B. CONTENTMENT PACKARD,
married Isaac, son of Eliphalet Kingman —[*See Cary*, p 19
They had a son Robert, and perhaps other children.

No 15 VII B MARY PACKARD,
a sister of the preceding, married a Prince, and it is said
had a large family

THIRD BRANCH.

No 1. PHILIP THAYER,
a son of Ephraim and Sarah Thayer, married Mary Wilson of Braintree, 1 April, 1718, and settled in Braintree,
afterwards removed to Norton or Mansfield. Their children were,

1 Sarah,	born 17 Nov	1719	4 Ephraim,
2 Elisha,	" 27 Nov	1721	5 John,
3. Philip,	baptized	1724	6 Christopher.

No 2 I A SARAH THAYER,
married Stephen Grover Their children were, 1 Judith
—2. Sarah—3 Jedidiah

No 3 II A ELISHA THAYER,
married Anna Grover, and settled in Mansfield, Mass
Their children were,

1. Anna,	born 1 April 1763	8. Archippus,	born 30 Mar 1779
2. Ebenezer,	" 21 March 1765	9. Abigail,	
3. Susannah,	" 11 July 1767	10. Rachel,	" 2 Sept 1781
4 Isaac,	" 31 Aug 1769	11 David,	" 21 Sept 1784
5 Zenas,	" 21 Dec 1771	12. Jonathan,	
6. Lois,	" 6 March 1774	13 Sylvia,	" 9 Sept 1786
7. Jacob,	" 22 April 1777		

The 4 first, the 6th, the 9th and 10th, are dead—the 5th
and 8th are supposed to be dead.

No. 4. III B SUSANNAH THAYER,
married Scott Fuller, and had one child Caleb, and perhaps others.

No 5. IV B ISAAC THAYER,
was said to have married and had one child

No. 6. VI B. LOIS THAYER,
married Levi Lane, and settled at Mansfield. Their chil-

dren were, 1. Lyman—2. Lewis—3 Lois—4 Levi—5
Granville.

No 7. V C.   GRANVILLE LANE,
married Roxana Wilber, and settled at Somerset, Mass.
Their children were, 1. Mary—2. an Infant

No 8 VII B   JACOB THAYER,
married Mary Anne Malonia, and settled in West Stock-
bridge, Mass   Their children were, 1 Gilbert—2 George
—3 Ebenezer—4 Mary Anne—5 Amanda Maria.

No 9 VIII B. ARCHIPPUS THAYER,
it was said married, but where he settled is not known
He is supposed to be dead

No 10 IX B   ABIGAIL THAYER,
married Ezekiel Fuller, and settled in Attleborough, Mass.
Their children were, 1 Hiram—2 Alfred—3 Ezekiel—4
Tisdale—5 Guilford—6. William—7 Sylvia.

No 11. XI B   DAVID THAYER,
is living in Attleborough, unmarried

No 12. XII B   JONATHAN THAYER,
married Keziah Turner, and settled in Worcester, N. Y
They had one son William
    His second wife was Nancy Bates

No 13 XII B   SYLVIA THAYER,
married George Brooks, and settled at Mansfield, Mass

No 41 IV A   EPHRAIM THAYER,
a son of Philip and Mary Thayer, went to sea when quite
young, returned to England and connected himself with
the British Navy   It is said, that by his perseverance and
good conduct, in the service of his sovereign, he was pro-
moted from grade to grade, until he was appointed Admi-
ral of one of His Majesty's fleets. He came to this country and visited his friends not long before the American
Revolution.

No 15 V A   JOHN THAYER,
a brother of the preceding, married Rachel Skinner Their
children were, 1. Ephraim—2. John—3 James.

No 16   VI A   CHRISTOPHER THAYER,

a brother of the preceding, married Bathsheba Skinner. Their children were, 1. Christopher—2. Bathsheba—3. Sally—4 Perne.

FOURTH BRANCH.

No. 1.   HANNAH THAYER,

a daughter of Ephraim and Sarah Thayer, married Nathaniel Blanchard,* and settled in Braintree. Their children were,

1. Ephraim,	born 18 March 1725	5. Nathaniel,	born 19 April	1734
2. Sarah,	" 8 April 1727	6. Nehemiah,	" 10 Feb	1736
3. Hannah,	" 1 March 1729	7. Joseph,	" 24 Jan	1739
4. Abigail,	" 28 Aug 1731			

Her second husband was William Noyes, married 8 May, 1765.

No. 2.   I A.   EPHRAIM BLANCHARD,

a son of the preceding, married Polly Hall. Their children were,

1. Elizabeth,			5. Polly,
2 Ephraim,	born	1754	6. Lucy,
3. Abigail,	" 3 July	1759	7. Chloe.
4. Joseph,			

His second wife was Anna Capen, married 3 Jan. 1779. 8. Joseph, born 16 Feb 1781.   (See 8 Branch, No. 42.) Ephraim Blanchard died 3 April, 1797, aged 72 years 15 days.   Anna, widow of Ephraim Blanchard, died 15 Oct. 1808, aged 72.

No. 3.   I B.   ELIZABETH BLANCHARD,

married Bartholomew Thayer, in 1789, and settled in Peterborough, N. H.   (See 11 Branch, No. 1, 12.)

No. 4.   II B.   EPHRAIM BLANCHARD, Jr.,

married Sarah Hayden of Braintree, 9 Jan. 1783, and settled at Braintree, and died in Oct. 1805, without issue.

---

* Nathaniel Blanchard was probably born in Weymouth, a son of Nathaniel and Dorothy Blanchard, who afterwards settled in Braintree.

Their children born in Braintree were, Hannah, born 14 March, 1710—Mary, born 22 Feb. 1713—John, born 22 March, 1715.

There was a Nathaniel Blanchard of Weymouth, in 1662.—[*Farmer.*]

No. 5. VI B.   LUCY BLANCHARD,
married John Blaisdel, and had three children, 1. Abigail
—2. Ephraim—3. Thomas Penniman

No. 6. VIII B.   JOSEPH BLANCHARD,
the son of Ephraim and Anna Blanchard, married Dorothy,
a daughter of Seth Spear, 31 May 1804, and settled in
Quincy. Mrs. Blanchard was born 16 Sept. 1778. Their
children were,

1. Mary Adams, born 27 Feb 1805 | 3. William Prior, born 30 Jan 1814
2. Hiram Washington, b 7 Jan 1811 |

Mrs Blanchard died 30 Jan. 1822, aged 43 years 8 mos.
Mr. Blanchard died 8 Aug. 1825, aged 44 years, 6 months.

No. 7. I C.   MARY ANN BLANCHARD,
married Charles Breck of Quincy, 2 May, 1827, and settled
in Milton. They have one child, Mary Elizabeth, born 26
May, 1829.

No. 8. III A.   HANNAH BLANCHARD,
perhaps a daughter of Nathaniel and Hannah Blanchard,
married Clement Hayden of Braintree, 26 Nov. 1762.

FIFTH BRANCH.

No. 1.   JOSEPH THAYER,
a son of Ephraim and Sarah Thayer, married Sarah Faxon
of Braintree, 16 Dec. 1725. Their children were,

1. Joseph, born 1 May 1727 | 3. Mehitable, born 19 Sept 1730
2 Sarah, " 1 Dec 1728 | 4 Sarah, " 17 April 1732
Died 11 Oct 1730. | 5. Abigail, " 26 Oct 1733

His second wife was Eunice Ludden, married 16 Nov.
1738.

6. Huldah, born 12 Aug 1739 | 10. Betty, born 25 March 1747
Died 19 April 1752. | Died 11 May 1749.
7. Reuben, born 27 Jan 1741 | 11. Timothy, 2d born 4 March 1748
8. Timothy, " 17 Oct 1743 | 12. Betty, 2d " 23 May 1751
Died 23 July 1749. | Died 4 April 1752.
9. Eunice, born 3 July 1745 |

No. 2. I A.   JOSEPH THAYER, Jr.,
married Zilpah Lane, and settled in Stoughton. His sec-

ond wife was Sarah Richards   Mr Thayer died in Jan.
1818, without issue Mrs Thayer afterwards married Dea
Zacheus Thayer of Randolph   (See 11 Branch, No. 11.)

No. 3   IV A   SARAH THAYER,

a sister of the preceding, married Moses, son of Ephraim
and Moses Jones   (See Copeland, No. 57, 2.)   They had
one son, 1 Moses, born 30 May, 1759.   Mr Jones married
a second wife Dorothy   Their children were,

Abraham,	born 4 Dec	1760	Joseph,	born 12 Feb	1766
Sarah,	" 26 Dec	1762	Prudence,	" 7 Jan	1768
John,	" 3 June	1764	Mary,	" 10 Feb	1770

Sarah was the wife of Capt. William Thayer. (13 Branch,
No 30.)

No. 4   V A.   ABIGAIL THAYER,

a sister of the preceding, married Christopher Capen of
Stoughton, (now Canton)   (See 8 Branch, No. 42)

No. 5.   VII A.   REUBEN THAYER,

a brother of the preceding, married Sarah Linfield of Braintree, 17 Sept. 1768, and settled at Braintree   Their children were,

| 1. Caleb, | born 5 Aug | 1770 | 3 Joseph, | born 25 Aug 1785 |
| 2. Timothy, | " 2 Feb | 1773 | | |

No. 6.   I B.   CALEB THAYER,

a son of the preceding, married a Tileston, and setttled in
Sterling, Conn   They had six or more children.

No 7.   II B.   TIMOTHY THAYER,

a brother of the preceding, married and settled in Providence, R. I. where he died, leaving several children.

No. 8.   IX A.   EUNICE THAYER,

the surviving daughter of Joseph and Eunice Thayer, married John Wales, 29 Aug 1772.   (See Wales, No. 15, 8)
They had one son, 1 John, born 25 Oct 1774.   Her second husband was Jonathan Curtis of Stoughton, married
about 1785, by whom she had one son, 2. Jonathan, born
22 Oct. 1786.   Mrs. Curtis died March, 1808.

No 9.   I B.   Capt. JOHN WALES,

son of the preceding, married Olive Pendergrass, and settled in Randolph. Mrs Wales was born 4 Dec. 1774. Their children were, 1. Olive, who died about the year 1804—2. Varrannes—3 Apollos

No. 10. II C. VARRANNES WALES,

married Maria, a daughter of Capt. Thomas White of Randolph, and have one son John.

No. 11   III C.   APPOLLOS WALES,

married Lucinda Faxon of Randolph

No. 12.   II B.   JONATHAN CURTIS, Jr ,

was graduated at Dartmouth College in 1811; was settled in the ministry at Epsom, N H 22 Feb. 1815 ; dismissed 1 Jan. 1825, settled in Sharon, Mass 12 Oct. 1825 ; dismissed in 1834, and settled in Pittsfield, N. H 1 Oct 1834 He married Betsey Barker of Concord, N. H.   Their children were,

1 Jonathan Strong, b. 23 Dec 1817	5 Mary Kent, born 28 Dec 1825
Died 14 Feb 1819	6. Elizabeth, " 24 Jan 1828
2. Sarah Barker, born 28 Sept 1819	7. Theodore Alden, b 23 Jan 1831
3 Jona Strong, 2d b 11 June 1821	8 Ellen Annette, b. 23 March 1833
4. Thos.W.Thompson,b 18Apr 1823	

SIXTH BRANCH.

No. 1.   SHADRACH THAYER,

a son of Ephraim and Sarah Thayer, married Rachel, a daughter of Samuel and Anna White of Braintree, 2 May, 1723. (See White, No. 14, 8, first part.)   Their children were,

1 Uriah, born 15 Oct 1724	3 Noah, born 30 Dec 1727
2. Jonathan, " 31 Jan 1726	4 Rachel, " 1 April 1730

Mr. Thayer died 17 Feb. 1783, in the 82 year of his age.

No. 2. I A.   URIAH THAYER,

married Deborah Copeland of Braintree.   (See Copeland, No. 12.)   Their children were,

1. Ebenezer, born 27 July 1749	8 Abner, born 28 Sept 1760
2 Uriah, " 22 Dec 1750	9 Hannah, " 16 July 1762
3. Deborah, " 25 May 1752	10. Abner, 2d , " 31 May 1764
4. Rachel, " 15 Feb 1754	11. Titus, " 26 Jan 1766
Died unmarried 29 Jan 1798, æ. 44	12. Stephen, " 11 Nov 1768
5. Mary, born 7 Oct 1755	13. Ezra, " 25 Jan 1770
6 Samuel White, " 4 June 1757	14. Betsey, " 5 May 1773
7. David, " 18 Jan 1759	

Mr. Thayer died 10 March, 1797, aged 72 years 5 months, nearly. Mrs. Thayer died 21 Oct. 1805.

No. 3.　I B.　EBENEZER THAYER,

married Deborah Wild of Braintree, 15 Sept 1770. Their children were, 1. Deborah, born 25 May, 1772—2. Charlotte—3. Samuel—4. Ebenezer His second wife was Lydia West, married about 1779. Their children were,

5. Elihu,　　born 7 Aug　1784 | 6 Lydia,　　born 15 March 1787

Mr. Thayer died 4 April, 1800, aged 50 years 8 months. All the children of his first wife died young, except the oldest.

No. 4.　I C.　DEBORAH THAYER,

married Zenas Packard, a son of Simeon Packard, and grandson of Zacheus Packard of North Bridgewater, (see Alden, No. 36, first part,) and settled in N. Bridgewater. Mr. Packard was born 22 May, 1771. Their children were,

1. Deborah,	born	9 Jan	1795	6. Benjamin Alden, b. 5 Sept 1806
2. Charlotte,	"	2 Oct	1796	7. Mary Perkins, b. 8 May 1808
3. Zenas,	"	29 March	1798	8. Lorenzo Emerson. b 6 Aug 1810
4. Hosea,	"	19 March	1800	9. Horatio, born 26 Feb 1813
5. Rachel,	"	12 Sept	1803	10. Lydia Thayer, b. 21 April 1815

No. 5.　I D.　DEBORAH PACKARD,

married Samuel Holmes, and settled in East Bridgewater. Mr. Holmes was born 25 Aug. 1793. Their children were,

1. Alpheus,	born 11 July	1814	5. Mary Perkins, born 19 Jan 1822
2. Deborah,	" 28 May	1816	Died 13 Aug 1825
3. Elizabeth,	" 12 April	1818	6. Abner Hayden, born 11 Dec 1823
4. Sam'l Martin,	" 15 March	1820	7. Thomas Ellis, " 16 Jan 1828
			Died 21 March same year.

Mr. Holmes died 17 Dec. 1827.

No. 6.　II D.　CHARLOTTE PACKARD,

married Joseph Wild of Braintree, and settled in North Bridgewater. Their children were,

1. Zenas Packard,	born 16 Oct 1818	Susan Ann, died 7 Jan 1824.
2 Joseph Allen,	" 23 Mar 1820	5. Deborah, born 2 Oct 1824
3. Charlotte Temple,	" 2 Oct 1821	6 Susan A. Coburn, b. 2 Mar 1827
4. Susan Ann,	" 23 Mar 1823	7. Benjamin, born 15 March 1829

No. 7.　III D.　ZENAS PACKARD, Jr.,

married Jerusha, daughter of Isaac and Esther Norton, (see first part, Thayer, No. 21, 4,) and settled in North Bridgewater. Their children were,

1. Jerusha,   born 13 Mar 1822 | 4. Ezekiel Reed, born 13 Oct 1827
2. Betsey French, " 16 Apr 1823 | 5. Hermon, " 26 Nov 1830
3. Benjamin, " 23 Mar 1825 |

No. 8. IV D. HOSEA PACKARD,

married Roxana Holmes, and settled North Bridgewater.
Their children were,

1. Celia,	born 24 Feb	1819	Henry died 25 Aug 1828.
2. Hosea,	" 4 April	1821	5. Ebenezer, born 24 March 1828
3. Roxana,	" 21 Sept	1824	6 Jerome Henry, born 16 Aug 1830
4. Henry,	" 3 Dec	1825	

No. 9. VI D. BENJAMIN A. PACKARD,

married Rhoda Packard, and settled in North Bridgewater.
Their children were,

1. Benj. Winslow, b. 5 Sept 1829 | 2 Andrew Franklin, b. 13 Mar 1831

No. 10 VII D. MARY P. PACKARD,

married William Lewis, and settled in North Bridgewater.
Mr. Lewis was born Aug 1802. Their child, 1. Mary Elizabeth, born 1 Oct. 1831.

No. 11. II B. URIAH THAYER,

the second son of Uriah and Deborah Thayer, married
Phebe Hayden, and settled in Braintree. Their children
were,

1. Phebe,	born 31 Jan	1782	7. Joseph,	born 16 March 1796
2. Uriah,	" 13 March	1784	8. Thomas, died in infancy.
3. Rachel,	" 21 Jan	1786	9. William H. born 3 Aug	1799
4 Charlotte	" 25 Aug	1788	10. Relief,	" 7 Feb	1802
5. Ephraim,	" 31 May	1791	11. Albert,	" 26 March 1804
6. Sally,	" 22 June	1793		

Mr. Thayer, died 22 April, 1805, in the 55 year of his age.

No. 12. II C. URIAH THAYER,

married Thankful, daughter of Lieut. Peter Dyer, and
grand-daughter of Zachariah Thayer. (See first part,
Thayer, No. 55, 10.) Their children were,

1. Thankful,	born 7 Feb	1807	5. Elias,	born 10 April	1815
2 Uriah,	" 31 Dec	1808	6. Rachel,	
3. David,	" 8 April	1811	7. Richmond,	
4. Warren,	" 11 March 1813	8. Elias Appleton.	

No. 13. I D. THANKFUL THAYER,

married Titus Thayer, 2d. son of Stephen Thayer. (See
No. 64.)

No. 14. III C.   RACHEL THAYER,

a daughter of Uriah and Phebe Thayer, married William Cleverly, (now Coolidge,) and settled in Quincy. Mr Coolidge was born 26 July, 1787   Their children were,

1. Phebe Thayer, born 17 Mar 1805
2. William Beals,   "   30 Aug 1807
3. Charles,   "   9 July 1809
4. Lucy Ann,   born 3 Aug   1812   Died June 1813.
5. Lucy Ann.

No. 15. I D.   PHEBE T. COOLIDGE,

married Ebenezer Richards, and settled in Weymouth.

Their children were, 1. Charles Newcomb—2. *unknown* —3. Ebenezer—4. George.

No. 16. II D.   WILLIAM B COOLIDGE,

married Maria Tirrell, and settled in Weymouth.

No. 17. V D.   LUCY ANN COOLIDGE,

married Prince Nash, and settled in Weymouth.

No. 18. IV C.   CHARLOTTE THAYER,

a daughter of Uriah and Phebe Thayer, married Samuel Newcomb, and settled in Braintree. Mr. Newcomb born 15 Oct 1786. Their children were,

1. Charlotte,   born 11 Sept   1807
2. Nathaniel,   "   16 May   1810
3. Samuel Gardner, b. June   1813   Died Sept 1814
4. Mary Ann,   born Sept   1814
5. Abigail,   "   May   1819
6 Francis Henry,   "   Feb   1831

No. 19. I D.   CHARLOTTE NEWCOMB,

married Capt Levi White, and settled in Braintree. Their children were, 1. Levi—2. Southerland Douglas—3. an infant.

No. 20. II D.   NATHANIEL NEWCOMB,

married Harriet, daughter of Lemuel Bent, and settled in Braintree. They have one child, Harriet, born in 1833.

No 21. V C.   EPHRAIM THAYER,

a son of Uriah and Phebe Thayer, married Salome Burrill of Weymouth, and settled in Braintree   Their children were, 1 Salome—2 Nancy Ann—3. Charles Henry.

Mr. Thayer died of consumption, 22 Nov. 1832.

No. 22. VI C   SALLY THAYER,

a sister of the preceding, married Nathaniel Hayden, and

settled in Braintree. Their children were, 1. Nathaniel,
born 11 Nov. 1811—2. Sally, born 10 Nov. 1813—3. Jonathan—4 Joseph—5. William—6. Albert—7. Henry—8. Albert—9. Bartlett—10 *unknown*.

No. 23. VII C JOSEPH THAYER,

a brother of the preceding, married Drucilla Penniman, and
settled in Randolph She died without issue. His second
wife was Evelina Stetson (See No. 51, 2) Their children were, 1. Joseph Henry—2. George Washington—3.
Drucilla—4. Elmeda.

No. 24. IX C. WILLIAM H. THAYER,

a brother of the preceding, married Lucy Clark, and settled
in Randolph Their children were, 1 William—2. Lucy
—3. Napoleon—4. Atkins—5. *unknown*.

No 25. X C RELIEF THAYER,

a sister of the preceding, married Caswell Pool, and settled
in Randolph Their children were, 1 Caswell Gardner—
2. Thomas Atwood—3 John Phillebrown—4 Laura Ann
Relief—5. Charles Norris—6. George—7. Emmory.

No. 26. XI C. ALBERT THAYER,

a brother of the preceding, married Clarissa White, and
settled in Braintree or Randolph. Mrs. Thayer was born
8 Jan 1800.

No. 27. DEBORAH THAYER,

a daughter of Uriah and Deborah Thayer, married Sherebiah Arnold, 10 Aug. 1777, (see first part, Arnold, No. 13,)
and settled in Braintree. They had one son, 1. Sherebiah,
born 15 July 1778. Mr Arnold died 13 June, 1778 Mrs.
Arnold, a widow, died 10 May, 1793, aged 41 years.

No. 28 I C. SHEREBIAH ARNOLD,

married Rachel Wild Arnold, daughter of Joseph and Ruth
Arnold. (See first part, Arnold, No 15, 3.) Their chil-
dren were, 1 Rachel—2 Sherebiah Joseph—3. Ruth.
  He married a second wife and removed to Maine

No. 29. V B. MARY THAYER,

a daughter of Uriah and Deborah Thayer, married Samuel
Belcher, who are now living in Randolph Mr. Belcher
was born 3 Aug. 1761. Their children were,

1. Polly,	born 29 April	1784	5. Sarah,	born	1 Sept	1792
2. Samuel,	" 10 Oct	1786	6. Deborah,	"	12 Sept	1796
3. Jonathan,	" 6 Oct	1788	7. Linus,	"	27 Dec	1801
4. Elizabeth,	" 5 Jan	1790		Died in infancy.		

No. 30. I C.   POLLY BELCHER,

married Samuel Bass in 1802, (see first part, Bass No. 22, 2,) and settled in Braintree, Vt. Their children were,

1 Samuel Belcher, born 2 Jan 1804	6 James,	born 12 April 1814
Died 18 Jan 1805	7. Harriet,	
2. Samuel Belcher, b. 15 Nov 1805	8. Harriet, 2d,	
3 Jonathan Belcher, b. 26 Dec 1807	9. Josiah,	
4. Mary, born 27 Jan 1810	10. John Quincy Adams,	
5. Elizabeth, " 26 May 1812	11. Savill, died an infant.	

No 31. III D.   JONATHAN B BASS,

married Emily Kidder, and settled in Braintree, Vt.

No. 32   II C.   SAMUEL BELCHER, Jr ,

married Amanda Bill, and settled in Braintree, Vt. Their children were, 1. Samuel White, born 18 Aug. 1813—2. Linus, born 16 April, 1816—3. Amanda—4. Jonathan Wales. His second wife was Polly Hutchinson. 5. Sewall Hutchinson—6. Deborah—7. Samuel.

No. 33. III C. JONATHAN BELCHER,

married Sally, daughter of Col. Simeon White, (see first part, White, No. 25, 12,) and settled in Randolph. Mrs. Belcher was born 16 March, 1796. Their children were,

1. Sarah White, born 30 Nov 1821	3. Mary Thayer, born 18 Sept 1830
2. Jonathan White, " 14 Nov 1823	

No. 34. IV C. ELIZABETH BELCHER,

married Amos Wardner, and settled in Roxbury, Vt. Their children were, 1. Amos, born 10 Dec. 1815—2. George Washington, born 27 July, 1817.

No. 35. VI C. DEBORAH BELCHER,

married Jonathan Thayer, (No. 136,) and settled in Randolph.

No. 36. VI B. SAMUEL WHITE THAYER,

a son of Uriah and Deborah Thayer, married Esther French, 9 May, 1780, (see Ninth Branch, No. 35, 2,) and settled in Braintree ; afterwards removed to Wrentham, where he spent his days. Their children were,

1. Sam'l White, born 26 June 1783	6. Anna,	born 29 June 1796
2. Elisha, " 15 Sept 1785	7. a Son,	
3. Esther, " 19 Jan 1788	8. Silas,	" 21 Oct 1798
4. Mary, " 23 Jan 1791	9. Susannah,	" 9 Feb 1801
5. Ezra, " 18 Sept 1793	10 Sylvanus,	" 28 Nov 1803

Mr. Thayer died 3 Jan. 1816, in the 59th year of his age.

No. 37.   I C.   Dr. SAMUEL W. THAYER,

commenced the study of Medicine, under the tuition of Dr. Ebenezer Alden of Randolph, with whom he continued until about the time of his death in 1806. (See first part, Alden, No 40.) He completed his studies under the instruction of Dr. Elias Weld of Amesbury, Mass. about the year 1809, settled in Braintree, Vt. and afterwards removed to Thetford He married Ruth, the oldest daughter of Dea. Eliphalet Packard of Winthrop, Me. 7 Oct. 1813. She was born 19 Sept. 1786. Their children were,

1 Ruth Barrell, born 10 May 1816	6. Abigail Weld, born 10 Oct 1821
Died 11 May, same year.	Died 12 Oct same year.
2. Sam'l White, born 21 May 1817	7. Rushbrook, born 29 Sept 1822
3. Mary George, " 28 Dec 1818	8. Jas. Cary Barrell, b. 10 Aug 1824
4. Ruth, " 16 Nov 1820	9. Ruth Swan, born 30 April 1826
Died the same day.	Died 22 Aug 1827.
5. Elias Weld, born 10 Oct 1821	10. Darwin, born 2 Feb 1828
Died 11 Oct same year.	The 5th and 6th were twins.

No. 38.   II C.   ELISHA THAYER,

(the principal author of this Memorial,) was educated in Medical Science and Practice, under the instruction of Dr Jonathan Wales of Randolph, (see first part, Wales, No. 11, 4,) and settled first in Bethel, Vt. and in the autumn of 1815 removed to Dedham, Mass. He married Nancy Billings of Canton, 8 July, 1813. (See first part, Billings, No. 31, 4.) Their children were,

1. Nancy Billings, born 1 Sept 1814	4 John Henry Bass, b. 8 June 1830
2. Elisha French, " 2 Dec 1815	5. George Heber, born 18 Dec 1831
3. Maria. " 1 May 1821	

No. 39.   I D.   NANCY B. THAYER,

married John Bass Arnold of Braintree, 26 Nov. 1829, a son of Samuel V. Arnold, (first part, Arnold, No. 14, 3,) and settled in Braintree. Their children were,

1. Samuel Vinton, b. 21 April 1831	3. Maria Angenette, b. 8 Jan 1835
2. Edmund Soper, b. 13 March 1833	

No. 40.   III C.   ESTHER THAYER,

married Elias White of Attleborough, Mass. and settled in

Wrentham, afterwards removed to Bangor, Me. Mr. White was born 3 Oct 1787. Their children were,

1. Esther Thayer, b 2 April 1815 Died 23 Oct 1834.
2 Samuel Thayer, b. 26 Sept 1816
3 Charles French, b. 27 Sept 1818
4 Mary Ann, born 22 Feb 1820 Died 22 Oct 1834.

No 41.　IV C　MARY THAYER,

married Lewis George of Wrentham, with whom she lived about a year, and died 21 May, 1818, aged 27 years and 4 months, without issue.

The following lines, written by herself, and found among her papers, after her death, are indicative of the state of her mind

"No meaner things, their ravished eyes behold,
Than robes of white and crowns of radient gold—
Sceptres and thrones beyond the lofty sky,
With golden harps and palms of victory.
O may this soul, when stript of mortal clay,
Mount to those realms of bright celestial day ;
To dwell forever on that peaceful shore,
Where sighings cease, and sins disturb no more "

Capt. Lewis George died 11 June, 1834, aged 44 years. Capt George was a kind husband, and in his own neighbourhood, and wherever known, he was respected for his kindness and undissembled friendship

No. 42.　V C.　EZRA THAYER,

married Huldah Carpenter of Wrentham, and now lives in Taunton Mrs. Thayer was born 8 Nov 1794. Their children were,

1. Ezra George, born 8 March 1821
2 Elizabeth C. born 29 Nov 1822
3. William Walker, b. 8 May 1825
4. Esther French, born 31 Jan 1827
5 Abner, died the day of his birth
6 Ann Maria, born 10 July 1829 Died 24 Dec 1829
7 Charles Bradford, born Apr 1833
8. Sylvanus, born 31 March 1835 The 5th and 6th were twins.

No. 43.　VIII C.　SILAS THAYER,

married Rebecca Carr of Rhode Island, and lives in Sharon, Mass. Their children are,

1. John Alden, born 8 March 1823
2 Rebecca Davis, " 23 April 1825
3. Silas Lysander, born 28 Dec 1827
4. Anne Eliza, " Dec 1834

No. 44.　IX C　SUSANNAH THAYER,

married Otis Cheever of Wrentham Their children were,
1. Alonzo Williams, b. 27 Feb 1831 | 2. Ann F Malvina, b. 4 Sept 1833

No 45.　X C.　SYLVANUS THAYER,

married Rebecca Crossman of Taunton, and settled in

Wrentham. Mrs. Thayer was born 23 March, 1806. Their children were,

1 Harriet,	born 17 July 1827	3. Abby Elizabeth, b 18 Aug 1831	
2. Henry Allen,	" 11 May 1829	Died 14 Dec 1834.	

No. 46. VII B.   DAVID THAYER,

a son of Uriah and Deborah Thayer, married Anna French, 16 Oct. 1783, (see Ninth Branch, No. 36,) and settled in Braintree. Their children were,

1. David,	born 19 Feb 1784	2. Anna,	born 8 Aug 1785

Mr Thayer "died with a mortification on one of his fingers, 27 March, 1785, after a few days' complaint, viz : at meeting one Sabbath, and dead the next."—[*Records.*

Mrs Thayer afterwards married Dea. Eliphalet Packard of North Bridgewater, who removed with his family to Winthrop, Me.

No 47 I C   DAVID THAYER,

died in the flower of his age, with Diabetes, 27 April, 1806, at the age of 22 years and 2 months, much lamented by all his connexions and acquaintance.

No. 48. II C.   ANNA THAYER,

married Samuel Floyd of New Sharon, Me. and now lives in Winthrop. Their children were,

1 Eliza Ann,	born 11 Aug 1815	3 Silas Thayer, born 10 Oct 1820	
2. Sally,	" 9 Nov 1817	4. Albion, " 27 June 1823	

VIII. B. ABNER THAYER, a son of Uriah and Deborah Thayer, died 29 Aug. 1762, at the age of 1 year and 11 months.

No. 49. IX B.   HANNAH THAYER,

a daughter of Uriah and Deborah Thayer, married John White of Randolph, 25 Oct 1781. (See first part, White, No. 25, 5.) Their children were,

1. John,	born 31 May 1782	4. Ruth,	born 13 Nov 1787
2. Hannah,	" 18 March 1784	Died in infancy.	
3. Charlotte,	" 3 Jan 1786		

Mrs. White died 6 Jan. 1788, aged 25 years 6 months.

No. 50. I C.   JOHN WHITE,

married Olive Linfield, (see first part, White, No. 24,) and settled in Thetford, Vt. Mrs. White was born 17 May, 1786. Their children were,

26

1. a Son, } born 5 April 1811 | 4 Olive,
2. Daughter, } | 5 John,
3. Sarah Ann, " 15 June 1813 | 6 John.

No. 51. II C. HANNAH WHITE,

married Jeremiah Stetson, 1 Dec 1803, and settled in Weymouth. Mr. Stetson was born 1 Sept. 1776. Their children were,

1. Mary,	born	5 Oct	1804	6 Harriet Newell, b. 2 March 1815	
	Died 18 Oct same year.			7. David Brainard, b 1 Feb 1817	
2 Evelina,	born 25 Nov		1805	8 Anson,	born 18 Jan 1821
3. Hiram,	" 14 Nov		1807	9. Julia Ann,	" 14 Dec 1823
4. Lucinda,	" 17 Jan		1811	10. Henry Martin, " 18 Dec 1825	
5. Louisa,	" 8 July		1813		

II D. EVELINA STETSON,

married Joseph Thayer, (see No. 23,) and settled in Randolph.

No. 52. IV D. LUCINDA STETSON,

married William Burrill, and settled in Weymouth. They have one child.

No. 53. III C. CHARLOTTE WHITE,

married Benjamin Thayer, and settled at Weymouth. (See 10 Branch, No. 5) Her second husband was Stephen Blanchard, by whom she had one child.

No. 54. X B. ABNER THAYER, 2^d

a son of Uriah and Deborah Thayer, married Persis Turner, and settled in Turner, Me. Their children were,

1. Abner,	born 22 May	1791	10. Mary,	born	6 May	1807	
2. William,	" 27 Nov	1792	11. Lucius,	"	28 Feb	1809	
	Died 5 Aug 1803.		12. Jane,	"	1 Oct	1810	
3. Sarah Rand,	born 31 Aug	1794	13 Emma,	"	17 Jan	1812	
4. Persis,	" 27 June	1796		Died Feb 1833.			
5. Charles,	" 8 Aug	1798	14 Francis,	born 28 Sept		1814	
6 Rushbrook,	" 23 May	1800	15. Harriet,	" 7 March		1817	
7. John,	" 16 Jan	1802	16. Henry,	" 5 Sept		1819	
8. Evelina,	" 17 Oct	1803		Died 4 Sept 1820			
9. William,	" 20 Aug	1805	17. Henry,	born 1 March		1821	

No. 55. I C. ABNER THAYER,

was a Master Mariner, in which occupation he was employed many years ; but in consequence of a long series of misfortunes, he abandoned the sea, purchased a farm, and now lives in Bangor, Me. He married Elizabeth H. Taber of New Bedford, and settled in the city of New York. They had one child born there, viz : 1. Harriet Eliza, born 17 Feb. 1819 or 20. Mrs. Thayer died June, 1821. He has since married a second wife.

No. 56   III C.   SARAH R. THAYER,
married Charles Cushing, and settled in Turner. Their children were,

1 Mary E.	born 28 June	1822	5. Persis,	born 15 June	1828
2 Sarah,	" 5 Nov	1823	6. Charles,	" 28 Oct	1829
3 Francis,	" 13 Feb	1825	7. John T.	" 30 Sept	1831
4 Deborah T.	" 18 Jan	1827			

No 57.   V C   CHARLES THAYER,
married Amelia Towne, and settled in Foxcroft, Me   They have one child, Persis T. born 13 March, 1830.

No 58.   VI C   RUSHBROOK THAYER,
married Harriet Walker in 1833, and settled in Foxcroft.

No 59.   VII C.   JOHN THAYER,
married Temperance F Cushing, and settled in Turner. Their children were,

1. Elizabeth Tabei, b. 7 March 1829 | 2 Lydia Ann T. b. 5 March 1830

No. 60.   VIII C   EVELINA THAYER,
married Elisha Daggett, and settled in Foxcroft. Their children were,

| 1 Mary T. | born 13 March 1828 | 3 Evelina, | born 1 June | 1831 |
| 2. Matilda, | " 17 May 1829 | Mrs. Doggett died 2 Oct 1831. | | |

No. 61.   XI B.   TITUS THAYER,
a son of Uriah and Deborah Thayer, married Susannah Sprague of Boston, and settled in Braintree. Their children were,

1. Susannah, born in 1794	3. Susannah, born 24 Dec 1798
Died 8 Jan 1798 aged 3 years 6 mos.	4. John Hancock, } " 12 July 1801
4. John Hancock, born in 1796	5. James, }
Died 12 July 1798, aged 2 years.	

No. 62.   III C.   SUSANNAH THAYER,
married Robert Milton Thayer of Braintree. Mr. Thayer was born 17 Dec. 1799. Their children were,

1. Susannah, born 9 Sept 1818 | 2. Lydia Jane, born 29 March 1820

No. 63.   IV C.   JOHN H. THAYER,
married Louisa Holbrook of Randolph, and settled in Brain-

tree. Mrs. Thayer born 16 Oct. 1802. Their children were,

1. Quincy Adams, b 10 Mar 1825
2. Lucinda Ann, born 2 Nov 1826
3. Lois Livia, born 30 Dec 1828
4 an Infant, " 14 Sept 1832

No. 64. XII B. STEPHEN THAYER,

a son of Uriah and Deborah Thayer, married Sally, daughter of Ezra and Hannah Shaw of Abington, (see Copeland No. 15, first part,) and settled in Braintree. Their children were,

1. Stephen, born 6 Jan 1794
2. Betsey, " 25 Jan 1796
3. Sally, " 8 Dec 1798
   Died 1 Aug 1809.
4 Hannah, born 15 March 1801
5. Stephen, 2d., born 14 May 1803
6 Titus, " 22 Sept 1805
7. Mary, " 6 March 1807
8 Sally, " 19 Sept 1810

His second wife was Mary Shaw, sister of his first wife. Lieut. Stephen Thayer died Oct. 1823.

No. 65. II C. BETSEY THAYER,

married Ezra Shaw of Abington, by whom she had one child, 1. Henry.

No. 66. V C. STEPHEN THAYER,

married Sarah Shaw, and settled in Abington. Their children were,

1. Sarah Ellis, born 20 Aug 1827 | 2 Mary, born Dec 1830

No. 67. VI C. TITUS THAYER, 2d.,

married Thankful Thayer, (See No. 13, I. D,) and settled in Braintree. Their children were,

1. Betsey Jane, born May 1827
2. a Daughter, " 28 Aug 1829
3 John, born 9 Dec 1830

No. 68. VII C. MARY THAYER,

married John H. Thayer, a son of Charles Thayer, and settled in Braintree.

No. 69. II A. JONATHAN THAYER,

the second son of Shadrach and Rachel Thayer, married Dorcas Hayden, and settled in Braintree. Their children were,

1. Nehemiah, born 11 Aug 1748
2. Dorcas, " 11 Dec 1752
3. Lydia, " 20 Nov 1755
4. Jonathan, born 15 June 1758
   Died in infancy.
5 Jonathan, born 10 April 1761

Capt. Jonathan Thayer died 18 Jan. 1805.
Mrs. Thayer died in Jan. 1814.

No. 70. I B.   NEHEMIAH THAYER,
married Sarah Hobart of Pembroke, Mass. in 1785. Their
children were,
1. Sally,   born 20 July   1787 | 2. an infant,   died 11 Jan 1792
Mrs. Thayer died 6 Jan. 1792. His second wife was
Mary Nash, married 2 July, 1798 Their children were,
3. Mary,   born 8 Jan   1800 | 4. Clarissa,   born July   1805

No 71. I C.   SALLY THAYER,
married Capt Isaac Dyer, a son of Leiut Peter Dyer of
Braintree Capt Dyer was born 8 Nov 1782' Their children were,
1. Jane Bailey, born 13 March 1807 | 4. Nehemiah Franklin,b.10 Jan1813
2. Isaac,   " 23 May   1809 | 5 Lorenzo.
3. Lavinia,   " 15 Feb   1811 |

No 72 I D   JANE B DYER,
married Warren Mansfield of Braintree   (See 13 Branch,
No 12)

No 73. III D   LAVINIA DYER,
married Hiram Wild of Braintree. They have one child,
1 Lavinia Ann, born 12 July, 1831.

No. 74 III C   MARY THAYER,
a daughter of Nehemiah and Mary Thayer, married Joseph
Dyer, a brother of Capt Isaac D and settled in Braintree.
Their children were, 1 Clarissa Thayer—2 Joseph—3.
Mary—4. Sarah—5. Eunice—6 Sarah, 2d —7 Lavinia—
8 Nehemiah

No. 75. IV C.   CLARISSA THAYER,
married Samuel Sanborn, and settled in Northfield, Vt.
Their child, 1. Samuel Roby.

No. 76 II B.   DORCAS THAYER,
a daughter of Jonathan and Dorcas Thayer, married Alexander White about 1778, and settled in Braintree. Their
children were,
1. Samuel, | 4. Thomas,   born 3 Jan   1786
2. Alexander,   born 12 Jan 1781 | 5. Dorcas,   "
3. Lydia, | 6. Jonathan,   " 13 Oct   1795
Mr. White died in Sept. 1814

No. 77 I C.   SAMUEL WHITE,
married Mary Hayward about 1801, and settled in Brain-

tree   Their children were, 1. Samuel—2. Edward—.3
Sarah C.—4. John—5 Bartimeus—6 Nehemiah—7. Mary.

No. 78. II C   ALEXANDER WHITE,
married Betsey Faxon, and settled at Braintree. Their
children were,

1. an infant, who died 23 Jan 1806 | 2. Elizabeth A   born 11 Mar 1807

Mrs. White died 23 March, 1807. His second wife was
Tirzah ——, who was born 14 Nov 1795. Their children
were,

3 Alexander,	born 14 Feb 1818	6 Nathaniel,	born 8 Dec 1824
4 Henry Augustus,"	13 Oct 1819	7 Caroline,	" 12 Feb 1828
5 Maria Fay,	" 31 July 1821	8. Jacob,	" 30 July 1831

No 79. III C.   LYDIA WHITE,
married James Bowditch of Braintree. Their children were,
1. Alexander—2 Dorcas—3. James—4. Alden—5. Mary—
6. Lydia—7. Almira.

No. 80. IV C   THOMAS WHITE,
married Matilda ——, who was born 8 July, 1786. Their
children were, 1 Ira Thomas, born 15 March, 1818—2.
Alexander

No 81. V C.   DORCAS WHITE,
married Benjamin Bowditch of Braintree. Their children
were, 1 Caroline—2 Benjamin F —3. Adoniram.
His second wife was Lydia Thayer. (See No 83, 1.)
Their children were, 4. Eunice—5. George—6. Gilbert.

No 82 VI C.   JONATHAN WHITE,
married Susannah ——, who was born 24 June, 1798, and
settled in Braintree. Their child, 1. Susan, born 26 May,
1827.

No. 83. III B   LYDIA THAYER,
a daughter of Jonathan and Dorcas Thayer, married Abraham Thayer of Braintree. (See first part, Thayer, No.
48, 7) Their children were,

1. Lydia,	born 12 Sept 1787	4. Nehemiah,	born 5 Jan 1795
2. Sarah,	" 15 Aug 1789		Died in youth.
3 Abraham,	" 24 Dec 1791	5 Jonathan,	born 27 April 1797
		6 Relief,	" 24 Feb 1799

Mr. Thayer died in Jan. 1819.

I C. LYDIA THAYER, married Benj. Bowditch. (See No. 81.)

No. 84.   II C.   SARAH THAYER,

married Charles Hayward of Braintree, had one child, 1.
Sarah Thayer, born 18 Jan. 1818. Mrs. Hayward died 15
Feb. 1818.

No. 85.   III C.   Col. ABRAHAM THAYER,

married Mary Nash Arnold, probably a grand-daughter of
Samuel Arnold, (first part, Arnold, No. 6,) and settled in
Weymouth   Their children were,

1 Nehemiah, born 12 Oct 1814	4 Mary Weston, born 25 Mar 1820	
2. Charles Hayward, b 12 May 1816	5 Abraham, " 10 Apr 1822	
3. Sarah Hayward, b. 18 Mar 1818	6. Cornelia, " 23 Aug 1824	

Mrs. Thayer died 1 Feb. 1825. His second wife was
Abigail ——, who was born 11 July, 1802.   Their children
were,

7. Benj. Bowditch, b. 5 July 1828 | 8 Caroline Cottonton, b. 14 Jan 1832

· No 86.   V C.   JONATHAN THAYER,

married Ruth Penniman, and settled in Braintree.   Their
children were, 1. Lucinda—2. Jonathan—3. Joseph Parker
—4. an infant.

No. 87.   VI C.   RELIEF THAYER,

married Gardner Penniman, a brother of Jonathan's wife,
and settled in Braintree. Their children were, 1. Lydia
—2. Catharine—3. Mary Relief—4. Sarah—5. Gardner—
6. Eliza.

No. 88.   V B.   JONATHAN THAYER,

the youngest son of Jonathan and Dorcas Thayer, married
Betsey Faxon, 9 May, 1780, settled in Braintree , afterward removed to Windsor, Vt then to Amherst, N H.
     Their children were,

1 Beulah, born 17 April 1781	6 Ludovicus, born 3 June 1793	
Died 9 Aug 1782.	Died 9 March 1794.	
2 Barnabas, born 28 Aug 1783	7. Ludovicus, 2d , born 17 Mar 1796	
3. Jonathan, " 6 Jan 1786	8 Joel F. " 3 Oct 1797	
4 Betsey, " 12 Aug 1788	9 Betsey, 2d , " 6 Jan 1800	
Died 8 March 1796	10 Lavinia, " 22 Feb 1802	
5. Beulah, 2d , born 22 Nov. 1790		

No. 89.   II C.   BARNABAS THAYER,

married Susannah Packard, and settled in Windsor, Vt. ;
afterwards removed to South Boston, Mass.
     Their children were,

1. Geo. Washington, b 28 Jan 1806 | 4 Eliza Hayden, born 15 June 1814
2 Edward Sumner, b. 19 Nov 1809 | 5. Joel—6. Susan.
3. Maria, who died 21 Aug   1813

No. 90. III C   JONATHAN THAYER,

married Sally Thayer, and settled in Braintree. Their children were,

1 Elizabeth F. born 21 Dec 1806 | 4. Sally Maria, born 10 March 1812
2 Jonathan L   " 8 Sept 1808 | 5. Almira,   " 21 March 1814
3. Joel E.   " 11 Nov 1809 | Died 10 March 1815.

No. 91. V C   BEULAH THAYER,

married David Holbrook, Esq of Braintree. Mr. Holbrook was born 6 Aug. 1782. Their children were,

1 Adeline,   born 19 Aug   1807 | 3 Joel Edwin,
2. David Alfred, " 11 March 1809 | 4. Elizabeth.

No 92. I D. ADELINE HOLBROOK,

married a Mr. Eales, and settled at Detroit in Michigan. Their child, 1. George.

No. 93. III D. JOEL EDWIN HOLBROOK,

married Susan, daughter of Capt Ralph Arnold of Braintree, 4 April, 1832   (See first part, Arnold No.   )

No. 94. IV D   ELIZABETH HOLBROOK,

married Elbridge Gerry Hayden of Quincy. (See 12th Branch, No.   .)

No. 95   VII C. LUDOVICUS THAYER,

married Rhoda Penniman of Windsor, Vt and settled there; afterwards moved to Orono, Me. Children not known.

No 96. VIII C   JOEL F. THAYER,

married Charlotte Fessenden of Boston, and settled in Woburn. After having studied the Science of Medicine, he relinquished the practice and is now a Druggist. Their children were,

1. Frederic Fessenden, born 17 Dec 1820—2. George Augustus, born 19 Oct 1824—3 Charles Edward, born 14 June 1828—4. Charlotte Ann, born 22 June 1834.

No. 97. IX C. BETSEY THAYER,

married Luther Damon of Hartland, Vt. and settled there. Their children not known.

No. 98. III A. NOAH THAYER,

a son of Shadrach and Rachel Thayer, married Margaret, a daughter of William and Sarah Harmon, who was born 23 April, 1731. Their children were,

†
1. Zachariah Marquand, born 1752
2. Noah, born
3. Margaret, " 8 Feb 1757
4 Shadrach, " 18 May 1759
5. Experience, " 28 April 1761
6. Michal, born 13 May 1765
7. Tamar, "
8. Meribah, " 1 May 1769
9 Mechech, " 29 March 1772
10. Leah, " 8 April 1774

Mrs. Thayer died in March, 1794.

No. 99. I B. ZACHARIAH M THAYER,

married Judith Crane, and settled in Braintree Their children were, 1. Ruth—2. Deborah His second wife was Sarah Gardner of Hingham, married about 1792. Mr. Thayer died 24 May, 1808, aged 56.

No. 100. I C. RUTH THAYER,

married a Williams, and had two children, names not known, nor where settled.

No. 101. II C. DEBORAH THAYER,

married Zachariah Godfrey, and had several children whose names are not known, nor where settled.

No. 102. II B ½ NOAH THAYER, Jr,

married Dorothy Hunt, 15 March, 1775, and settled in Randolph. Their children were, 1. Dorothy—2. Polly—3 Sally—4. Susannah—5. Tamar—6. Betsey—7 Leah, born 17 Feb 1788—8. Peter, born 23 Nov. 1789—9. Noah, born 20 July, 1792. Mr. Thayer died in May, 1803.

No. 103. I C DOROTHY THAYER,

married Issachar Everett, and settled in Wrentham. Mrs. Everett died in Oct. 1833.

No 104. II C. POLLY THAYER,

married Isaac Tower and settled in Randolph. Their children were, 1. Orimel—2 Isaac—3. Mary—4. Benjamin Franklin, born 24 April, 1806—5. Sally, b 25 Dec 1807—6 Elmira, b 11 July, 1810—7. Luther, b. 22 Feb 1813—8. Silas, b. 23 Sept. 1815—9. Lorenzo, b 14 May, 1820.

No 105. I D. ORIMEL TOWER,

married Phebe Thayer, and settled in Randolph. They

27

had one child born 8 Aug 1821.   Mrs Tower died 26 Jan.
1833, aged 33 years
" Her disease succeeded an extensive burn, which de-
stroyed nearly all the integuments and muscles of the feet.
She endured the spasms of this truly frightful disease with
a remarkable degree of fortitude ; and while perfectly sensible of the rapid approach of death, anticipated the event
with composure, and in the end calmly resigned herself
into the hands of her heavenly father.—[*Norfolk Advertiser.*

No. 106.   II D.   ISAAC TOWER, Jr.,
married Minora Brackett, and settled in Randolph.

No. 107.   III D.   MARY TOWER,
married Hiram Alden, a son of Simeon Alden, (see first
part, Alden No. 59, 1,) and settled in Randolph   Their
children were, 1 Hiram—2 Julia Ann—3. Charlotte—4.
an infant

No. 108.   IV D.   BENJAMIN F. TOWER,
married a Hollis, and settled in Randolph, and have children, names not known.

No 109   V D.   SALLY TOWER,
married Melvin Orr, and settled in North Bridgewater.

No. 110.   VI D.   ELMIRA TOWER,
married Winslow B Cushman, and settled in N. Bridgewater   It is said that all of the name of Cushman in New
England, are descendants of Elder Thomas Cushman, who
came to this country in 1620 or 21. His sons were Thomas,
Isaac, Elkanah and Eleazer —[*See Alden's Coll. 3, 253.*

No. 111.   III C.   SALLY THAYER,
a daughter of Noah and Dorothy Thayer, married Amos
Aldrich, and settled in Wrentham.   Mr. Aldrich was born
10 Feb. 1785.   Their children were,

| 1. Artemas, | born 3 Jan | 1809 | 4. Anson T. | born 14 Nov | 1814 |
| 2. Harriet E. | " 2 Nov | 1811 | | | |

No. 112.   I D   ARTEMAS ALDRICH,
married Jane T. Mann, and settled in Randolph.   Mrs.
Aldrich was born 23 March, 1808.   Their child, 1. Sarah
Jane, born 17 July, 1832

No. 113. IV C. SUSANNAH THAYER,

a daughter of Noah and Dorothy Thayer, married Isaac Spear, and settled in Boston Their children were, 1. Thomas Jefferson—2. George—3. Isaac—4. William—5. Henry, and five others, names not known.

No. 114. VI C. BETSEY THAYER,

a sister of the preceding, married Elisha Jones, and settled in Boston. Their children were,

1. Elisha,   born 3 Aug.   1804 | 2 James S.   born 7 Feb   1806

No. 115. VII C   LEAH THAYER,

a sister of the preceding, married the same Elisha Jones as above. Their children were,

1. George W. born 7 May 1808 | 3 Elizabeth, born 5 April 1812
2. Henry,   "   11 Feb   1810 | Died 17 April 1831.
       Died 16 April 1816. |

Her second husband is Dr. Paul R. Metcalf of Wretham
4. Paul S. born 7 May, 1828

No. 116. VIII C. PETER THAYER,

married Betsey Bird of Stoughton, and settled in Boston. Their children were, 1. Washington—2. Clarissa, who died an infant—3 Elizabeth—4 Peter.

No. 117. IX C.   NOAH THAYER,

married Amelia Howard, and settled in Randolph. They have had one child, 1. Amelia, born 6 April, 1817   Mrs Thayer died 6 April, 1817, aged 21 years   His second wife was Joanna, daughter of Meshech Thayer. (See No. 137.) Their children were,

2. Washington, born 21 Feb 1820 | 4. Elisha,   born 16 Aug   1823
3. a son,   "   22 Sept 1821 | Died 22 Sept 1825 .
     Died an infant of 6 hours. | 5. Luther Aldrich, b 12 Dec 1825
                              | 6.   born 28 Aug   1828

No. 118. III B. MARGARET THAYER,

a daughter of Noah and Margaret Thayer, married Joseph Steele, and settled in Washington, N. H. Their children were, 1. Tamar—2. Nancy—3 Hannah, 4 Margaret, twins —5. Zachariah, and others, names not known

No. 119. IV B. SHADRACH THAYER,

a son of Noah and Margaret Thayer, married Ruth Vinton, 18 Oct. 1779, (see first Branch, No. 25,) and settled in Monson, Mass. Their children were,

1 Betsey,	born 30 July	1780	5 John,	born 7 March 1788
	Died 13 July 1800.		6 Zachariah Mark, b. 16 Aug	1793
2. Ruth,	born 2 Dec	1781	7. Sally,	born 17 Feb	1795
3. Polly,	" 5 Jan	1784	8 Isaac,		
	Died 22 April 1804		9. Rebecca,	" 10 Jan	1797
4 Relief,	born 27 Feb	1786	10. Shadrach,	" 17 Aug	1799
	Died 17 April 1817.		11. Timothy,	" 16 June	1806

No. 120.   V B.   EXPERIENCE THAYER,

a sister of the preceding, married Samuel Crane, and settled at Bradford. Their children were,

1 Betsey,	born 5 March 1784	4. Samuel,	born 27 Jan	1795
2 Polly,	" 29 Oct	1787	5. Joshua,		
3. Sally,	" 11 Oct	1789	6. Ebenezer,	" 15 May	1798

No. 121. I C.   BETSEY CRANE,

married Micah Smith, and settled in Stoughton. Their children were, 1 Betsey Drake, born 14 Jan. 1810—2. Samuel Crane—3. Asahel—4. Ansel—5. Mary—6. Martha.

No. 122. II C.   POLLY CRANE,

married Gideon Denton, and settled in Braintree. Their children were, 1. Mary Francis—2. Anna Alden Loring—3. Jacob and Elizabeth, twins. Mr. Denton died in the prime of life.

No. 123. III C   SALLY CRANE,

married Dea Seth Littlefield of Easton, and settled in New Grantham, N. H

No. 124. IV C   Dea. SAMUEL CRANE,

married Roxana, daughter of Ebenezer and Abigail Crane of Stoughton. Mrs. Crane was born 8 Sept. 1796. Their children were,

1. Francis Bradford, b. 30 Mar 1817	3. Roxana,	born 8 June	1824
2 Samuel Lewis, born 28 May 1821		Died 16 Sept same year.	
	4 Ebenezer Austin, b. 18 Mar 1830	

No. 125. V C.   JOSHUA CRANE,

married Sally, a sister of Roxana, above named, and settled in Bradford, N. H. Mrs. Crane was born 11 July, 1798. Their children were, 1 Hannah Maria—2. name not known.

No. 126. VI C. EBENEZER CRANE,

married Mary Dyer Crane, another daughter of Ebenezer and Abigail Crane, and settled in Stoughton. Mrs. Crane was born 15 April, 1802. Their children were, 1. George Leonard—2. Henry Baxter—3. Mary Francis

No. 127. VI B. MICHAL THAYER,

daughter of Noah and Margaret Thayer, married Lemuel Capen of Stoughton, (perhaps No. 21, 5, Capen, first part,) and settled in Winthrop, Me. Their children were, 1. Hannah—2. Uriah—3. Dorcas, and others names not known.

No 128. VIII B. MERIBAH THAYER,

a sister of the preceding, married Aaron Littlefield of Randolph. Mr. Littlefield was born 2 Aug. 1759. Their children were,

1. Micah,	born 12 July	1786		7. Samuel, 2d.,	born 27 Feb	1802
2. Hannah,	" 26 Aug	1789		8 William,	" 11 April	1804
3. Samuel,	" 28 April	1791		9. Sally,	" 17 Nov	1806
Died 16 Aug same year.				10. John,	" 30 Mar	1809
4 Polly,	born 18 Nov	1794		11. a son,	" 24 Nov	1811
5. Thomas,	" 19 Feb	1796		Died in Dec same year.		
6. Aaron,	" 9 Oct	1798		12. Fanny,	born 29 Mar	1814

No. 129. II C. HANNAH LITTLEFIELD,

married William Linfield, 3d. of Randolph. (See 1st Branch, No 17.) Their children were,

1. Charles,	born 30 Oct	1808	3. Lucinda,	born 5 Sept	1813
Died Sept 1809.			4. Zilpha,	" 12 Feb	1820
2 Hannah,	born 22 Sept	1810	Died 5 Sept 1822.		

No. 130. IV C. POLLY LITTLEFIELD,

married John Wild of Randolph, son of William and Rachel Wild. (See first part, Thayer No. 35, 4) Their children were,

1. Mary,	born 24 Aug	1814	4. Daniel,	born 6 Sept	1820
2 Hannah,	" 2 March	1816	5. William,	" 26 Aug	1825
3. Malinda,	" 27 April	1818	Mrs. Wild died 8 Dec 1827.		

No. 131. V C. THOMAS LITTLEFIELD,

married Lucinda Sherman, and settled in Randolph. Their children were,

1. Anna Sherman, b. 29 May 1819	3. George Thomas, b. 11 Feb 1823
Died 9 Sept same year.	4. Seth, born 30 March 1825
2. John Sherman, b. 23 Sept 1820	5. Joseph Dana, " 8 Sept 1827
	And others, names not known.

No. 132. VI C. AARON LITTLEFIELD, Jr ,

married Emily Wales, (see first part, Wales No. 14,) and settled in Randolph. Their children were,

1. Ephraim Wales, b. 25 Nov 1821	4. Emily,	born 30 March 1827
2. George Wales, born 19 June1824	5 a daughter,	" 10 Sept 1829
4. Aaron, " 2 Sept 1825	6. a son,	" 19 May 1831

No. 133.   VII C.   SAMUEL LITTLEFIELD,

married Ruth Alger, and settled in Randolph. Their children were,

1. Eliza Ann, born 5 Oct 1827 | 3   born 21 April 1831
2.   " 29 July 1829

No. 134.   IX B.   MESHECH THAYER,

a son of Noah and Margaret Thayer, married Anna, daughter of Dea Zacheus Thayer, (see 11 Branch No. 11,) and settled in Randolph. Their children were,

1. Zacheus,	born 2 Aug 1795	4 Irene,	born 17 Sept 1804
2. Jonathan,	" 3 Feb 1797	5 Rachel,	" 27 May 1807
3. Joanna,	" 5 June 1799	6. Ephraim,	" 15 Sept 1812

No. 135.   I C.   ZACHEUS THAYER,

married Phebe, daughter of Micah White, Esq. of Randolph. (See first part, White No. 20) Their child, 1. Nancy, born 13 April, 1831

No. 136.   II C.   JONATHAN THAYER,

married Deborah Belcher. (See No 35.) Their children were,

1. Jonathan Edwards, b 9 Nov1823 | 3.
2. Calvin, born 3 April 1826

No. 137   III C.   JOANNA THAYER,

married Noah Thayer of Randolph. (See No. 117.)

No. 138.   IV C.   IRENE THAYER,

married Lyman Thayer of Randolph. (See 11th Branch, No. 5)

No. 139.   X B.   LEAH THAYER,

a daughter of Noah and Margaret Thayer, married Joshua Bradley, and removed to Middlebury, Genesee Co N Y. Their children were, 1. Malinda—2. Lucinda—3. Fanny—4. Joshua—5. Sapphira.

No. 140.   IV A.   RACHEL THAYER,

daughter of Shadrah and Rachel Thayer, married Capt. Eliphalet Sawin, a brave revolutionary officer, and settled in Randolph. He was probably a son of Joseph and Lydia

Sawin. (See first part, Paine No. 6, II B) Their children were, 1. Rachel, born 18 Sept. 1748—2 Sarah—3. Shadrach—4. Naomi—5. Amasa—6. Shadrach, 2d —7. Eliphalet—8. Eliphalet, 2d. Capt S. died 21 June 1802.

No. 141   I B.   RACHEL SAWIN,

married Isaac Thayer of Braintree, (see first part, Thayer No 55, 2,) and settled in Randolph. Their children were,

1. Vashti,	born 21 Feb	1771	4. Rachel,	
2 Shadrach,	" 22 July	1776	5 Eliphalet,	
3. Eunice,	" 21 Aug	1778		

No. 142   I C.   VASHTI THAYER,

married Ephraim Hunt, and settled in Canton. Their children were,

1. Vashti,	born 16 March 1791	6. Ephraim,	born	3 Feb	1803
2 Mary,	" 21 Feb	1794	7. Warren,	"	15 Feb	1805
3. John,	" 26 Jan	1796	8. William,	"	2 March 1807
	Died 8 Dec 1799.		9 Hannah,	"	8 May	1809
4 Nancy,	born 24 April	1798	10. Nathaniel,	"	26 Jan	1811
5. Ruth,	"	5 Nov	1800			

No. 143. I D.   VASHTI HUNT,

married Paul Thurston, settled in Canton ; afterwards removed to Boston, thence to Dorchester. Mr. Thurston was born 5 Feb 1788. Their children were,

1. Caroline,	born 11 March 1808	5. Mary Ann,	born 24 Dec	1815
2. Louisa,	" 25 Nov	1809		Died 19 March 1816.
3. Albert,	" 17 Jan	1812	6. Calvin,	born 5 Sept	1817
4. William,	" 29. Dec	1813		Died 15 Nov. same year.

Mr. Thurston died 20 Sept. 1821, aged 33 years. Her second husband was Luther Gates of Dorchester born 4 May 1800,

7. Henrietta,	} born 17 April 1825	9 Emily,	born 17 April	1828
8. Henry,	}	10 Vashti,	" 7 May	1830
	Died 9 Aug same year.	11. Wm. Warren	" 27 March 1832

NO. 144.   I E.   CAROLINE THURSTON,

married Josiah Blake and settled in Dorchester, Mr Blake was born 4 July 1808. Their children were,

1 William Josiah,	born 20 Oct 1828	3 Edward Francis, b. 3 Sept 1832
2. Henry Willard	" 6 Sept 1830	

NO 145   II E.   LOUISA THURSTON,

married Elnathan Cushing and settled in Scituate Mass. Their children were,

1. Louisa Maria, born 4 Dec 1826	William T died April 1832
2. Wm. Thurston " 18 Aug 1828	3. Isabella Jane, born 12 Aug 1831

No 146. II D.   MARY HUNT,
married William Andrews, and settled in Boston, had one child, 1 Charlotte born 7 March 1811, the wife of Abel Oakes of Providence R. I Their children are Mary and Charles Billings

No. 147. IV D.   NANCY HUNT,
married Benjamin Gates of Dorchester. Their children are,

1. Mary Ann, born 10 Aug 1817 | 2. Vashti, born 8 June 1819

    Mrs. Gates died 1 July 1829 aged 31 years

No. 148. V D.   RUTH HUNT,
married Lemuel Munroe of Boston, who was born 6 Feb. 1794, and died 19 Aug 1821. She had one child stillborn in Oct. 1821.

No. 149. VI D.   EPHRAIM HUNT,
married Elizabeth Holmes and settled in Milton Their children, were,

1. Nancy Elizabeth, born Nov 1829 | 2. Mary Davenport, born Jan 1832

No. 150. VII D.   WARREN HUNT,
married Ruth Dickerman and settled in Canton. Their child 1 Infant born 1 Jan. 1833 died 4 Jan. same year.

No 151. II C.   SHADRACH THAYER,
a son of Isaac and Rachel Thayer, married Dorothy Thayer daughter of Paul Thayer, (See first part Thayer No. 70, 3,) and had one son, 1 Peter born 8 March 1796, died 28 Nov. same year. Mrs Thayer died 25 Sept. 1796 aged 23 years.

    His second wife was Hepzibah Howard, born 13 Aug. 1773. Their children were,

1. Loring Howard, b 17 June 1798   Eliza died 4 Jan 1831
2. Joshua,   " 22 July 1800   6 Mary Ann, born 2 Dec 1808
3. Ansel,   " 14 July 1802   7 Simeon,   " 7 May 1811
4 Sarah,   " 24 Sept 1803   8. Harriet,   " 31 July 1813
5. Eliza,   " 19 Sept 1805   Died 9 Nov. 1823.

No. 152. I D.   LORING H. THAYER,
married Louisa daughter of Jonas Howard and settled in Randolph. Their children were,

1. Ann,   born 21 Aug 1822 | 3. Elisuna,   born 12 Oct 1829
2. Loring Williams, " 14 Feb 1824 |

No. 153. II D   JOSHUA THAYER,

married Malinda, daughter of Silas Alden, (See first part
Alden No 59, 3,) born 9 March 1803, and settled in Randolph. Their children were,

1 George Henry, born 30 Sept 1824 | 3. Augusta,   born 18 Oct 1830
2. Sarah Elizabeth, "   8 Feb 1829 |

No. 154. III D.   ANSEL THAYER,

married Sarah, daughter of John V Arnold, (see first part,
Arnold No 14, 1,) and settled in Randolph. Their children were,

1 Maria,   born 8 Jan 1825 | 3 Ansel,   born
2 John Vinton,   " 14 Oct 1826 | 4   " 13 Feb   1831

No 155. IV D   SARAH THAYER,

married Isaac Spear, and settled in Randolph. Their children were,

1. Isaac,   born 8 Sept   1822 | 3 James,   born   1826
2. Mary,   "   30 April 1825 | 4   "   1832

No. 156. V D.   ELIZA THAYER,

married Joseph Tower, and settled in Randolph   Their
children were,

1. an infant, who died. | 2 Abraham,   born Sept   1830

Mrs. Tower died 4 Jan 1831.

No. 157. VI D. MARY ANN THAYER,

married Charles Alden, son of Silas Alden, Jr., and grandson of Silas Alden, (see first part, Alden No 59, 3,) and
settled in Randolph. Mr. Alden born 28 Feb. 1810. Their
children were,

1. George Frederic, born 1 Oct 1829 | 2. Simeon,   born 2 Aug   1831
                                    | Died Sept same year.

No 158   III C. EUNICE THAYER,

a daughter of Isaac and Rachel Thayer, married Asa Howard, and settled in North Bridgewater. Mr. Howard was
born 24 Sept. 1776. Their children were,

1. Ephraim,   born 19 April 1798 | 6. Asa,   born 4 July 1813
2. Samuel,   "   12 July 1800 | Died 7 Oct 1814.
3. Charles,   "   18 April 1803 | 7. Asa,   born 28 Aug 1815
4 Isaac Thayer, "   7 May   1805 | Died 10 Sept 1817.
     Died 11 Sept 1822. | 8. Elizabeth, born 22 Feb 1818
5. Mary Ann,   born 24 Feb   1808 | 9 Martha Jane, " 15 June 1820

Mr. Howard died 23 Aug. 1828.

28

No. 159. I D. EPHRAIM HOWARD,
married Lydia Cary, and settled in N Bridgewater. Their
children were, 1. Lucian, born in Sept. and died in Dec.
1821—2 an infant daughter, born in Nov. and died in Dec.
1823. Mrs. Howard died 22 Feb. 1831.

No. 160. II D. SAMUEL HOWARD,
married Mary Carlton, and settled in North Bridgewater.

No. 161. III D. CHARLES HOWARD,
married Lavina Round, and settled in North Bridgewater.

No. 162. V D. MARY ANN HOWARD,
married William Faxon of North Bridgewater, and settled
there. Their children were,

1. Mary Ann, born 3 July 1826	3. Mary Ann, born 18 Oct 1830
Died 11 Sept 1826	4. Charles Howard, " 1 Sept 1832
2. William Henry, born 8 Apr 1829	

No. 163. VIII B ELIPHALET SAWIN, Jr.,
married Eunice Wild of Randolph, (see first part, Bass No
31, 6.) and settled there   Their children were, 1 Eliphalet—2. Daniel.

No 164 I C ELIPHALET SAWIN,
married Mary Adams of Milton, and settled there   Their
children were,

1. Henry, born 4 Jan 1805	4 Mary, born
2. Daniel Adams, " 10 June 1807	5. Arabella, " 15 April 1816
3. Lucy, died young.	Died young.

No. 165 II D DANIEL A. SAWIN,
married Sarah Mann of Randolph, and settled there.

No. 166. II C. DANIEL SAWIN,
a son of Eliphalet and Eunice Sawin, received his professional education under the instruction of Dr Jonathan
Wales of Randolph, and settled in practice in East Bridgewater   He married Hannah, daughter of Major Barrell of
the same town. Their children were, 1. Hannah Barrell
—2 Eliza
    Mrs. Sawin lived but few years after her marriage, but
while she lived she was an ornament to that circle in which
she moved ; not only as a wife, a mother, a friend to the
poor and needy, but as a *christian*, and died in the triumphs

of that religion she professed, greatly lamented.   Her
christian character and exalted virtues were the subject of
eulogy in the public prints after her decease   Dr. Sawin
married again and by his second wife had one son, 3 Daniel

Dr Sawin was eminent as a Practitioner in Medicine,
and in Surgery but few of his age excelled him   In all his
social relations he was highly esteemed, even before he
professed to be a subject of that religion, which became
the spring of all his actions in subsequent life, his solace in
death,and the foretaste of endless felicity beyond the grave
" His path was like that of the righteous, shining brighter
and brighter unto the perfect day."   He died in the midst
of life and usefulness

SEVENTH BRANCH.

No. 1.   CHRISTOPHER THAYER,

a son of Ephraim and Sarah Thayer, married Mary Morse,
and settled in Braintree   Their children were,

1. William,	born 22 Aug	1736	5 Amos,	born	5 April	1745
	Died 27 Jan	1756	6. Abigail,	"	20 Aug	1747
2 Sarah,	born 2 May	1738	7. Elizabeth,	"	14 March	1749
3. Christopher,	" 27 April	1741	8. Ruth,	"	1 July	1752
4. Mary,	" 7 April	1743	9. Susannah,	"	5 April	1755

Mr. Thayer died 10 Dec. 1787.

No. 2.   II A.   SARAH THAYER,

married James Collins, and settled in Boston.   Their children were, 1. John Morse—2. Sarah.

No. 3.   I B.   JOHN M COLLINS,

married Betsey Brackett of Peterborough, N. H. in 1798.
Their children were, 1. Sarah C.—2. John—3. Samuel—4.
Rebecca—5 Eliza.

No. 4.   II B.   SARAH COLLINS,

married a Mr. Partridge, residence unknown.

No. 5.   III A.   CHRISTOPHER THAYER, Jr.,

married Bethiah, a daughter of Ebenezer and Bethiah Hunt
of Weymouth, 12 Sept. 1766, (see first part, Adams No. 25,)
and settled in Peterborough, N. H   Mrs Thayer was born
30 Nov. 1744.   Their children were,

1 William,   born 25 Nov 1767
2 Mary, who died an infant.
3 Mary,   born 8 July 1771
4. Eber,   "   17 Aug 1773

5 Christopher, born 26 Dec 1776
6 Sarah,   " 12 Feb 1779
7 Joseph Adams, " 18 May 1781
8. Elihu,   "   1 May 1783

Mr. Thayer died 28 Sept. 1823   Mrs Thayer died 28 Feb. 1817.

No. 6. I B.   WILLIAM THAYER,

married Abigail daughter of Abijah Wyman of Ashby Mass 11 March, 1792, and settled in Peterborough, N H. Mrs Thayer was born 6 Sept 1774   Their children were,

1. Abijah Wyman, born 5 Jan 1796
2 Cephas Prentice, " 6 Sept 1797
3 Abel Wyman,   " 21 Sept 1799
          Died 27 Sept 1800
4. Stephen Wyman, b. 1 Aug 1801

5 Elizabeth Stearns, b. 23 Mar 1803
          Died 18 Jan 1817.
6 Abigail Smith, born 3 Dec 1804
7. Sarah Wingate,   "   6 July 1806
          Died 22 Jan 1807.

Mr. Thayer died 6 Aug 1807   Mrs Thayer died 11 July, 1818.

No 7. I C.   ABIJAH W. THAYER,

Editor and Publisher of the Essex Gazette at Haverhill, Mass married Susan, daughter of Jonathan Bradley of Andover, 9 Nov. 1824   Their children were,

1. Sarah Bradley, b 11 Sept 1825
          Died 3 July 1826.
2 Sarah Smith, born 6 Oct 1827

3 William Sidney, b 15 April 1829
4 James Bradley, " 15 Jan 1831
5 Susan Bradley, " 7 Oct 1833

No. 8. II C.   CEPHAS P THAYER,

married and lives in Cambridge, is also a Printer.

No. 9 IV C. STEPHEN W THAYER,

married and lives in Lunenburgh, Mass

No 10   VI C   ABIGAIL S THAYER,

married Royal B Hancock of Cambridge, in June, 1832, and on the 29 of the same month embarked for India, in the Missionary service at Maulmein, in the Burman empire.

No. 11   IV B.   EBER THAYER,

a son of Christopher and Bethiah Thayer, married Elizabeth, daughter of Dea Ebenezer Jaquith of Washington, N H. 16 June, 1805, and settled in Peterborough. Mrs. Thayer was born 25 April, 1780, died 30 Oct 1805. His second wife was Sarah Everett, who was born 21 May, 1785, married 8 May, 1817. Their children were,

1. Maria Everett, born 10 Mar 1818
2. Joseph Adams, " 25 Nov 1819
3. Richard Everett, " 21 Mar 1821
          Died 31 May same year.

4. Elizabeth Jaquith, b. 21 Oct 1822
5. Abigail,   born 27 July 1824
6. Stephen,   " 28 Oct 1827
          Died 20 Aug 1828

No 12. VI B. SARAH THAYER,
a sister of the preceding, married Elihu Penniman, Jr and
settled in Fitzwilliam, N H Their child, 1 Jos Adams.

No 13 VIII B. ELIHU THAYER,
a brother of the preceding, married Susan Everett, and
settled in Peterborough Their children were, 1 Eliza
Ann—2. William—3 Susannah—4 John—5 Sarah Penniman, who died in 1826—6. Martha—7 Charles, who died
in 1826—8. Nancy, who died in 1827—9 George.

No 14. IV A MARY THAYER,
daughter of Christopher and Mary Thayer, married John
Hunt, and settled in Belchertown, Mass Their child, 1.
Mary, and perhaps others

No 15. V A AMOS THAYER,
a brother of the preceding, married Hannah Damerell, and
settled in Braintree Their children were, 1 William—2
James—3 Susannah—4 Mary
  Mr Thayer died in Jan 1819

No 16 III B SUSANNAH THAYER,
married John G Holland, and settled in Boston. Their
children were, 1. William—2 Susannah G—3 James—4
name not known

No 17. IV B. MARY THAYER,
married Stephen Gore of Boston, and settled there Their
children were, 1 Mary—2 Hannah—3 Stephen—4 Za-
biah—5 Abigail—6. Lucretia—7 Susan—8 Samuel

No. 18 VII A ELIZABETH THAYER,
a daughter of Christopher and Mary Thayer, married John
Scudder of Boston, 13 Oct 1774 Their children were, 1
John, born 29 July, 1776—2. Abigail—3. Elizabeth—4 Polly
—5. James—6 name unknown.

No 19 I B JOHN SCUDDER, Jr,
married and settled in the city of New York He had by
his first wife one son John, and two daughters, who live
in New York He is the owner of an extensive Museum.

No. 20 VIII A. RUTH THAYER,
daughter of Christopher and Mary Thayer, married John

Field of Braintree, 11 Nov 1775, and settled in Peterboro.'
Mr Field was born in Quincy, 16 April, 1752. Their children were,

1. John,   born 27 Oct   1777
2. an infant who died.
3. William,   born 18 Nov   1782
4. Elisha,   "   2 Aug   1784
5 a son that lived two months

6. Jabez, who was drowned at the age of 4 years and 5 months.
7. Sally,   born   March 1791
8 Otis,   "   12 Jan   1794
9. Ruth,   "   3 April   1796
10. Mary,   ·   "   10 March 1798

No 21   I B.   JOHN FIELD, Jr,
married Beulah Reed, 20 June, 1802, who was born at New Ipswich, N H 15 Nov 1778, and settled in Peterborough. Their children were,

1 Adeline,   born 29 April 1803
2 Isaac,   "   11 July   1804
3. Louisa,   "   20 March 1806
4 Sylvina,   "   21 Dec   1807
5. Ruth,   "   22 June   1809
6 John,   "   22 Nov   1810
7. Horatio Nelson, b. 25 March 1813
8. William,   "   27 April 1814

9. Mary Ann,   born 22 Nov 1815
        Died 4 April 1816
10. Mary,   born 13 Jan   1817
11 Marcy Calista, " 23 Dec   1817
12. Sarah Thayer, "   3 Aug   1819
13 Louisa Jane,   " 14 June 1821
14. a son,   " 26 June 1822
        Died 8 Sept same year.

No. 22   I C.   ADELINE FIELD,
was married to James B Nichols, 4 Feb 1830 Their children were,
1. John Field, born 7 Jan   1831 | 2 James,   born 1 April 1833

No 23   III B.   WILLIAM FIELD,
married Mary McAllister, and settled in Peterborough They had fifteen children, 1. William Jackson, born 4 Jan 1808—2. Alexander Hamilton—the rest unknown

No. 24.   IV B.   ELISHA FIELD,
a brother of the preceding, has no children.

No 25.   VII B   SALLY FIELD,
married Noah Youngman, and has had five children.

No. 26.   VIII B   OTIS FIELD,
married Lydia Dodge, by whom he has had six children.

No 27.   IX B.   RUTH FIELD,
married David Youngman, had one son and died.

No 28.   X B.   MARY FIELD,
married Timothy Bruce, and has had four children.

No. 29 IX A. SUSANNAH THAYER,

the youngest daughter of Christopher and Mary Thayer,
married Lemuel Field, 19 Dec 1774, and he settled in
Belchertown, Mass They had one child, 1 Peter, born
and died in Braintree, in consequence of being scalded
His mother died about the same time He married again,
and has a number of children

EIGHTH BRANCH.

No. 1. RUTH THAYER,

a daughter of Ephraim and Sarah Thayer, married John
Capen, 20 Sept. 1722, and settled in Braintree. Their
children were,

1. John,		7 Elizabeth, born 22 May 1739
2. Esther,		8. Sarah,
3. Nathaniel, born in 1729		9. Ephraim, ⎫
4. Ruth,		10. Philip, ⎬ born 24 Mar 1745
5. Christopher, 1 May 1730		11. Samuel,
6. Anna, born 20 March 1737		12. Rebecca.

No. 2. I A. JOHN CAPEN, Jr ,

married Mary Williams, and settled in Dorchester. Their
children were,

1. John,	5 Mary,
2. Eunice,	6 Esther,
3. Elizabeth,	7. Susannah,
4. Ruth,	8. Sarah.

No. 3 III B ELIZABETH CAPEN,

a daughter of the preceding, married William Hobart, by
whom she had a family of children ; number and names
unknown.

No. 4. II A. ESTHER CAPEN,

a daughter of John and Ruth Capen, married Benjamin
Ludden of Braintree, and settled in Chesterfield Their
children were,

1. Esther,	born in	1746	8. Daniel,	born 6 Sept	1759
2. Anna,	" 23 Feb	1748	9. Ruth,	" 3 July	1761
3. Asa,	" 8 Feb	1750	10. Eunice,	" 29 April	1763
4. Esther,	" 9 Aug	1752	Died 15 Feb 1766.		
5 Eli,	" 3 June	1753	11. Milcah,	born 7 April	1765
6. Daniel,	" 3 May	1755	12 Eunice,	" 26 April	1767
7. Bezer,			13. Elisha,	" 10 March	1773

No 5. II B   ANNA LUDDEN,
married Sands Niles, about 1780, and settled at Fairlee,
Vermont. Their children were,

1. Nancy,	born 5 April 1781	4. Benjamin,	born 30 Aug 1787
2 Samuel,	" 28 Aug 1782	Died 18 July 1829.
3 Sands,	" 25 Oct 1785

  Mr. Niles died in Oct 1823.

No. 6 I C   NANCY NILES,
married Asa Southworth, and settled at W Fairlee Their
children were, Albert, Samuel, Asa, Nancy, Benjamin.
   Mrs Southworth died in Nov 1824.

No 7 II C.   SAMUEL NILES,
married for his first wife Betsey Kezer, and for his second
Abigail Wild, and settled at Thetford, Vt. Their children
were,

1. Harvey Hale, born 1 Oct	3. Edward Munroe, born Oct
2. George W.	" 11 Mar 1817	Mr Niles died 7 Jan 1827.

No 8 I D   HARVEY H NILES,
married Lucy C Heaton, and settled at Thetford, Vt.

No 9 III B   Dea ASA LUDDEN,
a son of Benjamin and Esther Ludden, married Deliverance Paine, and settled at Williamsburgh Their children
were, 1. Daniel—2 —— His second wife was a Moulton.
Their children were, 3 Betsey—4 Polly—5 Sally—6
Amelia—7 Judith, 8 ——.
   Mrs Ludden died 14 Feb 1830, aged 80 years

No. 10 IV B   ESTHER LUDDEN,
a sister of the preceding, married a Brown, and settled in
New Hampshire.

No. 11 V B   ELI LUDDEN,
a brother of the preceding, died in Aug. 1775, aged 22 years.

No 12 VII B.   BEZER LUDDEN,
married and settled at Chesterfield His children were,
1. Ruth, 2 Cynthia, 3. Bezer, 4. Clarissa He died at the
age of 58 years

No 13 VIII B DANIEL LUDDEN,
married and has nine children, and was living in 1833, in
Lower Canada, at the age of 74 years.

No 14 IX B   RUTH LUDDEN,
married a Damond, and died soon after, aged 22 years

No. 15. XI B   MILCAH LUDDEN,
married for her first husband a Brown, and for her second
a Gates, and settled at New York   Their children were,
1 Joseph B 2 Esther G 3 Joseph Brown, 4. Forest, and
two names unknown

No 16 XII B   EUNICE LUDDEN,
married Ralph Southworth, and settled in Fairlee, Vt
   Their children were,

1. Phinehas,	born 12 May	1792	5 Nancy,	born 11 June 1799
	Died 19 April 1831.		6 Elisha Niles,	" 2 Feb 1801
2 Irene,	born 12 Sept	1793	7 Horace,	" 2 Nov 1803
3 Milcah,	" 1 Feb	1795	8 Fidelia,	" 1 Nov 1805
4 Joseph,	" 11 Oct	1797	9 Ralph Bowen,	" 4 Aug 1809

No 17 III C   MILCAH SOUTHWORTH,
married Asa Baldwin, and settled at West Fairlee, Vt
Their children were, 1 David Martin. 2 Asa Lyon, 3
Thomas Porter, 4 Horace, 5 Calvin Bliss, 6. Nancy Ce-
mantha, 7. Rolin Malary

No 18 IV C   JOSEPH SOUTHWORTH,
married Susannah Jenkins   Their children were, 1 Pa-
renelia, 2 Joseph, 3 Edmund Chapell, 4 Susannah, 5.
Eliza

No 19 V C   NANCY SOUTHWORTH,
married John Holbrook, and settled at New York. Their
children were, 1 John, who died, aged 9 years, 2. Adelia
Maria, 3 Nancy Lavinia, 4 Mary Salina

No 20 VII C   HORACE SOUTHWORTH,
married Dolly Holbrook   They had one child.

No. 21 XIII B.   ELISHA LUDDEN,
a son of Benjamin and Esther Ludden, married a Strong,
and had three children

No 22 III A. NATHANIEL CAPEN,
a son of John and Ruth Capen, married Deborah Curtis,
and settled at Braintree   Their children were, 1 Phebe,
2 Rhoda, 3. John, 4. John, 5 Nathaniel, 6. Nathaniel, 7
29

Deborah, 8 Samuel   Mr Dapen died 27 April, 1806, aged
77 years. Mrs Capen died 7 Aug 1797, aged 66 years

No. 23. II B.   RHODA CAPEN,
married Levi Wild, and settled at Braintree. (See Thayer
No. 21. 2.) They have no children.

No. 24. VIII B.   SAMUEL CAPEN,
married Allice Adams, (see Adams No. 30, 6,) and settled
in Braintree. Their children were,

1. Clarissa,	born 6 July	1796	3. Maria,	born 7 July	1800
2. Nathaniel,	" 7 Feb	1798	4. Sam'l F Moseley, b 3 Oct		1811

No. 25. I C.   CLARISSA CAPEN,
married Charles Hayward, settled in Braintree, and has
two children, 1. Charles—2 Clarissa.

No 26 III C.   MARIA CAPEN,
married Livingston White, (see White No. 20,) settled in
Braintree, and has four children, 1. George—2 Maria Mann
—3. Caroline—4. Ataline

No. 27. IV A   RUTH CAPEN,
a daughter of John and Ruth Capen, married Benjamin
Thayer. (See Thayer No. 24, 1st part.) They had 15
children, viz :

1. Ruth,	baptized in	1742	9. Benjamin,
2 Ruth,			10. Benjamin,
3 Susannah,	born 30 Sept	1747	11 Lewis,
4. Phebe,			12. Lewis,
5. Phebe,			13 Timothy,
6. Benjamin,	baptized in	1751	14. Levi, born 27 March 1795
7. Benjamin,			15 Elizabeth.
8. Benjamin,			

They all died young except the three last named   There
is no record to show that they were all born in the order
in which they are here placed. His second wife was Bethiah Thayer, (See 10 Branch, No 2,) who died in Oct.
1816.   He died in 1807

No 28. XIII B. TIMOTHY THAYER,
married Hannah Thayer of Weymouth, about 1777, and
had one daughter, 1. Hannah. His second wife was Phebe
Kingman, married about 1783. They had two children,
2. Elihu, born 24 Sept. 1784—3. Ruth, born 26 Aug. 1788.

No. 29.   I C.   HANNAH THAYER,
married William Madan of Randolph, and had several children, William, Hannah, Jonathan, and others.

No. 30.   II C.   ELIHU THAYER,
married Betsey Savill, settled in Dorchester, and has children, 1 Elihu, born 25 Oct. 1811, and others.

No. 31.   III C.   RUTH THAYER,
married Joseph Wales, and settled in Quincy or Milton.
Their children are, 1 Elihu T —2. Susannah.

No. 32   I D.   ELIHU T WALES,
married Emily Crane, and settled in Dorchester.

No. 33   II D.   SUSANNAH WALES,
married Calvin Alden, Jr., a grandson of Silas Alden. (See
Alden No 59, 3, first part)

No. 34.   XIV B   LEVI THAYER,
a son of Benjamin and Ruth Thayer, married Elsey or Allice Belcher, in 1787, and settled in Randolph.
Mrs. Thayer was born 29 March, 1770.   Their children
were,

1· Lydia B.	born	3 Oct	1790		Died in 1817.		
2 Nathaniel B	"	7 Aug	1792	6 Daniel,	born	19 April	1804
3 Otis,	"	13 May	1794	7 Elizabeth,	"	2 June	1806
4 Hosea,	"		1796	8 Roxana,	"	10 Dec	1808
	Died in 1800			9. Cyrus,	"	7 Jan	1812
5. Elsey or Allice,	born	1802					

No. 35.   I C.   LYDIA B. THAYER,
married Eliphaz Sprague, 4 June, 1823, and settled in Randolph.   Mr. Sprague was born 24 April 1789.   Their children were,

1. Alvan H.	born	12 April	1824	4. Nathaniel P.	born	21 Nov 1829
2. Eliza Ann,	"	6 Sept	1825	5 Quincy,	"	25 Sept 1831
3. Lydia J	"	15 June	1827			

No. 36.   II C.   NATHANIEL B THAYER,
married Charlotte Wade of Braintree, 4 July, 1813, and
settled in Randolph.   Mrs. Thayer born 4 July, 1793.
Their children were,

1 Charlotte,	born	20 Oct	1814	3 Susan,	born	21 Feb 1820
2. Sophronia H	"	23 May	1817			

No. 37. III C. OTIS THAYER,

married Lucy Pendergrass, 13 April, 1813, and settled in Randolph. Mrs. Thayer was born 16 Feb 1796 Their children were,

1 Abram,	born 7 May 1814	4 Mary B born 30 Sept 1828
2 Lucy Ann,	" 8 March 1816	5 Eliza J " 5 Feb 1831
3 Julia Ann,	" 16 Feb 1825	

No. 38. VI C. DANIEL THAYER,

married Sally Orcutt, 5 April, 1825 ; settled in Randolph. Mrs Thayer born 10 Jan. 1804 Their children were,

1. Roxana,   born 26 Dec   1825 | 2. Daniel Webster, b 26 April 1829

No. 39 VII C ELIZABETH THAYER,

married Abiel Orcutt, 14 Dec. 1824, and settled in Abington. Mr Orcutt born 9 May, 1802. Their children were,

1 Betsey,	born 23 Aug 1825	3 Henry, born 22 Aug 1828
	Died 28 Aug same year	4. Abiel Newton, " 8 Mar 1830
2 Cyrus,	born 8 Sept 1826	

No. 40. VIII C. ROXANA THAYER,

married William Gurney, and settled in Abington. Mr. Gurney born 7 Sept 1807. Their children were,

1 Lysander,	born 1 Oct 1828	3 Francis M. born 25 Feb 1832
2. Alice E	" 31 July 1830	

No. 41 IX C. CYRUS THAYER,

married Esther Orcutt, 19 Dec. 1831, settled in Randolph. Mrs Thayer born 26 Aug. 1812.

No. 42. V A CHRISTOPHER CAPEN,

a son of John and Ruth Capen, married Abigail, daughter of Joseph and Abigail Thayer, (fifth Branch, No. 4,) and settled in Stoughton, (now Canton) Their children were,

1. Mehitabel,	born 20 May 1755	Died 7 April 1767
2 Abigail,	" 16 Oct 1756	8. Oliver, 2d , born 10 April 1768
3. Joseph,	" 13 May 1758	Died 23 April 1771.
	Died 22 Oct 1768.	9. Anna, born 7 Sept 1770
4 Samuel,	born 20 Nov 1760	10 Joseph, 2d , " 23 Aug 1772
5. Christopher,	" 18 Oct 1762	11. Jabez, " 24 Feb 1774
	Died 8 Oct 1792.	Died 2 Jan 1779.
6. Sarah,	born 31 Jan 1765	12 Ephraim, born 28 Dec 1777
	Died 27 Nov 1792	13. Jabez, 2d., " 9 May 1780
7. Oliver,	born 31 Aug 1766	

    Mr Capen died 20 Oct 1809 Mrs Capen died 16 April, 1816

No. 43 I B. MEHITABEL CAPEN,

married David Talbot, and settled in Canton Mr Talbot was born 8 March, 1746 Their children were, 1 Gratis, who married a Warren, had 4 children, and died at the age of 45 years. 2 Saloma, born 16 Feb 1791, who was murdered by Jack Batters, a Mulatto, in June, 1804 Mrs. Talbot died 7 Jan. 1830.

No. 44. II B. ABIGAIL CAPEN,

married Robert Bancroft, 28 Dec. 1779, and had children.

No. 45. IV B. SAMUEL CAPEN,

married a Childs, by whom he had five children, three of whom are living, and settled in Dorchester. His second wife was a White, who had by him four children, all living.

No. 46. IX B. ANNA CAPEN,

married Samuel Clap of Stoughton, and settled in Dorchester. She had four children ; but one is now living.

No. 47. X B. JOSEPH CAPEN,

married a Williams, and settled in Dorchester, had nine children, six of whom are now living

No. 48. XII B. EPHRAIM CAPEN,

married Milly, daughter of Jonathan Capen, perhaps granddaughter of Jonathan Capen, Jr. of Stoughton, (see Capen No. 19, first part,) and settled in Canton They had four children, 1. Edwin—2 George—3. Jerusha, and another, two of whom are now living.

No. 49. XIII B. JABEZ CAPEN,

married Mary Wood, and settled in Dorchester. Their children were, 1. Mary—2 Abigail, now living. Mr. Capen died 24 Sept. 1815.

No. 50. VI A. ANNA CAPEN,

daughter of John and Ruth Capen, married Ephraim Blanchard of Braintree. (See fourth Branch, No. 2.)

No. 51. VIII A. SARAH CAPEN,

a sister of the preceding, married Nathaniel Moseley of Stoughton, about 1742, and settled in Pomfret, Ct Their children were, 1. Nathaniel—2 Flavel—3. Joseph—4.

Thomas—5 Uriel—6. Elisha—7. Hannah—8. Beulah—9. Sarah—10. Betsey, and five others, names not known.

N. B. This article should have been placed as No. 3 or 4 in this Branch, which was not discovered till too late to correct it

No 52. IX A. EPHRAIM CAPEN,

married Dorothy Thayer, and settled in Dorchester; afterwards removed to Connecticut, had three children, 1. Sally—2. Phebe—3 Philip R and perhaps others.

Mr. Capen died at the age of seventy-five years

NINTH BRANCH.

No 1 ESTHER THAYER,

a daughter of Ephraim and Sarah Thayer, married Moses French, (see French No. 31, first part,) and settled in Braintree. Their children were,

1 Moses,	born 16 Sept	1731	4 Sarah,	born 15 Jan	1738
2 Elisha,	" 12 Jan	1734	5 Jonathan,	" 19 Jan	1739
3. Esther,	" 21 Dec	1735	6 Deliverance,	" 7 Nov	1742

Mr. French died 19 Sept. 1768, in the 69 year of his age. Mrs. French died 13 Dec. 1800, aged 95 years, 5 months

No 2 I A MOSES FRENCH, Jr.,

married Elizabeth Hobart of Braintree, 11 Aug 1756, (see Hobart No 17, first part,) and settled in Braintree. Their children were,

1 Caleb,	born 15 Dec	1757	7. Moses,	born 29 Oct	1769
2. Zenas,	" 15 April	1760	8 Jonathan,	" 29 April	1772
3 Sylvanus,	" 6 June	1763	9 Asa,	" 16 April	1775
4 Abijah,	" 11 Sept	1766	10. Charles,	" 24 April	1778
5 6 } twins, who died in infancy			11. Elizabeth,	" 13 May	1780
			Died 6 March 1796		

Mr. French was a Deacon in the church at Braintree many years, and was much employed in public business

Dea French died 19 Jan 1807, aged 75 years 3 months. Mrs. French died 25 Dec 1822, aged 84 years 8 months.

No. 3 I B. CALEB FRENCH,

married Relief Faxon of Braintree, 9 July, 1784, and settled there. He died 15 July, 1823, aged 65 years 7 months, without issue.

No 4.   II B.   ZENAS FRENCH,

married Relief Thayer of Braintree, (see Thayer No. 48, 8, first part,) and settled in Randolph.   Their children were,

1. Sally,   born 24 Jan   1783 | 3. Avis,   born 31 May   1789
2. Relief,   "   19 Feb   1785 | Mrs. French died 22 Aug 1790.

His second wife was Ruth White   (See White No 24, 2, first part.)   They were married 30 Oct 1791.   Their children were,

4. Joseph W.   born 23 Sept   1792 | 9 Aaron,   born 17 May   1805
   Died 27 Oct 1818. | Died 10 May 1830
5 Elizabeth,   born 18 Oct   1794 | 10 Alvan,   born 27 Dec   1806
   Died 1 Nov 1800 | Died 20 May 1807.
6 Zenas,   born 7 Feb   1798 | 11 Charles,   born 15 Jan   1809
7. Ruth,   "   3 Sept   1799 | 12 Caleb,   "   18 Oct   1811
8 Moses,   "   2 Feb   1802 | Died 9 Feb 1816.

No 5.   I C.   SALLY FRENCH,

married Jacob Whitcomb, Jr. and settled in Randolph. Mr. Whitcomb was born 6 Nov. 1780   Their children are,

1 Jacob,   born 23 Jan   1807 | 3. Sarah Ann,   born 25 April 1822
2 Charles F.   "   2 Oct   1813 | Mr Whitcomb died 9 Sept 1825.

I D.   JACOB WHITCOMB, 3d ,

married Abigail T. Holbrook, daughter of Capt. Abia Holbrook, and grand-daughter of Capt Isaac Thayer, (No. 48, 1, first part,) and settled in Randolph.   Mrs Whitcomb was born 1 Jan. 1811.   Their child, 1. Jacob Henry, born 17 Aug. 1830

No 6.   II A   RELIEF FRENCH,

married John Adams, son of Lemuel Adams of Milton, in 1802 ; settled in Milton   Mr. Adams was born 1 Dec 1780. Their children were,

1 Hannah Relief, b 31 Dec   1803 | 5 Ruth White, born 23 June 1816
2. Susannah Davenport, b 1 May 1806 | Died 1 Nov 1817.
3 Lemuel Zenas,   b 24 April 1808 | 6. Caroline French, b 23 Jan 1821
   Died Jan 1827. | Died in 1829.
4. Betsey French, b 18 Nov   1810 |

No 7.   I D   HANNAH R ADAMS,

married Simeon Faxon of Randolph, and settled there
   Mr. Faxon was born 24 Feb. 1803.

No 8.   II D.   SUSANNAH D. ADAMS,

married Oliver B. Alexander, and settled in Boston.   Their children were, 1. Lemuel Zenas, born 30 Jan. 1827—2. Sarah Elizabeth, born 22 April, 1831.

No 9   IV D.   BETSEY F ADAMS,
married William N. Gardner, and settled in Milton.   Their
children were, 1. John Adams, born 20 April, 1828—2
Caroline R. born 6 May, 1830.

No. 10.   III C   AVIS FRENCH,
married Parmenas Brett, and settled in N Bridgewater.
Mr. Brett was born 3 Nov. 1782.   Their children were,

1 Simeon,   born 8 March 1805 | 4. Lucinda,   born 11 July 1813
2 Elizabeth F "   19 March 1807 | Died 19 Jan 1814.
3. Susannah Relief, b 7 June 1809 |

No. 11.   I D.   SIMEON BRETT,
married Lodency Wallis, and settled in N. Bridgewater.
Their children were, 1. Erastus W. born 2 Sept. 1829—2.
Betsey Jane, born 2 Sept 1832.

No. 12.   II D.   ELIZABETH F BRETT,
married Philander Holmes, and settled in N Bridgewater.
Their children were, 1 George N. born 21 Oct. 1828—2.
Susan W. born 2 Feb 1830.

No. 13.   III D.   SUSANNAH R. BRETT,
married Erastus Wales, and settled in N. Bridgewater.

No 14.   VI C.   ZENAS FRENCH Jr.,
married Julia Tower of Canton, and settled in Randolph
Mrs. French was born 18 July, 1802. Their children were,

1. Julia Ann,   born 23 July 1827 | 3. Mary Holbrook, b. 14 Aug 1831
2. Elizabeth Porter," 16 Jan 1829 |

No 15.   VII C.   RUTH FRENCH,
married Samuel Whitcomb and settled in Randolph.   Mr.
Whitcomb was born 4 June, 1788   Their children were,
1 Samuel, born 18 April, 1819—2. Ruth F. born 12 March,
1827.

No 16   VIII C.   MOSES FRENCH,
married Susannah Faxon, and settled in Randoldh.   Mrs.
French was born 25 Nov. 1804.   Their child, 1. Susan E.
born 5 Nov. 1828.

No. 17   III B.   SYLVANUS FRENCH,
a son of Moses and Elizabeth French, married Hannah,
daughter of Abraham Thayer, (see Thayer No. 48, 10, first

part,) and settled in Randolph, had one son, 1 Joseph, who died 15 Oct 1792, aged about 4 years His second wife was Azubah Penniman, born 5 May, 1770, married 28 April, 1791. Their children were, 2. Joseph—3 Hannah —4 Sally

No. 18 IV C SALLY FRENCH,

married Rhodolphus Porter, and settled in Randolph Mr. Porter was born 25 Jan 1794. Their children were,

1. Isaac,	born 19 April 1821	5 Sarah F	born 7 Oct 1827
2 Rhodolphus,	" 5 Sept 1822	6 Lucinda,	" 11 Sept 1829
3 Joseph F	" 28 April 1824	7. Azubah Ann,	" 2 Jan 1832
4 Lewis,	" 25 Jan 1826		

No 19 IV B. ABIJAH FRENCH,

son of Moses and Elizabeth French, married Sarah Clark, 11 Nov 1790, and settled in Boston Mrs. French was born 29 March, 1766 Their children were,

1. Abijah,	born 3 Nov 1791		Died 4 Sept 1796
Died at Cincinnati, Ohio		4 Willard,	born 29 Sept 1796
2 Elizabeth,	born 15 March 1793	5 Catharine, }	
3. Willard,	" 16 Nov 1794	6. Caroline, }	" 29 July 1798

Mrs French died 7 Oct 1798, aged 32 years His second wife was Sarah Billings, who died 9 Dec. 1809. Mr. French died in Jan. 1811.

No 20 II C. ELIZABETH FRENCH,

married George Guild of Dedham, 24 June, 1813, and setted in Boston Mr Guild was born 20 March, 1788 Their children were, 1 George French, born 31 March, 1814— 2 James Edward, born 25 June, 1816, died 5 May, 1817.

Mr Guild died 15 Feb 1817, aged 29.

No 21 V C CATHARINE FRENCH,

married George Washington Thayer of Randolph, son of Capt Luther and Olive Thayer, (see Thayer No. 48, 1, first part,) 8 Sept. 1818, and settled in Boston. Mr. Thayer was born 11 Feb 1793 Their children were,

1 George Luther, b 7 June 1819	5 Charles French," 24 Nov 1825
2 David Dudley, " 26 May 1821	6 Francis, born 7 Sept 1827
Died 23 Sept 1822	Died 8 Sept 1827
3. Olive Turner, born 7 May 1823	7. Catharine French, b 20 Aug 1828
4. James Edward, " 24 Aug 1824	8 James Henry, born 12 Dec 1829
Died 21 April 1825.	9 " 11 Feb 1832

VI C. CAROLINE FRENCH,

married Benjamin V French, 22 Sept. 1817, (see No 23,) and settled in Boston

30

No 22   VII B   MOSES FRENCH, Jr,
married Eunice Vinton, 9 Dec 1790, and settled in Braintree   Their children were,

1. Benj. Vinton,	born 29 July 1791	5 Charles,	born 14 Sept	1802
2 Moses,	" 7 June 1794	6 Edward,	" 28 Dec	1809
3 Caleb,	" 1 Nov 1797		Died 16 March 1834	
4 John Allen,	" 15 June 1800	7 Eunice Elizabeth, b 1 July 1812		

No. 23   I C   BENJAMIN V FRENCH,
married Caroline French, 22 Sept, 1817   (See No 19, 6, VI C.

No 24   II C   MOSES FRENCH, Jr,
married Azubah Cleverly of Quincy, and settled in Boston
Their children were,

1 Benj Vinton, born	5 Oct 1821	4. Susan Whitney, b 28 Jan	1827
2. Caroline, "	4 Aug 1823	5. Mary Azubah, " 14 July	1829
3 Sarah Cleverly, "	27 July 1825		

Mrs. French died 27 Jan 1830, aged 35 years   His second wife was Elizabeth Cleverly, who was born 27 Dec. 1804, married 3 March, 1831.

No. 25.   III C.   CALEB FRENCH,
married Nancy Parmenter in 1822, who was born 31 Aug 1797.   Their children were,

1 Caroline Elizabeth, b 25 Oct 1822 Died 30 Nov 1823	4 Gronvill Ellis, born 9 Oct 1827 Died 13 July 1828
2. Jane Bates, born 14 Dec 1823	5 Cynthia Brown, b 24 July 1829
3 Maria Haskell Thayer, born 17 Feb 1826	6 Ann Elizabeth, b 11 July 1831 Died 10 Feb 1832

Mrs. French died 3 Oct 1831, aged 34 years

No. 26.   IV C   JOHN ALLEN FRENCH,
married Lucy Perkins Spear, 6 Dec 1826, who was born 13 Jan. 1805, and settled in Boston   Their children were,

1. Ellen Maria, born 1 Dec 1827		Died 24 July 1829
2. John James, " 12 Feb 1829	3 Mary Elizabeth, b 30 June 1831	

No. 27.   V C   CHARLES FRENCH,
married Cynthia Brown, and settled in Boston   Mrs. French died 24 Nov. 1827, aged 23 years. His second wife was Catharine L daughter of Charles French of Braintree. (See No 34, 1)

No. 28   EUNICE E FRENCH,
married Thomas J Noyes of Lebanon, N H. 25 Feb. 1830,

and settled in Braintree Their child, 1 Aaron Davis Weld French, born 4 Oct 1830.

No 29 VIII B JONATHAN FRENCH,

a son of Moses and Elizabeth French, married Ann Weld of Boston, and settled there Their children were, 1 Jonathan, born 1 Oct 1803—2 Aaron Davis Weld, born 25 June, 1813, died 25 Oct 1830, aged 17 years 4 months.

No. 30. IX B. ASA FRENCH, Esq,

married Mehitabel Hollis, and settled in Braintree Mrs French was born 11 Aug, 1779 Their children were,

1 Elizabeth, born 12 May 1800 Died 20 Nov 1820.	3 Mehitabel Ann, b 22 June 1806	
2 Jonathan, born 22 March 1802	4 Lucinda, " 5 Oct 1810 Mrs. French died 22 Aug 1819.	

No. 31. II C JONATHAN FRENCH,

married Sarah B Hayward, and settled in Braintree Their children were,

1 Eliza, born 25 Sept 1825	3 Asa, born 21 Oct 1829		
2. Jonathan, " 19 Aug 1827			

No 32 III C MEHITABEL ANN FRENCH,

married Capt Samuel D Hayden, and settled in Braintree Their daughter, 1. Sarah Mehitabel, born 25 Aug 1832

No. 33. IV C. LUCINDA FRENCH,

married Isaac Willett, and settled in Braintree

No. 34. X B CHARLES FRENCH,

the youngest son of Moses and Elizabeth French, married Sally Lush, and settled in Braintree. Their children were,

1. Catharine Lamb, b. 23 Jan 1816	3. Charles Andrew
2. Ann Weld, " 22 Aug 1817	

No 35 II A. ELISHA FRENCH,

a son of Moses and Esther French, married Mary, daughter of John and Mary Ludden, (see Thayer No 13, 2, first part,) and settled in Braintree Their children were,

1. Esther, born 10 Feb 1757 Died 3 Aug 1760	3 Anna, born 7 Aug 1763		
2 Esther, born 3 Nov 1761	4 Elisha, " 5 Nov 1768		

Mrs French died 20 June, 1805 Mr French died 19 Oct. 1818

II B   ESTHER FRENCH,

married Samuel White Thayer of Braintree   (See No. 36, sixth Branch.)

No. 36   III B.   ANNA FRENCH,

married David Thayer of Braintree   (See No 46, sixth Branch) Her second husband was Dea Eliphalet Packard, formerly of N Bridgewater, married 11 Oct 1800, by whom she had,

1 Betsey,	born 1 Sept	1801	3 Esther	born 5 Aug 1809
2 Mary,	" 19 June	1805		

Dea E Packard died 16 Jan 1819, aged 61 years and 21 days

No 37   IV B   ELISHA FRENCH, Jr ,

married Susannah, daughter of Robert Hayden, Esq of Braintree, 16 May, 1794, (see French No 51, 2, first part,) and settled in Braintree , afterwards removed to Boston Their children were,

1 Hervey,	born 24 June	1795	6 Susannah,	born 23 May	1803
2 Elisha,	" 7 May	1797	7 Charles,	" 8 Oct	1809
3 Robert,	" 11 Dec	1798		Died 11 Dec 1810	
1. and 5. died in infancy.					

Mrs French died 12 Aug 1818   His second wife was Mary Noyes of Boston   Maj E French died 4 Aug 1826

No 38   I C   HERVEY FRENCH,

married Nancy Keith of Easton, Mass and settled in Braintree   Their children were, 1 Hosea Edson, born 22 Feb 1822—2 Robert Hervey, born 16 Feb 1824   Mr French died in the flower of his age, much lamented

No 39   II C   ELISHA FRENCH, 3d ,

married Lucinda White, and settled in Braintree   Their children were,

1. Elisha,	born 7 May 1820		Died 26 Aug same year
2 Lucinda Ann,	" 16 Feb 1826	3 Charles Austin, born 12 Dec 1827	

No. 40.   VI C   SUSANNAH FRENCH,

married William Reed, and settled in Braintree   Their children were, 1 Susannah, born 11 Oct 1825—2 Clarissa, born 11 Sept 1829

No 41   III A   ESTHER FRENCH,

a daughter of Moses and Esther French, married Richard

Thayer, (see Thayer No 18, first part,) and settled in Braintree   Their children were,

1. Henry,	born 28 Oct	1756	7	Obadiah,	born 23 Feb	1772
2 Moses,	" 26 July	1758	8	Zebadiah,	" 5 June	1774
3. Isaiah,	" 10 Nov	1760	9	Lydia,	" 22 Sept	1776
4. Elisha,	" 31 Aug	1764	10	Nath'l Emmons,"	29 May	1778
5 Theodora,	" 5 Nov	1766	11.	Abigail,	" 20 Aug	1781
6 Richard,	" 21 March	1769				

Mr Thayer died 23 March, 1823, aged 92 years

No 42   I B   HENRY THAYER,

married Phila daughter of Jacob Packard of N Bridgewater, 27 Jan about 1780, (see Cary's gen p 24,) and settled in Winchester, N H Mrs Thayer was born 15 Sept 1756 Their children were,

1 Hezekiah,	born 25 Oct	1783	3 Dorothy,	born 20 May	1787
2. Nancy,	" 26 July	1785	4 Emmons,	" 16 May	1789
	Died 30 April 1803		5. Esther,	" 21 Dec	1791

No 43   I C   HEZEKIAH THAYER,

married Harriet Meiggs, 16 Oct 1808, and settled in Troy, N Y   Their children were,

1 Mary Spring,	born 6 Aug	1809	6	Laura Porter,	born 30 Aug	1820
	Died 2 Nov 1810		7	Levi Parsons,	" 9 Nov	1823
2 Harriet,	born 22 June 1811		8	Samuel,	" 24 Apr	1826
3 Henry French,	" 14 May	1813	9	David Porter,	" 29 Feb	1828
4. Asa Packard,	" 15 April 1815		10	Hezekiah E	" 15 Dec	1829
5 Philena Perkins,	" 30 July	1817	11	Edw Phinehas,	" 15 Nov	1831

No 44   III C   DOROTHY THAYER,

married Ebenezer Conant, 22 Nov 1806, and settled in Winchester, N H   Mr Conant was born 23 July, 1779 Their children were,

1 Edna,	born 8 Sept 1807	6	Louisa,	born 16 Sept	1818
2 Huldah P	" 4 May 1809	7.	Eunice,	" 26 Dec	1821
3 Hezekiah,	" 17 Feb 1811	8	Ebenezer,	" 23 Nov	1823
4 Louisa,	" 6 Jan 1814	9.	Sarah Davis,	" 11 April	1826
	Died 10 Aug 1816.	10.	Chas. Bennett,	" 11 Sept	1828
5 Philena,	born 1 May 1816		Mr. Conant died 20 June 1832		

No 45   IV C   EMMONS THAYER,

married Barbara Emerson of Warwick, 19 April, 1815, born 19 Sept 1797   Their children were,

1 Maria,	born 16 Sept	1816	3 Benj Emerson,	b 12 Nov	1820
2 Edward,	" 10 Aug	1818	4 Cereno Taylor,	" 21 Dec	1826

Mr Thayer died 26 Oct 1826

No 46   V C   ESTHER THAYER,

married Alpheus Kingman, 6 April, 1807 and settled in

Winchester, N H   Mr Kingman was born 9 July, 1786.
Their children were,

1 Alvan,	born 4 July 1807	6 Nancy Thayer, b 27 Feb 1815
2 Eliza,	" 9 July 1809	7 Emeline P. born 11 Nov 1816
3 Pliny,	" 22 May 1811	8 Pliny Emerson, b 7 Nov 1818
	Died 4 Jan 1814	9 Marshal, born 26 May 1820
4 Emerson,	born 11 Aug 1812	10 Warren E born 16 April 1827
	Died 2 Dec 1812	11 Ellen Mehitabel, b. 27 Jan 1829
5 Sidney,	born 18 Oct 1813	12 Louisa Francis, b. 17 Aug 1831

On the 20 April, 1833, the House and other buildings of
Mr Kingman were consumed by fire, and in 12 days he
had another raised by the active benevolence of the people in that vicinity

1 ALVAN KINGMAN, married Lucinda Rugg of Keene, 21
Feb 1832

ELIZA KINGMAN, married Caleb Sawyer Graves of Keene,
1 Nov 1832

No 47   II B   MOSES THAYER,

a son of Richard and Esther Thayer, married Anna Ayres
Allen, and settled in Boston   Their children were,

1. Henry.	born 24 Feb 1784	2 Moses,	born 17 Oct 1786
	Died in infancy.		Died young
		3 Nancy,	born 18 Oct 1788

No 48   III C   NANCY THAYER,

married John Minchen, and settled in Boston , afterwards
removed to N Y and was drowned   Their children were,
1 John Henry, born 19 Sept 1809—2 William—3 Edward
—4 Eliza—5 Margaret Ann—6 Paul Jones

No 49   III B   ISAIAH THAYER,

a son of Richard and Esther Thayer, married Tamar Bayley of Weymouth, 11 May, 1786, and settled in Sterling,
Mass   Their children were,

1. Sybil,	born 2 March 1787	4 Deborah,	born 23 Aug 1793
	Died 14 March 1828.		Died 24 Sept 1832.
2 Sarah,	born 6 April 1789	5 Eliza,	born 14 Oct 1795
3 Nathaniel,	" 23 May 1791	6 Isaiah,	" 6 Jan 1798

Mrs Thayer died 29 Sept 1812   His second wife was
Rhoda Stetson of Braintree, married 17 June, 1817   Mr
Thayer died 10 Nov 1827

No 50   III C   NATHANIEL THAYER,

married Fanny Drury, and settled in Brighton, Upper
Canada   Their children were.

1 Edward Bayley, b. 10 Sept 1827 | 2 Eliza, born 10 April 1829
Died in Oct 1827 | 3 Isaiah, " 10 Sept 1833

Isaiah Thayer, brother of the preceding, also resides at Brighton Sarah and Eliza live in Sterling

No 51 IV B ELISHA THAYER, Esq,

a son of Richard and Esther Thayer, married Irana Holbrook, and settled in W Fairlee, Vt

No. 52. V B THEODORA THAYER,

married Benjamin Wales, 27 June, 1797, (see Wales No 7, 7, first part,) and settled in Braintree She was his second wife

No 53 VI B. RICHARD THAYER, Jr,

married Martha Appleton, and settled in Boston Their children were,

1 Thomas Appleton, b 1 Mar 1799 | 5 George Henry, born 6 Aug 1807
2 Martha Appleton, " 9 Mar 1801 | 6 Lydia Wells, " 9 Aug 1809
3 Richard French, b 19 Mar 1803 | 7 Charles Edward," 28 May 1812
4 Mary Ann, born 5 Sept 1805 |

No 54 I C THOMAS A THAYER,

married Betsey, daughter of Benjamin Wales, No 52, and settled in Boston. Their children were,

1. Thomas Albert, b 13 June 1827 | 3 Richard Benj born 22 Aug 1830
2 Maria Elizabeth, " 17 Feb 1829 |

No 55 IV C. MARY ANN THAYER,

married Samuel Lucas Hay, and settled in Boston

No 56 VII B OBADIAH THAYER,

a son of Richard and Esther Thayer, married Elizabeth Vinton, and settled in Braintree Mrs Thayer was born 2 April, 1781 Their children were,

1. Elisha, born 18 Aug 1799 | 3. Hezekiah, born 8 Nov 1804
Died 6 April 1831. | 4. Simeon, " 2 June 1809
2 Richard, born 20 Oct 1801 | 5. Joseph Warren, " 6 Aug 1815

Mrs Thayer died 6 Sept 1823 His 2d wife was Mary Field, born 10 April, 1779

2 RICHARD, married Esther Penniman, settled in Braintree, and died 26 Oct 1824, without issue

No 57 VIII B. ZEBADIAH THAYER,

a brother of the preceding, married Lucy, widow of Ben-

jamin Parker, Jr of Andover, and had by her one daughter,
1 Elizabeth   Mrs Thayer had one daughter Lucy by her
first husband   They live in Wiscasset, Maine

No 58   X B   NATHANIEL E THAYER,

married Deliverance, daughter of Dea Eliphaz Thayer,
(see 13 Branch, No 53, also Thayer No 12, 4, first part,)
and settled in Braintree   Their children were,

1 Esther,	born 8 May	1803	5 Irene,	born 5 May	1811
	Died 20 Jan 1808.		6 David,	" 19 July	1813
2. Lydia,	born 16 March	1804	7 Sarah Eleanor, "	May	1815
	Died 20 March same year		8 Moses,	" 10 Aug	1817
3 Emmons,	born 1 Nov	1806		Died 11 Nov 1822	
4 Esther,	" 7 Dec	1808			

No 59   III C   EMMONS THAYER,

married Jerusha Holbrook, and settled in Braintree

No 60   V C   IRENE THAYER,

married Nahum Bunker, and settled in Braintree   Their
children were, 1 George—2 Albert—3 ——

No 61   XI B   ABIGAIL THAYER,

a daughter of Richard and Esther Thayer, married Hezekiah Goodnough, and settled in Boston   Their children
were, 1 Hezekiah—2 Nancy T —3 Asa

No 62   V A   Rev JONATHAN FRENCH,*

the youngest son of Moses and Esther French, was married
to Miss Abigail Richards, 26 Aug 1773   Her father was
Dr Benjamin Richards of Weymouth   Her mother was
Abigail, the youngest of the children of Ephraim and Sarah
Thayer   (See 14th Branch, No 3)   Their children were,

1 Sarah,	born 18 Nov 1774	4 Mary Holyoke, born 6 Aug 1781
	Died 25 same month .	5 Sarah, 2d,	" 13 Dec	1784
2 Abigail,	born 29 May 1776		Died 2 April 1788.	
3. Jonathan,	" 16 Aug 1778			

*The Rev Jonathan French of Andover, Mass was born at Braintree,
on the 30 Jan 1740, N S   When about seventeen years old he entered the
army employed against the French and Indians, and in March, 1757, repaired to Fort Edward   Debilitated by the small pox and the fever and
ague, he returned home in October.

He was afterwards stationed at Castle William, in the capacity of a ser-
geant, the chief care of the garrison often devolving upon him.   In that
situation his life was twice in great jeopardy   An Indian servant at the
Castle, to whom he had refused rum, assailed him with a drawn knife.
With great presence of mind and agility he avoided the weapon and
brought his antagonist to the earth   The Indian completely vanquish-

No 63   H B   ABIGAIL FRENCH,

married 9 May, 1797, to the Rev Samuel Stearns* of Bedford, Mass   Their children were,

1	b. 18 Aug 1798	8 Elizabeth W	b 29 July 1810
	Died 2 Nov same year	9 Josiah Atherton,	} b 1 Sep 1812
2 Abigail French,	b 7 Jan 1800	10 Geo Washington,	
3 Samuel Horatio,	" 12 Sept 1801	George W. died 12 Oct 1812	
4 Sarah Caroline,	" 15 April 1803	11 Charlotte Esther b 17 Sept 1814	
5 Wm Augustus,	" 17 Mar 1805	12 Ann Catharine, b 10 Oct 1816	
6. Mary Holyoke,	" 14 Nov 1806	13 Eeben'r Sperry, b 23 Dec 1819	
7 Jonathan French,"	4 Sept 1808		

Mrs Abigail French died 28 Aug in the 80th year of her age.

---

ed, and surprized that his life was spared, was ever after grateful and obliging

In the other instance, at great hazard, he seized an Indian prisoner who had escaped from confinement, and armed with a large club, threatened the life of any one who should attempt to take him.

Contemplating the practice of Physic and Surgery, his leisure was employed in the study and so much did he enjoy the confidence of the faculty, that the medicines and care of the sick were often entrusted solely to him

At a time when Boston harbour was so frozen as to prevent the passing of a boat, but not so as to be safe for any one on foot, a case occurred which required immediate attention Articles were necessary which must be procured in Boston Mr French, with his characteristic resolution and perseverance, as he could not procure a man who was willing to venture, furnished himself with a long pole, and holding it horizontally, went and returned safely, though often in great danger, and was considered the instrument under Providence of saving the patient's life

He afterward prepared for College, and on the last day of his service at the garrison, gave up his commission as commanding officer for the day, and entered Harvard University in the humble station of Cutler's freshman He graduated in 1771

He had contemplated a mission to the Indians, but was led in Providence, to settle in the ministry in the South Parish in Andover, where he was ordained 22 Sept 1772

Mr French's ministry was laborious His manner of preaching was serious, solemn, and impressive. Though his life was a continued scene of fatigue, he was remarkably cheerful at almost all seasons He was given to hospitality His company was eagerly sought by the young and the old, and his house was the abode of friendship, harmony, and love

In religious sentiment, he was such a Calvinist as the first fathers of New England He had a strong attachment to the Assembly's Catechism, in which he regularly instructed the children, in the 7 districts of his parish

He was one of the founders of the Massachusetts Society for the promotion of christian knowledge

He was very much esteemed by the Churches of New England, as a wise, prudent, and judicious counsellor, as appeared from the great number of Ecclesiastical Councils he was called to attend

He died of a paralytic affection, 28 July, 1809, in the seventieth year of his age, and the thirty-seventh of his ministry A sermon was delivered at his funeral from John 14. 28, by Rev. Mr. Stone of Reading

---

*Rev Samuel Stearns of Bedford, Mass descended from an ancient and

31

No. 64. II C. ABIGAIL F. STEARNS,

married Jonas Monroe of Bedford ; died Jan. 1833, leaving a daughter Ellen Maria.

No. 65. III C. SAMUEL H. STEARNS,

was graduated at Harvard University in 1823, and ordained pastor of the Old South Church in Boston, 16 Apr. 1834.

No 66. IV C. SARAH C. STEARNS,

married Rev Forest Jefferds of Epping, N. H Resettled in Middleton, Mass. Their children were, 1. Abigail Jane —2. Sarah Caroline—3. Samuel Stearns—4. Olive Maria.

No 67. V C. WILLIAM A STEARNS,

was graduated at Harvard University in 1827, was settled as Pastor of a church in Cambridgeport He married Rebecca Alden Frasier, a descendant of the pilgrim John Alden. Their child, Eliza Chaplin.

No. 68. VIII C. ELIZABETH W. STEARNS,

married Dea Charles James of Medford, Mass.

No. 69. III B Rev. JONATHAN FRENCH, Jr.,

was graduated at Harvard University in 1798, ordained at

very respectable family in Billerica, Mass His grandfather, John Stearns, married Miss Esther Johnson, daughter of the celebrated Capt. Edward Johnson, principal founder of the town and church of Woburn, and author of the history of New England, entitled, " Wonder-Working Providence of Sion's Saviour in New England "

Rev. Josiah Stearns, son of John and Esther Stearns, was born at Billerica, 20 Jan. 1732, was graduated at Harvard College, in 1751, ordained at Epping, N H. 8 March, 1758, and died there in 1788.

Rev Samuel Stearns of Bedford, the subject of this Memoir, was son of Rev Josiah Stearns of Epping, N H by his second wife, a daughter of Rev Samuel Ruggles of Billerica. He was born at Epping, 8 April, 1770; fitted for College at Phillips Exeter Academy, and graduated at Harvard University in 1794. His theological studies he pursued under the direction of Rev Jonathan French of Andover, whose daughter, Abigail, he afterwards married. He was ordained over the Church and Society in Bedford, 27 April, 1796, and died 26 Dec 1834, after a ministry of almost thirty-nine years Mr. Stearns was an able and faithful minister. He was very clear and decided in his views of religion In him, Orthodoxy and Charity were eminently united He was a man of prayer, leading apparently a life of communion with God.

In his last sickness it was a great privilege to be near him, so heavenly was his conversation, so submissive was his deportment, so calmly would he speak of his approaching dissolution, and so firmly would he express himself of the Glory that was to follow (See funeral sermon, by Rev Samuel Sewall, from John, 11—25, 26)

North Hampton, N. II. 18 Nov. 1801, married 4 Dec. 1804, to Rebecca, daughter of Dea. Samuel Farrar of Lincoln, Mass. Their children were,

1. Jonathan,	born 13 Dec 1805	7. John Farrar, born 10 Feb 1818
2. Rebecca Mercy, "	2 Feb 1807	8. Sarah, " 25 May 1820
3. Sam'l Farrar, "	11 Jan 1809	9. Eben'r Sperry, " 9 Jan 1823
4. Abigail, "	4 Aug 1810	10. Lucy Ann, " 5 Sept 1825
5 Mary Holyoke, "	23 Nov 1812	11. Elizabeth Dorcas, b 26 Jan 1829
6. James, "	1 April 1815	

No. 70. V C. MARY H. FRENCH,

married 16 Apr. 1833, to Jonathan Hobbs of NorthHampton.

No. 71. IV B. MARY H. FRENCH,

daughter of Rev. Jonathan French of Andover, married to Rev. Ebenezer Peek Sperry ; ordained at Dunstable, N. H. Installed at Wenham, Mass.

No. 72. VI A. DELIVERANCE FRENCH,

the youngest daughter of Moses and Esther French, married Rev. Nathaniel Emmons, D. D. 6 April, 1775, and settled in Franklin, Mass. Dr. Emmons was born 1 May, 1745. Their children were,

1. Nathaniel, born 14 April 1776	2 Diodate Johnson, b. 22 June 1777
Died 8 Sept 1778.	Died 8 Sept 1778.

Inscriptions on the tomb stones of Mrs. EMMONS, and her two children, Franklin, Mass.

" In Memory of Mrs DELIVERANCE EMMONS, consort of the Rev. NATHANIEL EMMONS, who departed this life June 22, 1778, in the 36 year of her age.

> In that dark hour all serene she lay
> Beneath the openings of celestial day ,
> Her soul retires from sense, refined from sin,
> While the descending Glory wrought within—
> Then in a sacred calm resigned her breath,
> And as her eyelids closed she smiled in death.

O Death, where is thy sting ? O Grave, where is thy victory ?"

" In Memory of NATHANIEL EMMONS and DIODATE JOHNSON EMMONS, sons of the Rev. NATHANIEL EMMONS, both of whom died Sept. 8, 1778, the eldest aged 2 years 4 months and 24 days, the youngest aged one year 2 months and 16 days. They were lovely and pleasant in their lives, and in their death they were not divided "

TENTH BRANCH.

No 1   NEPHTALI THAYER,

a son of Ephraim and Sarah Thayer, married Bathsheba. daughter of Dea Samuel Bass of Braintree, 3 Feb 1732, (see Bass No. 27, first part,) and settled in Braintree, (now Randolph.)   Their children were.

1. Bathsheba,   born 14 April 1733 | 4 Hannah.
2 Bethiah,   "   4 Nov 1734 | 5 Susannah,   born 26 May 1743
3 Naphtali,   " 30 July 1739 |

No. 2   II A   BETHIAH THAYER,

married Benjamin Thayer. 24 Dec 1794   (See 8th Branch No 27)   Mrs Thayer died in 1816, without issue

No 3   III A   NAPHTALI THAYER,

married Elizabeth, daughter of Benjamin and Ruth Thayer, (see 8th Branch, No 27,) 8 April 1763, and settled in Randolph   Their children were,

1. Robert,   born 22 June 1765 | 3 Benjamin
2 Bethuel,   "   1 Aug 1771 | 4 Rebecca

Mr. Thayer died

No. 4   I B.   ROBERT THAYER,

married Rebecca, perhaps a daughter of Richard Thayer of Weymouth, (see Thayer No 27, 6, first part,) in 1785, and settled in Randolph   Their children were, 1. Benjamin, born 20 Nov 1786—2 Rebecca—3 John, born 11 April, 1790—4. Davis—5 Ebenezer—6 Rebecca, 2d —7. Nahum—8 Elizabeth

No. 5   I C   BENJAMIN THAYER.

married Charlotte White. (see 6 Branch, No 53,) and settled in Weymouth   They have one child, 1 Charlotte
    Mr. Thayer died in Aug 1821.

No. 6.   II B   BETHUEL THAYER,

married Anna, a daughter of Richard Thayer of Weymouth, (see Thayer No 27, 9, first part,) in 1792, and settled in Randolph   Their children were, 1 Anna—2 Silas—3 Silas, 2d —4. Mehitabel—5 Belinda—6 Ephraim—7 Dorothy and 8 Susannah, twins—9 Dorcas—10. Richard—11 Luther—12. Jonathan

No 7 I C.   ANNA THAYER,
married John Hollis of Randolph, and settled there Their children were, 1 Anna, who died an infant—2 Lavina—3. James—4 Ephraim—5 Lucinda—6 Rebecca Ann

No 8 IV C MEHITABEL THAYER,
married Samuel Howland, and settled in Bridgewater Their children were, 1 Calvin, born 28 July, 1817—2. unknown

No. 9 VI C   EPHRAIM THAYER,
married Abi Paine, daughter of Zeba Paine, (see Paine, No 16, 3, first part,) and settled in Randolph.

No 10 VII C DOROTHY THAYER,
married William Madan, Jr of Randolph, (see 8 Branch, No. 29,) who died without issue Her second husband was Danforth Chandler, by whom she has had four children, (1827,) names unknown

No 11 VIII C SUSANNAH THAYER,
married James Tower, of Braintree and settled there, and has had five children, (1831,) names unknown

No 12 XI B LUTHER THAYER,
married Catharine Paine, sister of Abi P. above named, and settled in Randolph

ELEVENTH BRANCH.

No. 1   Dea PETER THAYER,
married Anna Porter of Norton, 1 June, 1732, and settled in Braintree, afterwards removed to Peterborough, N H. Their children were,

1 William,	born 26 July,	1733	7 Anna,	born 29 Sept	1744
Died the same day.			Died 25 Nov 1711		
2 Peter,	born 5 May	1735	8. Anna, 2d,	born 9 April	1746
Died 6 July 1736			9 Jabez,	" 7 July	1748
3 Peter,	born 3 April	1737	10 Phebe,	" 11 Feb	1750
4. William,	" 26 Jan	1739	11 Ruth,	" 23 Aug	1753
5. Ephraim,	" 16 Feb	1740	12 Bartholomew,	" 15 July	1757
6 Zacheus,	" 27 Dec	1742			

Dea. Thayer died 27 Sept 1798, aged 90 years.

No. 2. III A.   PETER THAYER, Jr ,
married Polly Withington, and settled in Randolph. Their
children were, 1. John—2. Polly—3. Peter—4 Mordecai—
5 Asa—6. William, born 26 March, 1777—7. Elisha.

No 3. II B   POLLY THAYER,
married Joseph Kingman, 8 April, 1792.   Their children
were, 1. Mary—2. Joseph—3. William.

———————

No 4 III B   PETER THAYER,
married Unity Hixon of Sharon, and settled in Randolph.
Their children were, 1. Lyman—2 Unity—3. Harriet—4.
Peter—5. Mary—6. Avaline.

No 5. I C.   LYMAN THAYER,
married Irene, daughter of Meshech Thayer, (see 6th
Branch, No. 138,) and settled in Randolph.

———————

No. 6. IV B   MORDECAI THAYER,
son of Peter and Polly Thayer, married Rachel, daughter
of Dea Zacheus Thayer, (see No. 13,) and settled at
Hampden, Me   Their children were, 1. Rachel, born 18
Oct. 1797—2. Mordecai—3. Alvan—4. Nancy—5 Zacheus
6. Seth Mann.

———————

No. 7. V B.   ASA THAYER,
married Olive Mann, and settled in Randolph.   Their children were,

1. Asa,	born 21 Sept	1802	4. Olive,	
2. Olive,	" 9 April	1805	5 William	
3 John,	" 24 Nov	1809		

No 8. I C   ASA THAYER, Jr.,
married Susan Thayer, and settled in Randolph   Their
children were, 1. Susan Jane, born 25 June, 1821—2. Asa
French born 21 July, 1823—3. Hosea—4 Susan Jane, 2d.

———————

No. 9. VI B.   WILLIAM THAYER,
married Sarah Whitcomb of Randolph, and settled in Thetford, Vt   Their children were,

1. Sarah,	born 26 Feb	1805	4. Loren,	born 7 July	1815
2 Relief,	" 4 May,	1807	5 Jane,	" 10 June	1818
3. Wm. Withington, b. 3 June 1809			6.		

No. 10. V A.   EPHRAIM THAYER,

son of Dea. Peter and Anna Thayer, married Phebe Porter of Stoughton, 3 Dec. 1762, and settled in Randolph,
afterwards removed away   Their children were,

1. Anna,	born 12 Oct	1763	4. Archippus,
	Died 13 June 1764.		5. Jonathan,
2 Porter,	born 19 Aug	1765	6. Jabez.
3. Ephraim,	" 2 Aug	1767	

No. 11. VI A.   Dea ZACHEUS THAYER,

married Deborah Mann, 30 June, 1770, and settled in Randolph.   Their children were,

1. Anna,	born 10 April	1772	4. Ruth,	born 15 Sept	1781
2 Deborah,	" 15 May	1774	5. Betsey,	" 18 June	1783
3. Rachel,	" 1 March	1778			

His second wife was Sarah, widow of Joseph Thayer,
deceased. (See 5th Branch, No 2)

No. 12. I B.   ANNA THAYER,

married Meshech Thayer. (See 6th Branch, No. 134)

No. 13. III B.   RACHEL THAYER,

married Mordecai Thayer, No 6, and settled in Hamden,
Maine.

No. 14. IV B   RUTH THAYER,

married Zeba Smith, and settled in Randolph.   Their children were,

1. Ruth,	born 13 May	1801	6. Judson,	born 3 April	1811
2. Lucinda,	" 27 April	1805	7. Isaac,	" 24 May	1813
3. Avis,	" 1 Feb	1807	8 Charles,	" 17 May	1815
4 Zeba,	" 28 Jan	1809	9. Adoniram,	" 20 Sept	1818
5. Elmira,			10.	" 18 July	1822

No 15 I C.   RUTH SMITH,

married Elisha Mann of Randolph, Vt. Mr. Mann was
born 28 March 1805. Their children were, 1. Elisha—2
Seth--3. Judson—4. Hosea—5. Stillman.
    Mr. Mann died in 1835.

No. 16 II C   LUCINDA SMITH,

married Francis Hollis, and settled in Randolph.

No. 17. V B.   BETSEY THAYER,

daughter of Dea Zacheus Thayer, married Bela Jordan,
and settled in Randolph   Mr. Jordan was born 11 April,

1783   Their children were, 1 John, born 9 Feb 1805—2 Betsey, born 23 Feb 1807

No 18   I C   JOHN JORDAN,
married a Phillips of Hanson, Mass and settled in Randolph

No 19   X A   PHEBE THAYER,
a daughter of Dea Peter and Anna Thayer, married Abraham Cummings of Topsfield, in 1781 Their children were, 1 Phebe—2 Ebenezer—3 Jabez

No 20   VII B   ELISHA THAYER,
son of Peter and Polly Thayer, No 2, 7, married a Tyler, and settled at Frankfort, Me

No 21   XII A   BARTHOLOMEW THAYER,
a son of Dea Peter and Anna Thayer, married Elizabeth Blanchard of Braintree, in 1789, (see 4th Branch, No 3,) and settled in Peterborough Their children were, 1 Ephraim—2 Jabez, who died in childhood

No 22   I B   EPHRAIM THAYER,
married and removed to Coshocton, Ohio, and has a family of children

TWELFTH BRANCH.

No 1   PRISCILLA THAYER,
a daughter of Ephraim and Sarah Thayer, married 11 July, 1732, to Elijah Hayden* of Braintree, (now Quincy) Their children were, 1 Elijah, born 22 March, 1733—2 Enoch, born 24 March, 1734

Her second husband was Joseph Ford   Their children were,

3 Joseph,   born 18 Sept 1740 | 5 Nathaniel,   born 23 June 1746
4 James,   " 13 June 1743 |

Her third husband was William Spear, married in 1781 Mrs Priscilla Spear died about the year 1795

*The progenitor of this family in Braintree, was JOHN HAYDEN, and his wife Susannah, whose children were, 1 John—2 Samuel, probably born before they settled in Braintree—3 Jonathan, born 19, 3, 1640—4. Hannah, b 7, 2, 1642—5 Ebenezer, b 12, 7, 1645—6 Nehemiah, b 14, 12, 1647.
JOHN HAYDEN and Hannah Ames were married by Gov Endicott, 6, 2,

No. 2. I A   ELIJAH HAYDEN, Jr.,

married Mary Faxon, and settled in Boston. Their children were, 1. Elijah—2. Mary—3. Lot—4. Elihu—5. James—6 Esther.

No. 3. III B.   LOT HAYDEN,

married Sally Cole, and settled in West Cambridge. Their children were, 1. Mary—2. Nancy—3. Elijah.

No. 4. II A.   ENOCH HAYDEN,

second son of Elijah and Priscilla Hayden, married Amy Thayer, (perhaps daughter of Zachariah Thayer, No 54, 3, first part,) and settled in Quincy. Their children were,

1. Enoch,	born 23 Feb	1756	5 Nathaniel,	born 11 July 1763
2. Priscilla,	" 27 April	1757	6. Elijah,	
3. Caleb,	" 17 May	1759	7. Abel,	
4. Amy,	" 19 Feb	1761	8. Elisha.	

No. 5. I B.   ENOCH HAYDEN,

was blind many years, having lost his sight in consequence of the small pox, and was supported by the town. His mind, however, was well stored with useful knowledge, being blessed with a good memory, and few men enjoyed the pleasure of joining in the Music and devotion of public worship more than he, while he was able to attend. The genealogy of this Branch was principally furnished by him, whose memory alone afforded the particulars, whether correct or not, must be left for others to determine.

He died in 1831.

No. 6. III B.   CALEB HAYDEN,

a brother of the preceding, married Bathsheba Howard, and settled in Quincy ; afterwards removed to Chelmsford, Mass. Their children were, 1. Elijah—2 Samuel—3 Hannah—4. Caleb—5. Josiah—6. Lois—7. Solomon—8. Mary—9. James.

No. 7. I C.   ELIJAH HAYDEN,

married Nancy Crocksford, and settled in Quincy. Their children were, 1. Elijah—2. Eli—3. Elbridge Gerry.

1660. Their children were, 1. Hannah, born 3, 11, 1660—2. Sarah, b 9, 5, 1662—3 Josiah, b. 19, 4, 1669.

SAMUEL HAYDEN and Hannah Thayer were married by Maj Lusher, 8, 2, 1664. (See Thayer No. 1, first part.) Their children were, 1 Samuel, born 6, 6, 1665, died 27 of the same month—2. Susannah, b. 27, 7, 1666—3. Sarah, b. 25, 1, 1658.

JONATHAN HAYDEN, with his wife Elizabeth, had 1. Margaret, born 11, 3, 1670—2. Amey, b 16, 7, 1672.

32

No. 8   III D   ELBRIDGE G HAYDEN,

married Elizabeth Holbrook of Braintree, (see 6 Branch, No. 94,) and settled in Quincy.

No 9.   III C   HANNAH HAYDEN,

daughter of Caleb and Bathsheba Hayden, married Thomas Newcomb of Quincy, and settled there.   Their children were, 1. Eliza—2. Thomas—3. William.

No. 10.   V C.   JOSIAH HAYDEN,

a brother of the preceding, married Betsey Miller, and settled in Quincy.   Children not known

No 11.   VII C   SOLOMON HAYDEN,

married Louisa Miller, and settled in Quincy.   Children not known.

No. 12.   VIII C   MARY HAYDEN,

married Joel Bemis, and settled in Quincy.

No. 13.   V B.   NATHANIEL HAYDEN,

son of Enoch and Amy Hayden, married Allice Peakes, and settled at South Boston.   Their children were, 1 Oliver—2. Mary—3 Isaac—4. Ambrose—5. Peter—6. Philip—7. Nathaniel—8 Allice—9. William.

No 14.   VII B   ABEL HAYDEN,

a brother of the preceding, married Lydia Niles, and settled in Quincy.   Their children were, 1 Nancy—2. Elizabeth—3. George—4. Mehitabel—5. Abel Thayer—6. Mary Niles

No 15.   VIII B.   ELISHA HAYDEN,

the youngest brother of the preceding, married Rebecca Finney.   Their children were, 1 Lewis—2. Elisha—3. Joseph—4. Thomas—5. Mary—6. Charles—7. Eliza.

No 16.   III A   JOSEPH FORD,*

son of Joseph and Priscilla Ford, married Mary Roberts, and settled in Boston   They had one daughter Mary, who was the wife of Mr Freeman, attorney at law at Barnstable, Mass, and died without issue

---

*Mr Nathaniel Ford, son of David Ford of Weymouth, says, his ancestors of the name of Ford, who came from England were NATHANIEL,

No. 17. IV A. JAMES FORD,

a brother of the preceding, settled in the city of New York, and is supposed to have left a large family.

No. 18 V A. NATHANIEL FORD,

the youngest brother of the preceding, went to the state of Maryland, leaving a daughter Joanna, born 6 June, 1765, in the care of his mother, by whom she was brought up, and nothing certain was known respecting him afterwards.

No. 19. I B. JOANNA FORD,

was married 22 April, 1787, to Isaac N. Field, who was born 27 April, 1765, and settled in Dorchester. Their children were,

1. Enos,	born 9 July	1788	6. Charlotte,	born	5 May	1796
2. Peter,	" 17 Nov	1789	7. Thomas M	"	31 Mar	1798
	Died 24 July 1792.		8. Aaron Davis,	"	10 Oct	1799
3 Joanna,	born 24 Aug	1791	9 Pearson H	"	19 Aug	1802
4. Isaac,	" 19 March	1793	10 Freeman,	"	3 Nov	1804
5 Lois,	" 8 Sept	1794	11. Harriet S.	"	30 Nov	1807
	Died 10 Oct 1795.					

No. 20. I C. ENOS FIELD,

married Elizabeth Blake, 10 May, 1818, and settled in Dorchester.

No 21. III C. JOANNA FIELD,

married Thomas Cox of Dorchester, and died 28 July, 1825.

No. 22. IV C. ISAAC FIELD,

married Emeline, daughter of Samuel Richards of Dorchester, 22 April, 1821. (See 14 Branch, No. 5.)

No. 23. VI C. CHARLOTTE FIELD,

married Ebenezer Bates, 24 Sept. 1823, and settled in Dedham. Mr. Bates died 14 May, 1828, leaving one child.

JOSEPH, ISRAEL, HANNAH, and ANN, the three last of whom died unmarried. JOSEPH lived and died in that neighborhood. His son Joseph married Priscilla Hayden, as before mentioned. David Ford of Weymouth, was son of Capt James Ford, Mariner, whose widow Deborah died about the year 1793, and grandson of Nathaniel Ford, who came from England.

Mr Farmer mentions "ANDREW FORD, Weymouth, freeman 1654, who had sons Samuel and Ebenezer. Twelve graduates of this name had been educated at the New England Colleges in 1825. ROGER (Ford or Foord) died at Cambridge, 24 April, 1644. THOMAS, Dorchester, admitted freeman 1631, removed to Windsor, Conn. WILLIAM was a proprietor of Bridgewater, 1645 "—[*Gen Reg.*]

No. 24.   VII C   THOMAS M FIELD,
married Esther Fuller, 23 April, 1820, and settled in Boston.

No 25.   VIII C.   AARON D. FIELD,
married Mary Ann Fessendon, 22 Dec. 1824, and settled
in Dorchester.

No. 26.   IX C.   PEARSON H FIELD,
married Susan N. Richards, 14 April, 1825, and settled in
Boston.

No. 27.   XI C.   HARRIET S. FIELD,
married Gardner E. Weatherbee, 13 Sept 1829, and settled in Dorchester.

THIRTEENTH BRANCH.

No. 1.   JAMES THAYER,
a son of Ephraim and Sarah Thayer, married Deborah
Arnold, (see Arnold No. 4, 10, first part,) and settled in
Braintree, on the farm of his ancestors.   Their children
were,

1. Ephraim,	born 14 Oct	1749	9. Deliverance, born 16 Aug	1762
2. Sarah,	" 1 Dec	1750	10. Demetrius, " 23 July	1764
3. James,	" 28 Aug	1752	11 Deborah, " 16 July	1766
4. Philip,	" 11 Nov	1753	12. Elizabeth, " 26 Dec	1769
5. Solomon,	" 10 Sept	1755	Died in infancy.	
6. Deborah,	" 9 March	1757	13. Elizabeth, born 3 Mar	1771
7. William,	" 8 March	1759	Died 4 Dec 1790, with consumption.	
8. Abigail,	" 4 Feb	1761		

Mr. Thayer died 19 June, 1790, aged 78 years 3 months.
Mrs. Thayer died 14 Dec. 1792, with small pox, aged 63
years.

No. 2.   I A.   EPHRAIM THAYER,
married Rebecca Porter, and settled in Boston. Mrs. Thayer was born 24 May, 1753.   Their children were,

1. Ephraim,	born 9 Sept	1781	4 Sally, born 19 Dec	1786
	Died 2 Feb 1782.		Died 22 July 1806.	
2. Ephraim,	born 15 April	1783	5 Betsey, born 13 June	1790
	Died 16 Nov 1819.		6. Lucretia, " 24 Nov	1793
3. Rebecca,	born 8 March	1785	7. Debby, " 19 May	1796
	Died 8 June 1796.			

Mrs. Thayer died 2 June, 1817, aged 64 years.

No. 3. VI B.   LUCRETIA THAYER,

married Stephen W. Jackson of Boston.   (See Jackson No. 18, 3, first part.)   Their children were,

1. George,	born 16 Feb	1814		6. Lucretia,	born	1 April	1824
2. Rebecca T.	" 21 Nov	1815			Died 22 Sept 1825.		
	Died 26 Dec 1816			7. Lucretia,	born 18 Dec		1825
3. Charles,	born 19 Oct	1817		8 Stephen W.	" 28 Feb		1829
4 Rebecca T.	" 3 Nov	1819			Died 14 Dec 1829.		
5. Stephen W.	" 1 Mar	1822		9. Sarah,	born 15 July		1830
	Died 17 Sept 1823.				Died 17 July 1830.		

No. 4. II A.   SARAH THAYER,

daughter of James and Deborah Thayer, married William Crane, 12 Sept. 1776, and settled in Boston.   Their children were,

1. William,	born 8 Jan	1778	3. Mary,	
2. Sarah,	" 16 Oct	1779		Died at the age of 4 years
			4. Betsey,	born 27 March 1783

Her second husband was Thomas Emmons.

No 5. I B.   WILLIAM CRANE,

married Dorcas Sawyer, and settled in Boston.   Their children were, 1. William, 2. Elizabeth, 3. Margaret.
Mr. Crane died 15 Jan. 1821, aged 43 years.

No. 6. II B.   SARAH CRANE,

married Amasa Murdock, and settled in Boston.   Their children were, 1. Mary, 2. Mary, 3. Amasa, 4. Sarah E. 5. John, 6. William, 7 Elizabeth, 8. Elizabeth.
Mrs. Murdock died in July, 1823, aged 44 years.

No. 7. III C.   AMASA MURDOCK,

married Jane Loring, and settled in Boston.   Their child, 1. Albert Loring, born 4 Sept. 1829.

No. 8. IV C.   SARAH EMMONS MURDOCK,

married Stephen W. Trowbridge, and settled in Newton. Their children were,

1. Sarah Jane,	born 7 Mar	1827	3. Eliza Davis.
2. Adeline Fuller,	" 23 Oct	1828	

No 9. IV B.   BETSEY CRANE,

married Capt. James Thayer of Quincy   (See No 14)

No. 10 III A   JAMES THAYER,

son of James and Deborah Thayer, married Mehitabel

Brackett, and settled in Braintree   Their children were,

1. Mary,   born 15 Dec   1776 | 2 James,   born 31 Oct   1778

His second wife was Mary, daughter of Thomas Thayer, married 26 Oct 1779   (See Thayer No 85, 4, first part) Their children were,

3 Thomas,   born 7 Oct   1780 | 5 Lydia,   born 29 Aug   1784
4 Jechonias,   " 25 Jan   1783 |

Mr. Thayer died 19 March, 1786, aged 33 years 7 months.

No 11   I B   MARY THAYER,

married Zenas Mansfield of Braintree, 14 April, 1794 Their children were, 1 Zenas, 2 James T who died 4 Oct 1797, 3 Mary, 4 Warren, 5 Mehitabel, 6. Betsey, 7 William, 8. George

No. 12.   IV C.   WARREN MANSFIELD,

married Jane B Dyer, (6 Branch, No 72,) and settled in Braintree   Their children are,

1. Charles W. born 19 Sept 1828 | 2 Sarah H.   born 17 June   1830

No 13   VI C   BETSEY MANSFIELD,

married Moses Ingalls of Boston, and settled there. Their child is 1 Mary Elizabeth.

No 14.   II B   Capt JAMES THAYER,

son of James and Mehitabel Thayer, married Betsey Crane, No 9, and settled in Quincy   Their children were,

1 Sarah Crane, born 16 May 1809 | 3 Elizabeth Emmons, b. 1 July 1813
2. Mary Brackett, " 14 Dec 1810 |

Capt Thayer died 17 Dec 1821, aged 43 years

No 15.   I C   SARAH C. THAYER,

married Ebenezer Underwood, and settled in Quincy

No 16   II C   MARY B THAYER,

married William Ditson, and settled in Quincy

No. 17.   V B.   LYDIA THAYER,

daughter of James and Mary Thayer, married Boylston Vinton, (see Adams No 29, 2, first part,) and settled in W Boylston, Mass   Their children were,

1. Lydia T.   born 8 Jan   1817 | 3 Mary Ann,
        Died in April 1833. | 4 John Quincy Adams
2. Louisa,

No 18   IV A   PHILIP THAYER,

son of James and Deborah Thayer, married Lydia Salisbury, and settled in Braintree   Mrs. Thayer was born 22 April, 1752   Their children were,

1 Stephen,	born 14 Sept	1778	5 Warren,	born 19 Jan	1789
2. Theodore,	" 29 Oct	1780	Died with bilious colic, 15 March,		
	Died at sea.		1810, sick but four days.		
3. Lydia,	born 4 May	1783	6 Elias,	born 30 April	1792
4 Philip,	" 4 Oct	1785	7 Mary,	" 13 April	1794

Mr Thayer died 20 Oct 1832

No 19   I B   STEPHEN THAYER,

married Nancy Leeds, and settled in Boston   Their children were,

1. Nancy,	born 10 March	1806	7 Edward,	born 5 Jan	1817
2. Stephen,	" 2 Feb	1808	8 Lucretia,	" 19 April	1819
	Died 1 Feb 1832		9 Henry,	" 29 Dec	1820
3. Sally,	born 12 Nov	1809		Died 1 Jan 1821.	
4 Warren,	" 18 Aug	1811	10. Wm. Henry, born 27 Dec		1822
5. Morgiana C. F.	" 21 Nov	1813	11 Theodore H.	" 23 Nov	1824
6 Elias,	" 11 Aug	1815	12. Alonzo,	" 11 June	1826

Mrs Thayer died 6 Dec 1826

No 20   I C.   NANCY THAYER,

married Charles Jarvis, and settled in Boston   Their children were,

1 Charles,	born 12 Sept	1825	2 Harriet,	born March	1827

Mrs Jarvis died 27 Jan 1831.

No 21   III B.   LYDIA THAYER,

daughter of Philip and Lydia Thayer, married Ezekiel White, and settled in Braintree   Their children were,

1 Lydia,	born 9 Dec	1805	Died 18 Nov 1824	
2. Sabra,	" 1 Nov	1808	3 Mary, born 1 July	1814

No 22   I C   LYDIA WHITE,

married Daniel Orcutt, and settled in Braintree.   Their children were, 1 Henry May, 2
Mrs Orcutt died in July, 1833, aged 27 years

No 23   IV B   PHILIP THAYER, Jr,

married Rebecca Leeds, and settled in Boston   Their children were, 1. Mary, 2 Frances Adeline, 3 Philip, 4. Almira Frances, 5. Lydia   Mr Thayer died 6 Dec 1827

No 24   I C   MARY THAYER,

married William Bird, and settled in Braintree   Their child 1 Rebecca Frances, was born 11 Aug 1831

No 25. VII B.   MARY THAYER,

daughter of Philip and Lydia Thayer, married Ezra Dyer,
and settled in Braintree   Their children are,

1. Ezra,   born 28 June   1819 | 3 Sabra Adams, born 21 Aug 1826
2. Mary,   "   12 July   1823 |

No 26. V A   SOLOMON THAYER,

son of James and Deborah Thayer, married Lydia, daugh-
ter of Ensign Thomas Thayer, 26 Oct 1779, (see Thayer
No 85, 7, first part,) and settled in Braintree, on the farm
of his ancestors. (See Appendix to first part, page 175.)
By her he had one son, 1 Theophilus, born 21 May, 1781.
Mrs Thayer died 19 March, 1783   His second wife was
Elizabeth, daughter of Abraham Thayer, (No 48, 6, first
part.)   Their children were,

2 Jechonias, born 24 July   1786 | 4. Solomon Alden, b 17 Dec 1792
3. Betsey,   "   26 May   1789 |

   Solomon Thayer, Esq died 1 Feb. 1835.

No. 27 I B   THEOPHILUS THAYER,

married Elizabeth Hall, and settled in Quincy Mrs Thayer was born 22 Jan 1780.   Their children were,

1. Harriet Ann, born 22 Dec 1804 | 2. George Alden, born 11 July 1807

   Mr Thayer died 14 June, 1814

No 28 II B   JECHONIAS THAYER,

married Eliza McClure, and was a Merchant in Boston
Their children were,

1. Eliza Ann,   born 15 July 1813 | Died 1 Aug 1821.
2. Mary Wilson,   "   4 Oct 1815 | 3. Sarah Hunter, born 17 April 1817

   Mrs. Thayer died 15 Aug 1818, aged 27   His second
wife was Abby Hurd. Their children were,

4. Mary Wilson, born 11 July 1821 | 7. Benjamin Hurd, b. 24 Sept 1825
5. Theophilus,   "   13 Aug 1823 | 8. Abby Hurd,
6. Jechonias,   "   1 Dec 1824 | 9. Harriet Louisa.
           Died 4 Oct 1831.

No 29. III B   BETSEY THAYER,

married Harlow Hooker, and settled in Boston.

No. 30. IV B. SOLOMON A THAYER,

married Abby Stetson, and settled in Braintree Their
children were, 1 Mary, born 29 Oct. 1818, 2. Ephraim, 3.
Harlow Hooker.

   Mr Thayer died in Oct 1828, aged 36 years.

No. 31.　VII A.　Capt. WILLIAM THAYER,

son of James and Deborah Thayer, married Sarah, daughter of Moses and Dorothy Jones, (see 5th Branch, No 3, also Copeland No 57, 2, first part,) in 1781, and settled in Braintree, near the great pond.　Their children were,

1. Mary,	born 27 April	1782	8 Betsey,	born	5 Dec	1795
2 William,	" 26 Oct	1783	9 Rebecca,	"	9 Aug	1798
3 Sally,	" 31 Oct	1785	10. Thomas,	"	4 March1801
4. Ruth,	" 1 Sept	1787	11 John Davis,	"	23 April	1803
5 Ruth, 2d,	" 10 Nov	1778	12 Lucretia,	"	15 Aug	1805
6. Prudence,	" 18 March	1791	13 Evelina,	"	19 Oct	1807
7. Deborah,	" 1 Sept	1793				

Mrs Thayer died 13 Oct. 1813, aged 51 years, nearly. Capt. Thayer died 17 March, 1822, aged 63 years.

No. 32　I B　　MARY THAYER,

married Thomas Hunt, and settled in Milton.　Their children were,

1 Mary,	born 14 Sept	1803	6 Charles K.	born 19 Dec	1813
2 Ruth Thayer,	" 28 April	1805	7 Joseph,	" 15 Dec	1815
3 Thomas,	" 17 April	1807	8 George,	" 12 Feb	1818
4 Sarah,	" 8 March 1809	9. Betsey Thayer,"	8 Jan	1822
5. Beulah,	" 19 Oct	1811	10 Wm. Alden, "	2 Nov	1826

No. 33.　I C.　　MARY HUNT,

married John Farrington of Milton　Their children were,

1. Sarah,	born 30 Oct	1826	2 Mary,	born 29 Jan	1828
	Died 12 May 1827		3 Sarah,	" 16 Dec	1830

No. 34.　II C.　　RUTH T. HUNT,

married Nathaniel Farrington, brother of the preceding, and settled in Canton.　Their child, 1. Nathaniel, born 3 June, 1831.

No 35.　III C.　　THOMAS HUNT Jr.,

married Augusta Crane, and settled in Milton.　Their child, 1 Augusta, was born 4 Jan. 1831.

No 36.　II B.　WILLIAM THAYER, Jr.,

married Sally, daughter of Josiah French, (see French, No. 46, first part,) and settled in Braintree.　Their children were, 1. Sally—2. David—3 Esther—4. Harriet—5 William—6. Elbridge—7. Joel—8. George—9. ——.

No. 37.　III B　　SALLY THAYER,

married Alpheus Thayer of Braintree, Vt.　Their children were,

33

1 Henry,	born 1 Aug	1801	4 Mary,	born 21 Jan	1812
2 Sarah,	" 9 Oct	1806	5 William,	" 11 Dec	1817
3 Ephraim,	" 9 Dec	1809	6. John Davis,	" 4 March	1823

No 38. V B.   RUTH THAYER,

married Christopher Kneeland of Boston   Their child, 1
Charles, was born 13 Aug. 1812, died 6 Nov 1814

Mr. Kneeland died 9 Feb 1814   Her second husband
was Thomas Emmons of Boston, a Cabinet Maker   Their
children were,

2. Thomas,	born 8 March	1816	4 John Alden,	born 31 Dec	1821
3. George,	" 5 Sept	1818	5. Alfred,	" 11 Sept	1823

Mr. Emmons died 17 April, 1825, aged 41 years

No. 39   VI B. PRUDENCE THAYER,

married Josiah Ames, and settled in Dracutt.   Their children were,

1. George,	born 5 Aug	1813	4 Harriet,	born 13 Sept	1819
2 Sarah Jones,	" 4 April	1815	5. John,	" 10 Dec	1821
3 Josiah,	" 17 Dec	1817	6		

No 40. VII B   DEBORAH THAYER,

married Alpheus Cary, Jr of Boston, son of Alpheus Cary,
who died in Milton, and grandson of Dea Jonathan Cary
of N. Bridgewater. [See Cary's Gen p 6.   Their children
are,

1. Alpheus,	born 5 Oct 1827	2. George W born 31 March 1830

No. 41. VIII B   BETSEY THAYER,

married Lewis Copeland of Milton   (See Copeland No 65,
8, first part)   Their children are,

1. Rebecca Thayer, b. 4 Feb 1823	3 Martha Emmons, b 9 May 1827
2. Charles Lewis, " 11 Feb 1825	

No 42. IX B   REBECCA THAYER,

married Stephen Lynch of Boston   Their children are,

1. Charles,	born 8 Oct 1825	2 Rebecca,	born 1 July 1827

No. 43   X B   THOMAS THAYER,

married Ann Locklin, and had by her one child, 1. Martha
Ann.

No. 44   XI B.   JOHN D. THAYER,

married Caroline Dexter, and settled in Quincy.   They
have two children

No 45. XII B LUCRETIA THAYER,
married Charles Coolidge, and settled in Boston.

No 46. VIII A ABIGAIL THAYER,
daughter of James and Deborah Thayer, married Silas
Wild, Jr of Braintree (See Thayer No. 20, 4, first part.)
Their children were,

1. Silas,	born 23 Jan	1787	7 Alden,	born Sept 1798
2 James T	" 16 Nov	1789	8 Lydia,	" 3 May 1801
3. Abigail,	" 17 June	1792	9 Washington, }	" 5 May 1802
4 Elisha,	" Jan	1794	10 Adams, }	
5 Betsey,	" 31 March	1795	Died 29 Jan 1803	
6 Polly Crane,				

Mrs Wild died 8 Jan. 1803, aged 43 years, nearly. His
second wife was Mrs Hayden, a daughter of Mr John
Noyes. Mr Wild died 12 Oct. 1828, aged 67 years, nearly.

No 47 I B SILAS WILD, Jr.,
married Ruth Reed of Braintree, and settled in Weymouth.
Their children are,

1 Abigail Thayer,	b 17 June 1811	5 Elizabeth Reed,	b 14 Aug 1821
2. Geo Washington,	" 29 Aug 1816	6 Mary Parker,	" 7 Mar 1823
3 Silas Franklin,	" 21 Aug 1818	7. Henry Martyn,	" 20 Dec 1825
4. Jona Sawyer,	" 29 April 1820		

No. 48 III B. ABIGAIL WILD,
married Pardon Keith of Bridgewater Their children are,

1. Willard,	born 6 June 1812	5 Betsey Ann,	b 31 Mar 1820
2 Nathan,	" 11 Feb 1814	6 Simeon Cary,	" 1 Sept 1822
3. Hannah,	" 30 Nov 1815	7. Abigail Thayer,	" 18 July 1826
4 Mary Wild,	" 10 Feb 1818	8 Howard Pardon,	" 13 June 1831

No 49. IV B ELISHA WILD,
married Caroline Healy, and settled in Braintree. Their
children are,

1 John Francis,	born 28 Dec 1820	3. Caroline,	born 13 Oct 1825
2 Rebecca,	" 21 Feb 1821		

No 50 VI B POLLY CRANE WILD,
married Jonathan Sawyer, and settled in Boston. Their
children were,

1 George,	born 26 July 1822	3 Mary Elizabeth,	b. 18 Sept 1828
2 Warren,	" 23 May 1825		

Mr. Sawyer died 7 Aug. 1831, aged 53

No. 51 VII B ALDEN WILD,
married Ann Cook, and settled in the city of New York.

Their children are, 1. Mary Ann—2. Harriet Newell—3. Caroline—4. Deborah—5 Elmira.

No. 52.   VIII B.   LYDIA WILD,

married Calvin Thayer, Jr , grandson of Nathaniel Thayer, (No 38, first part,) and settled in Braintree. Their children were, 1. Calvin—2 Lydia—3. Julia Ann. Mr. Thayer died in 1825

Her second husband was Robert Howe of Roxbury. Their children were, 1 Nancy Triplett—2 Abigail Thayer, who died 15 Jan 1832—3 Robert Harris, who died 23 Dec. 1831.

No. 53.   IX A   DELIVENANCE THAYER,

daughter of James and Deborah Thayer, married Deacon Eliphaz Thayer, (see Thayer No. 12, 4, first part,) and settled in Braintree. Their children were,

1. Deliverance,	born 14 May 1785			Died 25 Sept 1797.		
2. Sarah,	"	13 April 1787	7. Deborah,	born	7 Oct	1798
3. Isaiah,	"	2 Mar 1789	8. Lois,	"	11 Oct	1800
4. James,	"	29 Sept 1791	9 Eliphaz,	"	24 Feb	1803
5. Esther French,	"	12 Dec 1793		Died 11 Oct 1821.		
6. Eliphaz,	"	4 Feb 1796	10. Abigail,	born 27 Oct		1805

No. 54   I B   DELIVERANCE THAYER,

married Dea Nathaniel E. Thayer of Braintree. (See Ninth Branch, No. 58)

No. 55.   III B   ISAIAH THAYER,

married Sarah Hunt of Weymouth, and settled there.
Their children are,

1. Sally,	born 19 Jan 1814	4 William Alden,	born 16 May 1820
2 Deliverance,	" 6 Aug 1816	5. Sally Alden,	" 18 Aug 1822
3. Isaiah Warren,	" 2 Jan 1818	6 Susan S.	" 23 Nov 1824

No 56   V B.   ESTHER F. THAYER,

married Jonathan Hayward, and settled in Braintree.
Their children are,

1. Daniel,	born 13 May 1815	3 Jonathan Eliphaz, b. 24 Nov 1822
2 Esther,	" 20 Jan 1819	

No 57.   VII B.   DEBORAH THAYER,

married Sidney Johnson, and settled in Braintree. Their children are, 1. George Sidney, born 23 Oct 1815—2. Abigail—3 James—4 ——

No. 58.   VIII B.   LOIS THAYER,

married Nathaniel Seaver Spear, and settled in Quincy.
Their child, I. Daniel.

No. 59.   X A.   DEMETRIUS THAYER,

youngest son of James and Deborah Thayer, married Sarah
Blanchard of Weymouth, and settled there. Their children were,

1. Nicholas,	born 12 March 1801	Died 24 Aug 1825.
2 Sarah Hovey, "	3 Nov 1802	4. Chloe, born 3 April 1807
3 Charlotte, "	22 Aug 1804	5 Warren, " 29 Jan 1813

No. 60.   I B.   NICHOLAS THAYER,

married Thais Shaw, and settled in Weymouth Their
children are, 1. Noah—2. ——.

FOURTEENTH BRANCH.

No 1.   ABIGAIL THAYER,

the youngest daughter and child of Ephraim and Sarah
Thayer, was married 21 Nov. 1734, to Dr Benjamin Richards of Weymouth, and settled there. Their children were,

1 A son, } who died infants.	6. Sarah,	born 13 Oct 1744
2 A son, }	7. Joanna,	" in 1746
3 Benjamin, born 25 Dec 1739	8. Peter,*	" in 1748
Died in the army, 1757.	9 Ruth,	" 20 Aug 1750
4 Ephraim, born in 1741	Died 26 Sept 1833, aged 83	
5 Abigail, " 17 Nov 1742	10. Mary,	born 17 April 1753

Dr. Richards was an eminent Physician and a skillful
Practitioner in his day, especially in the throat distemper,
which, with the bloody flux, (dysentery,) were the fatal
epidemics and prevailed with uncommon mortality in the
years 1746, 7, 8, and 9.—[See *Alden's Coll* 2, 15.

Dr. Richards died 25 June, 1755, in the 41 year of his
age. Mrs Abigail Richards died 10 March, 1765, in the
52 year of her age.

No. 2.   IV A   EPHRAIM RICHARDS,

married Christian Rogers, a grand-daughter of Mr. Samuel Bass of Boston, (perhaps son of Samuel Bass, Sen., see
Bass No 3,3, first part,) and settled in Boston. Their children were, 1 Benjamin—2. Samuel—3. Lydia—4. Edmund
Quincy—5. Peter Hunt—6. Ephraim, who died young

---

*He was killed on board a privateer in 1778, aged 30 years.

Mr Richards died of the small pox in Boston, when that port was shut by the British, in 1774, aged 33 years.

No 3   I B.   BENJAMIN RICHARDS,
married and died in early life, leaving several children.

No. 4   II B   SAMUEL RICHARDS,
married Mary Wentworth, and settled in Dorchester. Their children were, 1 Emeline—2. Ansel Paca Pendleton, who left Dorchester in 1821, engaged in the U. S service, and has not been heard from for several years, it is presumed he is dead, and Administration on his estate was granted 14 Aug 1833—3 Laura—4 Warren Washington Hancock—5 Gerry Sullivan Gray, who was killed by the accidental discharge of a gun, while on a party of pleasure, near Squantum, in 1828 Mr Richards died about 1817.

No 5   I C   EMELINE RICHARDS,
married Isaac Field of Dorchester. (See 12 Branch No 22)

No 6   III C.   LAURA RICHARDS,
married Oliver Hall of Dorchester, and died 18 Nov 1832, aged 28 years

No 7   III B   LYDIA RICHARDS,
married first a Mr Hersey, settled in Charlestown, and after his decease, she married Capt William Rogers of Dorchester, of whom Rev William Rogers of Townsend, is adopted son

No 8   IV B   EDMUND QUINCY RICHARDS,
married and settled in Boston. Removed to Saco, Me had a large family Stephen, Edmund, John, Sarah and Lydia, twins, Abigail and others.

No 9   V B   PETER H. RICHARDS,
married Mary Duncan, 17 June 1792, and settled in Boston Their children were,

1 Christian Rogers b 27 Mar 1793	3 Peter H Richards, b 5 Jan 1797
2. Mary King, " 9 Sept 1795	4 Susannah Nazaro, " 2 Nov 1799

I C.   CHRISTIAN R RICHARDS,
was married 28 Oct 1812, to Marvin Marcy, and settled in East Cambridge. Their children were,

1 A son deceased.	3 Marvin Richards, b. 1 Dec 1816
2. Christian M born 11 Dec 1811	4 Mary Duncan. " 3 Oct 1818

5 Susannah Richards, b 3 May 1820 | 8 Daniel Grovsner, b 22 Oct 1825
6. Wm. Winchester, b 22 Aug 1822 | Died 5 Sept 1829
7. Howard Field,   " 22 Dec 1824 | 9 Lydia R Rogers, b 13 Sept 1830

II C   MARY K RICHARDS,

was married 16 Sept 1819, to Erastus Farnum   Their
children were,

1 George Macy, born 1 Nov 1820 | 2 Mary Richards, born 23 Aug 1820
      Mrs. Farnum, died 24 March 1825.

IV C   SUSANNAH N RICHARDS,

was married 14 April 1825, to Pearson H Field of Boston.
Their children were six, three of whom are now living.

1 *Pelans H* born   May 1826 | 3 Pearson H.   "   in 1833
2 Susannah L.   "   July 1827 |

No 10   V A.   ABIGAIL RICHARDS,

daughter of Dr. Benjamin and Abigail Richards, married
Rev Jonathan French of Andover   (See Ninth Branch,
No 62) Mrs Abigail French died 28 Aug 1821.

No 11.   VI A   SARAH RICHARDS,

sister of the preceding, married Leonard Miller of Boston,
son of John and Elizabeth Miller of Milton.   He was born
10 Dec 1743   Their children were, 1 Abigail, who married Nathaniel Lyttle of Boston, and died without issue--
2 George Ruggles, born 7 March, 1767, and died at Savan-
nah--3 Leonard--4. Joseph--5 Peter
      Mrs Sarah Miller died in 1802, aged 58 years.

No. 12   VII A   JOANNA RICHARDS,

sister of the preceding, married in 1766, to Lemuel Howe,
son of Dea Josiah and Sarah Howe* of Milton   Removed

---

* Epitaph on the tombstones of D n JOSIAH HOWE, and his wife
   Dea. Josiah Howe died Oct 3, 1792, in the 71 year of his age.

Here stands his Urn,	His body's dead,
He'll not return,	His spirit's fled,
He's gone to Christ above	His song's Redeeming Love.

SARAH HOWE died 13 Nov 1797, aged 81 years
      Tired with the troubles and ye cares,
      A long train of four score years,
      The pris'ner smiled to be released,
      She felt her fetters loose,
      And mounted to her rest

to Templeton, Mass   Mr Howe was born 5 Aug 1744. Their children were,

1. Joanna,	born 11 Jan 1768		4 Abigail Richards, b 29 May 1774
2 Sarah Preston,	" 19 May 1769		5 Elizabeth,	" 8 Apr 1782
3 Josiah,	" 19 Mar 1771		

Mrs Joanna Howe, died in 1819, aged 73 years

No 13   II B   SARAH P HOWE,

married Elisha Tucker of Winchendon, Mass   Their children were,

1. Mary,	born 17 Oct 1793		4. Joanna Howe, b 23 June 1799
2 Sarah Preston,	" 17 July 1795		5. Abigail Elizabeth, b 23 Apr 1803
3 Elisha,	" 24 July 1797		

No. 14   III B.   Dr JOSIAH HOWE,

brother of the preceding, Physician in Templeton, removed to Westminster, and married Lucy Barron, daughter of Dr Shattuck of Templeton, and sister of Dr Shattuck of Boston   Their children were, 1 Josiah, deceased—2. Benjamin Shattuck, deceased—3 Lemuel Barron—4 Lucy Barron—5 Rebekah Elizabeth—6. Josiah—7 George Cheyne Shattuck.

No 15   III C   LEMUEL B HOWE,

married Ruth Ann Richardson. Their children were, 1 Benjamin Shattuck, deceased—2 Lucy Shattuck and Catharine McFarland, twins.

No 16.   IV C   LUCY B HOWE,

married Dr John White of Westminster   Their children were, 1 Mary Lane, deceased—2 Lucy Shattuck, deceased—3 John Lane.

No 17   IV B   ABIGAIL R HOWE,

daughter of Lemuel and Joanna Howe, married Dea William Stearns of Epping, N H   Their children were, 1 William Ruggles, born 1 Nov 1809—2. Josiah Howe—3. Mary Elizabeth—4 Samuel Richards, deceased

No 18   V B   ELIZABETH HOWE,

married Joseph Upham of Templeton.

No 19.   X A   MARY RICHARDS,

youngest daughter of Dr Benjamin Richards, married Samnel Jones of Milton. Their children were, 1 Samuel—2 Benjamin Richards, who died young

3 Benj. Richards, b 28 Aug 1776		7 Sarah,	born 28 Nov 1786
4. Ruth,	" 21 Dec 1778	8. Lemuel Howe,	
5. Mary,	" 18 April 1781	9. Sophia.	
6. Stephen,			

Mrs. Mary Jones died in 1813, aged 60 years

No 20. I B   SAMUEL JONES, Jr ,

married Joanna Leasure   Their children were, 1 Benjamin Richards—2 Ann—3 Samuel—4 Peter Hunt Richards—5 Harriet—6. Abigail Howe—7. Elizabeth Brackett

No 21. III B   BENJAMIN R JONES,

married Mehitabel Lewis Hersey   Their children were, 1 Ebenezer Lewis—2 Mary—3. Sarah

No 22. IV B   RUTH R JONES,

married Dea Aaron Hayden of Eastport, Me   Their children were, 1 and 2 twins, deceased, 3 Aaron, deceased, 4 Hannah Claflin, wife of Mr Green, 5 Sally Leighton, wife of Mr Brooks of Salem, Mass , 6 Charles Henry, 7. Susan, 8. Aaron, 9. Emma and Sophia, twins, 11. Lucy Ann Sharp, 12 Daniel Sharp

No. 23. V B   MARY JONES,

married Edmund Johnson. Their children were, 1 Oliver Shed, 2 Sarah, 3. Mary, 4 Sophia Jones

No. 24 VI B   STEPHEN JONES,

married Elizabeth Brackett Young   Their child was John Young

No. 25 VII B   SARAH JONES,

was married, to whom, or where settled is not known.

No 26 VIII B   LEMUEL H. JONES,

was married, to whom, or where settled is also unknown.

No 27 IX B   SOPHIA JONES,

was married to a Mr. Gleason, but where settled, &c unknown.

34

Of the early settlers of New England of the name of Richards, there were EDWARD and SUSAN RICHARDS of Dedham, whose children were 1. Mary, born 28, 7, 1639—2 John, b 1, 5, 1641—3 Dorcas, b 24 7, 1643—4. Nathaniel, b 25, 11, 1648—5. Sarah, b. 25, 3, 1651 The children of John and Mary Richards were 1. John, born 20, 5, 1663, and perhaps others "EDWARD of Lynn, who died 20 Jan 1690, aged 74, leaving a son John (Lewis) JAMES, Mass admitted freeman 1652. JAMES, Conn was elected magistrate in 1665. JOHN, Dorchester, member of the Artillery Company 1644, its lieutenant in 1667, a captain and major, representative for Newbury from 1671 to 1673, 3 years, for Hadley 1675, of Boston 1679 and 1680; speaker Feb. 1680; was elected assistant 1680 to 1686; and one of the first counsellors under the charter of William and Mary, 1692 He died at Boston, 2 April, 1694 He married Elizabeth, widow of Adam Winthrop, 3 May, 1654. NATHANIEL, Cambridge, freeman 1632
[*Holmes Hist Cambridge.*

THOMAS, Mass was admitted freeman 1640. THOMAS, freeman 1645; member of the Artillery Company 1648. WILLIAM, Weymouth, 1658," (perhaps grandfather of Dr Richards)

"Of the name of Richards, 18 had graduated at the New England Colleges in 1828."—[*Farmer's Gen. Reg*

An extract from an article in Alden's Coll 2, 7, will at once give a recapitulation of the descent of these families from John Alden, and conclude the genealogy

"In the maternal line "*of these families,*" are traced to the Hon John Alden, one of the pilgrims of Leyden, who came to Plymouth in 1620, who was assistant to all the Governors of the Old Colony, except the first, who died at Duxbury in 1688, at the age of about eighty-nine years John Bass of Braintree, (now Quincy,) married Ruth, one of the daughters of John Alden Sarah, a daughter of Mr Bass, was the wife of Ephraim Thayer This happy couple, another Zacharias and Elizabeth, as to their life and conversation, were blessed with a numerous family of children, remarkable for their piety They were indulged the peculiar satisfaction of living to see fourteen children arrive at years of maturity, enter a family state, and unanimously make the noble resolution of Joshua; *as for me and my house, we will serve the Lord* On one communion occasion, they enjoyed the singular felicity of presenting themselves, with the fourteen children, God had graciously given them, at the table of the Lord, to receive the emblems of Redeeming Love ' A similar instance has seldom been found in the annals of the Christian Church "

CRITICAL REMARKS, ERRATA &c.

MEHETABEL is the true method of spelling a name which frequently occurs in the Family Memorial spelled *Mehitable.* It is a Hebrew name.
[*Rev. T. Alden.*

Page 21, third line from top, read *academical* for acidemical.

Same page 8th line after *and* insert *of*, so as to read and *of* whose numerous pupils, &c.

Page 48 No. 8, for "Harvey H Niles" read *Doct Harry H Niles.*

Page 49 No. 20, for "one child" read *no child.*

Page 23, Second Part, No 39, sixth branch, for, "Angenette" read *Ann Jenette.*

Page 87, third line, for "13 Sept" read 11 *Dec.* After "1830," same line, insert *Mr Marcy died* 17 *Jan* 1835. Same page, 7th line, for "1830" read 1820, and for "1820" read 1823

Page 119, 5th line from the bottom for item, read *idem.*

COPY OF THE WILL OF EPHRAIM THAYER.

IN the Name of God Amen   This 10th day of April Anno, 1755, I Ephraim Thayer, of Braintree in the County of Suffolk and Province of Massachusetts Bay in New England Weaver, being of perfect mind and memory thanks be given to God therefor, Calling to mind the mortality of my body Knowing that it is appointed to Man once to die, Do make and ordain this my last Will and Testament, Viz. Principally and first of all I give and recommend my Soul into the hands of that God that gave it, hoping and trusting through the merits of Jesus Christ my only Saviour, to have full and free pardon of all my sins, and to inherit everlasting life , and my Body I commit to the earth to be decently buried at the discretion of my Executors hereafter mentioned, Nothing doubting at the general resurrection I shall receive the same again by the mighty Power of God

And for the settling the temporal estate wherewith God hath blessed me I give and dispose of it in manner and form following, viz

IMPRIMIS.   I give and bequeath unto my well beloved Wife Mary the improvement of the best room in my house and what privileges she sees cause to improve in my garden if she continues at my house during her natural life ; and also I order my Executors after named to afford her a comfortable maintenance, but if she sees cause to move away, then I give her all the household goods she brought, and order my Executors to pay her yearly as much as she hath from her Sons Kingmands during her natural life

ITEM   I give unto my Son Ephraim 20s in money more than what he hath already received, to be paid in two years after my wife's decease.

ITEM.   I give unto my Son Philip the whole of my wearing apparel, both linen and woolen to be delivered him immediately after my decease and also 5£ to be paid in two years after my decease

ITEM   I give to my Son Joseph 1£ to be paid him in two years after my decease and also two bbls. Cider pr year for three years after my decease.

ITEM.   I give to my Son Shadrach my Ivory headed cane and also half my land in the first and second lott adjoining to the land I gave my Son Ephraim by Deed

ITEM   I give to my Son Naphtali the other half part of my land in the first and second lot adjoining to the lands I gave him by Deed.

ITEM.   I give to my Son Peter 20s in money to be paid him in five years after my decease

ITEM   I give to my Grand daughter Ruth Vinton the Daughter of my Daughter Sarah Dorman deceased a Cow to be delivered her in one year after my decease

ITEM.   I give to my Daughter Hannah Blancher one half an

acre of land adjoining to my Son Blancher's Land also two acres of meadow bounded Westerly on James Penniman's land, to run of an equal breadth, also my best feather bed and furniture belonging thereto

ITEM I give to my Daughter Ruth Capen 5 £ to be paid in two years after my decease she having received a Bed and furniture thereto belonging already

ITEM I give to my Daughter Esther French a feather bed and furniture belonging to it

ITEM. I give to my Daughter Priscilla Ford a Cow and 20s in money

ITEM. I give to my Daughter Abigail Richards my silver Cup.

ITEM I give to my five Daughters, viz Hannah, Ruth, Esther, Priscilla, and Abigail all the land I shall leave undisposed of to be equally divided among them, also all the Household moveables I shall leave undisposed of to be equally divided among them

ITEM I give and confirm unto my two Sons Christopher and James the whole of my homestead, viz Housing and Barn, with all the Lands both on the South and North side of the way, Christopher to have the West part of the land and James the East part, to be equally divided between them for quantity, and Christopher to have the East end of the Barn, and half the floor way and the Corn house to be equally divided between them and the Dwelling House to be divided as they shall agree to suit them both   I also give unto my Son Christopher 2½ acres meadow which I purchased of Capt Ebenezer Thayer; I also give unto my Son James, three acres of land, which I bought of John Mills, adjoining to Capt John Thayer's land, I also give to my Son James my Cart and wheels, yokes and chains and ploughs, &c. and also my great Bible.

FURTHERMORE I constitute ordain and appoint my two Sons Christopher and James my Executors of this last Will and Testament, Willing and Ordaining them to pay all my just debts and funeral expenses and the Legacies before mentioned, FINALLY, I do hereby utterly disallow, revoke and disannul all former Wills and Testaments

In Witness whereof I have hereunto set my hand and seal the day and year above written

EPHRAIM THAYER,   [SEAL]

Signed, sealed, published and declared by Ephraim Thayer,
to be his last Will and Testament in presence of

ISAAC NEWCOMB,
ELISHA NILES,
ANN NILES

Suffolk By the Honourable Thomas Hutchinson, Esq Judge of Probate, &c the within written Will being presented for Probate by the Executors therein named, Isaac Newcomb, Elisha Niles made oath that they saw Ephraim Thayer, the subscriber to this Instrument, sign the same and heard him publish and declare it to be his last Will and Testament and that when he so did he was of sound and disposing mind and memory, according to their deponents best discerning, and that they together with Ann Niles, now absent, set to their hands as Witnesses in the said Testator's presence   Boston, July 15, 1757

          T HUTCHINSON, Judge of Probate

Jno Cotton, Register

The following is here inserted as a mere antique curiosity

COPY OF THE LAST WILL AND TESTAMENT OF

Capt MYLES STANDISH, Gent

exhibited before the Court held at Plymouth the 4th of May, 1657, on the oath of Capt James Cudworth, and ordered to bee Recorded as followeth

Given under my hand this March the 7th, 1655

WITNESSETH these Presents that I Myles Standish, Senr of Duxburrow being in perfect memory yett deceased in my body and knowing the finall estate of man in his best Estate—I do make this to be my last Will and Testament in manner and form following—

1   My Will is that out of my whole Estate my funerall charges to be taken out and my body to be buried in a decent manner and if I die at Duxburrow my body to be layed as neare as conveniently may bee to my two dear daughters Lora Standish, my daughter and Mary Standish, my daughter in Law

2   My will is that out of the remaing pte of my whole estate that all my just and lawtul debts which I now owe or at the day of my death may owe bee paid

3   Out of what remains according to the Order of this Government my Will is that my dear and loving Wife, Barbara Standish have the third pte

4   I have given to my son Josias Standish upon his marriage, one young horse, five sheep and two heifers, which I must upon that contract of marriage make forty pounds, yett not knowing whether the Estate will bear it at present my will is that the residue remain in the whole stocke and that every one of my four sons, viz Alexander S Myles S Josias S and Charles S may have forty pounds apiece, if not that they may have proportionable to ye remaing pte bee it more or less

5   My Will is that my eldest son Alexander shall have a double share in land

6   My Will is that soe long as they live single that the whole be in partnership betwixt them

7   I doe ordain and make my dearely beloved wife Barbara S. Alexander S Myles S and Josias S joynt Exequtors of this my last Will and Testament

8 I doe by this my Will make and appoint my loving friends
Mr Timothy Hatherly and Capt James Cudworth, supervisors of
this my last Will, and that they will be pleased to do the office of
christian love, to be helpfull to my poor wife and children by their
Christian counsell and advice, and if any difference should arise,
which I hope will not, my will is that my said supervisors shall
determine the same and that they see that my poor wife shall have
as comfortable maintenance as my poor state will beare the whole
time of her life, which if you my loving friends please to do though
neither they nor I shall be able to recompense, I do not doubt
but the Lord will   By me,   MYLES STANDISH

Further my will is that Martha Mareye Robenson, whome I
tenderly love for her grandfathers' sake shall have three pounds
in something to go forward for her two years after my decease,
which my will is my overseers shall see performed

Further my will is that my servant John Irish, jr have forty
shillings more than his covenant, which will appear upon the town
Booke, alwaies provided that he continew till the time he coven-
anted be expired in the service of my executors or any of them
with their jointe consent   By me,   MYLES STANDISH
March 7, 1655

9 I give unto my son and heire aparant, Alexander S all my
lands as heire aparent by lawful descent in Ormistick Boisconge,
Wrightnyton Maudsley, Newburrow, Crawston and in the Isle of
Man and given to me as right heire by lawful descent but surrep-
ticiously detained from me my great Grandfather being a vond or
younger brother from the house of S of S

                  By me,   MYLES STANDISH
March 7, 1655
  Witnesseth by me JAMES CUDWORTH

*An extract from a Poem written by the first New England bard, the "learn
ed Schoolmaster and Physician," Dr. BENJAMIN THOMPSON, who
was born in Braintree, (now Quincy,) 11 July, 1642, died 13 April, 1714,
aged 72 years, will close our volume*

NEW ENGLAND'S CRISIS

"The times wherein old Pompion was a saint,
When men fared hardly yet without complaint,
On vilest cates, the dainty indian maize
Was eat with clamp-shells out of wooden trays,
Under thatch'd hutts without the cry of rent,
And the best sawce to every dish content
When flesh was food and hairy skins made coats,
And men as wel as birds had chirping notes.

When Cimnels* were accounted noble blood,
Among the tribes of common herbage food
Of Ceres' bounty formed was many a knack,
Enough to fill poor Robin's Almanack.
These golden times (too fortunate to hold,)
Were quickly sin'd away for love of gold.
'Twas then among the bushes, not the street,
If one in place did an inferior meet,
" Good morrow brother, is there aught you want?
" Take freely of me, what I have you ha'nt."
Plain Tom and Dick would pass as current now,†
As ever since " Your Servant Sir," and bow.
Deep shirted doublets, puritanic capes,
Which now would render men like upright apes,
Was comlier wear, our wiser fathers thought,
Than the cast fashions from all Europe brought
'Twas in those days an honest grace would hold,
Till an hot pudding grew at heart a cold.
And men had better stomachs at religion,
Than I to capon, turkey cock, or pigeon,
When honest sisters met to pray, not prate
About their own and not their neighbours's state
During Plain Dealing's reign, that worthy stud,
Of the ancient planters race before the flood—
Then times were good, merchants cared not a rush,
For other fare than Jonakin and Mush.
Although men fared and lodged very hard,
Yet innocence was better than a guard
'Twas long before spiders and worms had drawn
Then dungy webs, or hid with cheating lawne
New England's beautyes, which still seemed to me
Illustrious in their own symplicity.
'Twas ere the neighbouring Virgin-Land had broke
The hogsheads of her worse than hellish smoak
'Twas ere the Islands sent their presents in,
Which but to use was counted next to sin.
'Twas ere a barge had made so rich a fraight
As Chocolate, dust-gold and bitts of eight.
Ere wines from France and Moscovadoe to,
Without the which the drink will scarsly doe
From western isles ere fruits and delicasies
Did rot maids' teeth and spoil their handsome faces.
Or ere these times did chance, the noise of war
Was from our towns and herts removed far.
No bugbear comets in the chrystal air
Did drive our christian planters to despair.
No sooner pagan malice peeped forth
But valour snib'd it.   Then were men of worth
Who by their prayers slew thousands, angel like;
Their weapons are unseen with which they strike.
Then had the churches rest; as yet the coales
Were covered up in most contentious souls·
Freeness in Judgment, union in affection,
Dear love, sound truth, they were our grand protection "
                  [*Kettell's Specimens of Amer. Poetry, Vol. 1, 38.*

* Simuels   † Then

of and

married and settled in

(See No) Their

children were,

                    of   and
married   and settled in
                              (See No.   ) Their
children were.

of   and

married   and settled in
                    (See No   .)   Their

children were,

                 of   and
married   and settled in
                                (See No   )   Their
children were,

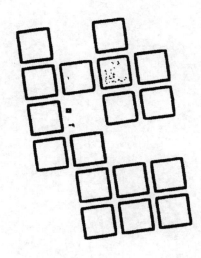

CPSIA information can be obtained
at www.ICGtesting.com
Printed in the USA
BVHW041036040122
625441BV00012B/449

9 781362 136255